O-Parts
HUNTER

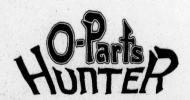

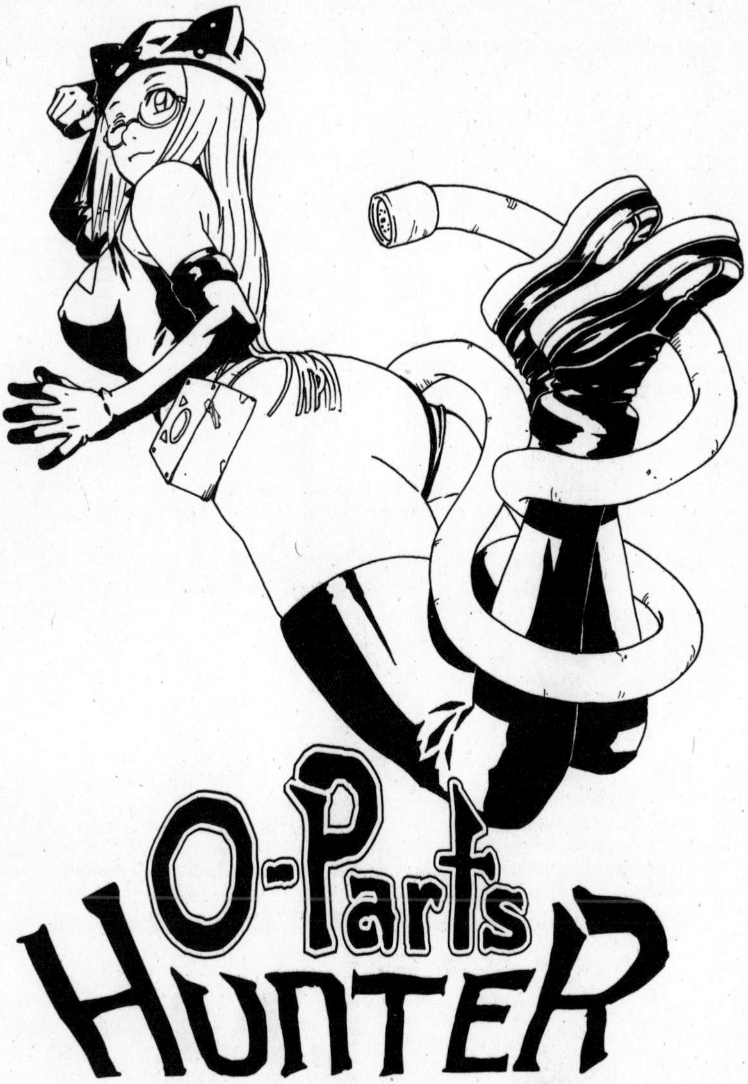

O-Parts HUNTER

SEISHI KISHIMOTO

8

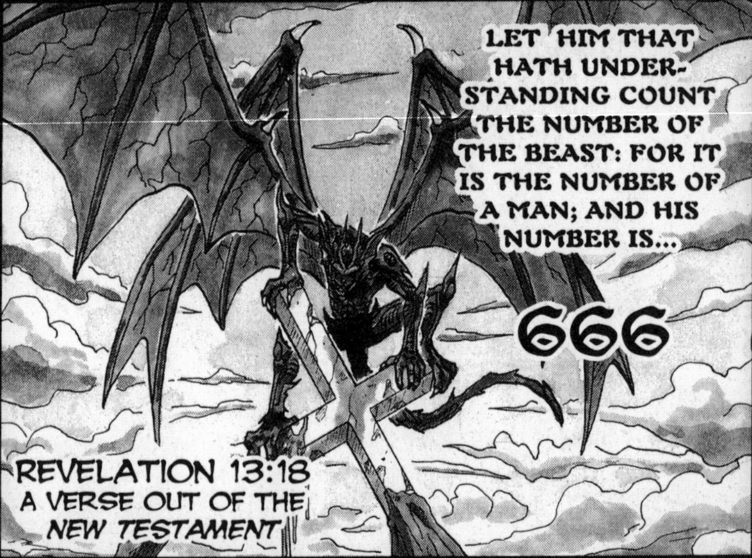
LET HIM THAT HATH UNDER-STANDING COUNT THE NUMBER OF THE BEAST: FOR IT IS THE NUMBER OF A MAN; AND HIS NUMBER IS...
666
REVELATION 13:18
A VERSE OUT OF THE *NEW TESTAMENT*

O-Parts Hunter

SPIRITS

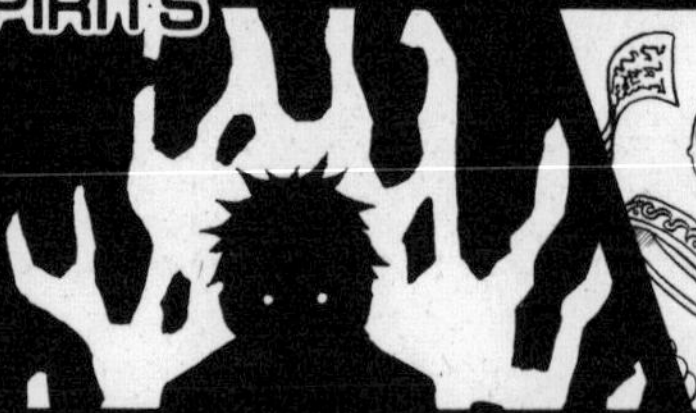

Spirit: A special energy force which only the O.P.T.s have. The amount of Spirit they have within them determines how strong of an O.P.T. they are.

O-PARTS

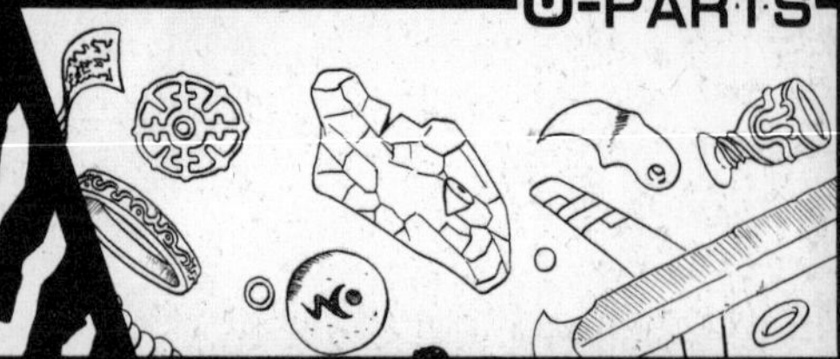

O-Parts: Amazing artifacts with mystical powers left from an ancient civilization. They have been excavated from various ruins around the world. Depending on their Effects, O-Parts are given a rank from E to SS within a seven-tiered system.

EFFECT

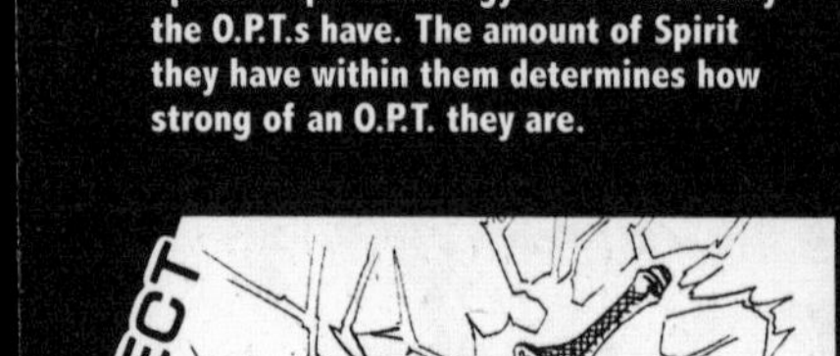

Effect: The special energy (power) the O-Parts possess. It can only be used when an O.P.T. sends his Spirit into an O-Part.

O.P.T.

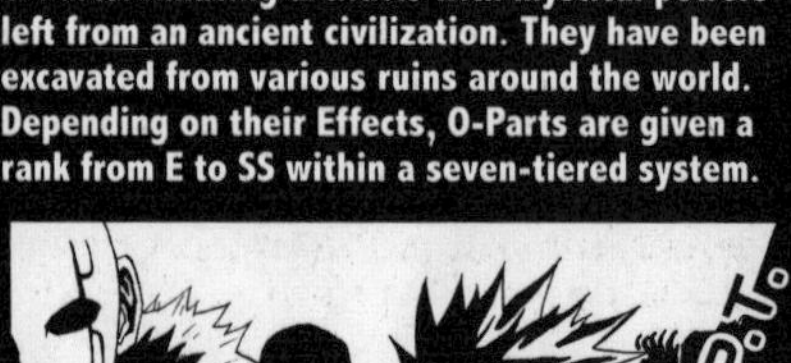

O.P.T.: One who has the ability to release and use the powers of the O-Parts. The name O.P.T. is an abbreviated form of O-Part Tactician.

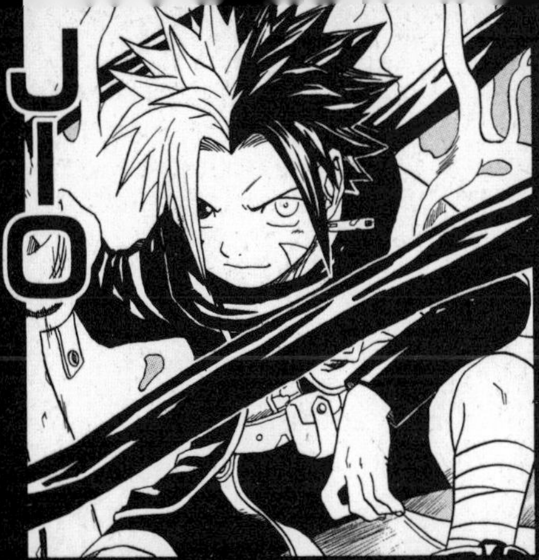
JIO

Jio Freed
A wild O.P.T. boy whose dream is world domination! He has been emotionally damaged by his experiences in the past, but is still gung-ho about his new adventures! O-Part: New Zero-shiki (Rank B)
Effect: Triple (Increasing power by a factor of three)

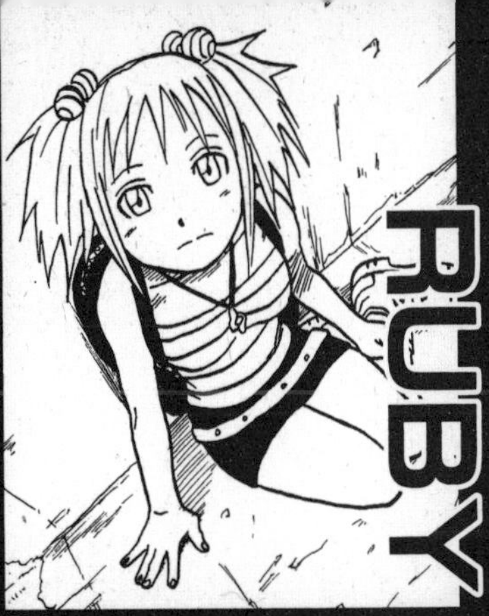
RUBY

Ruby
A treasure hunter who can decipher ancient texts. She meets Jio during her search for a legendary O-Part.

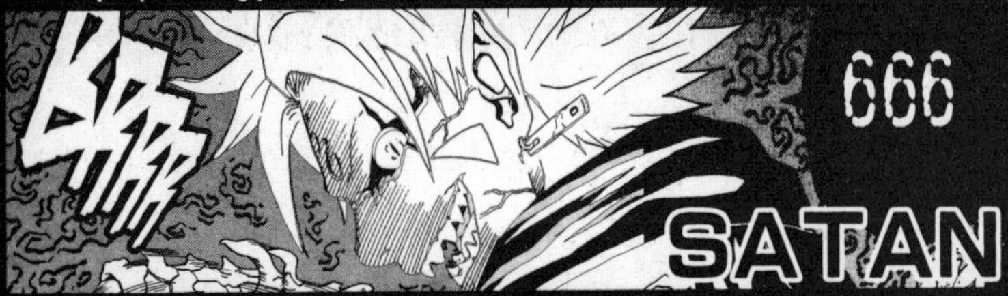
666
SATAN

Satan
This demon is thought to be a mutated form of Jio. It is a creature shrouded in mystery with earth-shattering powers.

STORY

Ascald: a world where people fight amongst themselves in order to get their hands on mystical objects left behind by an ancient civilization...the O-Parts.

In that world, a monster that strikes fear into the hearts of the strongest of men is rumored to exist. Those who have seen the monster all tell of the same thing–that the number of the beast, 666, is engraved on its forehead.

***

Jio, an O.P.T. boy who wants to rule the world, travels the globe with Ruby, a girl in search of a legendary O-Part and her missing father. They are joined by Ball, a novice O.P.T., and the three go to the Dastom Ruins where they meet Wick and Vercil, a couple who takes them in as their own. Wick tells them of the Kabbalah and how the O-Parts may have come from a different world. But then Kujaku of the Zenom Syndicate slaughters Wick and Vercil in an attempt to capture the O.P.T.s. Jio sets out for revenge and is almost killed, but is saved by Kirin, who turns out to be Kujaku's older brother. Our heroes then leave for the North Pole to see the Kabbalah for themselves. On the way, Ruby is attacked by thugs. Jio moves to save her–and so does Cross! Face to face for what should be the first time, the two have a nagging feeling that they've met before...

O-Parts Hunter

8

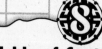

Table of Contents

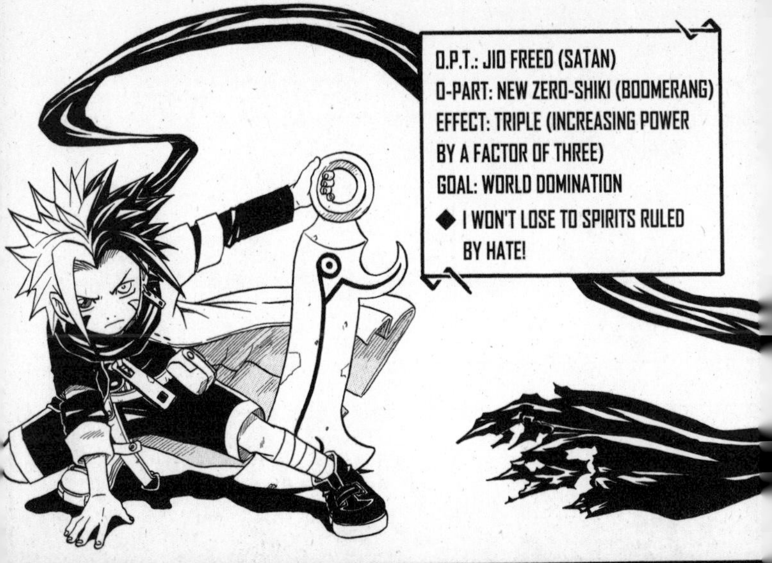
O.P.T.: JIO FREED (SATAN)
O-PART: NEW ZERO-SHIKI (BOOMERANG)
EFFECT: TRIPLE (INCREASING POWER BY A FACTOR OF THREE)
GOAL: WORLD DOMINATION
◆ I WON'T LOSE TO SPIRITS RULED BY HATE!

CHAPTER 29
THE FATED TWO

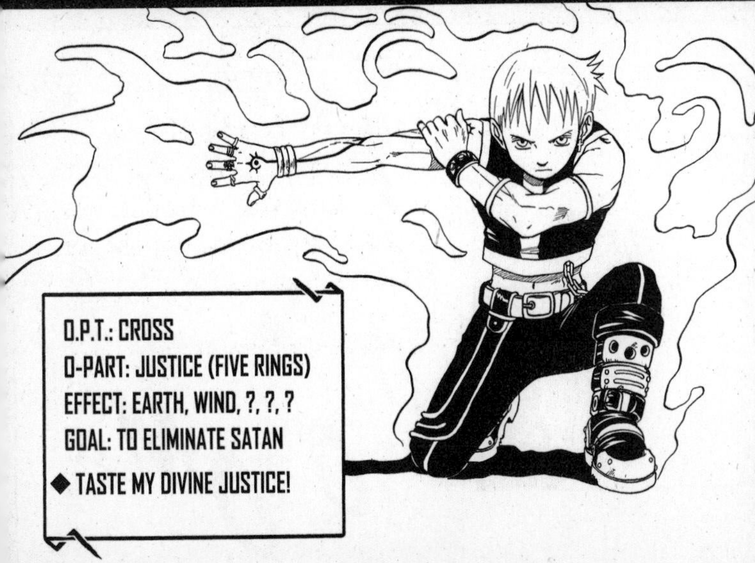
O.P.T.: CROSS
O-PART: JUSTICE (FIVE RINGS)
EFFECT: EARTH, WIND, ?, ?, ?
GOAL: TO ELIMINATE SATAN
◆ TASTE MY DIVINE JUSTICE!

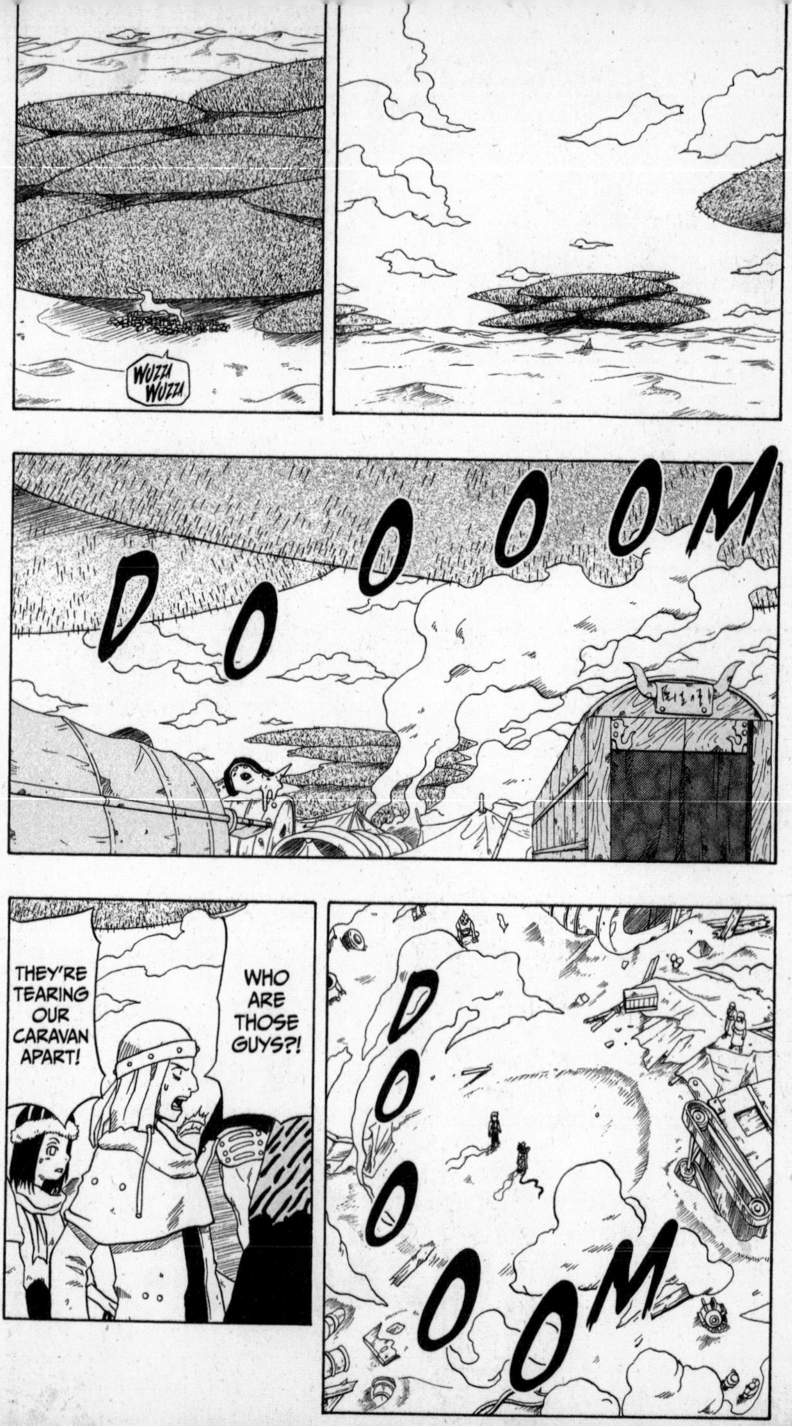
WUZZA WUZZA
DOOOOOM
DOOOOOM
WHO ARE THOSE GUYS?!
THEY'RE TEARING OUR CARAVAN APART!

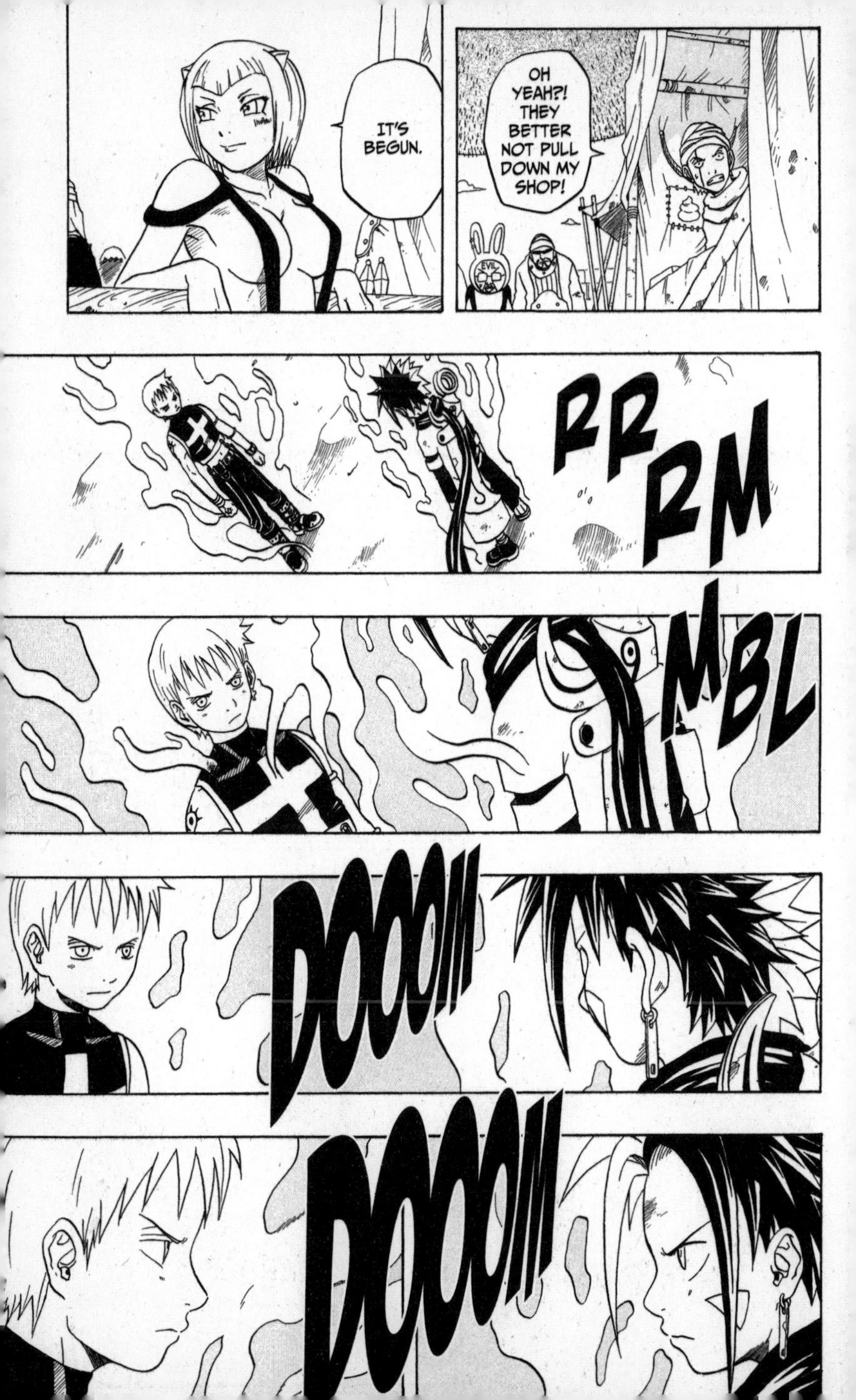
OH YEAH?! THEY BETTER NOT PULL DOWN MY SHOP!
EVIL
IT'S BEGUN.
RRRMMBL
DOOOM
DOOOM

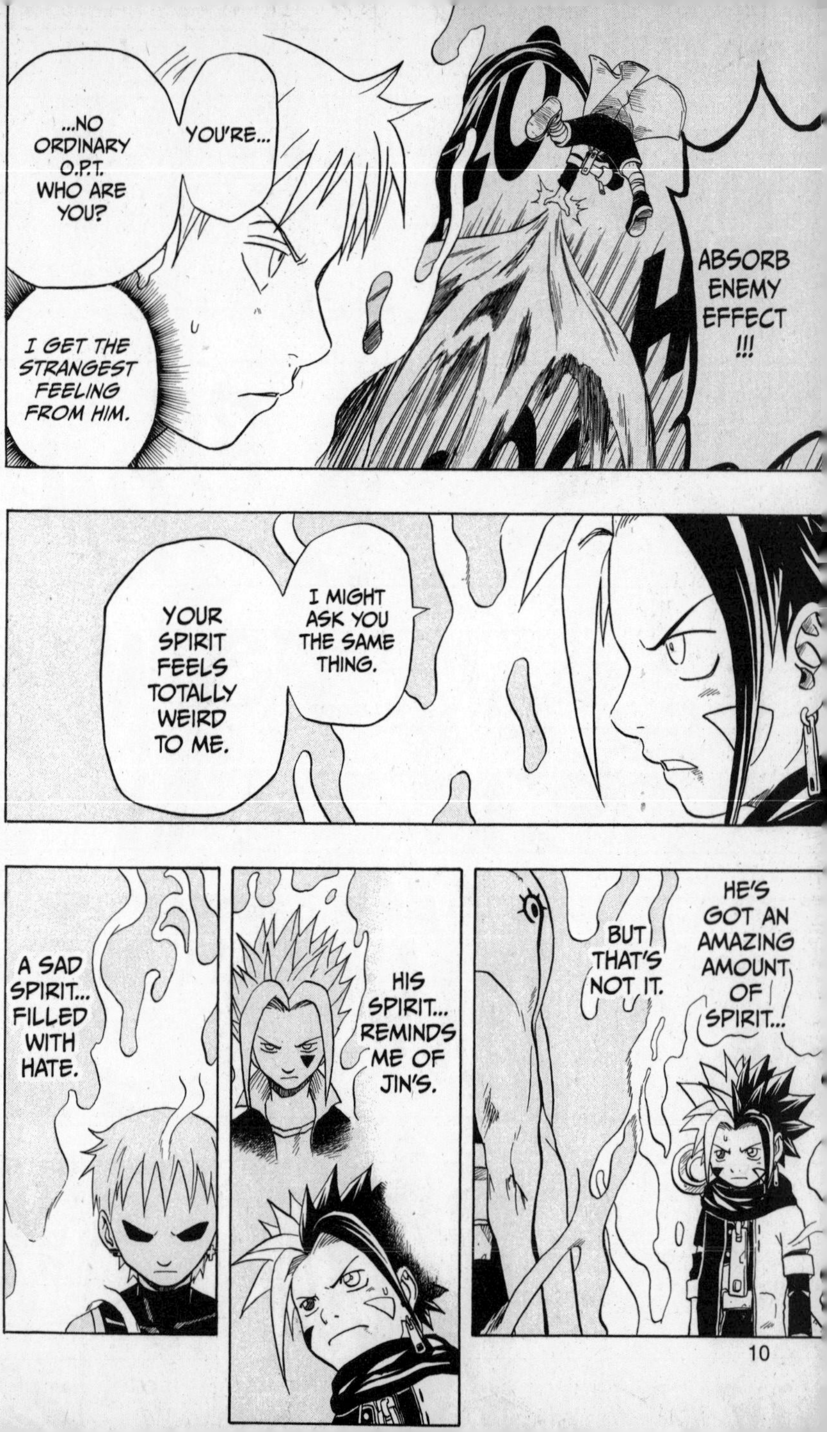
ABSORB ENEMY EFFECT !!!
YOU'RE...
...NO ORDINARY O.P.T. WHO ARE YOU?
I GET THE STRANGEST FEELING FROM HIM.
I MIGHT ASK YOU THE SAME THING.
YOUR SPIRIT FEELS TOTALLY WEIRD TO ME.
HE'S GOT AN AMAZING AMOUNT OF SPIRIT...
BUT THAT'S NOT IT.
HIS SPIRIT... REMINDS ME OF JIN'S.
A SAD SPIRIT... FILLED WITH HATE.

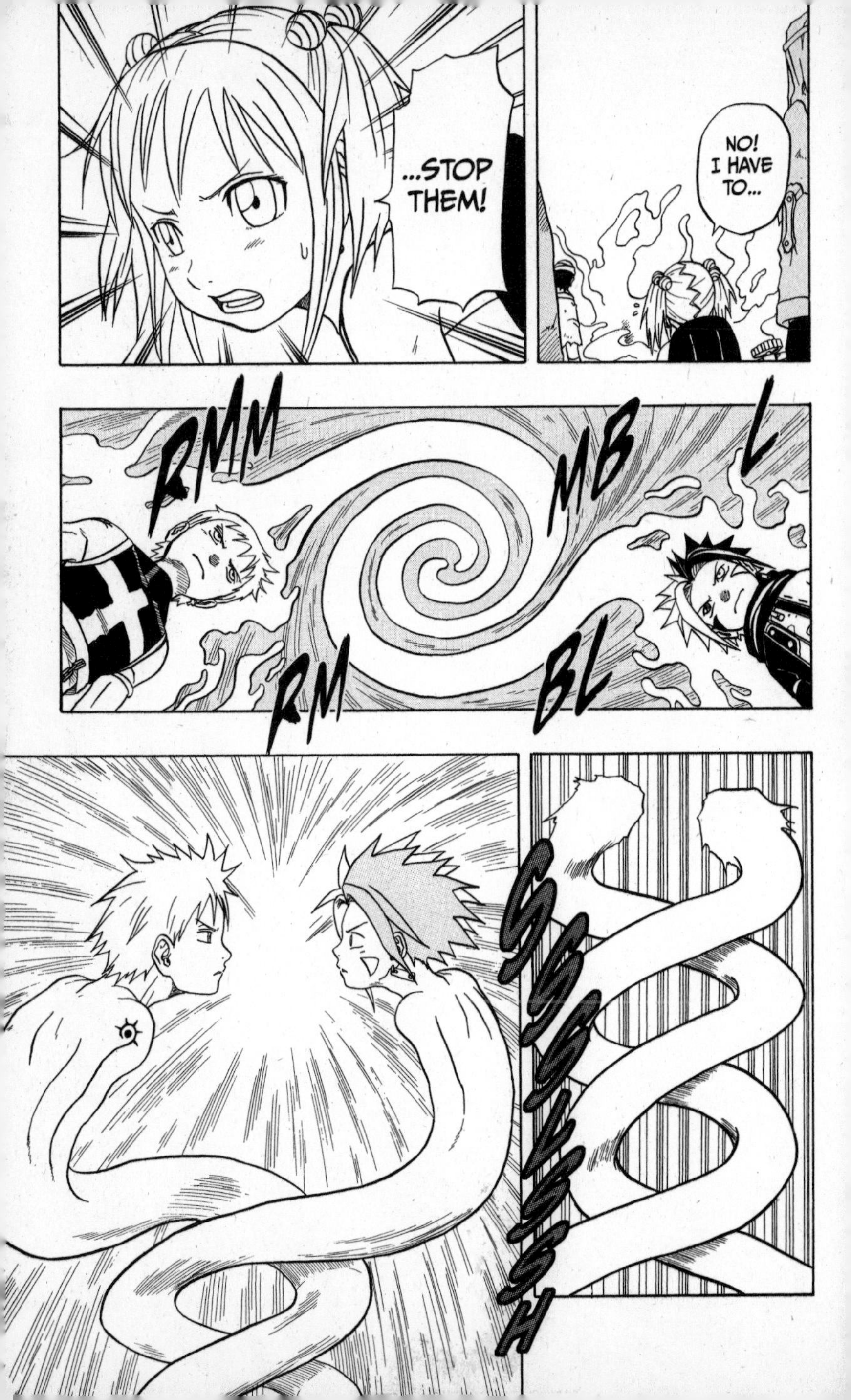
NO! I HAVE TO...
...STOP THEM!
L
MB
RMM
BL
RM
SSSSWSSH

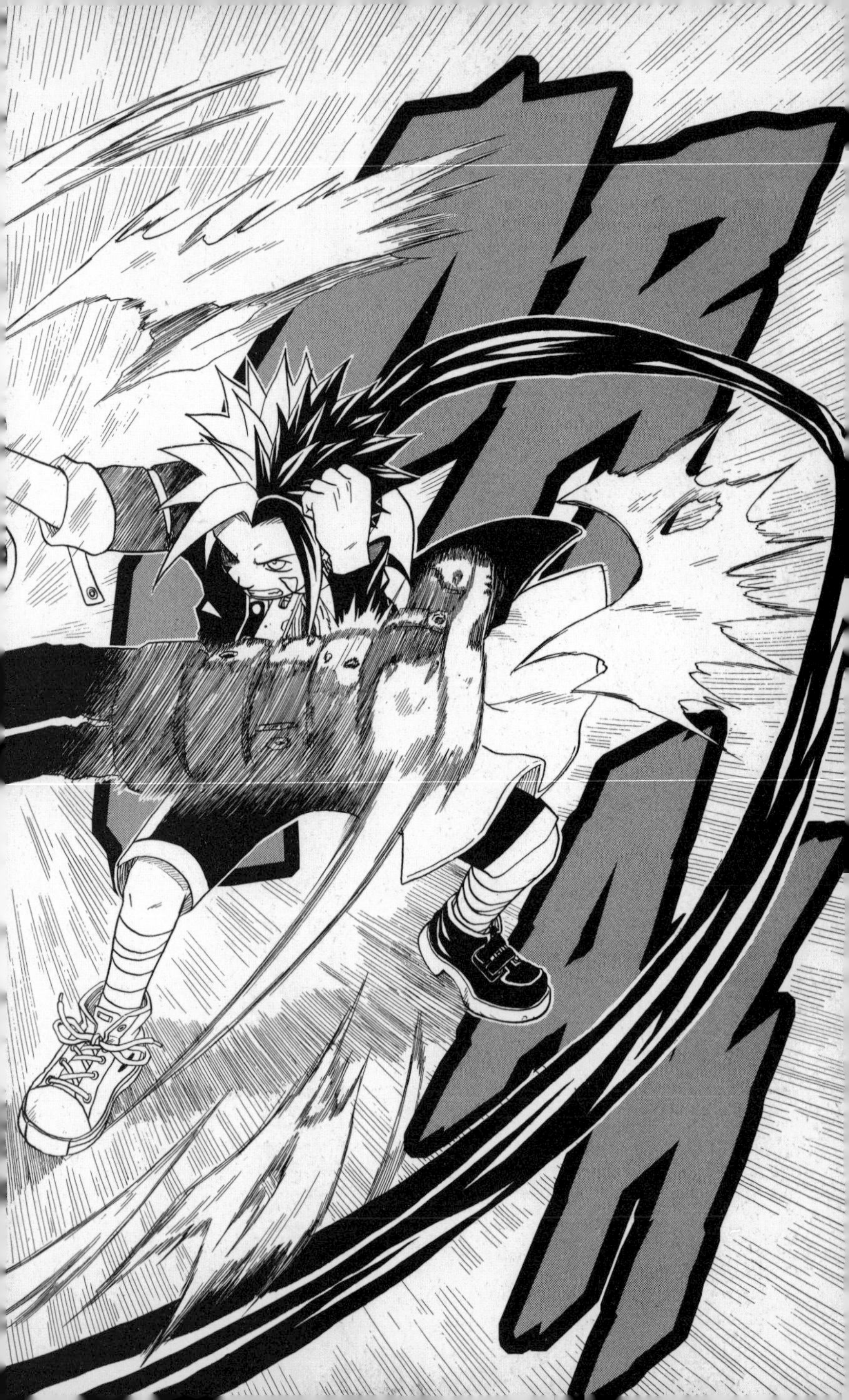

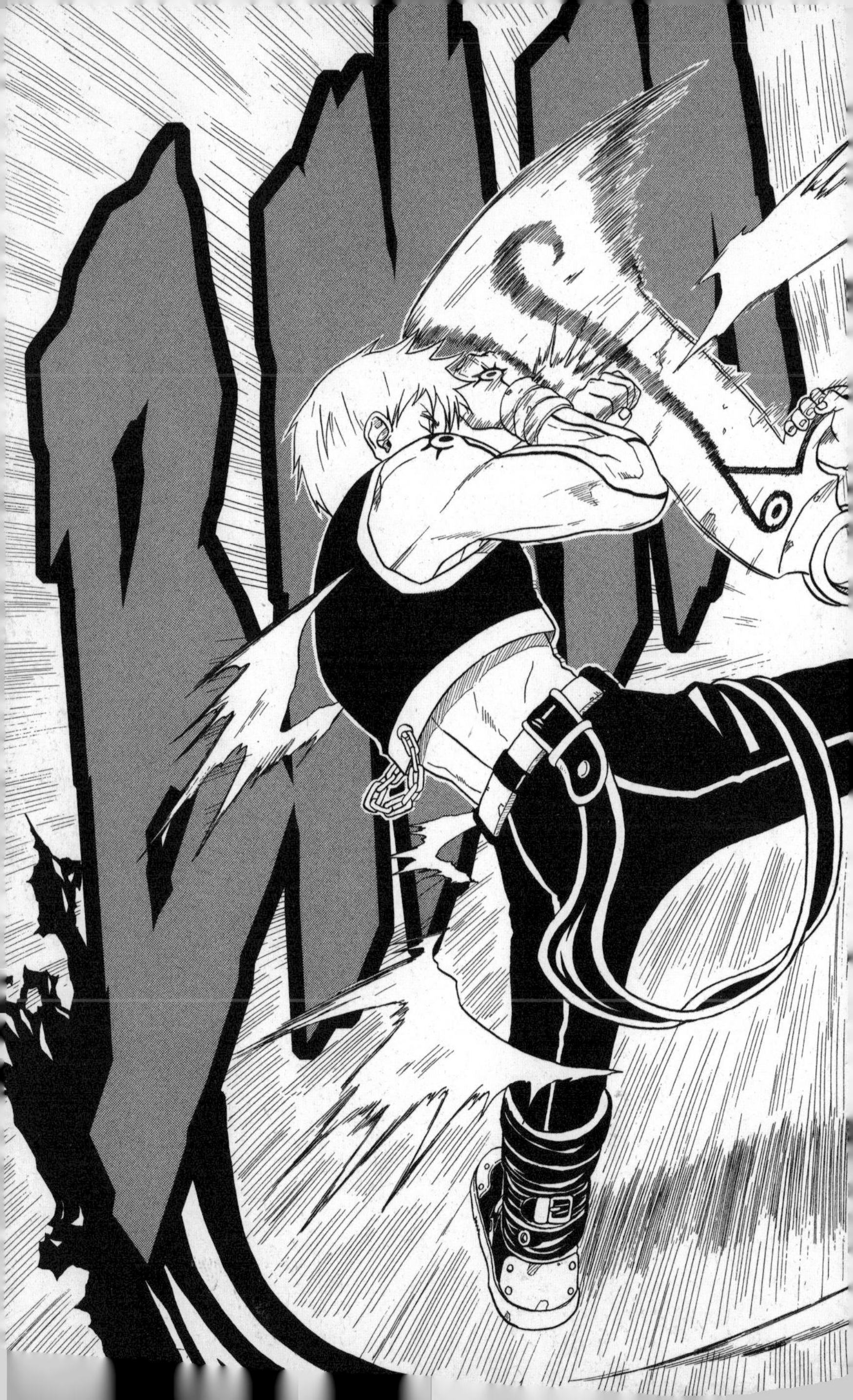

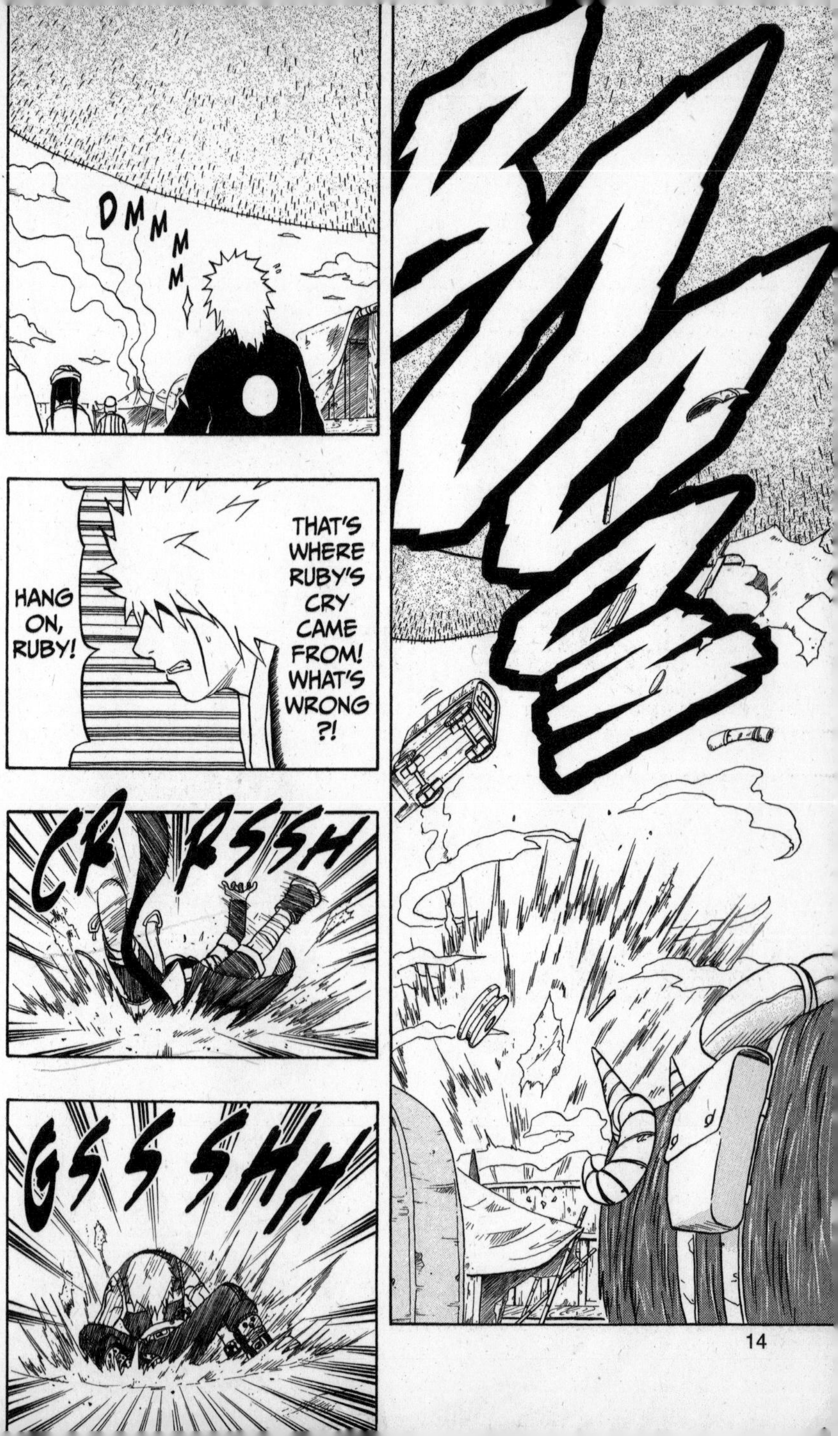
DMMMM
THAT'S WHERE RUBY'S CRY CAME FROM! WHAT'S WRONG?!
HANG ON, RUBY!
CRRSSH
GSSSHH

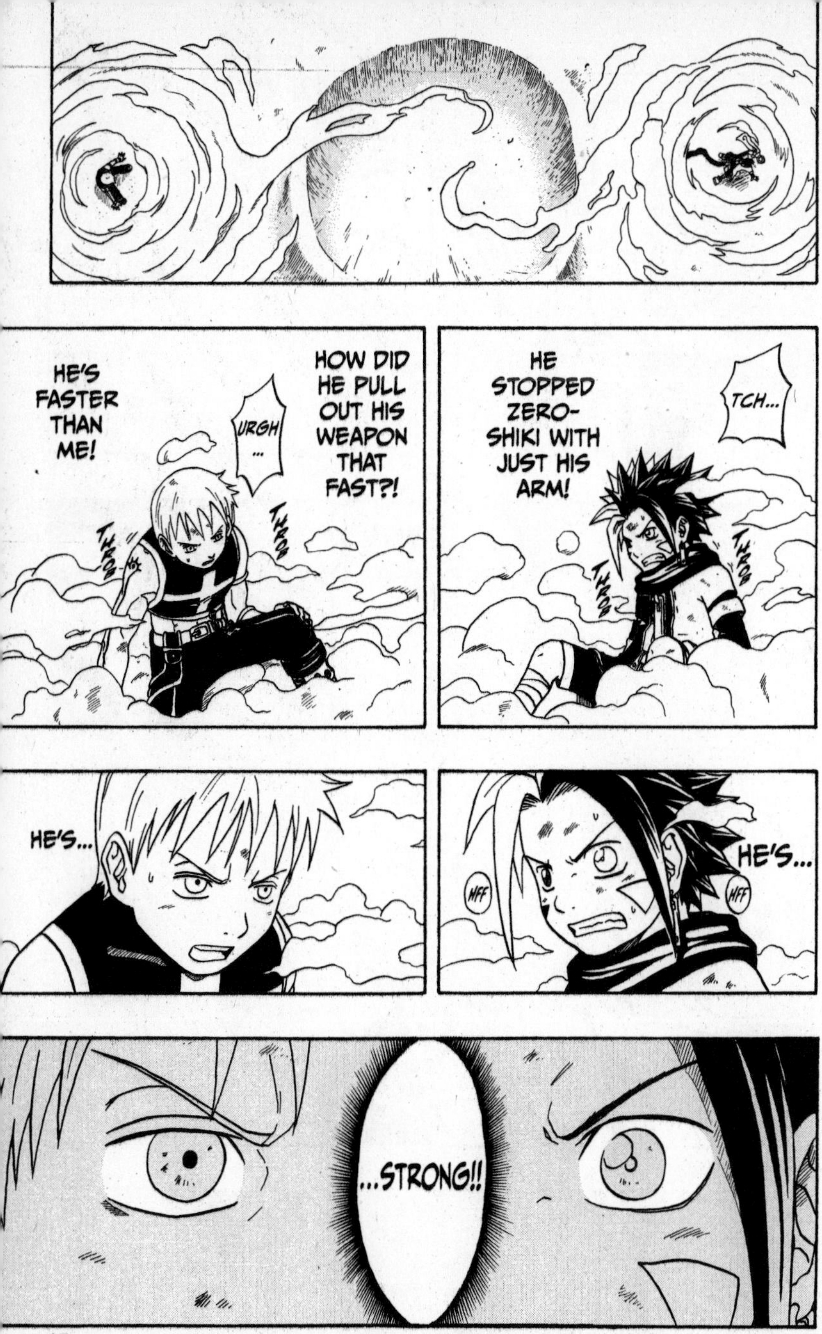
TCH...
HE STOPPED ZERO-SHIKI WITH JUST HIS ARM!
THROB
THROB
HOW DID HE PULL OUT HIS WEAPON THAT FAST?!
URGH...
HE'S FASTER THAN ME!
THROB
THROB
HE'S...
HFF
HFF
HE'S...
...STRONG!!

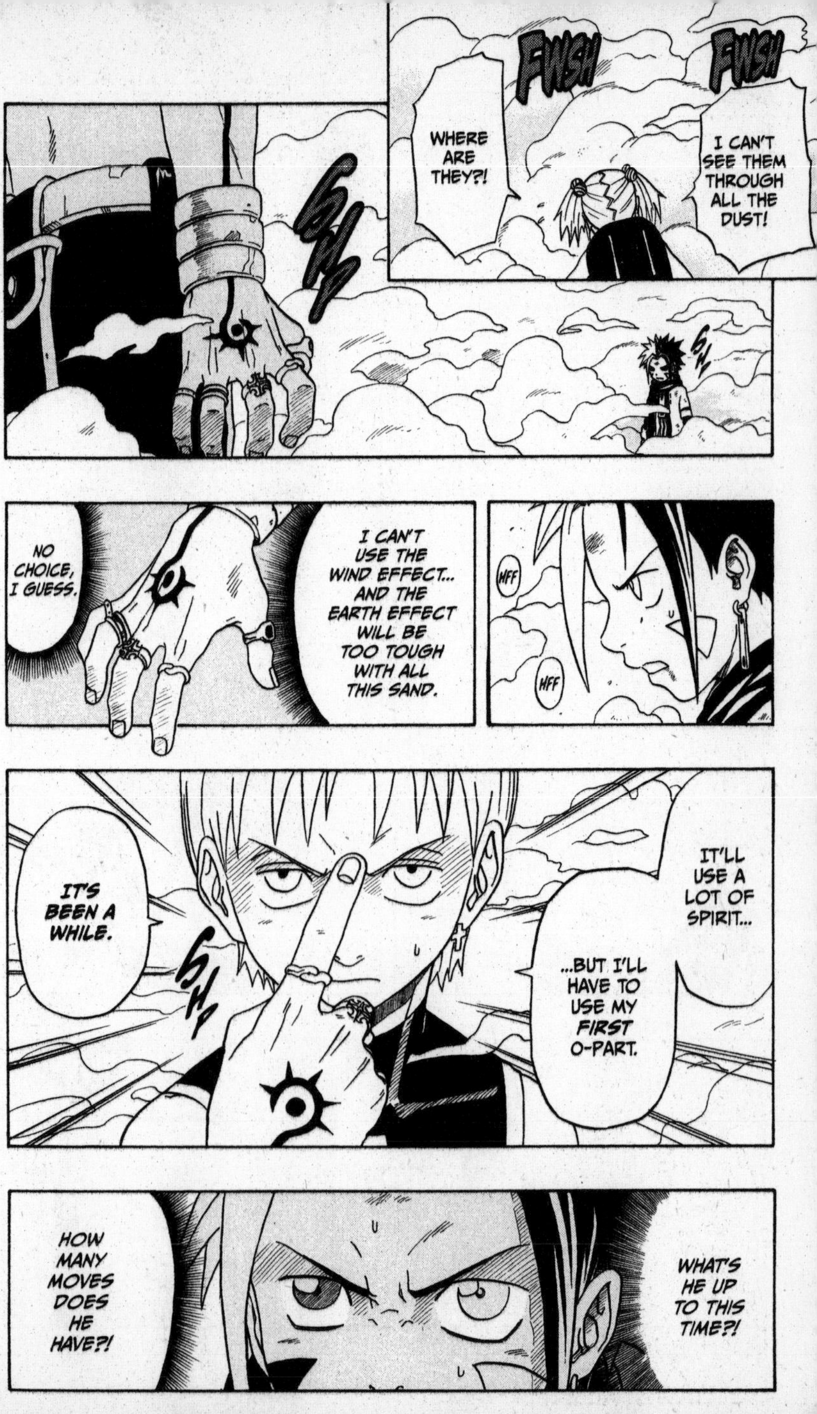
FWSH
FWSH
I CAN'T SEE THEM THROUGH ALL THE DUST!
WHERE ARE THEY?!
SHH
SHH
HFF
HFF
I CAN'T USE THE WIND EFFECT... AND THE EARTH EFFECT WILL BE TOO TOUGH WITH ALL THIS SAND.
NO CHOICE, I GUESS.
IT'LL USE A LOT OF SPIRIT...
...BUT I'LL HAVE TO USE MY FIRST O-PART.
SHH
IT'S BEEN A WHILE.
WHAT'S HE UP TO THIS TIME?!
HOW MANY MOVES DOES HE HAVE?!

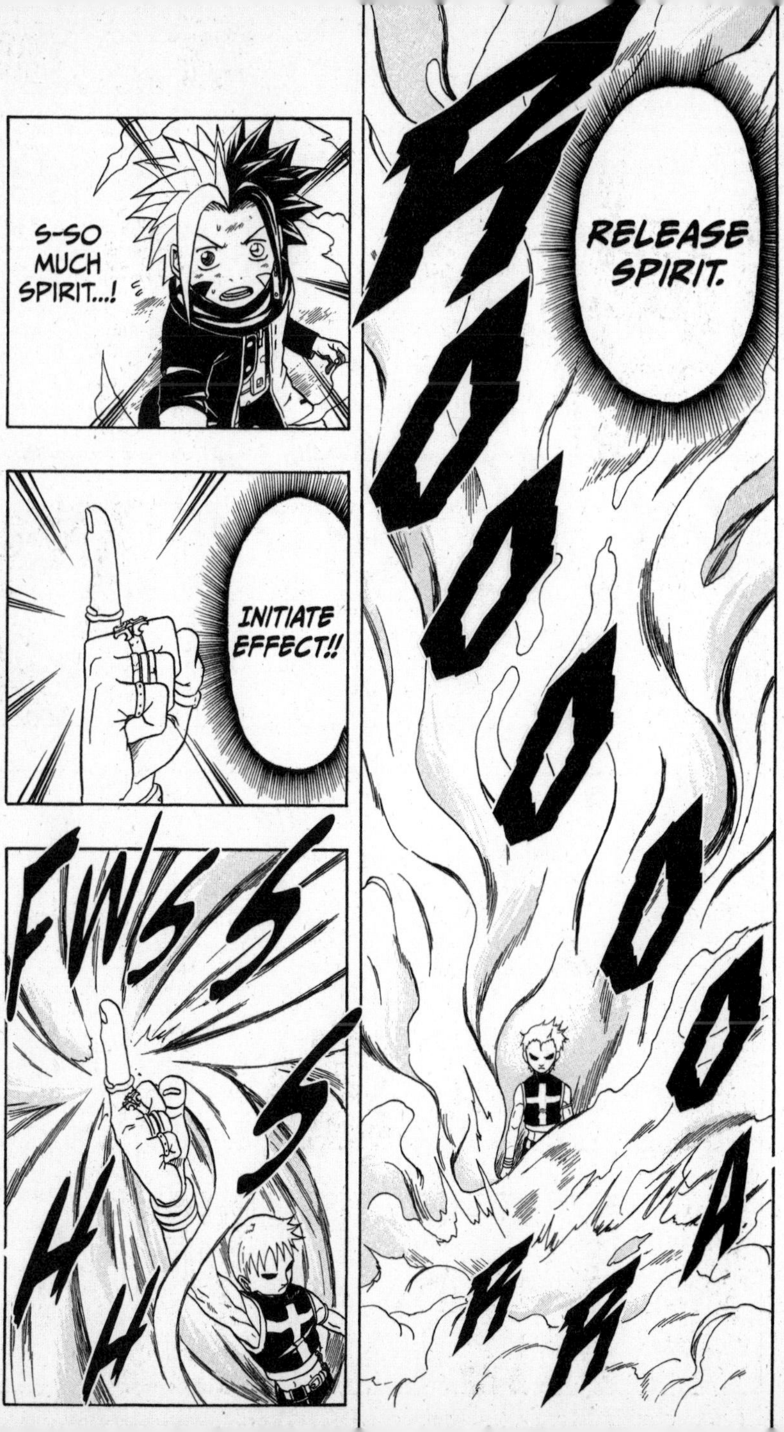
RELEASE SPIRIT.
ROOOOOARR
S-SO MUCH SPIRIT...!
INITIATE EFFECT!!
FWISSSHH

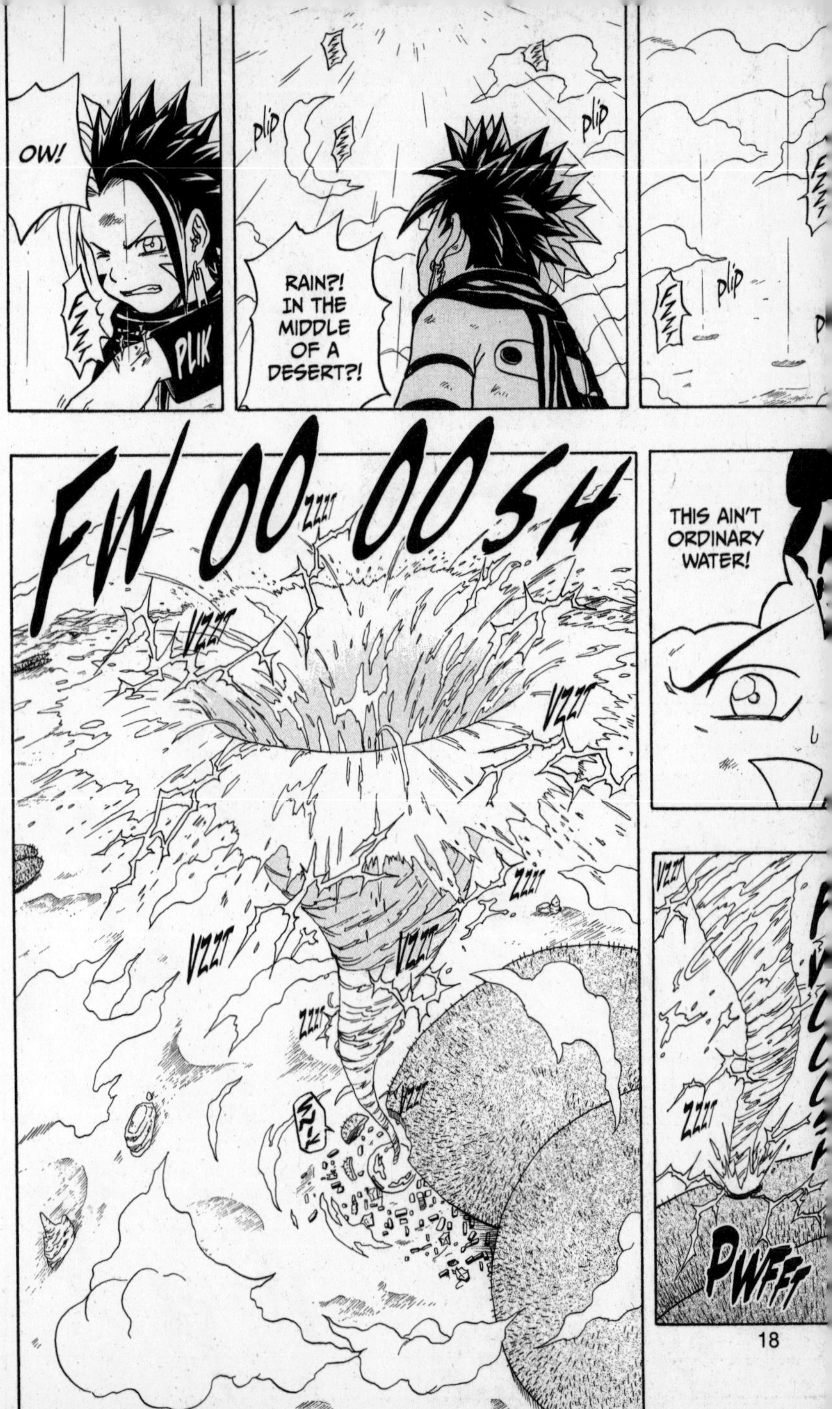
plip
plip
RAIN?! IN THE MIDDLE OF A DESERT?!
plip
OW!
PLIK
THIS AIN'T ORDINARY WATER!
VZZT
ZZZT
PWFFT
FWOOOOSH
ZZZT
VZZT
VZZT
ZZZT
VZZT
VZZT
ZZZT
VZZT

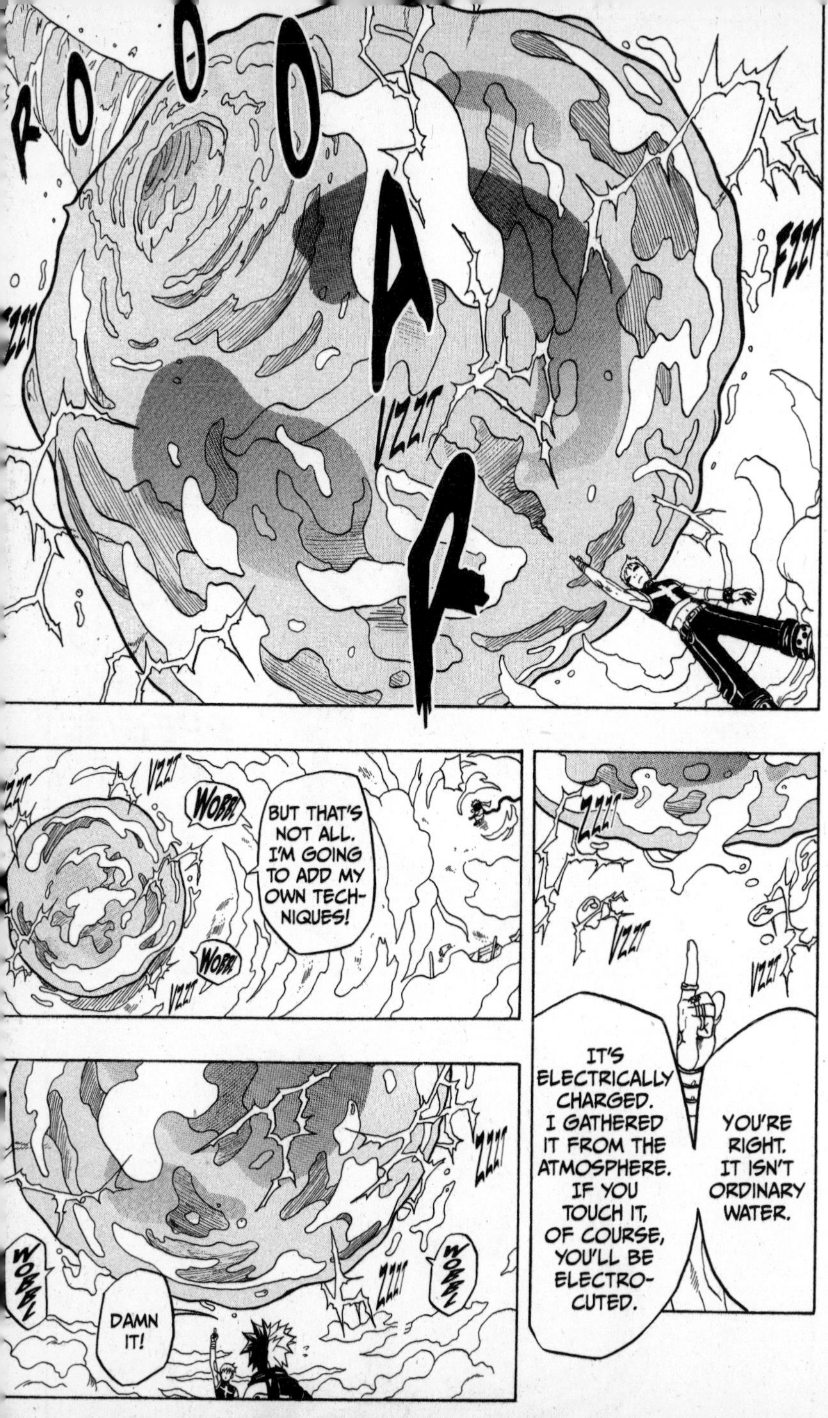
ROOOAR
FZZT
VZZT
ZZZT
ZZZT
VZZT
VZZT
YOU'RE RIGHT. IT ISN'T ORDINARY WATER.
IT'S ELECTRICALLY CHARGED. I GATHERED IT FROM THE ATMOSPHERE. IF YOU TOUCH IT, OF COURSE, YOU'LL BE ELECTROCUTED.
VZZT
ZZZT
WOBBL
BUT THAT'S NOT ALL. I'M GOING TO ADD MY OWN TECHNIQUES!
WOBBL
VZZT
ZZZT
WOBBL
ZZZT
WOBBL
DAMN IT!

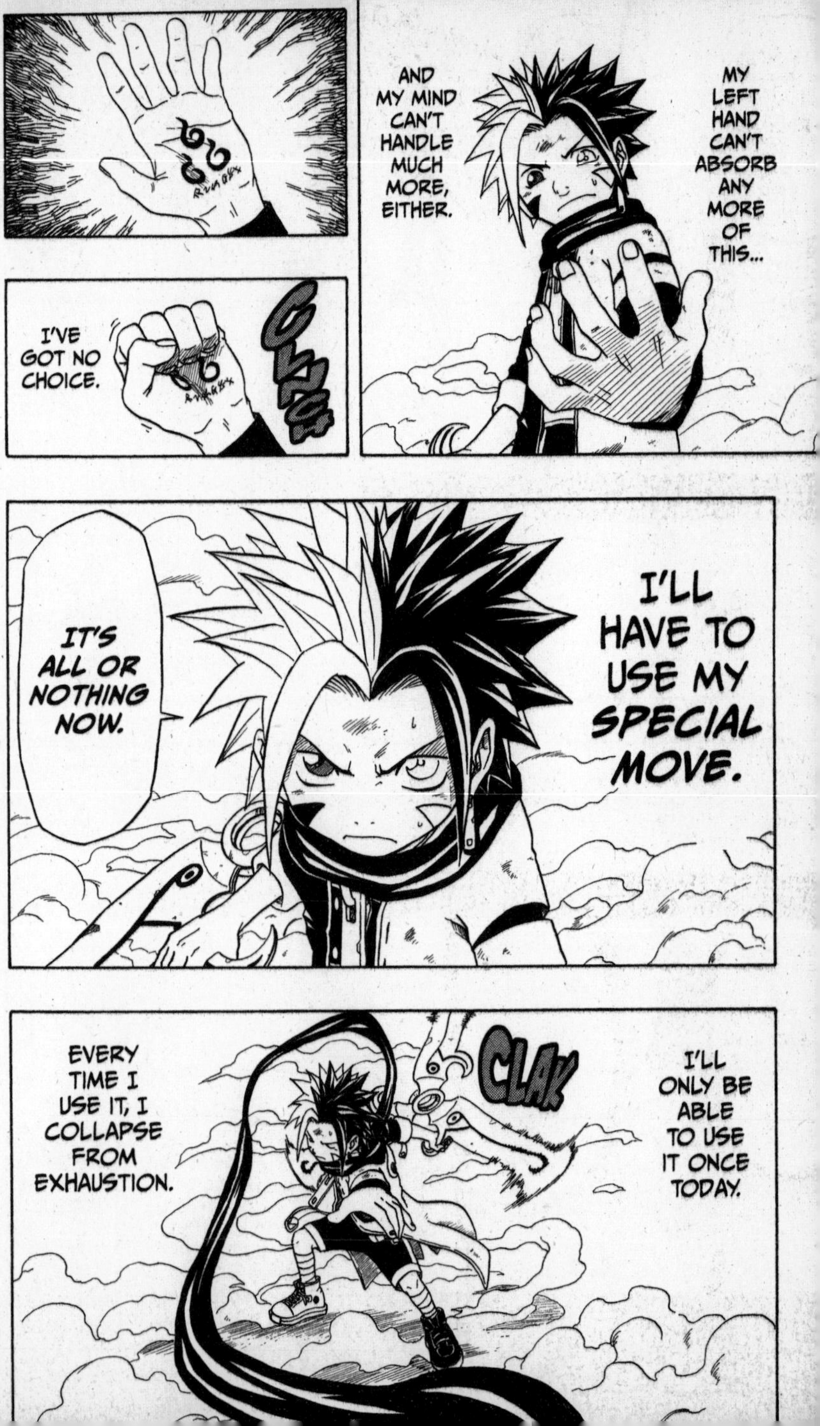
MY LEFT HAND CAN'T ABSORB ANY MORE OF THIS...
AND MY MIND CAN'T HANDLE MUCH MORE, EITHER.
CLNCH
I'VE GOT NO CHOICE.
I'LL HAVE TO USE MY *SPECIAL MOVE.*
IT'S ALL OR NOTHING NOW.
I'LL ONLY BE ABLE TO USE IT ONCE TODAY.
CLAK
EVERY TIME I USE IT, I COLLAPSE FROM EXHAUSTION.

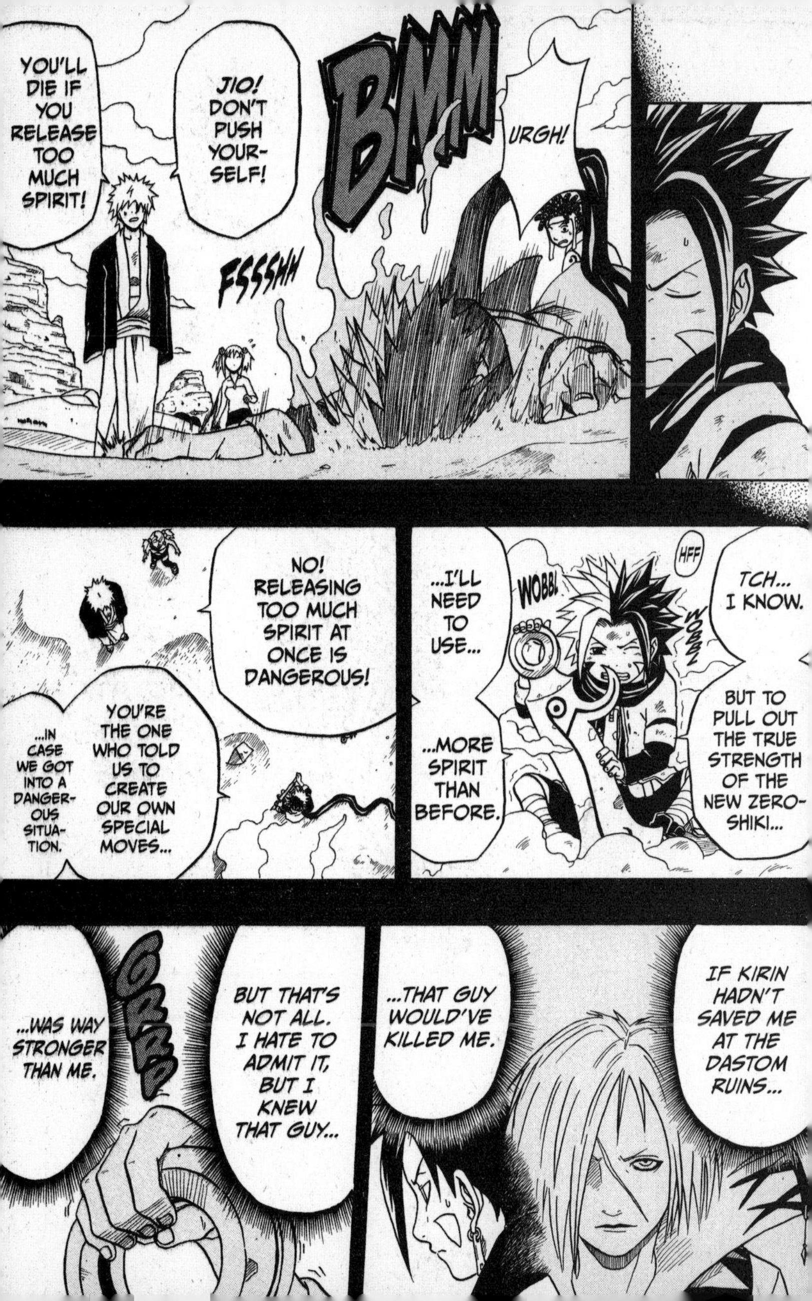
URGH!
BMM
JIO! DON'T PUSH YOURSELF!
YOU'LL DIE IF YOU RELEASE TOO MUCH SPIRIT!
FSSSHH
TCH... I KNOW.
HFF
WOBBL
WOBBL
BUT TO PULL OUT THE TRUE STRENGTH OF THE NEW ZERO-SHIKI...
...I'LL NEED TO USE...
...MORE SPIRIT THAN BEFORE.
NO! RELEASING TOO MUCH SPIRIT AT ONCE IS DANGEROUS!
YOU'RE THE ONE WHO TOLD US TO CREATE OUR OWN SPECIAL MOVES...
...IN CASE WE GOT INTO A DANGEROUS SITUATION.
IF KIRIN HADN'T SAVED ME AT THE DASTOM RUINS...
...THAT GUY WOULD'VE KILLED ME.
BUT THAT'S NOT ALL. I HATE TO ADMIT IT, BUT I KNEW THAT GUY...
...WAS WAY STRONGER THAN ME.

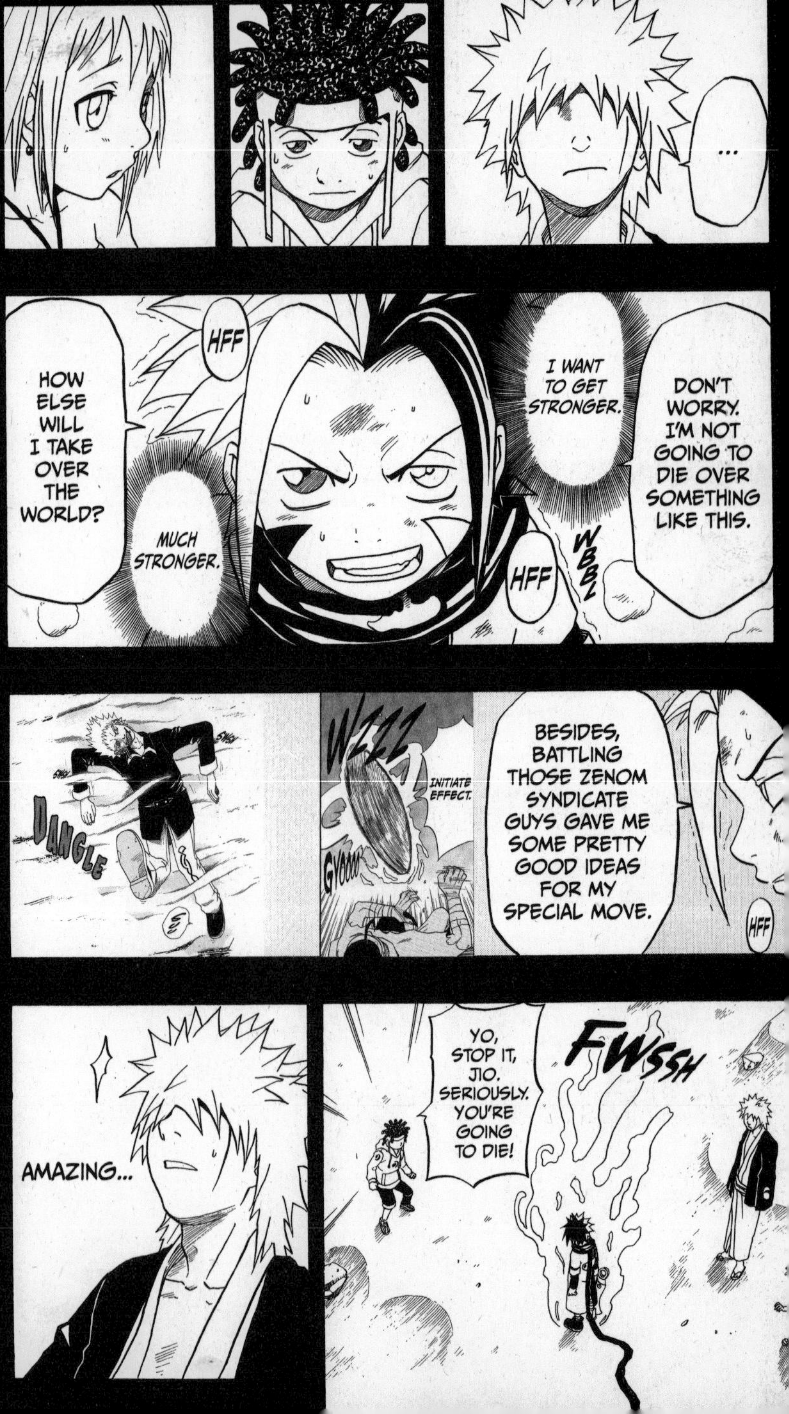
...
DON'T WORRY. I'M NOT GOING TO DIE OVER SOMETHING LIKE THIS.
I WANT TO GET STRONGER.
HFF
WBBL
HFF
HOW ELSE WILL I TAKE OVER THE WORLD?
MUCH STRONGER.
BESIDES, BATTLING THOSE ZENOM SYNDICATE GUYS GAVE ME SOME PRETTY GOOD IDEAS FOR MY SPECIAL MOVE.
HFF
WZZZ
INITIATE EFFECT.
GYOOOO
SWSH
SWSH
DANGLE
FWSSH
YO, STOP IT, JIO. SERIOUSLY. YOU'RE GOING TO DIE!
AMAZING...

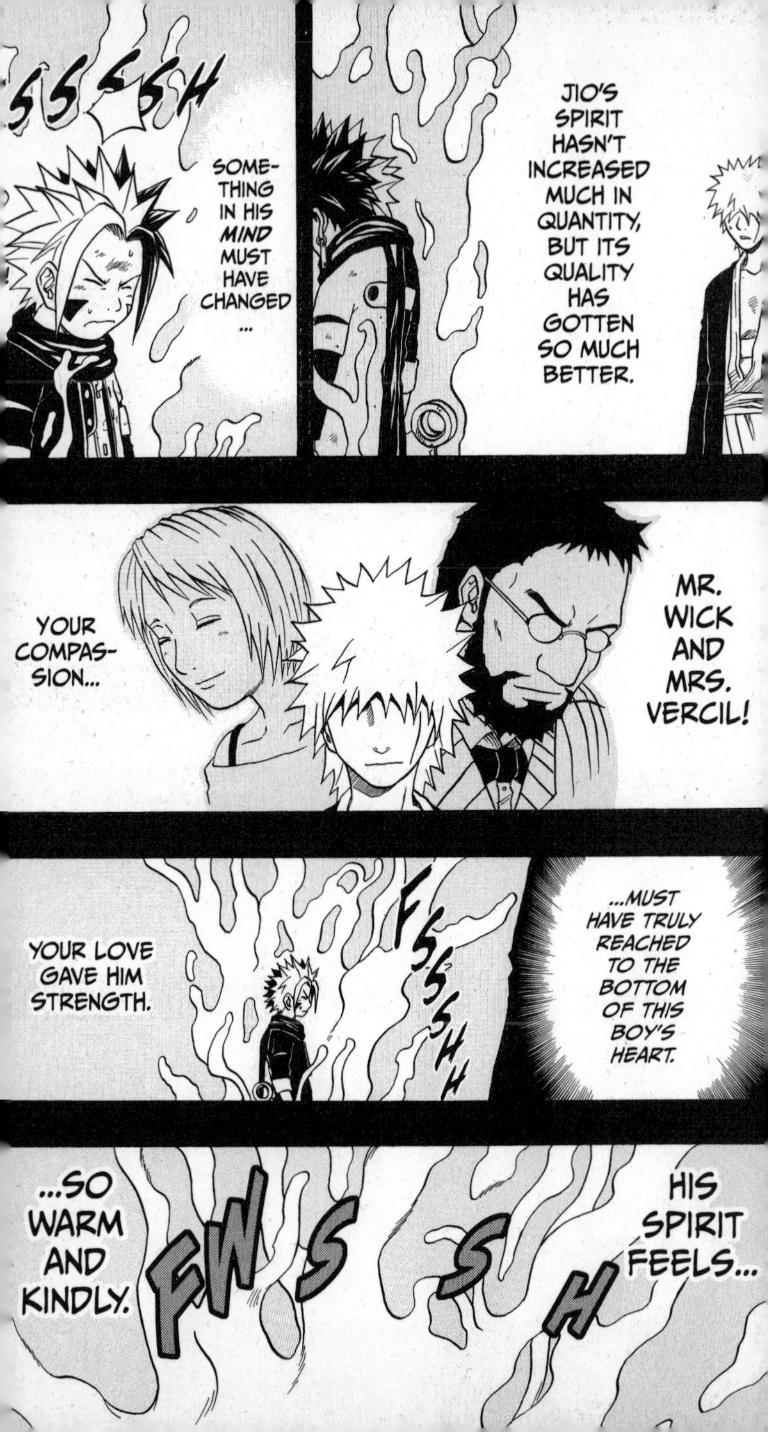
JIO'S SPIRIT HASN'T INCREASED MUCH IN QUANTITY, BUT ITS QUALITY HAS GOTTEN SO MUCH BETTER.
SSSSH
SOME-THING IN HIS *MIND* MUST HAVE CHANGED...
MR. WICK AND MRS. VERCIL!
YOUR COMPAS-SION...
...MUST HAVE TRULY REACHED TO THE BOTTOM OF THIS BOY'S HEART.
FSSSHH
YOUR LOVE GAVE HIM STRENGTH.
HIS SPIRIT FEELS...
FWSSH
...SO WARM AND KINDLY.

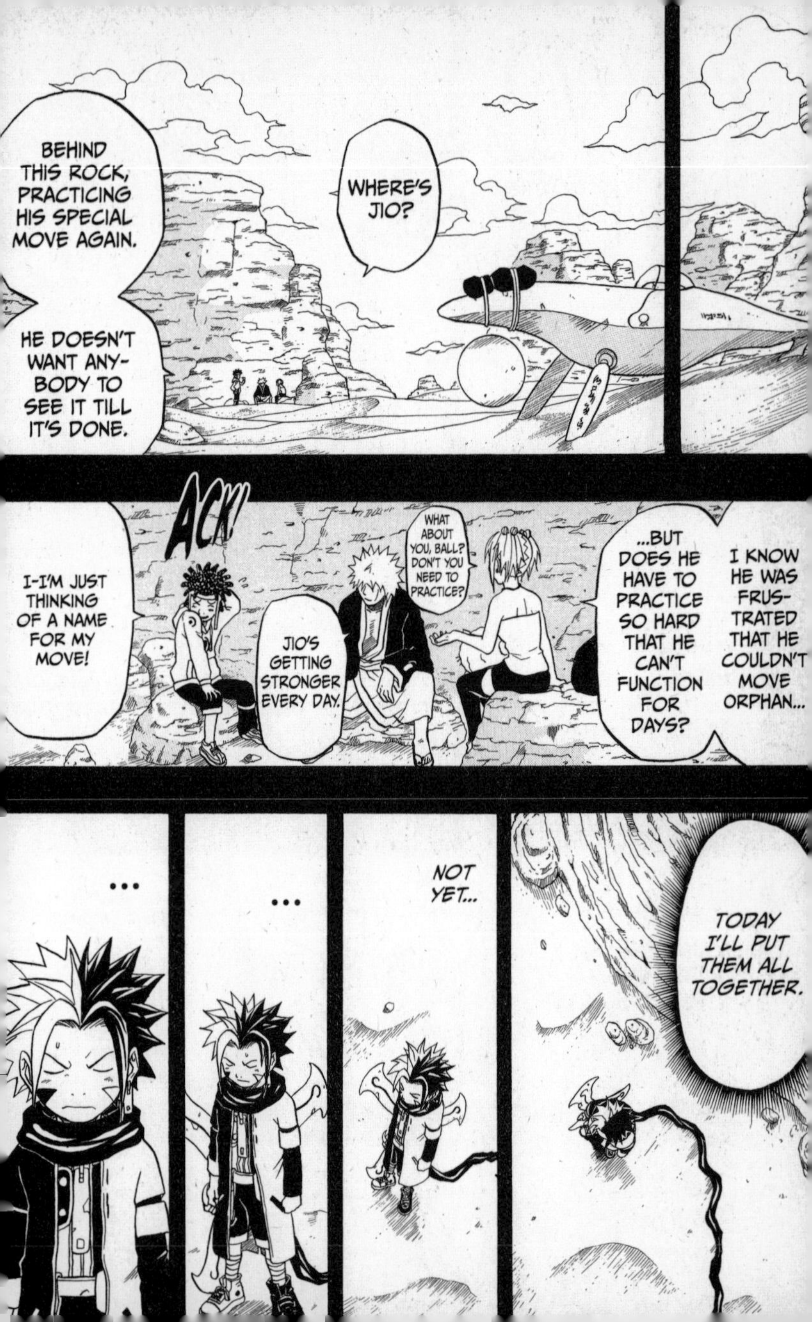
WHERE'S JIO?
BEHIND THIS ROCK, PRACTICING HIS SPECIAL MOVE AGAIN.
HE DOESN'T WANT ANY-BODY TO SEE IT TILL IT'S DONE.
I KNOW HE WAS FRUS-TRATED THAT HE COULDN'T MOVE ORPHAN...
...BUT DOES HE HAVE TO PRACTICE SO HARD THAT HE CAN'T FUNCTION FOR DAYS?
WHAT ABOUT YOU, BALL? DON'T YOU NEED TO PRACTICE?
JIO'S GETTING STRONGER EVERY DAY.
ACK!
I-I'M JUST THINKING OF A NAME FOR MY MOVE!
TODAY I'LL PUT THEM ALL TOGETHER.
NOT YET...
...
...

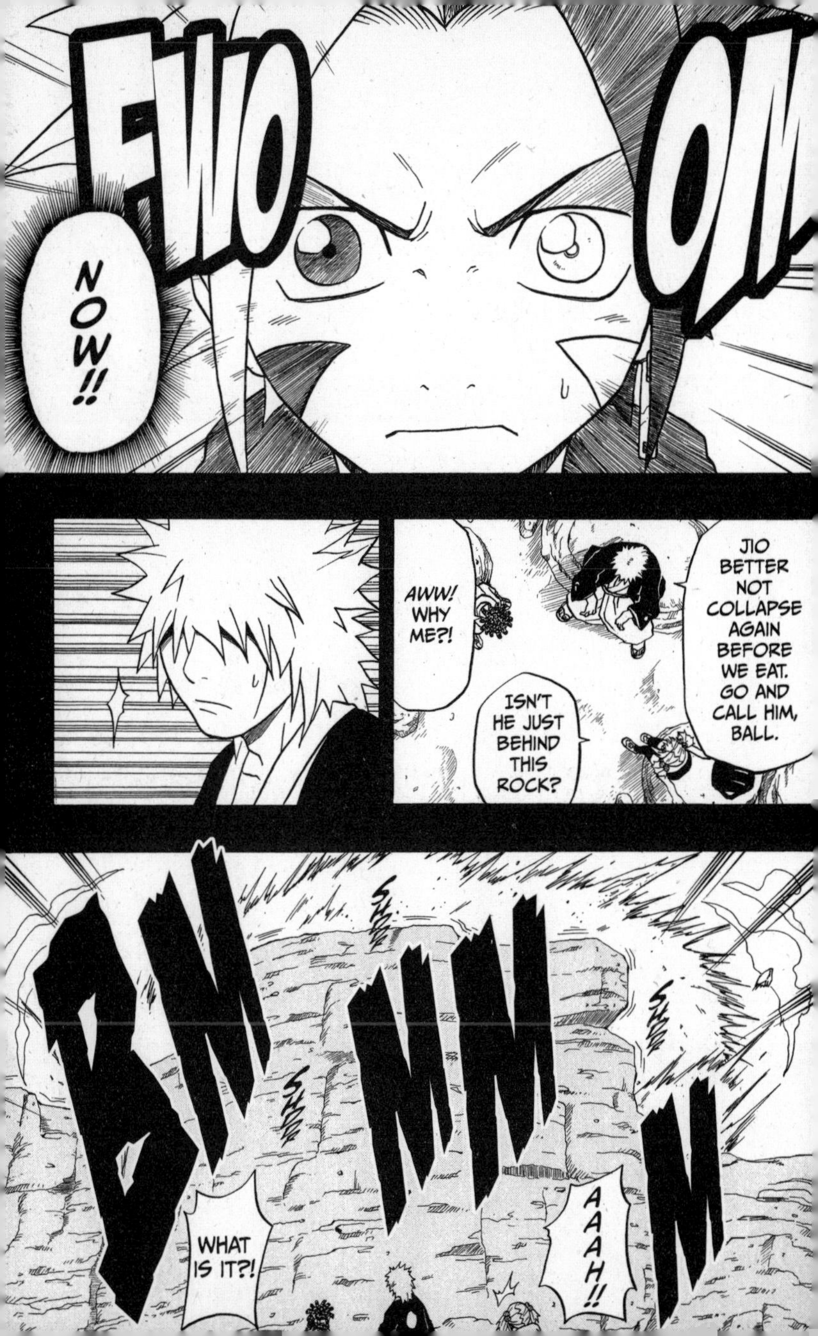
NOW!!
JIO BETTER NOT COLLAPSE AGAIN BEFORE WE EAT. GO AND CALL HIM, BALL.
ISN'T HE JUST BEHIND THIS ROCK?
AWW! WHY ME?!
AAAH!!
WHAT IS IT?!

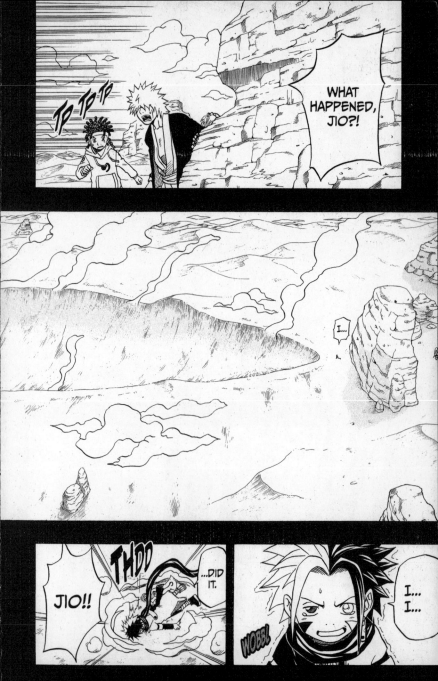

WHAT HAPPENED, JIO?!

I...

JIO!!

THDD

...DID IT.

I...
I...

WOBBL

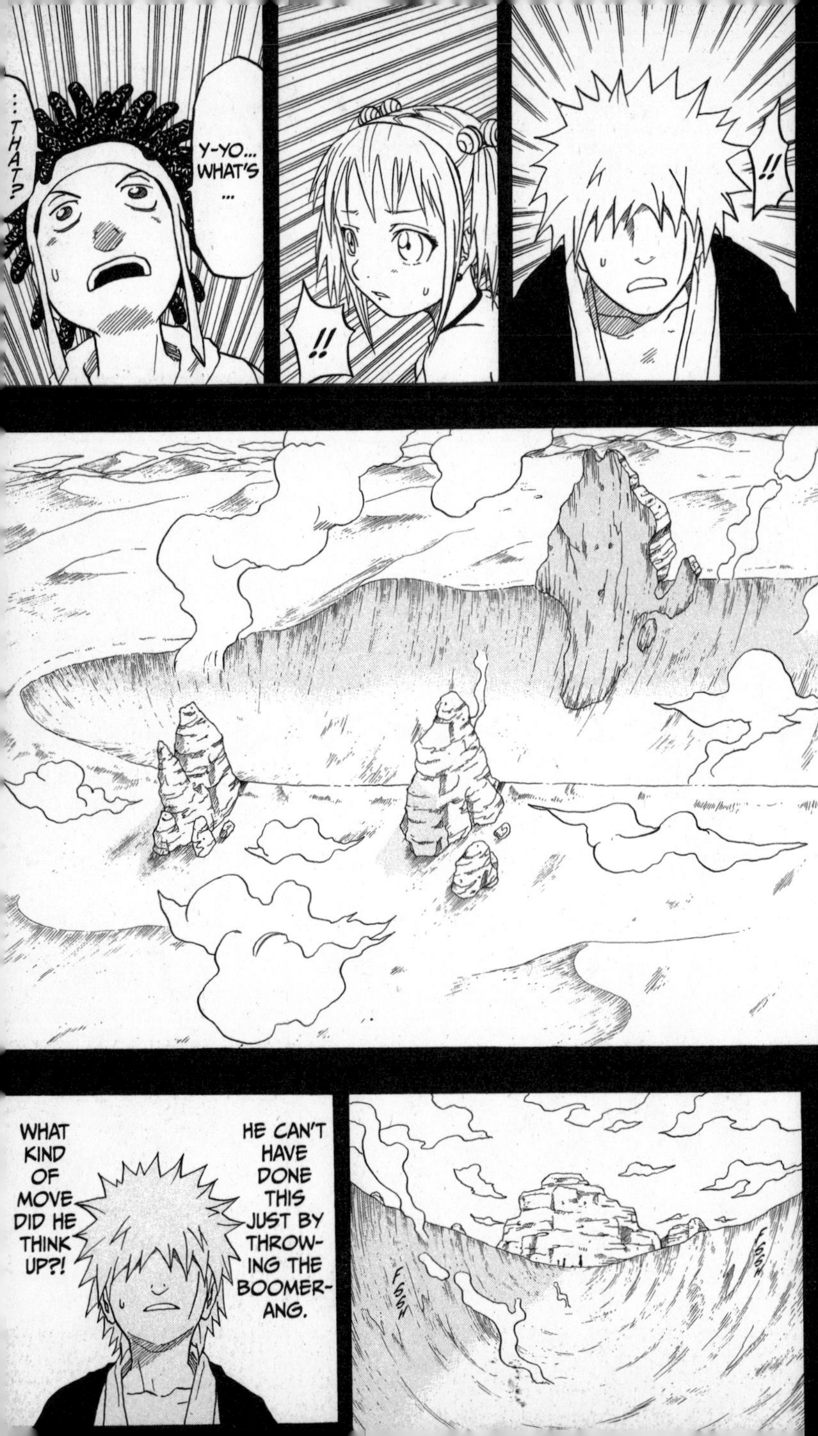
!!
!!
Y-YO... WHAT'S ...
... THAT?
FSSH
FSSH
HE CAN'T HAVE DONE THIS JUST BY THROW-ING THE BOOMER-ANG.
WHAT KIND OF MOVE DID HE THINK UP?!

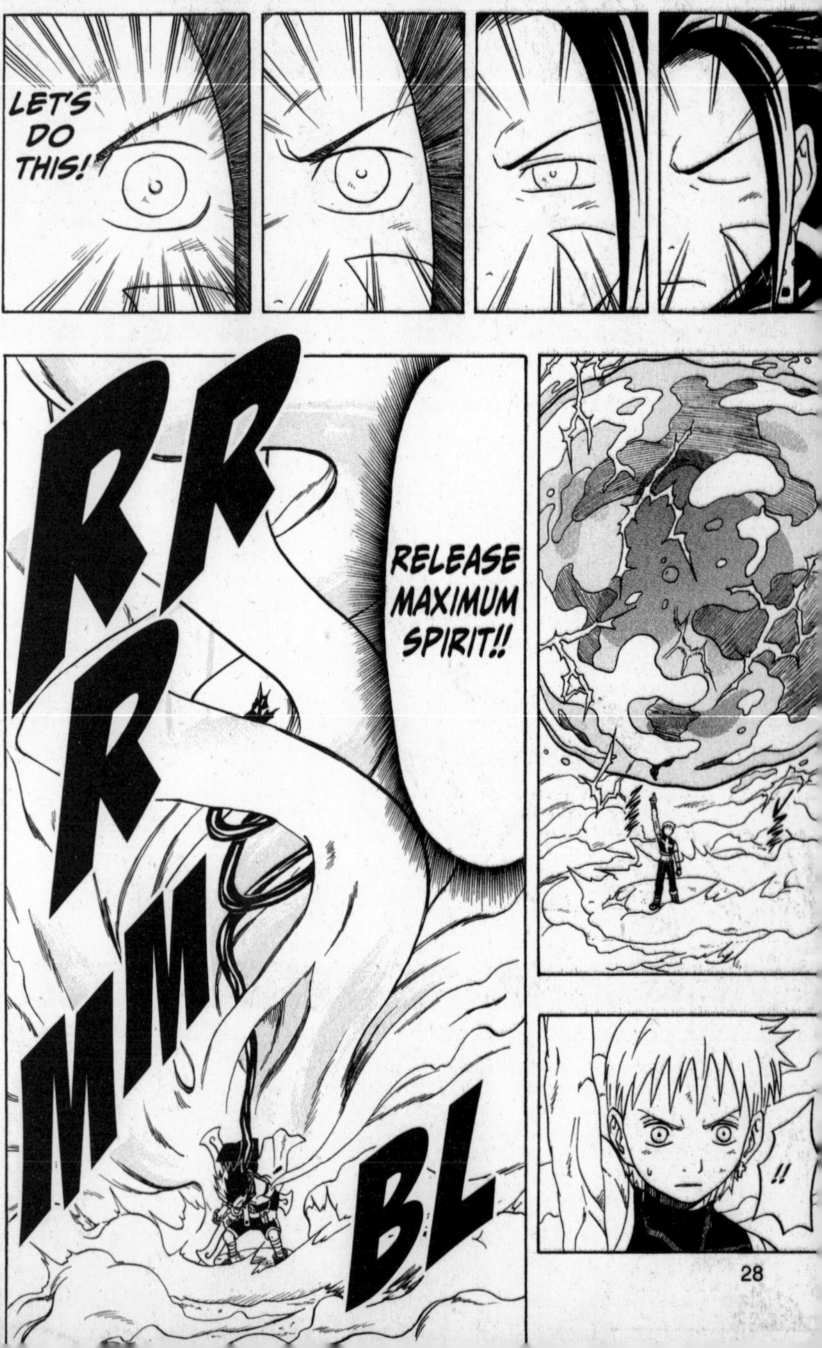
LET'S DO THIS!
!!
RELEASE MAXIMUM SPIRIT!!
RRRMMBL

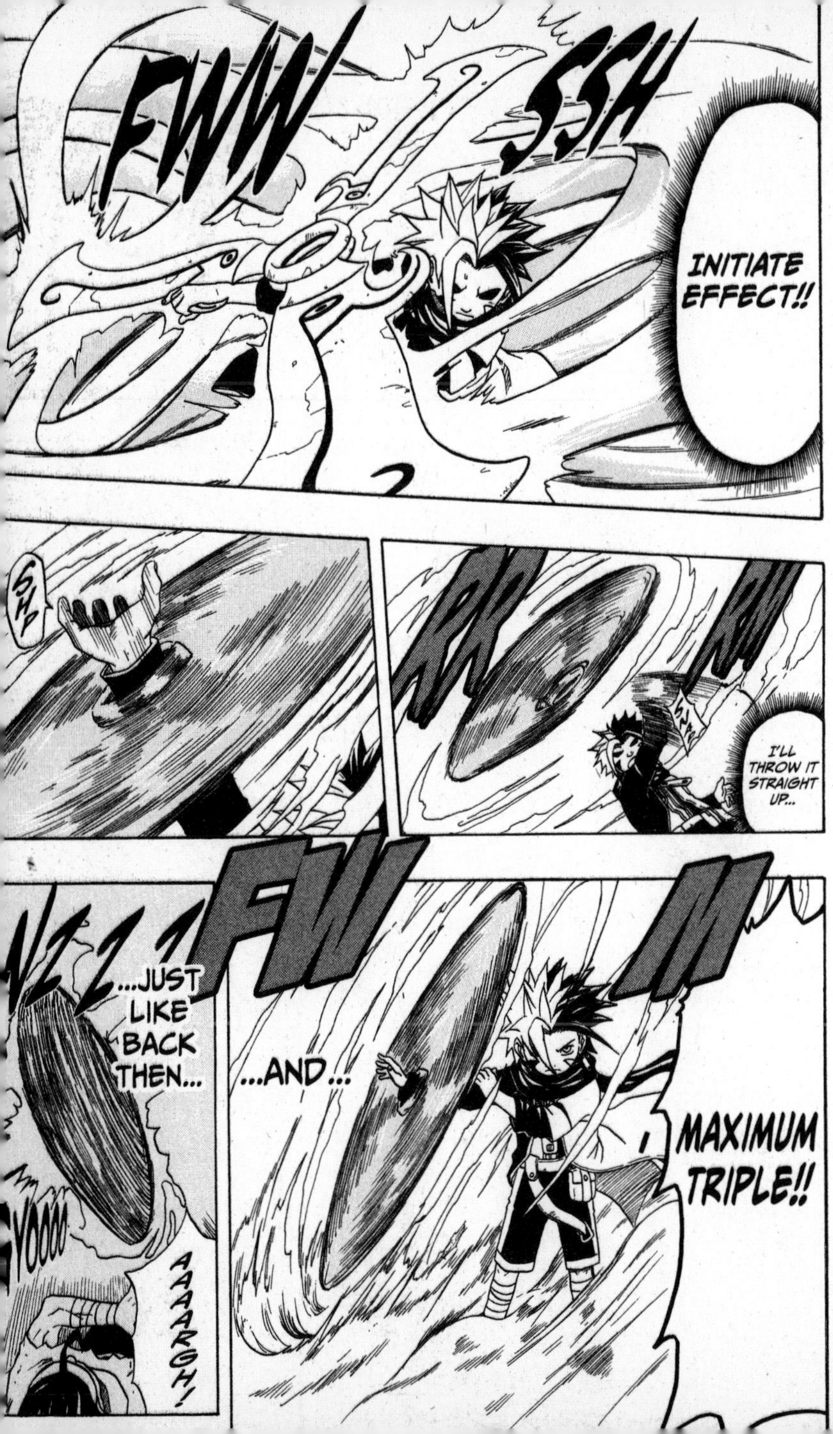
FWW
SSH
INITIATE EFFECT!!
I'LL THROW IT STRAIGHT UP...
...JUST LIKE BACK THEN...
...AND...
MAXIMUM TRIPLE!!
AAAARGH!

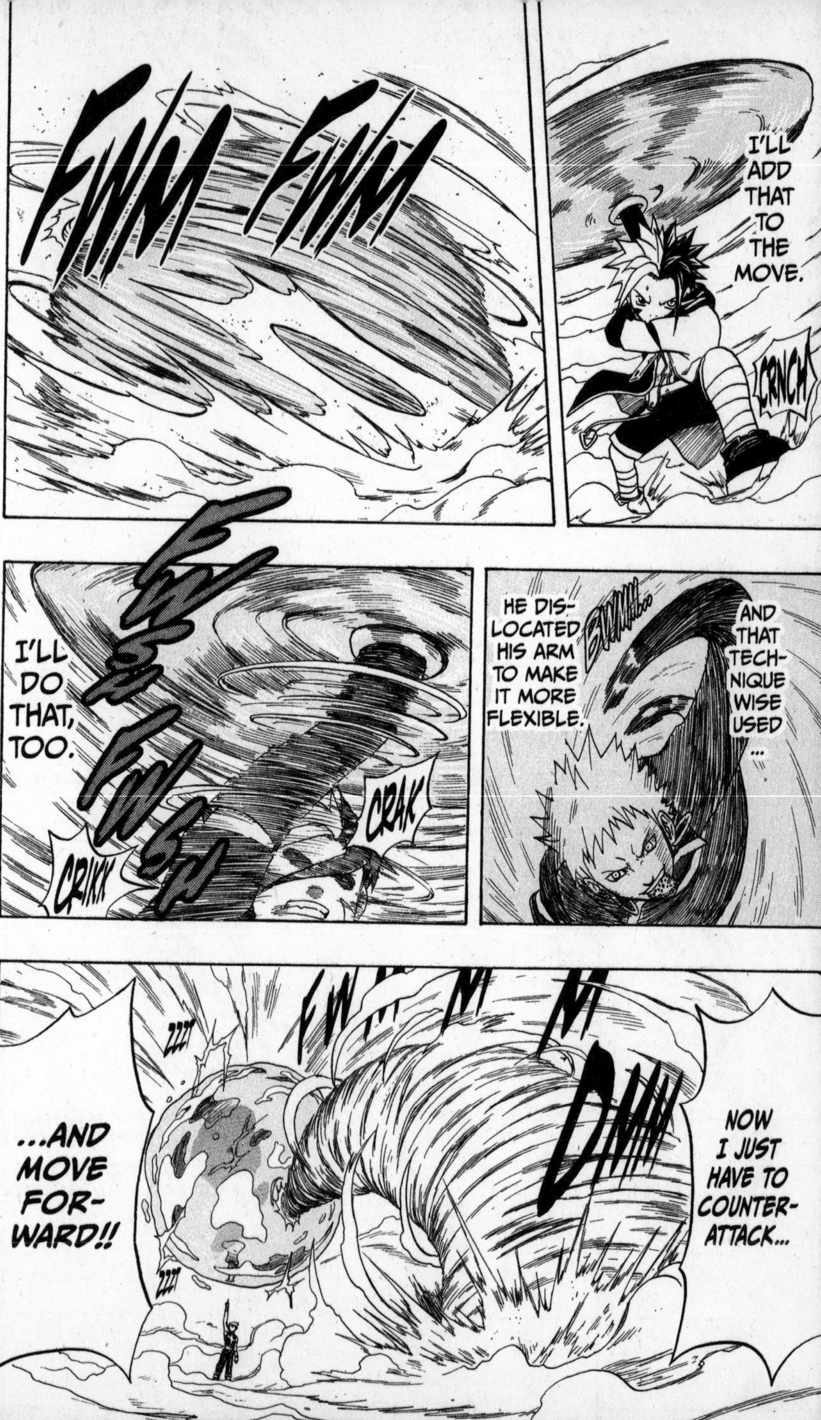

I'LL ADD THAT TO THE MOVE.
CRNCH
FWM FWM
AND THAT TECH-NIQUE WISE USED...
BVMMM...
HE DIS-LOCATED HIS ARM TO MAKE IT MORE FLEXIBLE.
FWSH FWSH
I'LL DO THAT, TOO.
CRAK
CRIKK
NOW I JUST HAVE TO COUNTER-ATTACK...
DMM
ZZZT
...AND MOVE FOR-WARD!!
ZZZT

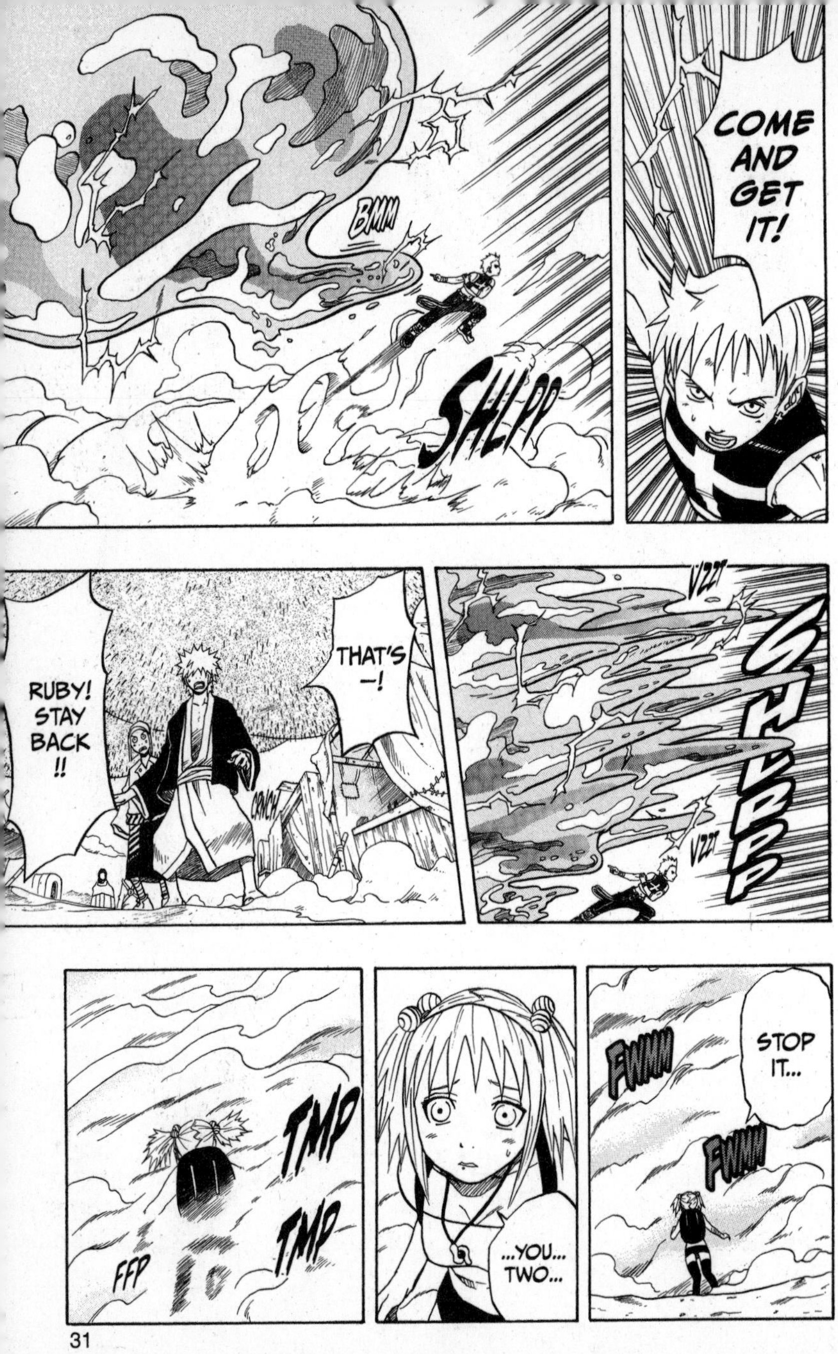
COME AND GET IT!
BMM
SHLIPP
VZZT
VZZT
THAT'S —!
RUBY! STAY BACK !!
CRNCH
STOP IT...
FWMM
FWMM
...YOU... TWO...
TMP
TMP
FFP

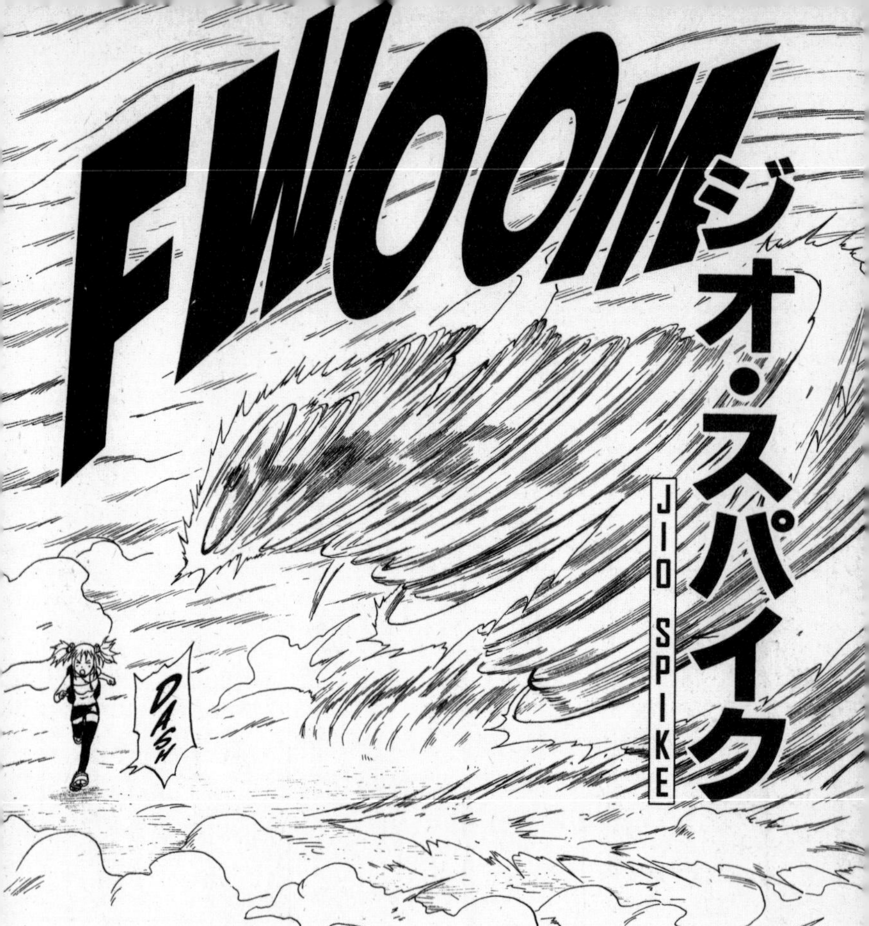
ジオ・スパイク
JIO SPIKE
FWOOM
DASH
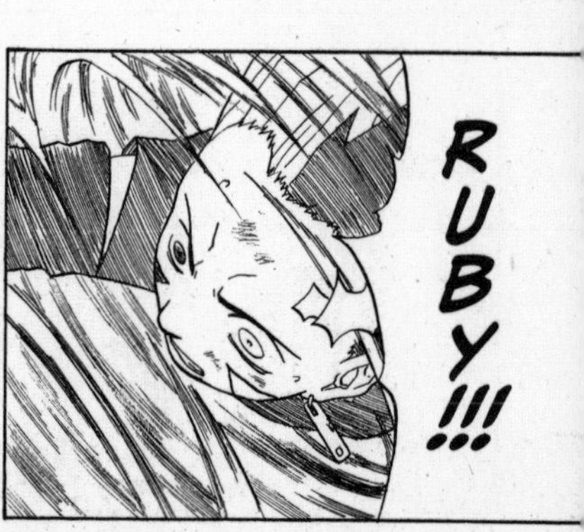
RUBY!!!
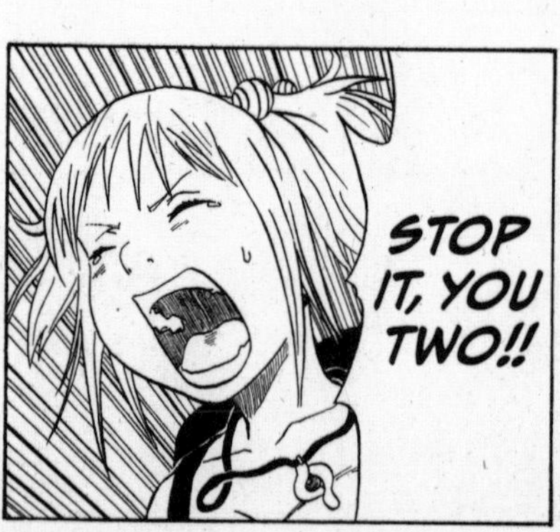
STOP IT, YOU TWO!!

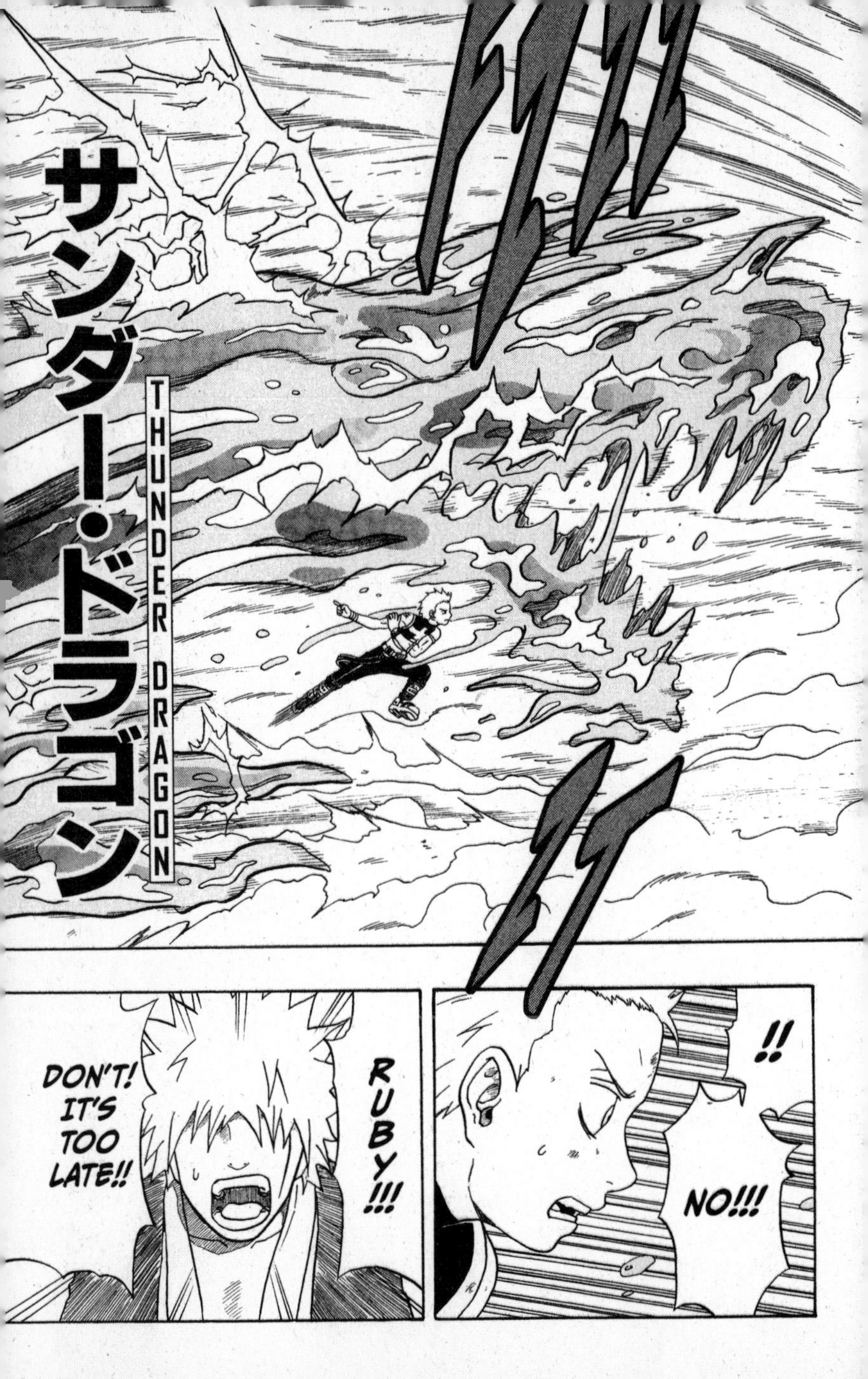
サンダー・ドラゴン
THUNDER DRAGON
!!
NO!!!
RUBY!!!
DON'T! IT'S TOO LATE!!

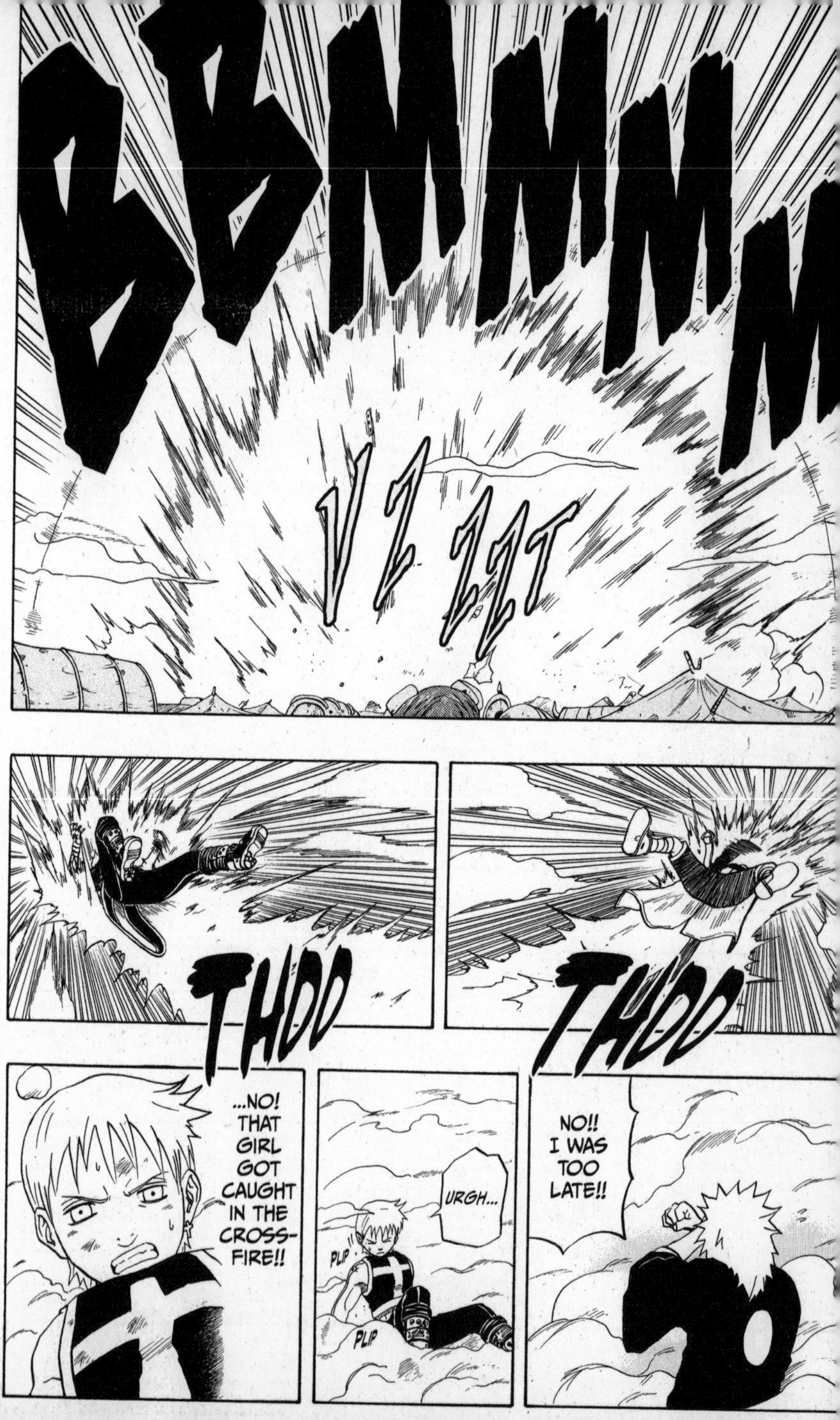
BBMMMM
VZZZT
THOD
THOD
NO!! I WAS TOO LATE!!
URGH...
PLIP
PLIP
...NO! THAT GIRL GOT CAUGHT IN THE CROSS-FIRE!!

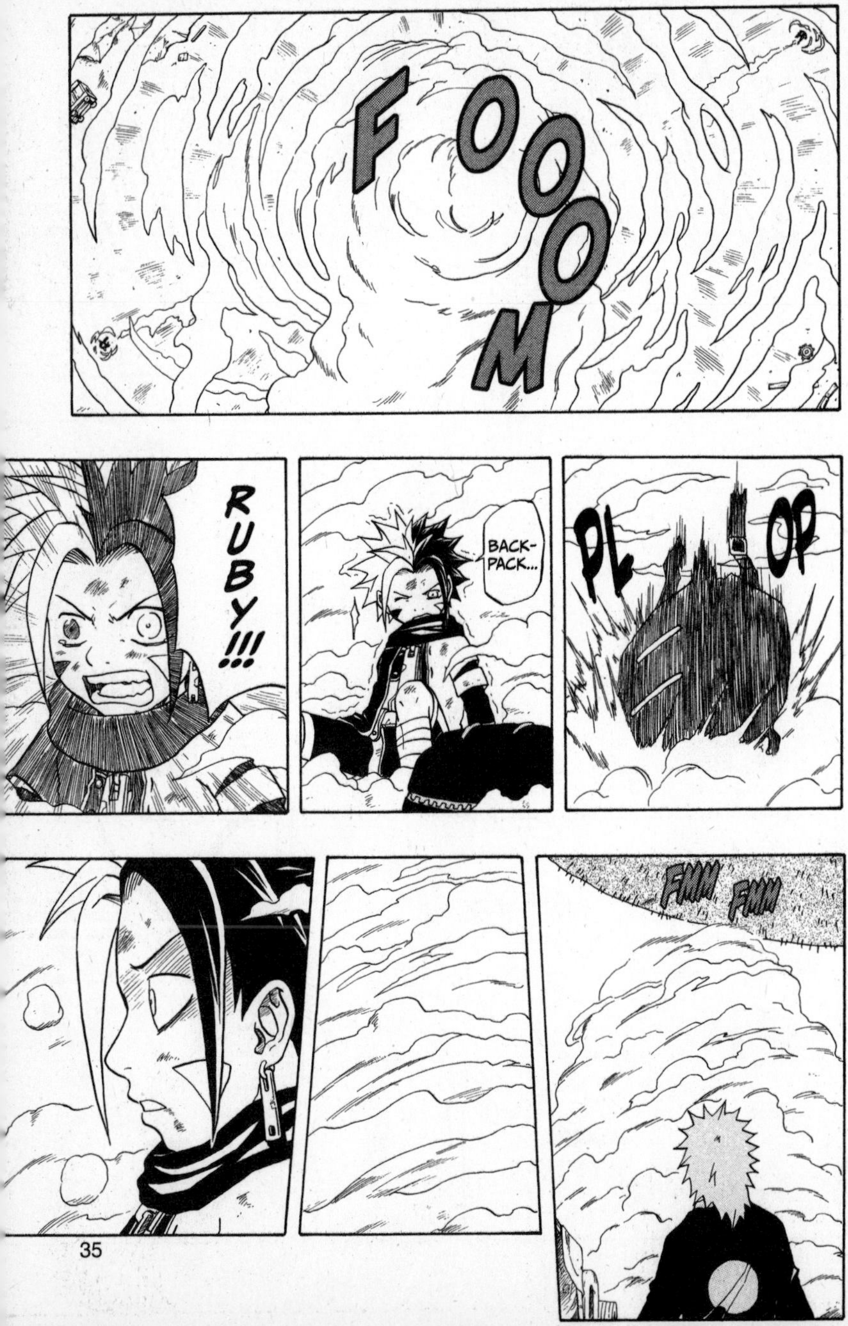
FOOOM
PLOP
BACK-PACK...
RUBY!!!
FMM FMM

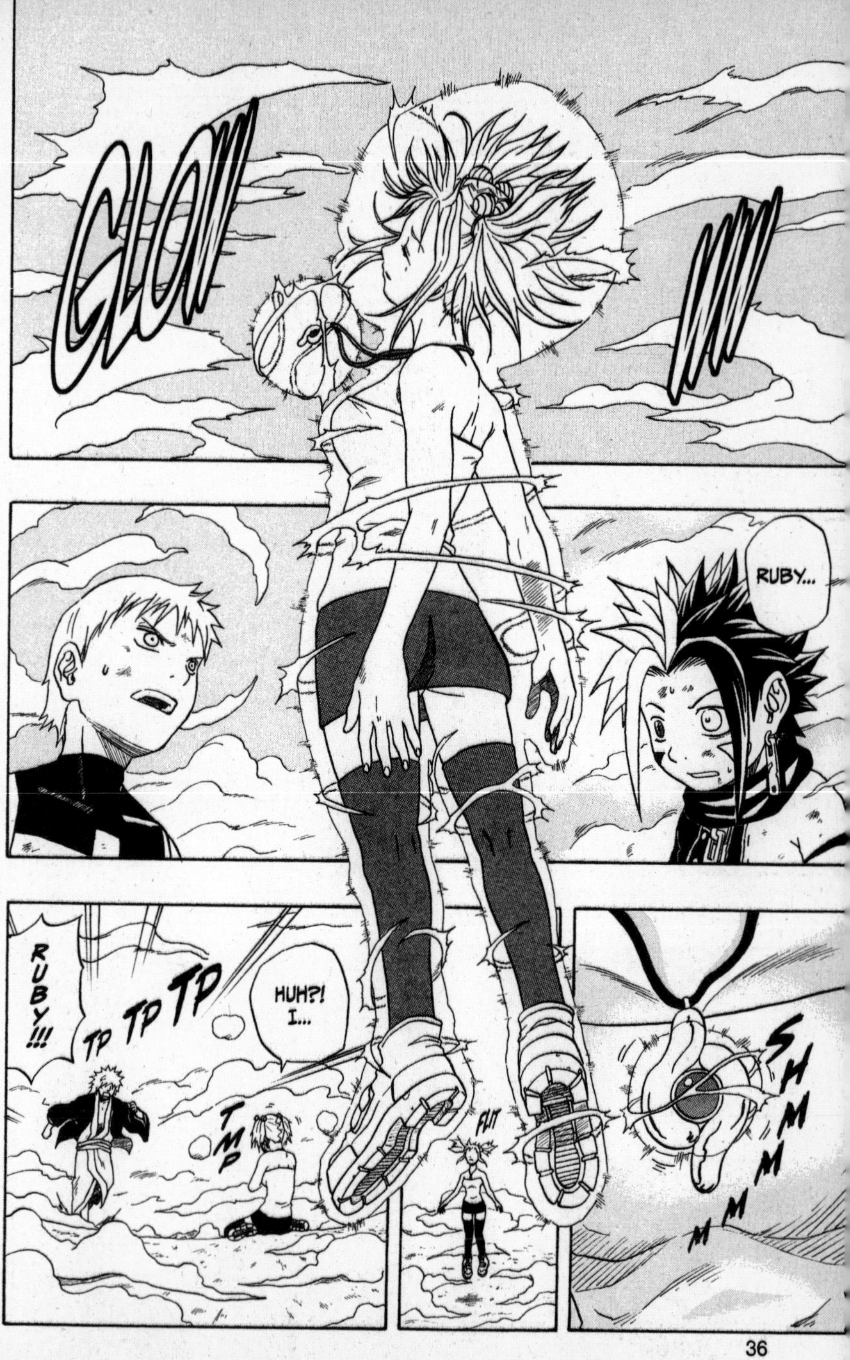
RUBY...
SHMMMMM
FLIT
HUH?! I...
TP TP TP
RUBY!!!
TMP

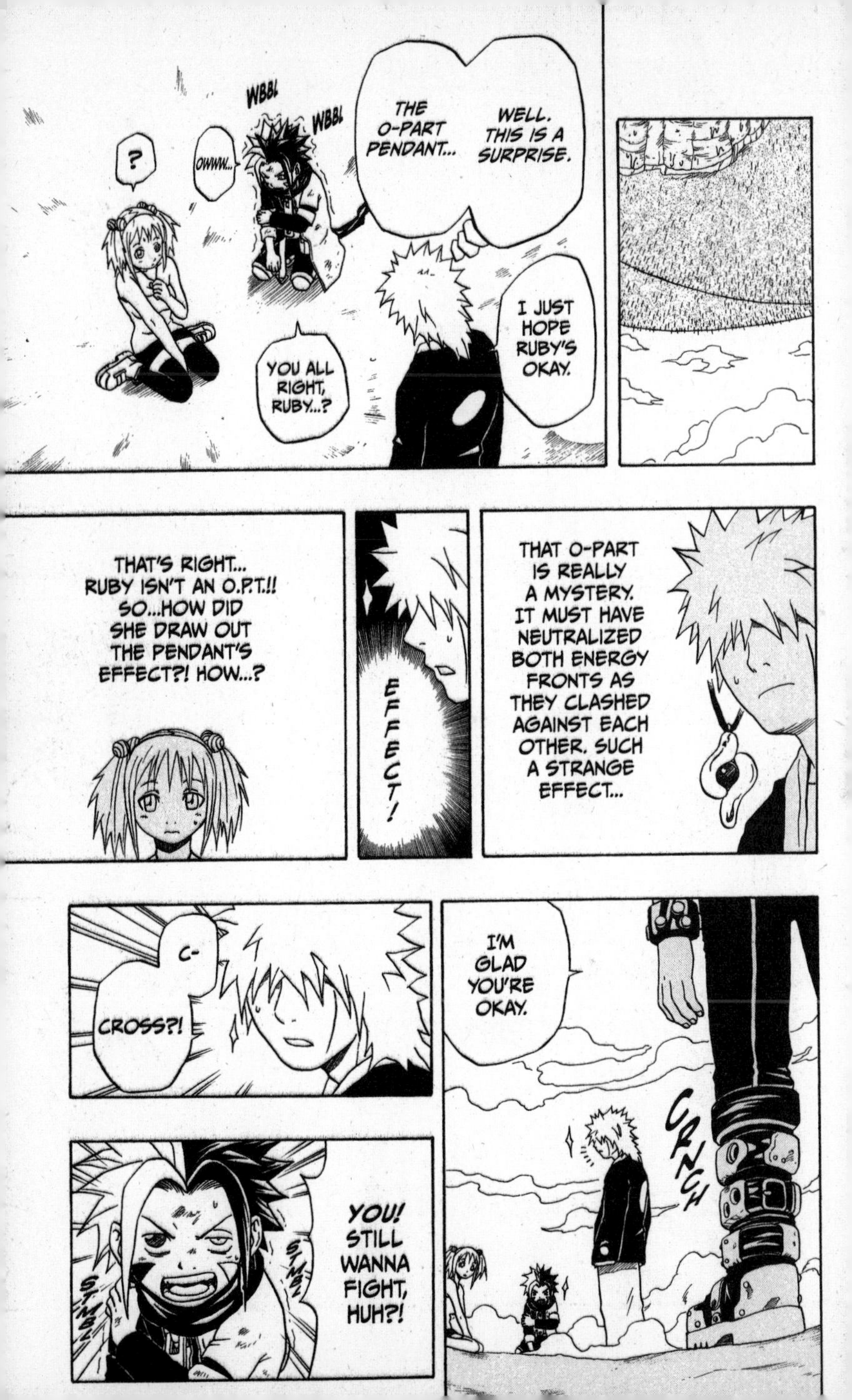
WELL. THIS IS A SURPRISE.
THE O-PART PENDANT...
WBBL
WBBL
OWWW...
?
I JUST HOPE RUBY'S OKAY.
YOU ALL RIGHT, RUBY...?
THAT O-PART IS REALLY A MYSTERY. IT MUST HAVE NEUTRALIZED BOTH ENERGY FRONTS AS THEY CLASHED AGAINST EACH OTHER. SUCH A STRANGE EFFECT...
EFFECT!
THAT'S RIGHT... RUBY ISN'T AN O.P.T.!! SO...HOW DID SHE DRAW OUT THE PENDANT'S EFFECT?! HOW...?
I'M GLAD YOU'RE OKAY.
CRNCH
C-
CROSS?!
STMBL
YOU! STILL WANNA FIGHT, HUH?!
STMBL

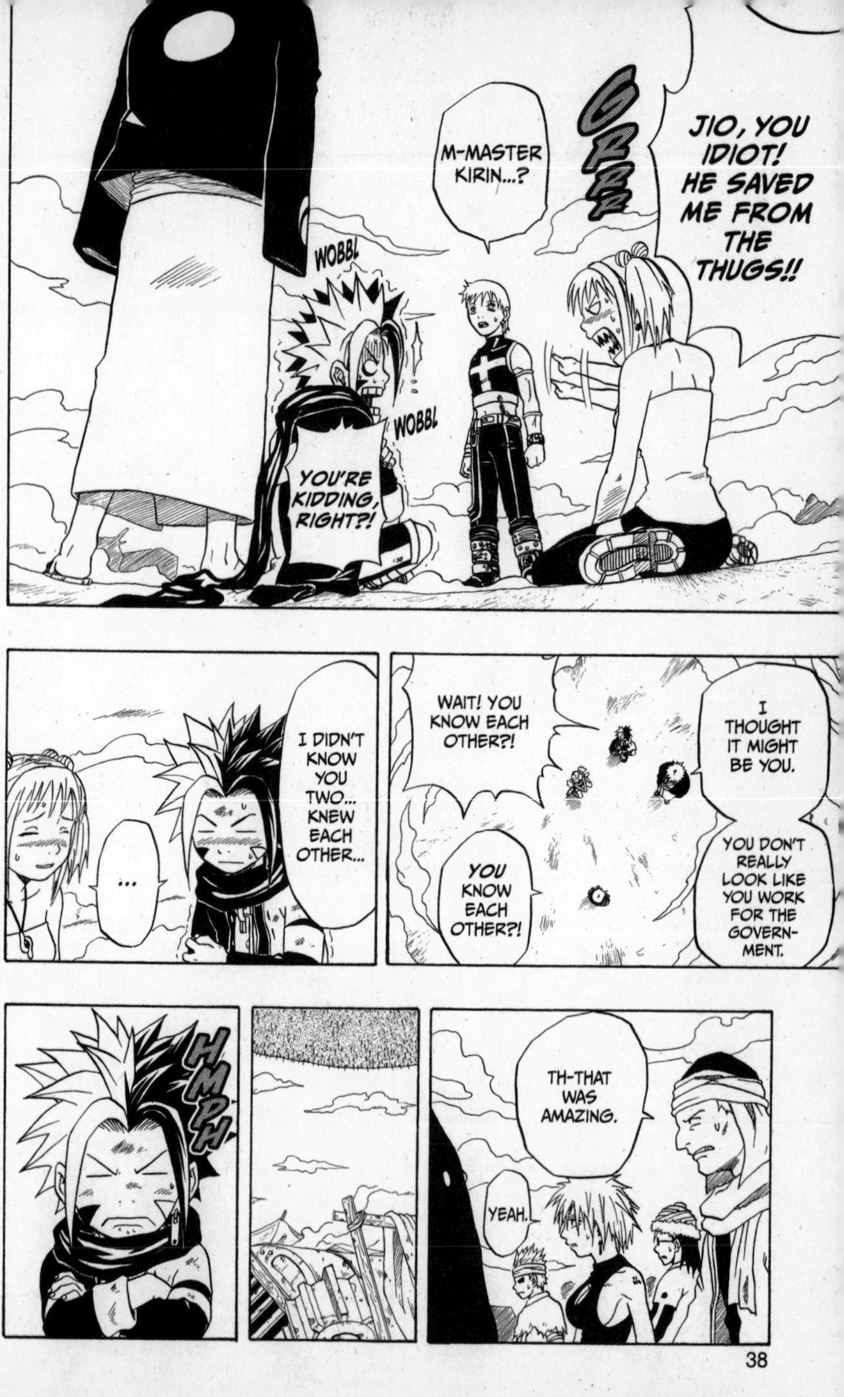
JIO, YOU IDIOT! HE SAVED ME FROM THE THUGS!!
M-MASTER KIRIN...?
WOBBL
YOU'RE KIDDING, RIGHT?!
WOBBL
I THOUGHT IT MIGHT BE YOU.
YOU DON'T REALLY LOOK LIKE YOU WORK FOR THE GOVERN-MENT.
WAIT! YOU KNOW EACH OTHER?!
YOU KNOW EACH OTHER?!
I DIDN'T KNOW YOU TWO... KNEW EACH OTHER...
...
TH-THAT WAS AMAZING.
YEAH.
HMPH

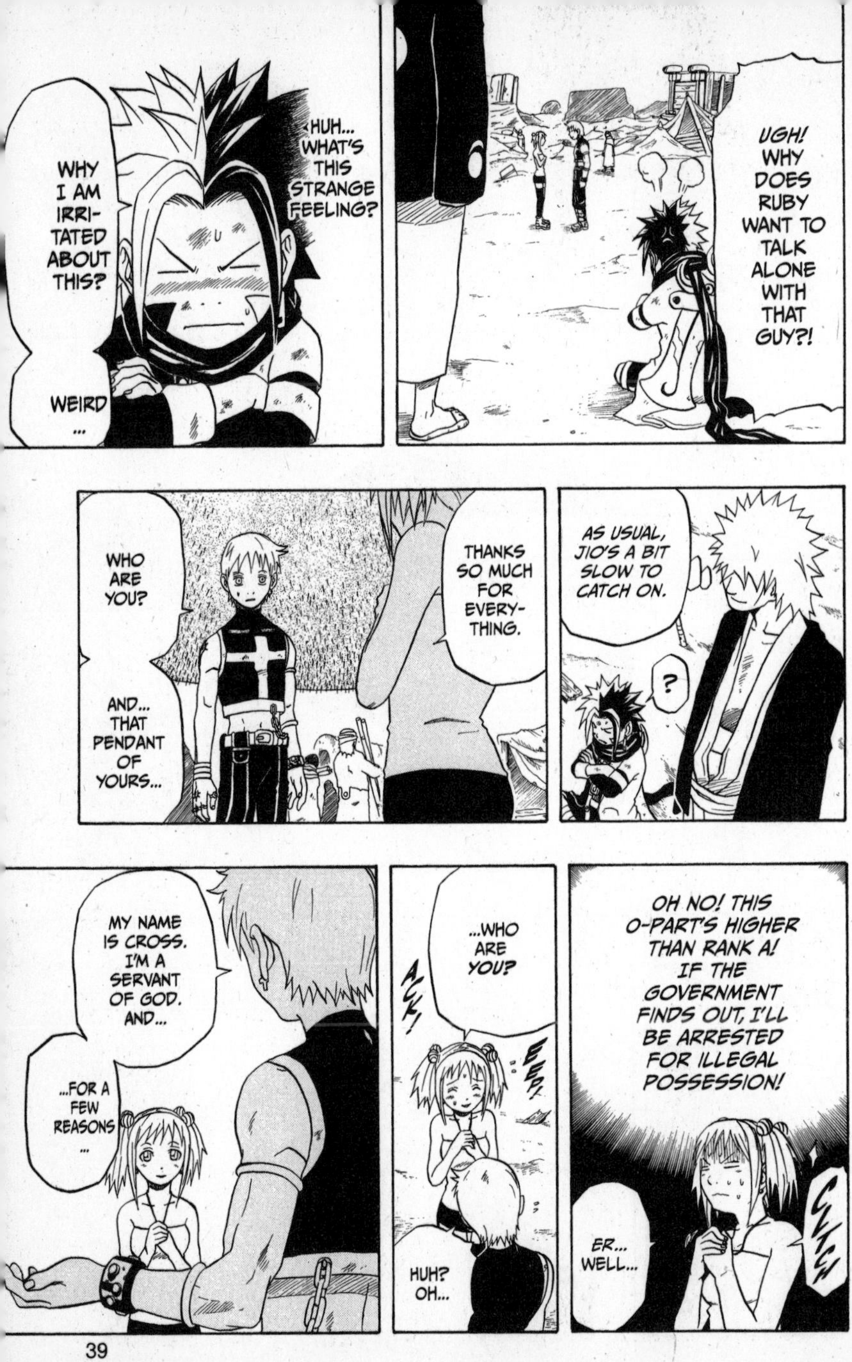
UGH! WHY DOES RUBY WANT TO TALK ALONE WITH THAT GUY?!
HUH... WHAT'S THIS STRANGE FEELING?
WHY I AM IRRI-TATED ABOUT THIS?
WEIRD...
AS USUAL, JIO'S A BIT SLOW TO CATCH ON.
?
THANKS SO MUCH FOR EVERY-THING.
WHO ARE YOU?
AND... THAT PENDANT OF YOURS...
OH NO! THIS O-PART'S HIGHER THAN RANK A! IF THE GOVERNMENT FINDS OUT, I'LL BE ARRESTED FOR ILLEGAL POSSESSION!
ER... WELL...
...WHO ARE YOU?
EEP!
ACK!
HUH? OH...
MY NAME IS CROSS. I'M A SERVANT OF GOD. AND...
...FOR A FEW REASONS...

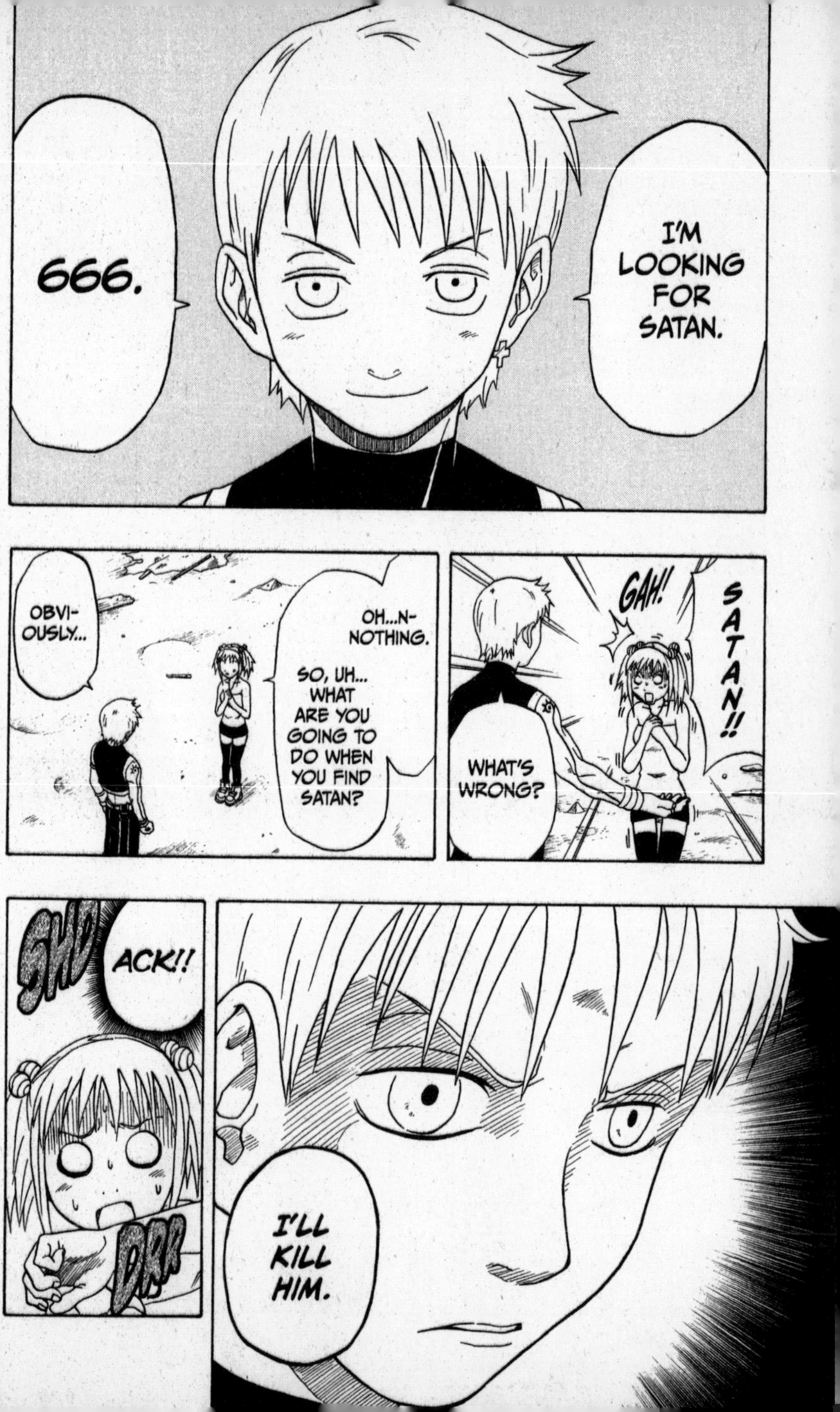
I'M LOOKING FOR SATAN.
666.
SATAN!!
GAH!
WHAT'S WRONG?
OH...N-NOTHING.
SO, UH... WHAT ARE YOU GOING TO DO WHEN YOU FIND SATAN?
OBVIOUSLY...
I'LL KILL HIM.
ACK!!

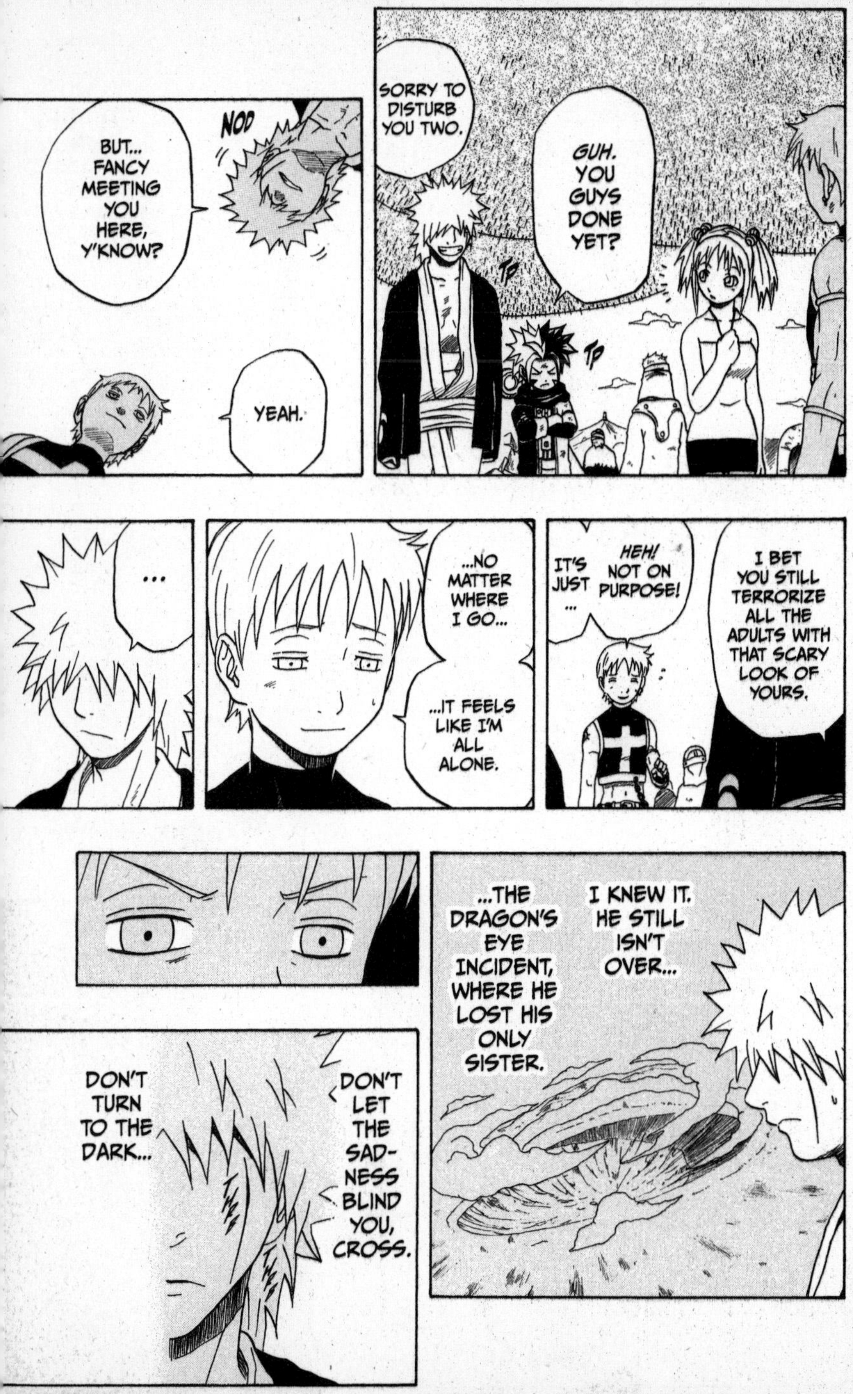
SORRY TO DISTURB YOU TWO.
GUH. YOU GUYS DONE YET?
TP
TP
NOD
BUT... FANCY MEETING YOU HERE, Y'KNOW?
YEAH.
I BET YOU STILL TERRORIZE ALL THE ADULTS WITH THAT SCARY LOOK OF YOURS.
HEH! NOT ON PURPOSE!
IT'S JUST ...
...NO MATTER WHERE I GO...
...IT FEELS LIKE I'M ALL ALONE.
...
I KNEW IT. HE STILL ISN'T OVER...
...THE DRAGON'S EYE INCIDENT, WHERE HE LOST HIS ONLY SISTER.
DON'T LET THE SAD-NESS BLIND YOU, CROSS.
DON'T TURN TO THE DARK...

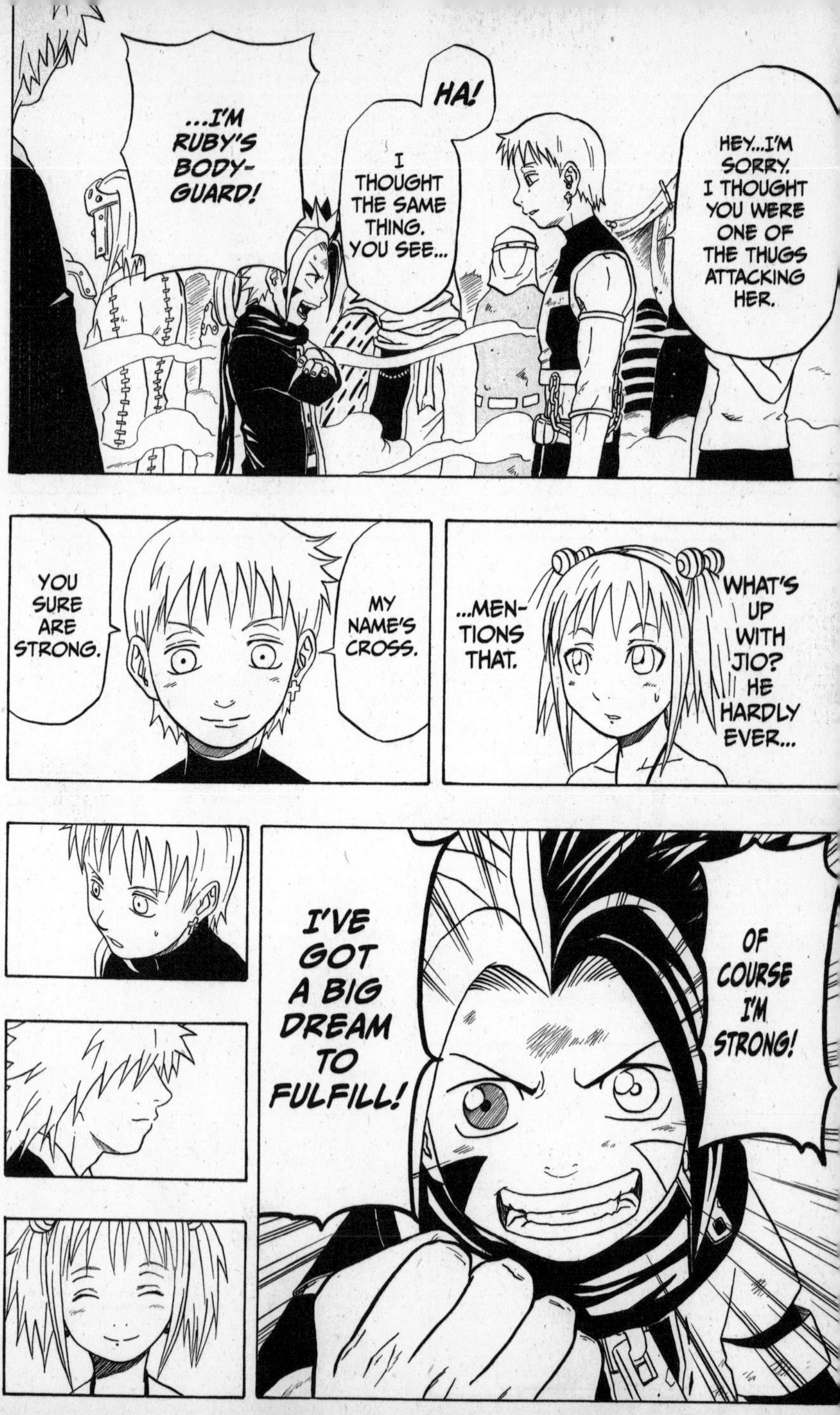
HEY...I'M SORRY. I THOUGHT YOU WERE ONE OF THE THUGS ATTACKING HER.
HA!
I THOUGHT THE SAME THING. YOU SEE...
...I'M RUBY'S BODY-GUARD!
WHAT'S UP WITH JIO? HE HARDLY EVER...
...MEN-TIONS THAT.
MY NAME'S CROSS.
YOU SURE ARE STRONG.
OF COURSE I'M STRONG!
I'VE GOT A BIG DREAM TO FULFILL!

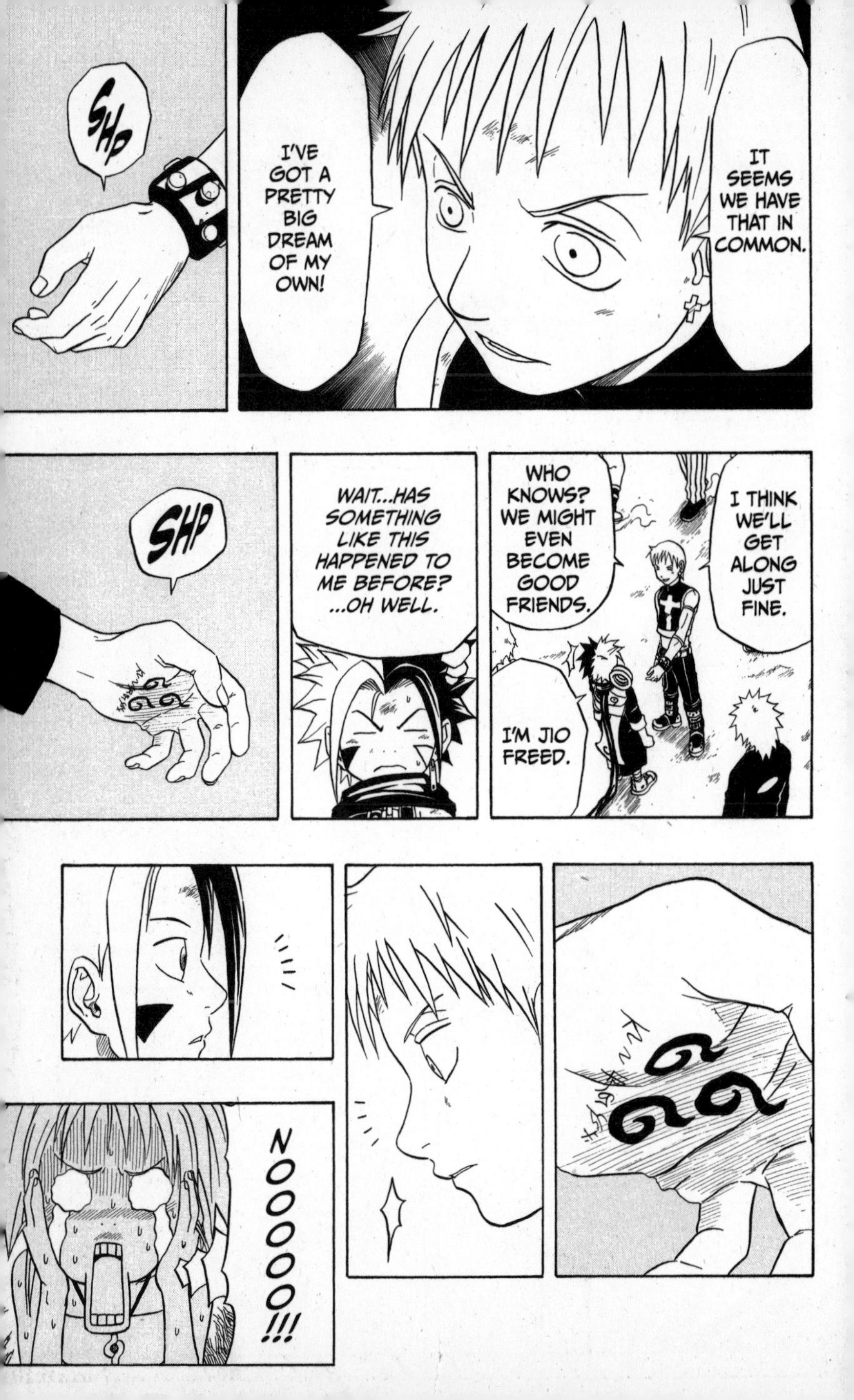
IT SEEMS WE HAVE THAT IN COMMON.
I'VE GOT A PRETTY BIG DREAM OF MY OWN!
SHP
I THINK WE'LL GET ALONG JUST FINE.
WHO KNOWS? WE MIGHT EVEN BECOME GOOD FRIENDS.
I'M JIO FREED.
WAIT...HAS SOMETHING LIKE THIS HAPPENED TO ME BEFORE? ...OH WELL.
SHP
NOOOOOO!!!

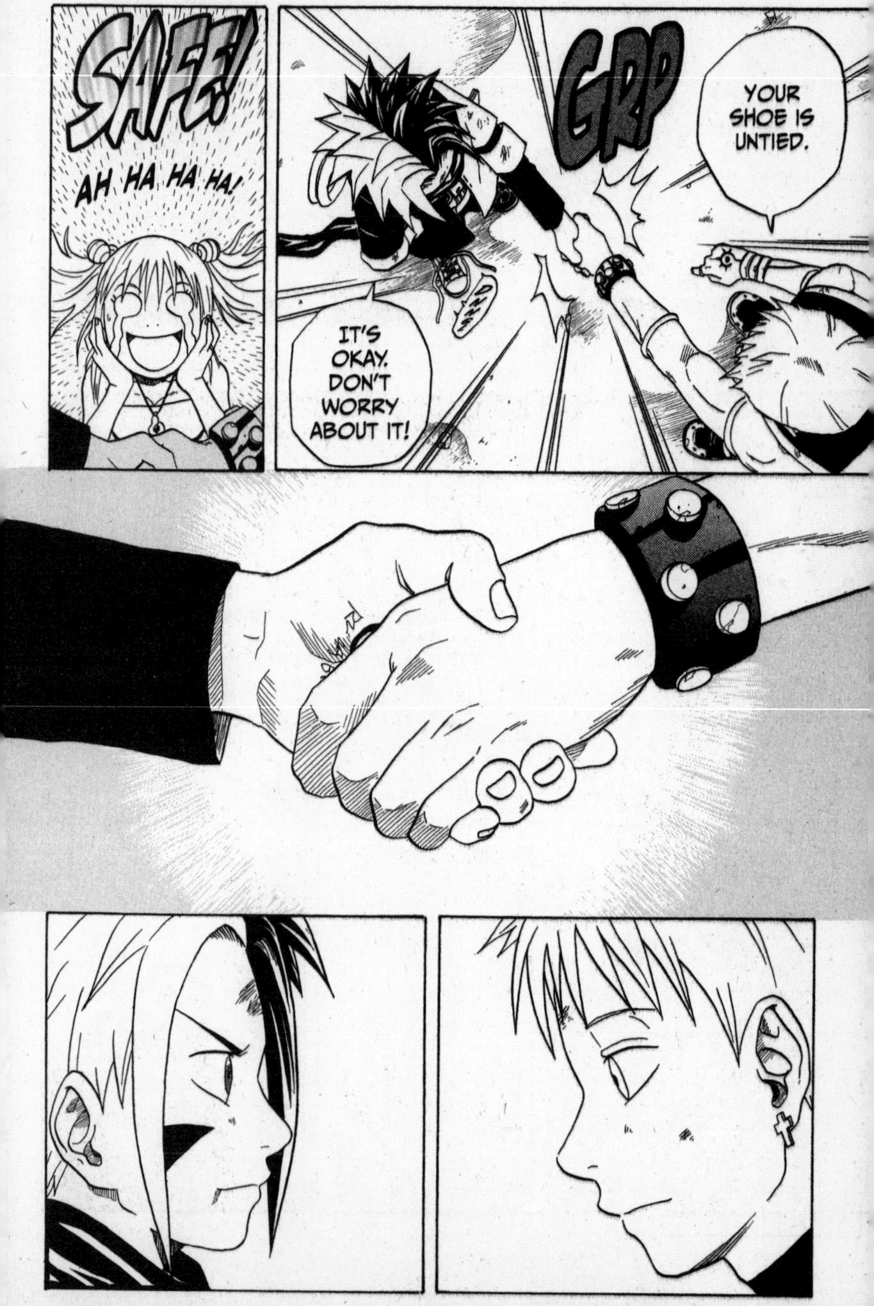
GRP
YOUR SHOE IS UNTIED.
IT'S OKAY. DON'T WORRY ABOUT IT!
SAFE!
AH HA HA HA!

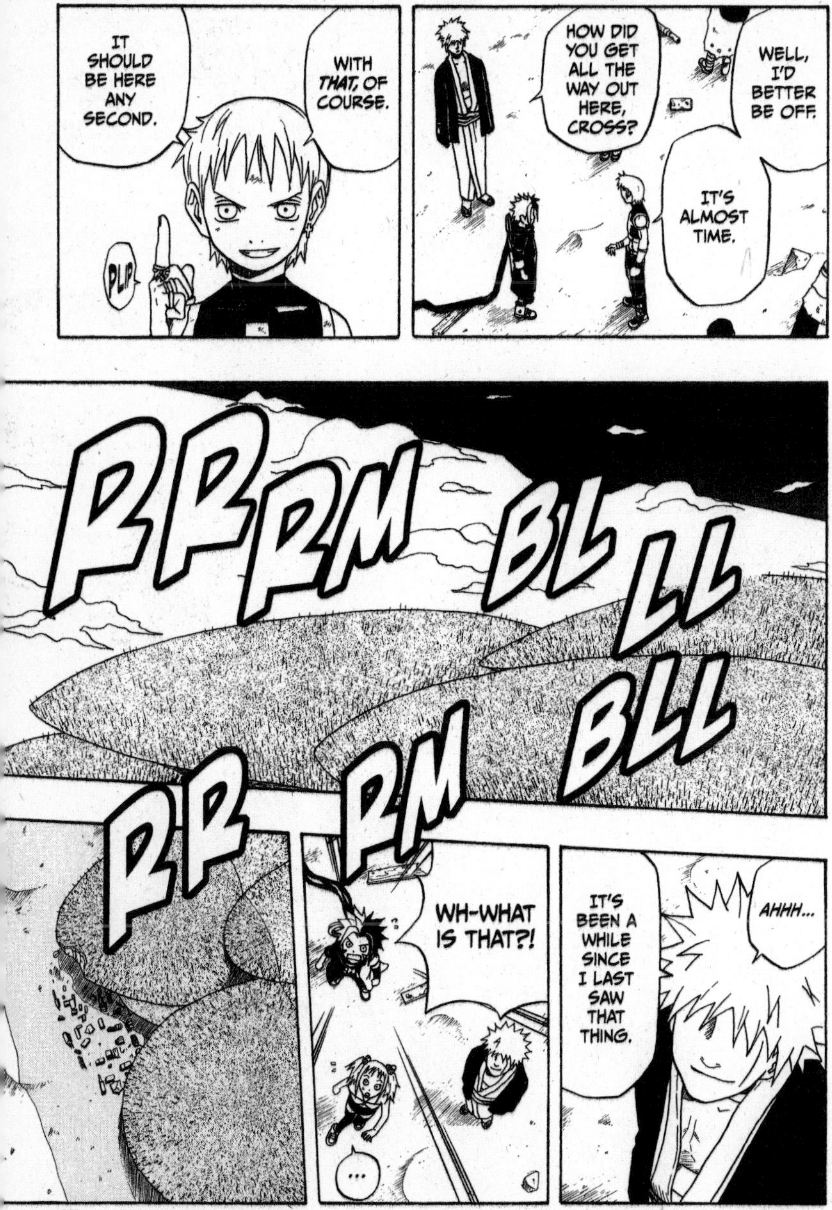
WELL, I'D BETTER BE OFF.
HOW DID YOU GET ALL THE WAY OUT HERE, CROSS?
IT'S ALMOST TIME.
WITH *THAT,* OF COURSE.
IT SHOULD BE HERE ANY SECOND.
PLIP
RRRM
BLLL
RRRM
BLLL
AHHH...
IT'S BEEN A WHILE SINCE I LAST SAW THAT THING.
WH-WHAT IS THAT?!
...

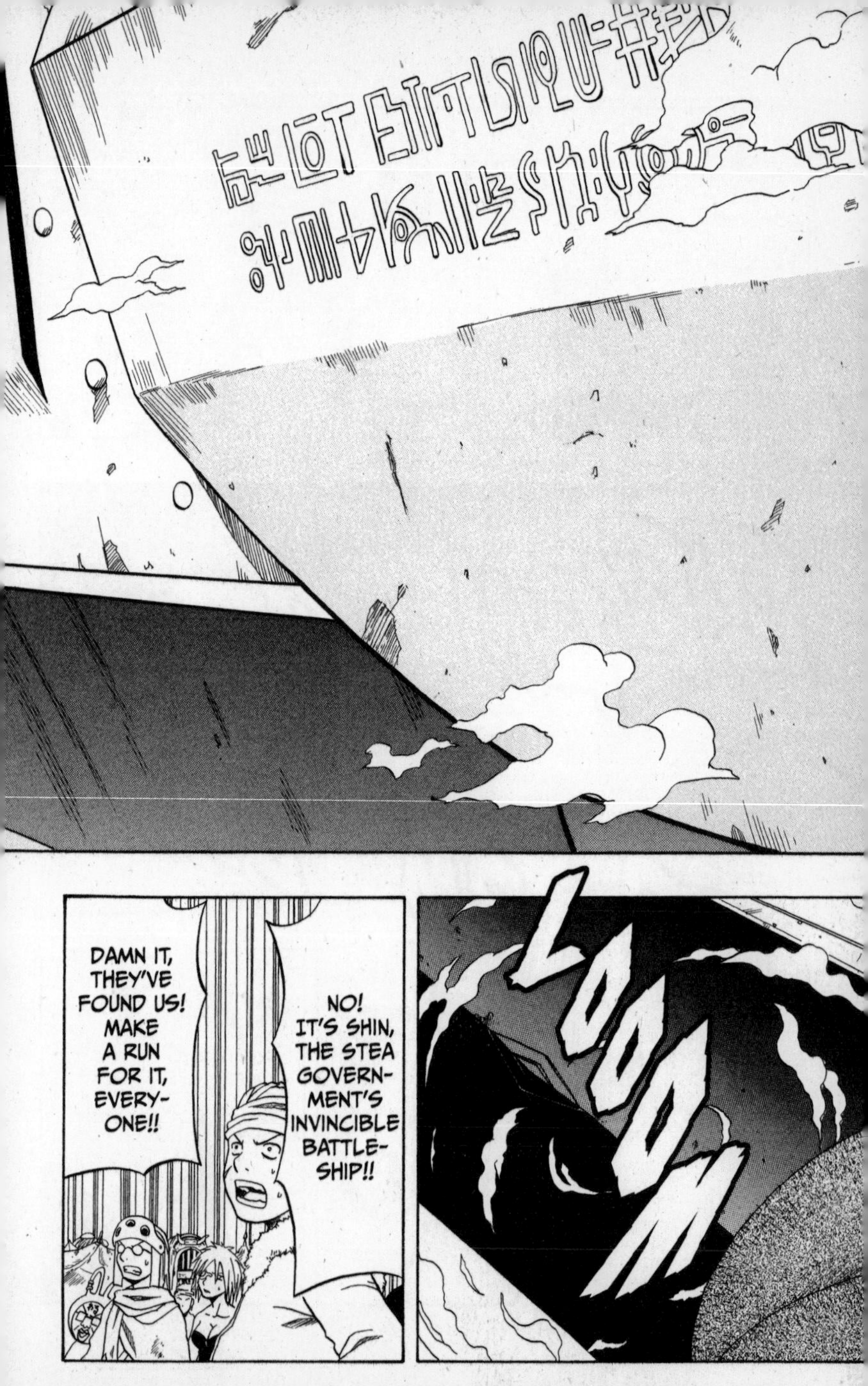
DAMN IT, THEY'VE FOUND US! MAKE A RUN FOR IT, EVERY-ONE!!
NO! IT'S SHIN, THE STEA GOVERN-MENT'S INVINCIBLE BATTLE-SHIP!!

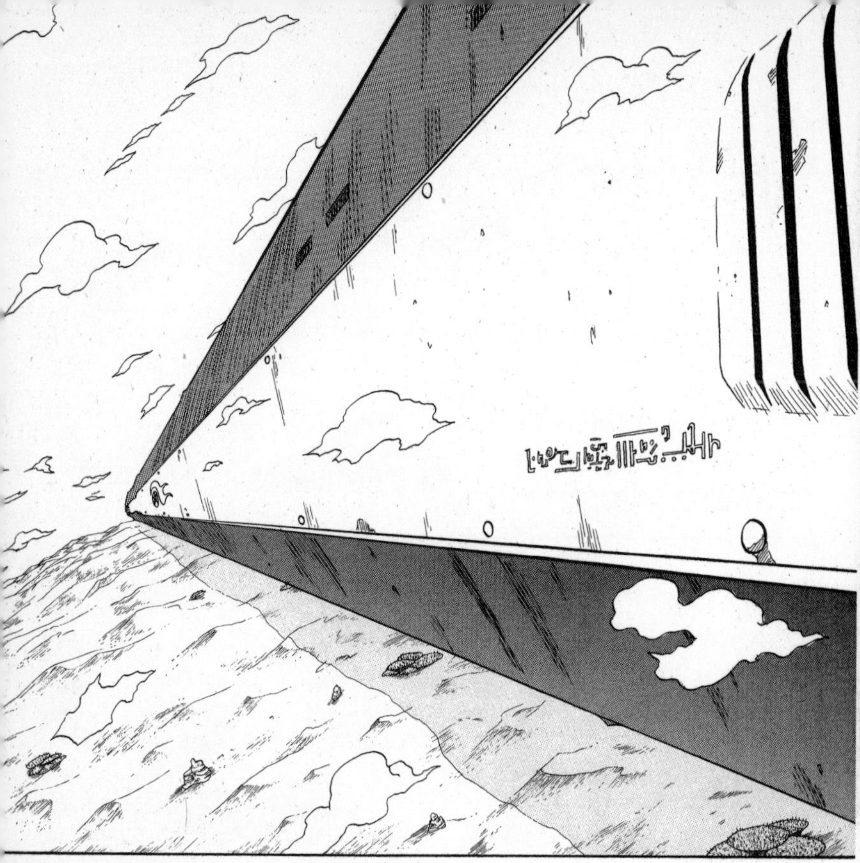

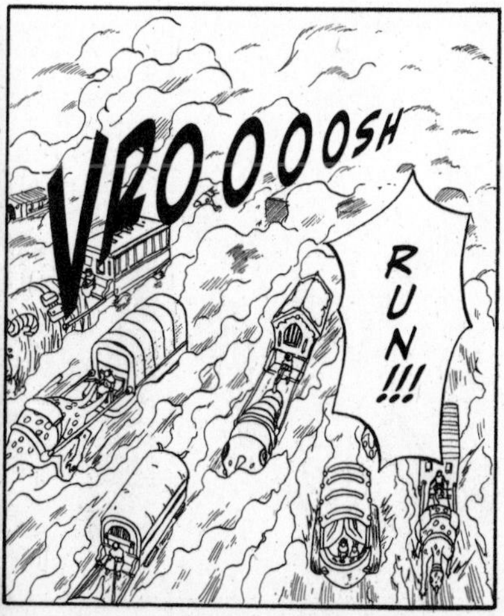
VROOOOSH
RUN!!!

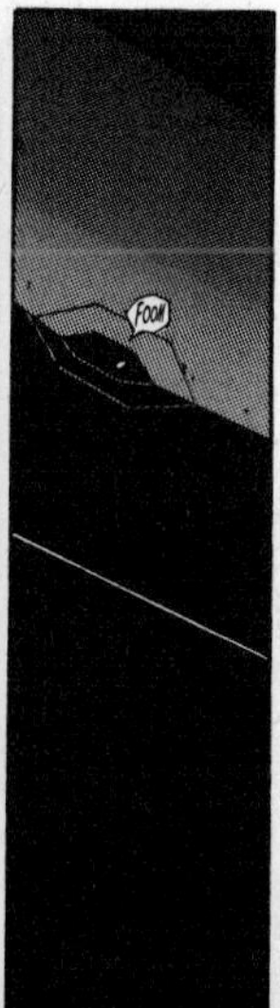
FOOM

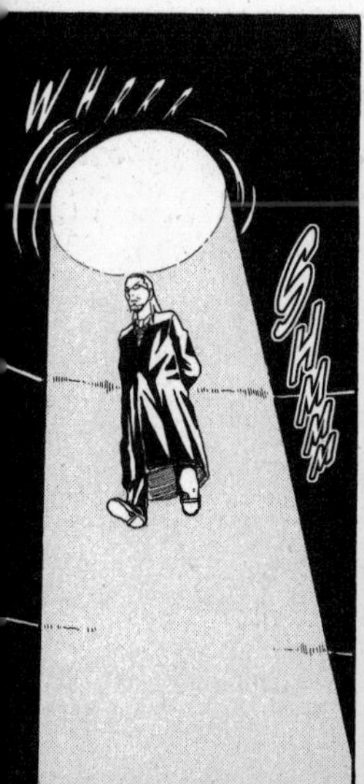
WHRRR
SHMMM

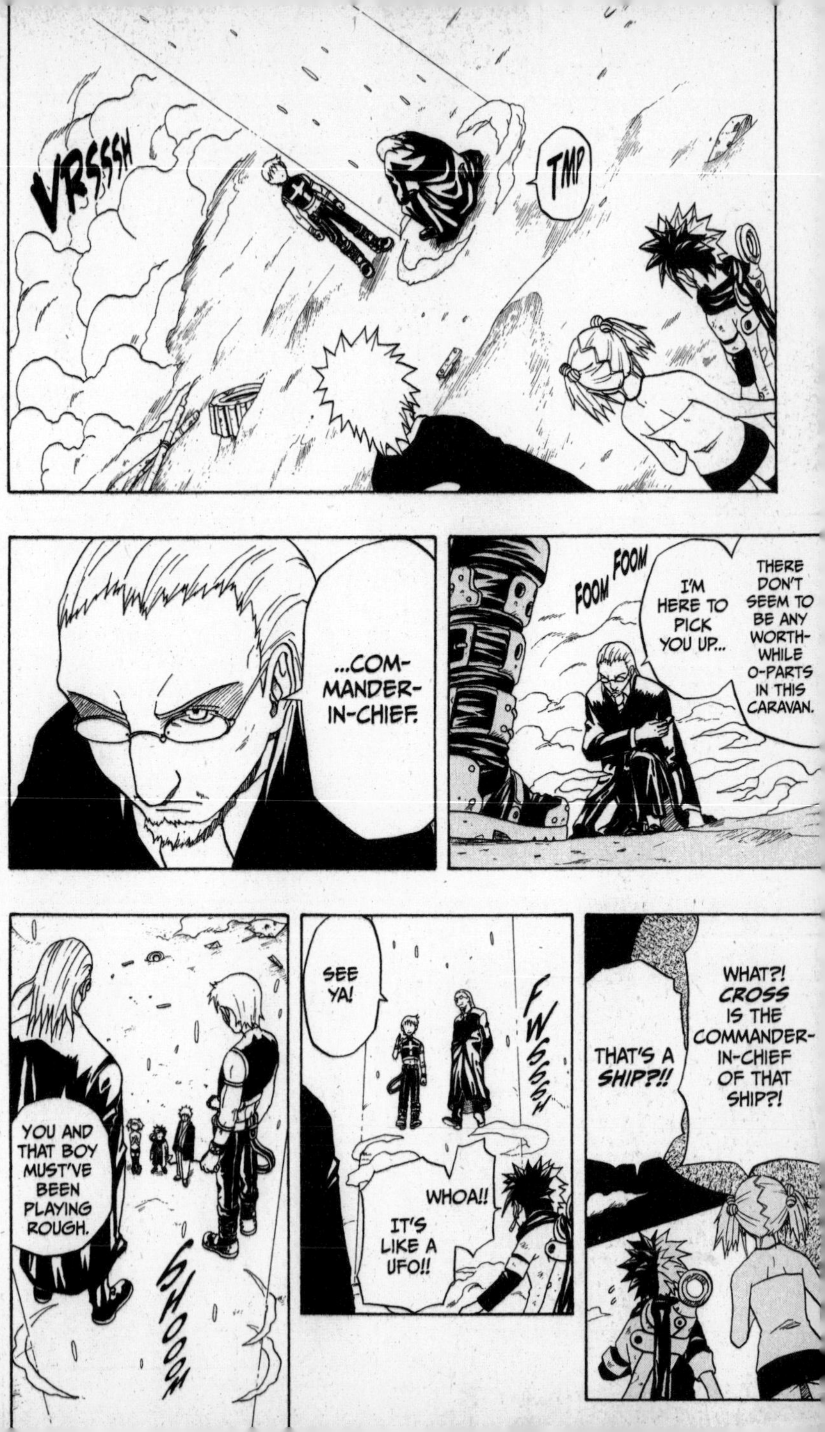
TMP
VRSSSH
THERE DON'T SEEM TO BE ANY WORTH-WHILE O-PARTS IN THIS CARAVAN.
I'M HERE TO PICK YOU UP...
FOOM FOOM
...COM-MANDER-IN-CHIEF.
WHAT?! CROSS IS THE COMMANDER-IN-CHIEF OF THAT SHIP?!
THAT'S A SHIP?!!
SEE YA!
FWSSSH
WHOA!!
IT'S LIKE A UFO!!
YOU AND THAT BOY MUST'VE BEEN PLAYING ROUGH.
SHOOOM

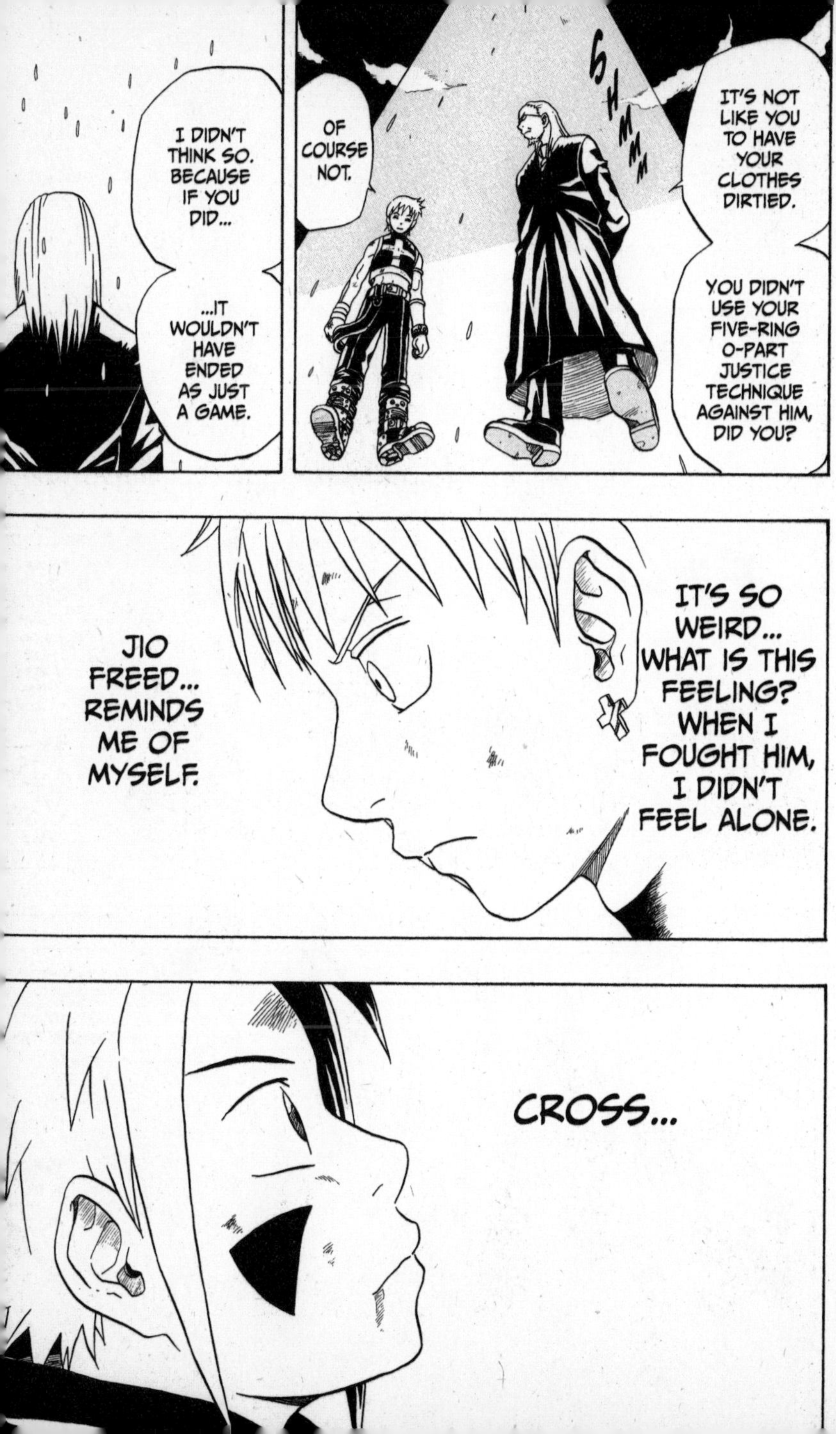
SHMMM
IT'S NOT LIKE YOU TO HAVE YOUR CLOTHES DIRTIED.
YOU DIDN'T USE YOUR FIVE-RING O-PART JUSTICE TECHNIQUE AGAINST HIM, DID YOU?
OF COURSE NOT.
I DIDN'T THINK SO. BECAUSE IF YOU DID...
...IT WOULDN'T HAVE ENDED AS JUST A GAME.
IT'S SO WEIRD... WHAT IS THIS FEELING? WHEN I FOUGHT HIM, I DIDN'T FEEL ALONE.
JIO FREED... REMINDS ME OF MYSELF.
CROSS...

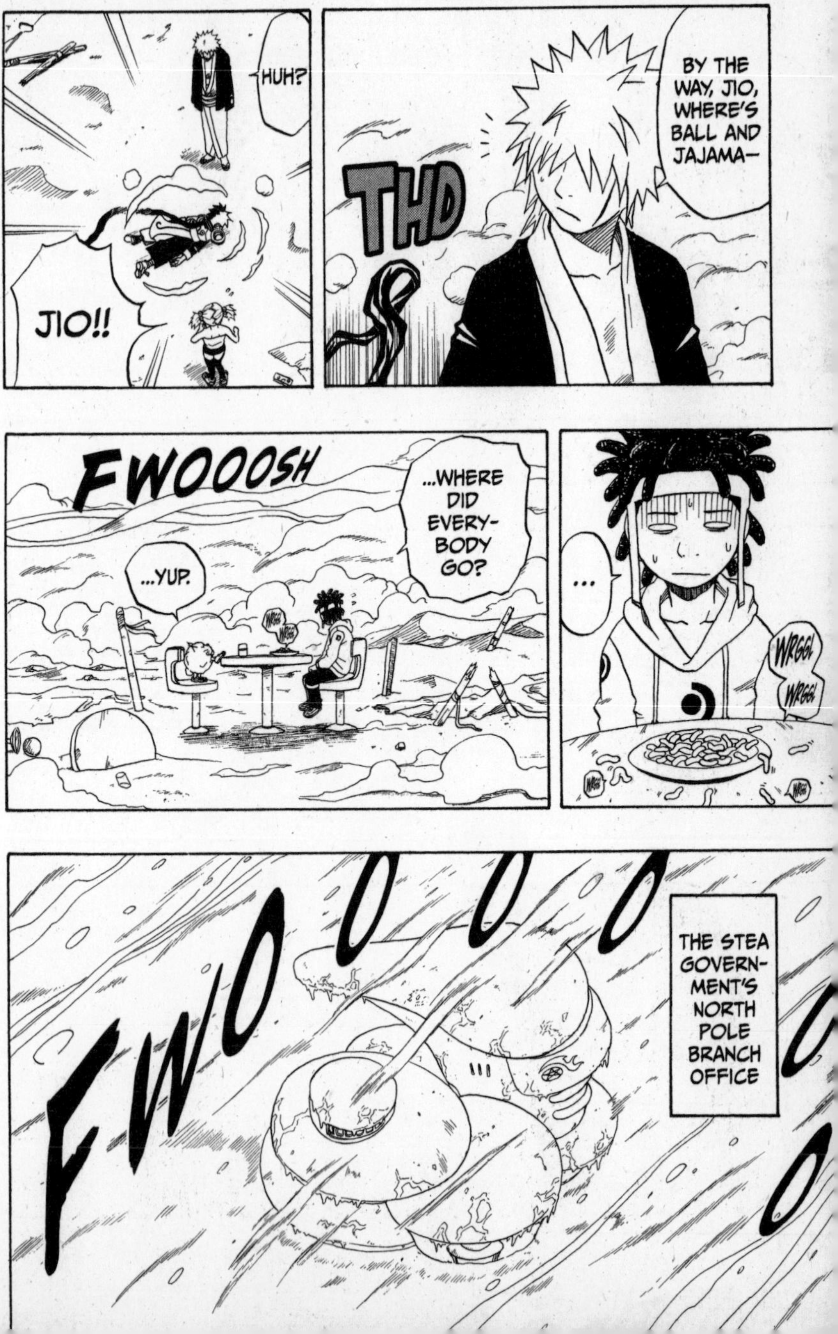
BY THE WAY, JIO, WHERE'S BALL AND JAJAMA—
THD
HUH?
JIO!!
...
WRGGL
WRGGL
FWOOOSH
...WHERE DID EVERY-BODY GO?
...YUP.
FWOOOOOO
THE STEA GOVERN-MENT'S NORTH POLE BRANCH OFFICE

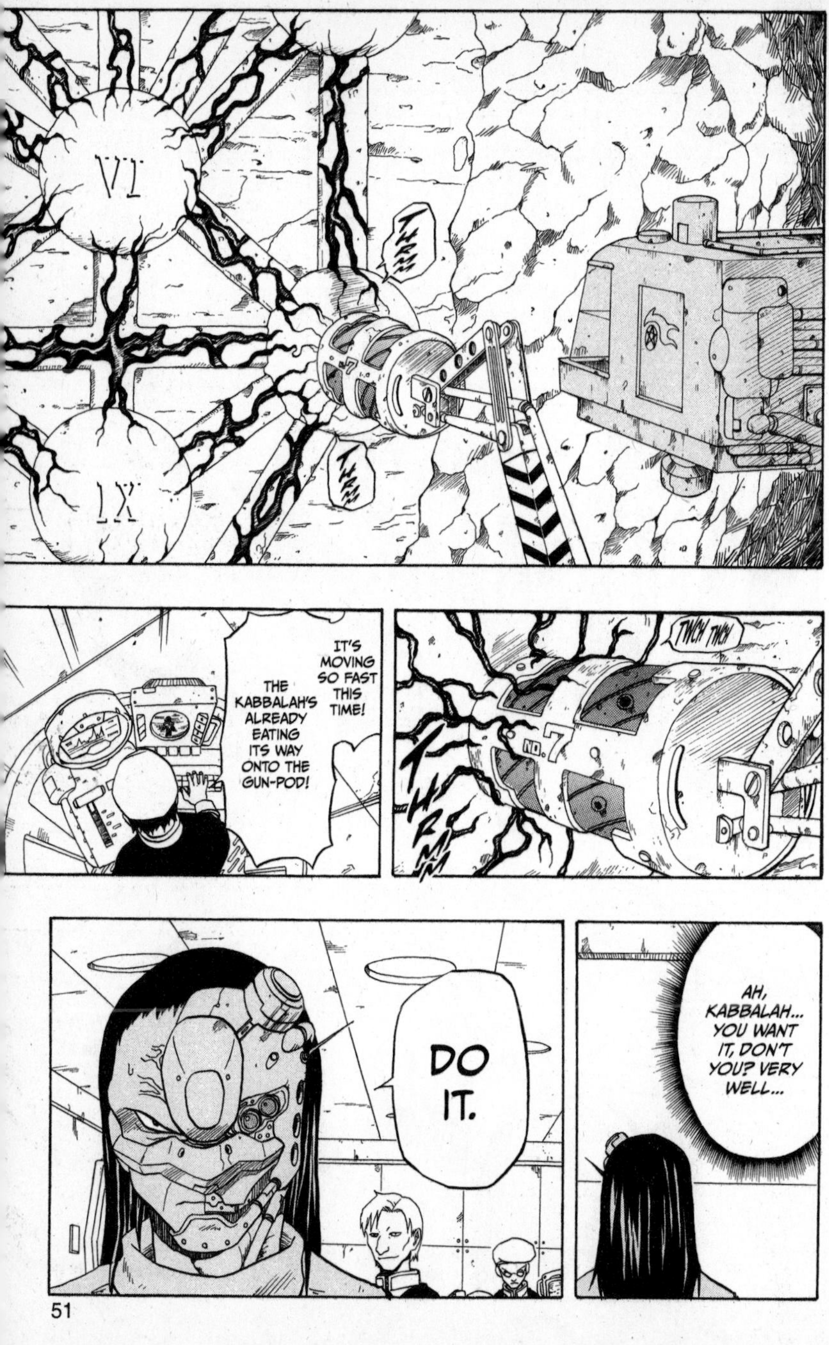

VI
THRM
THRM
IX
TWCH TWCH
No.7
THRMM
IT'S MOVING SO FAST THIS TIME!
THE KABBALAH'S ALREADY EATING ITS WAY ONTO THE GUN-POD!
AH, KABBALAH... YOU WANT IT, DON'T YOU? VERY WELL...
DO IT.

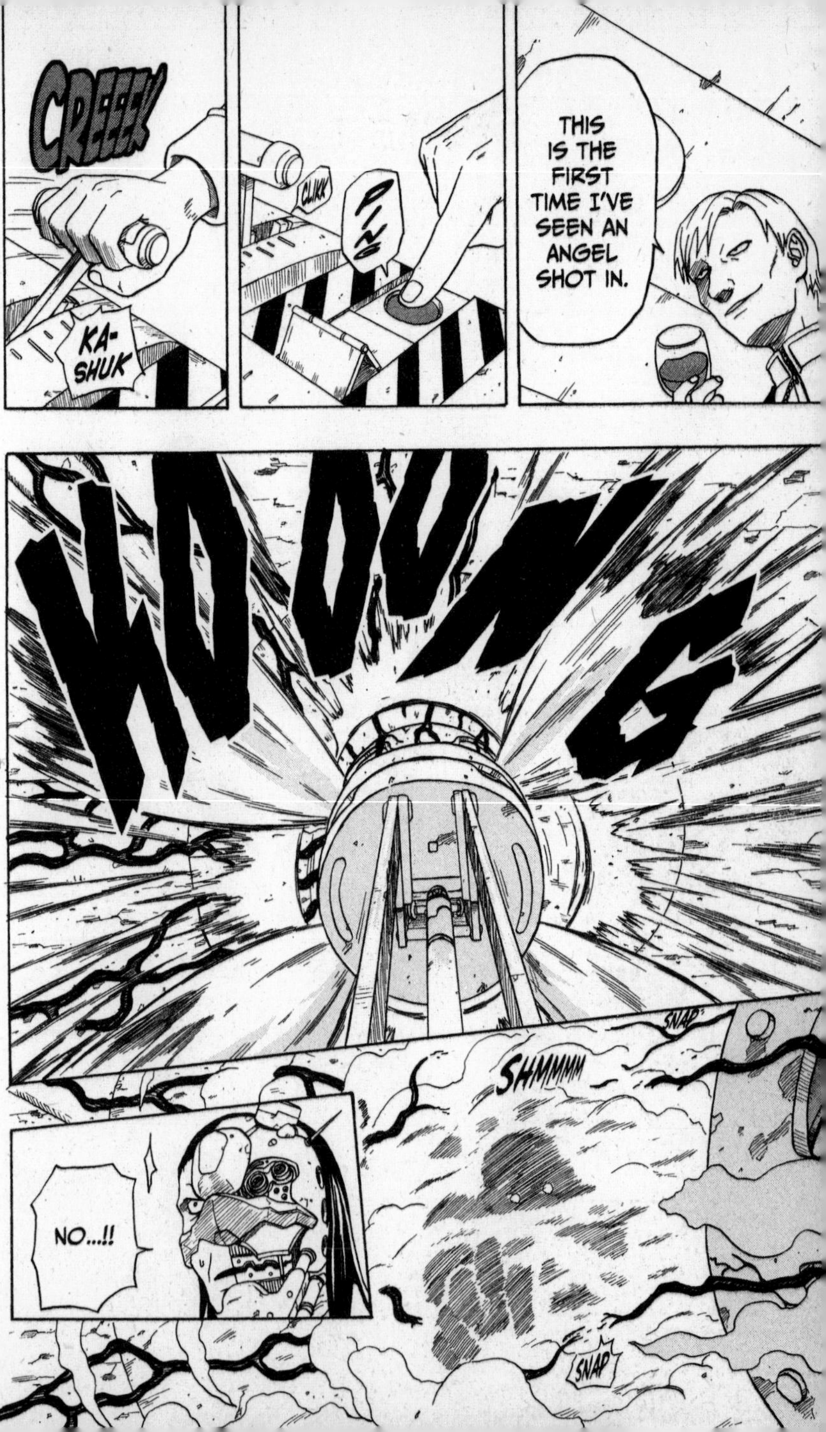
THIS IS THE FIRST TIME I'VE SEEN AN ANGEL SHOT IN.
PING
CLIKK
CREEEK!
KA-SHUK
WOOONG
SNAP
SHMMMM
NO...!!
SNAP

CHAPTER 30
THE KABBALAH'S ANGEL

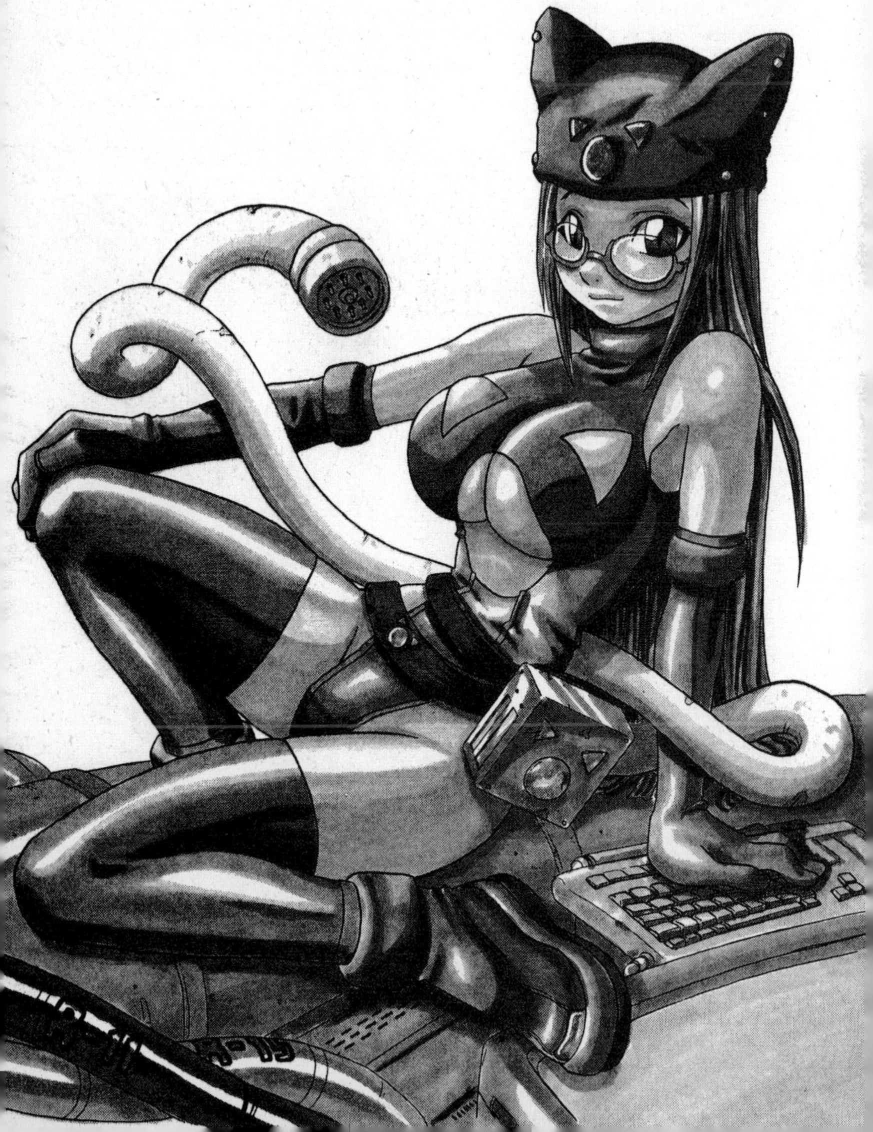

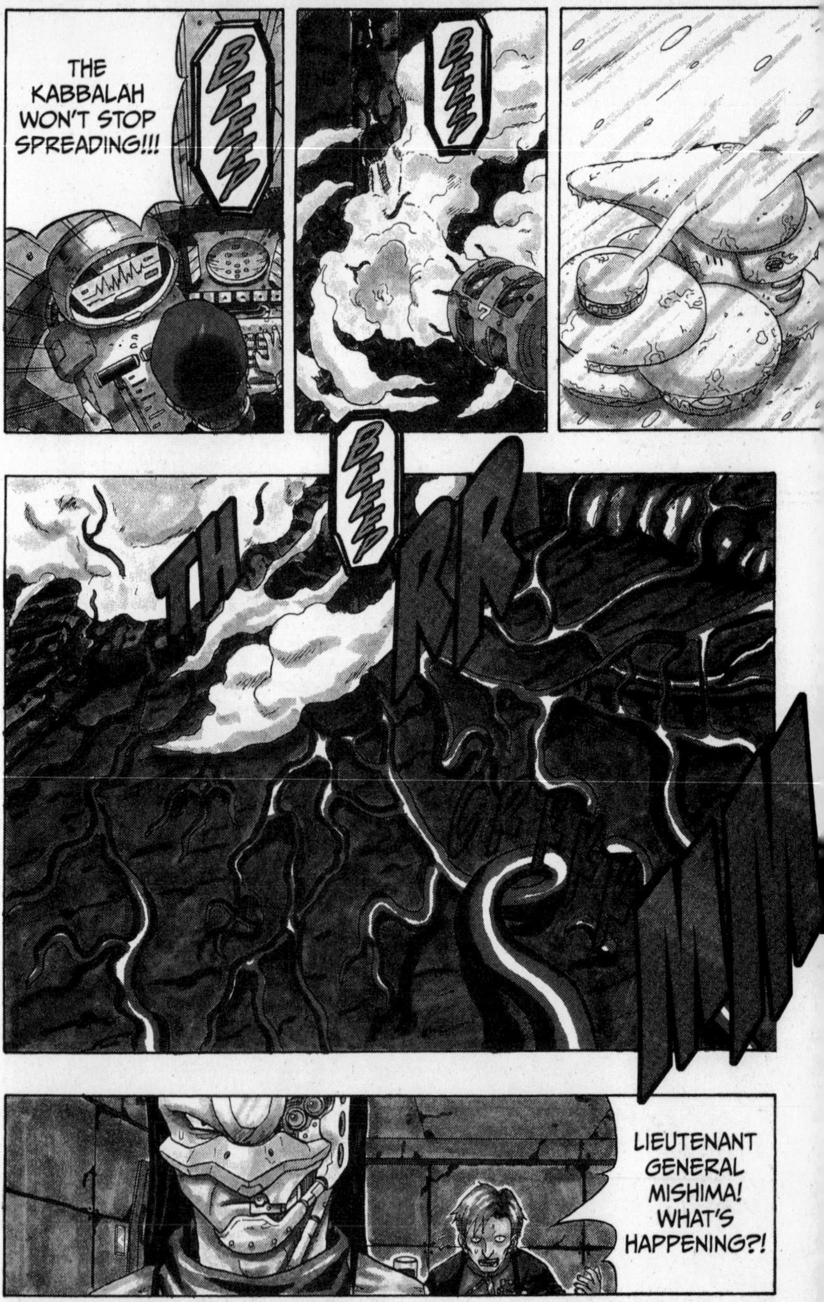
BEEEE
BEEEE
THE KABBALAH WON'T STOP SPREADING!!!
BEEEE
THRRMMMM
LIEUTENANT GENERAL MISHIMA! WHAT'S HAPPENING?!

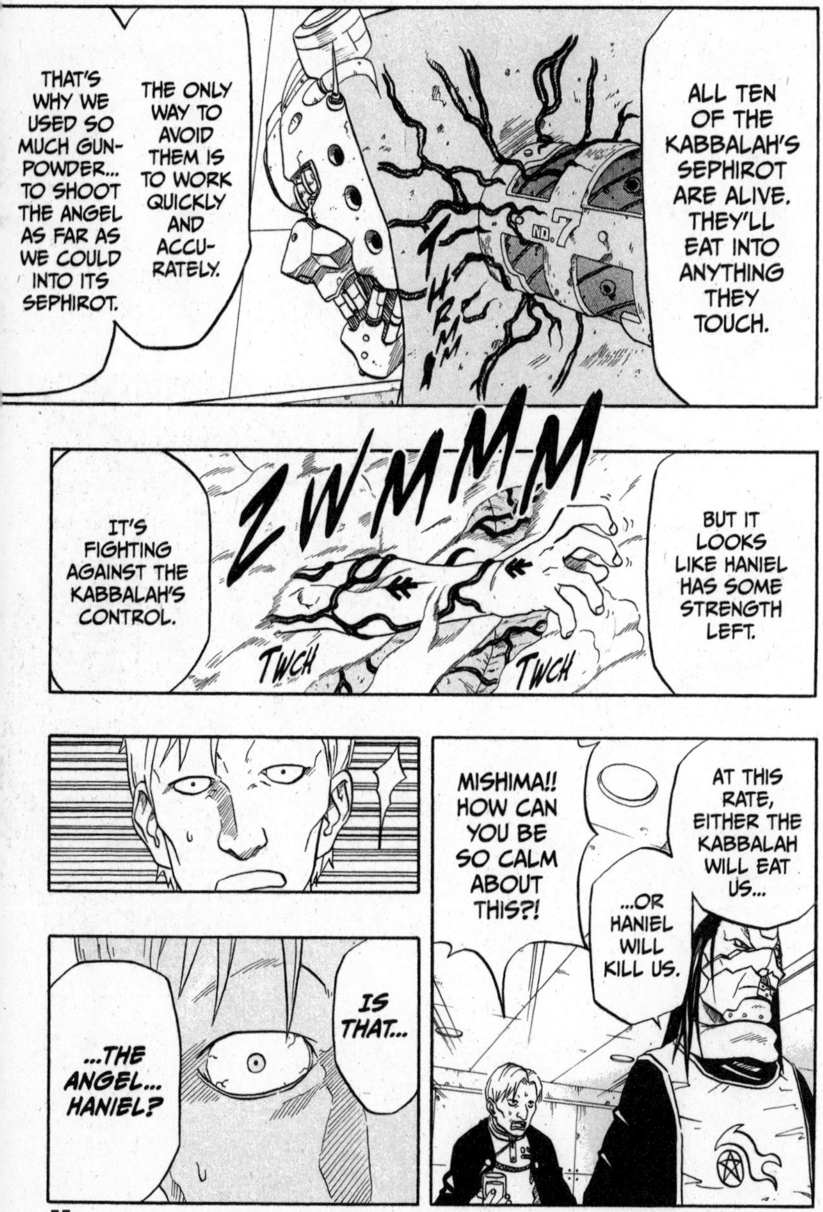
ALL TEN OF THE KABBALAH'S SEPHIROT ARE ALIVE. THEY'LL EAT INTO ANYTHING THEY TOUCH.
THRMM
THE ONLY WAY TO AVOID THEM IS TO WORK QUICKLY AND ACCU-RATELY.
THAT'S WHY WE USED SO MUCH GUN-POWDER... TO SHOOT THE ANGEL AS FAR AS WE COULD INTO ITS SEPHIROT.
BUT IT LOOKS LIKE HANIEL HAS SOME STRENGTH LEFT.
ZWMMM
TWCH
TWCH
IT'S FIGHTING AGAINST THE KABBALAH'S CONTROL.
AT THIS RATE, EITHER THE KABBALAH WILL EAT US...
MISHIMA!! HOW CAN YOU BE SO CALM ABOUT THIS?!
...OR HANIEL WILL KILL US.
IS THAT...
...THE ANGEL... HANIEL?

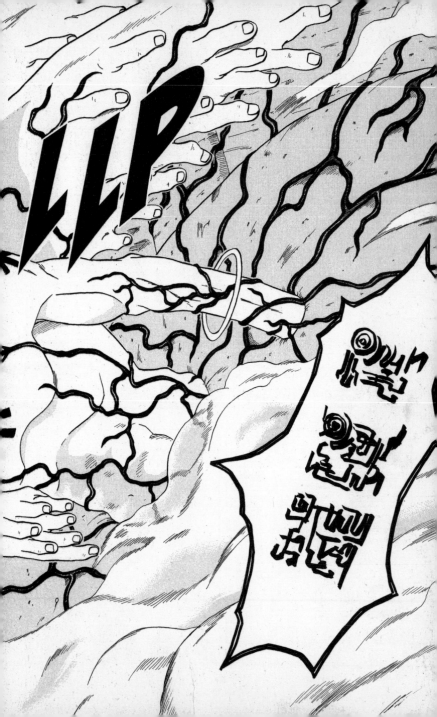

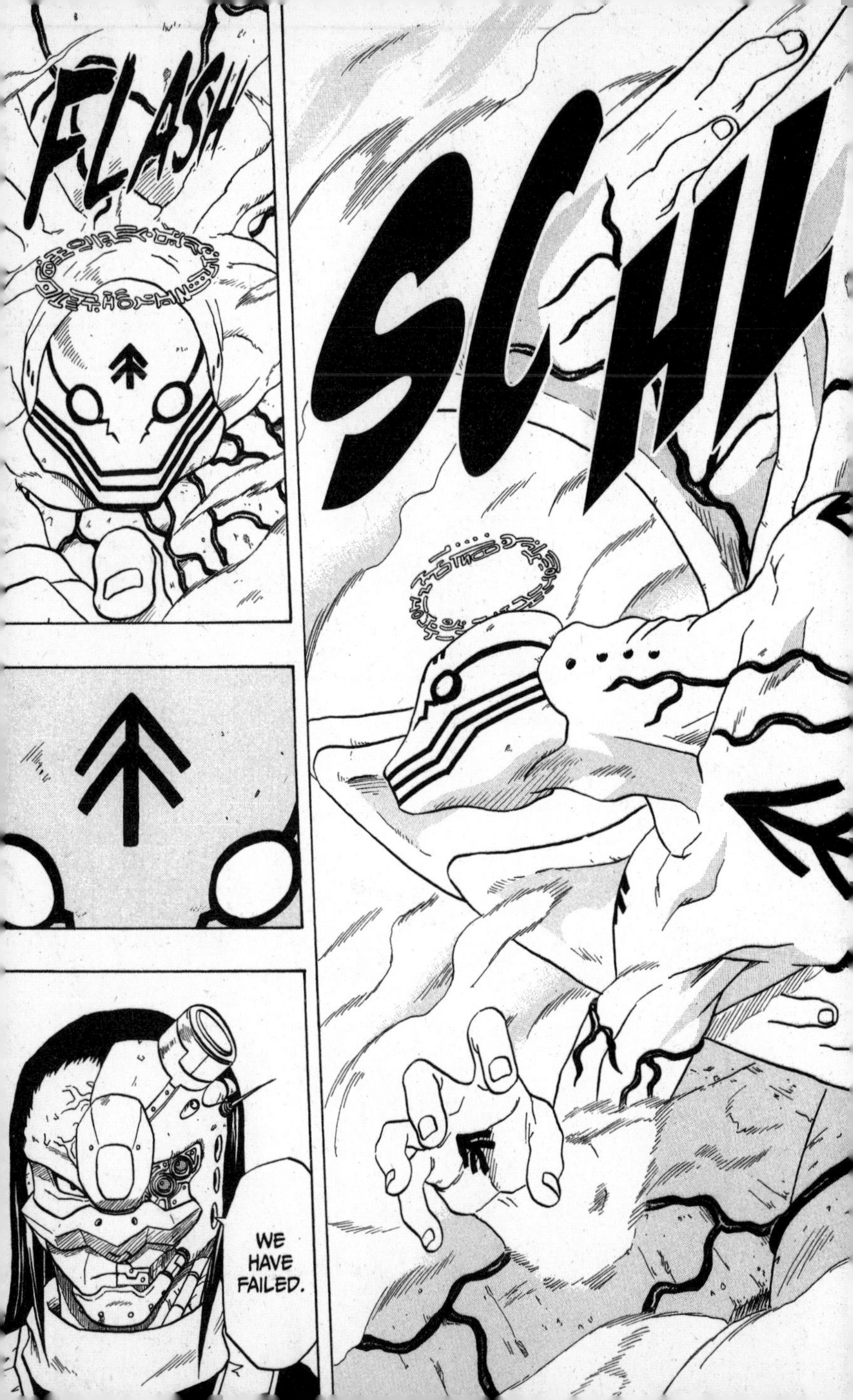
SCHL
FLASH
WE HAVE FAILED.

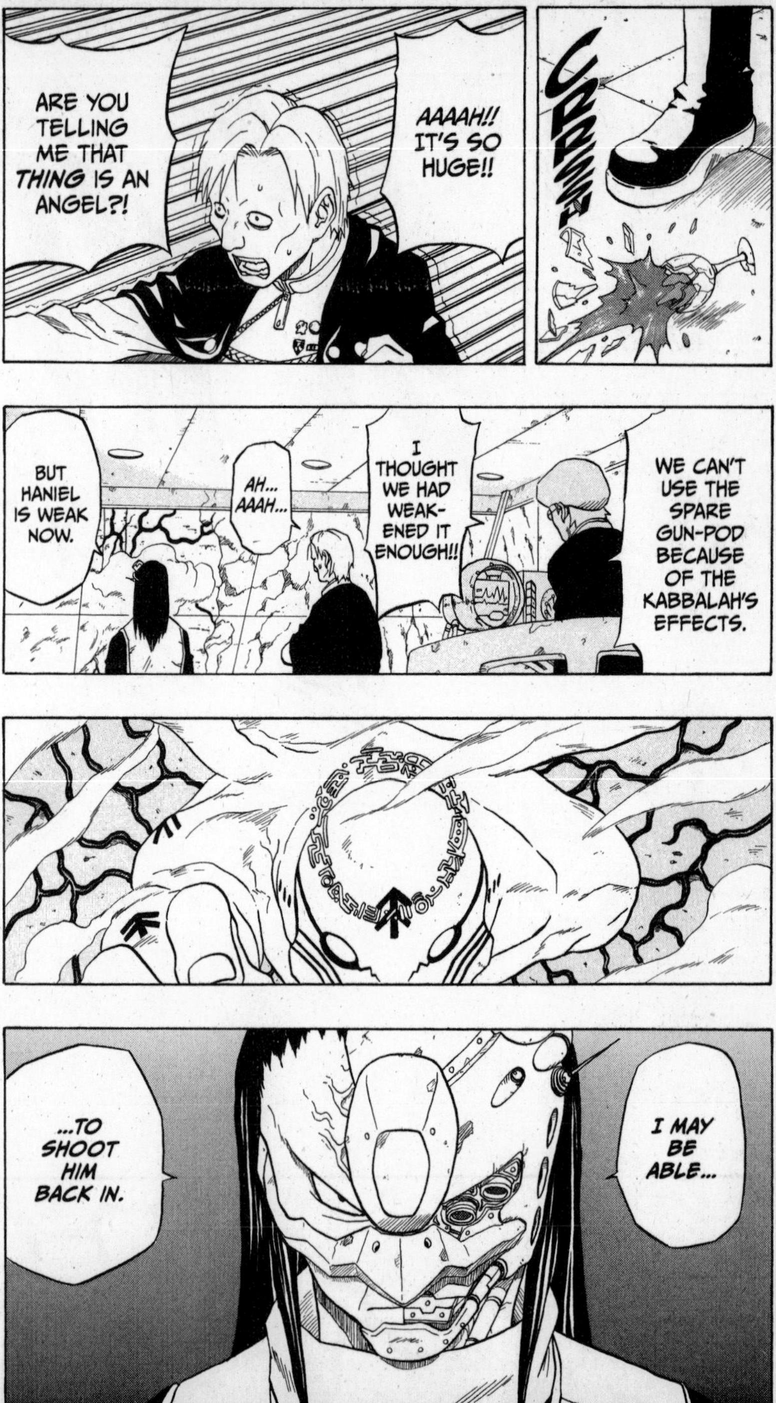
AAAAH!! IT'S SO HUGE!!
ARE YOU TELLING ME THAT THING IS AN ANGEL?!
WE CAN'T USE THE SPARE GUN-POD BECAUSE OF THE KABBALAH'S EFFECTS.
I THOUGHT WE HAD WEAK-ENED IT ENOUGH!!
AH... AAAH...
BUT HANIEL IS WEAK NOW.
I MAY BE ABLE...
...TO SHOOT HIM BACK IN.

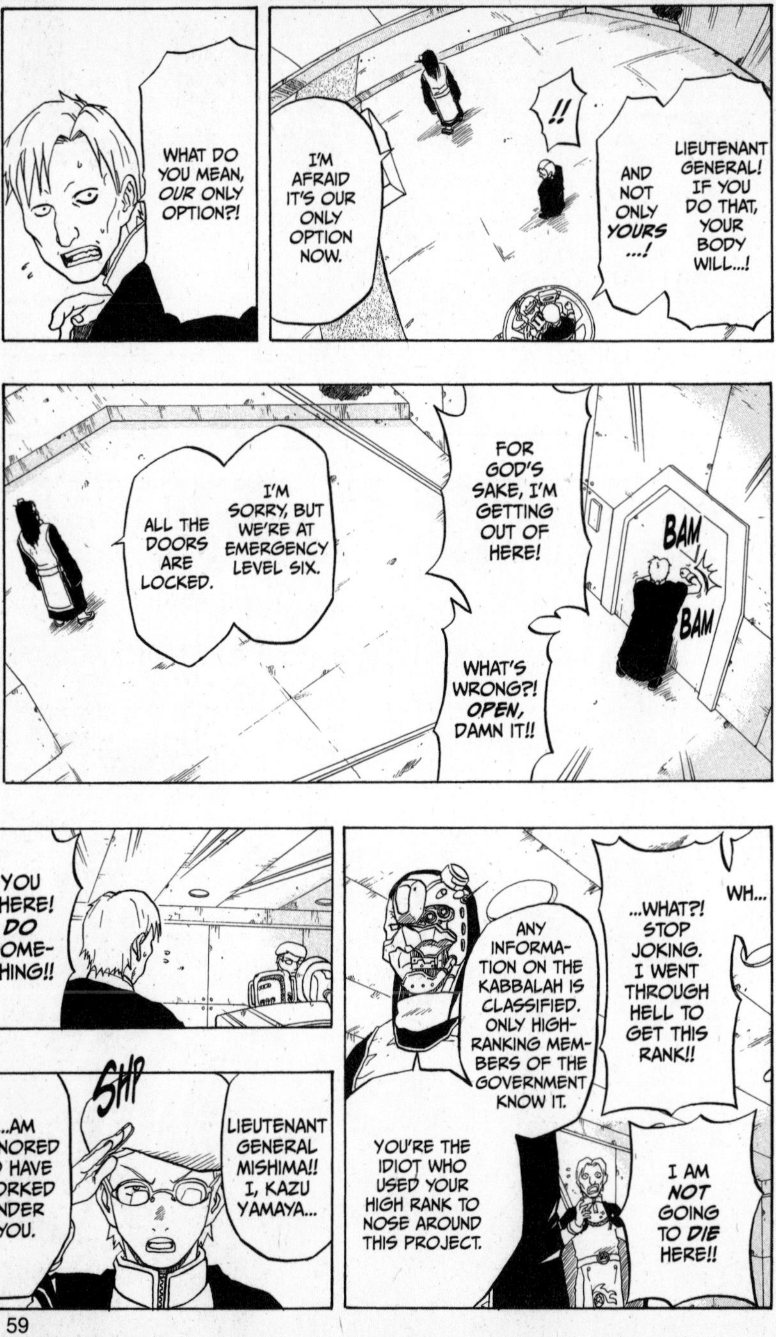
LIEUTENANT GENERAL! IF YOU DO THAT, YOUR BODY WILL...!
AND NOT ONLY *YOURS* ...!
!!
I'M AFRAID IT'S OUR ONLY OPTION NOW.
WHAT DO YOU MEAN, *OUR* ONLY OPTION?!
FOR GOD'S SAKE, I'M GETTING OUT OF HERE!
BAM
BAM
WHAT'S WRONG?! *OPEN*, DAMN IT!!
I'M SORRY, BUT WE'RE AT EMERGENCY LEVEL SIX.
ALL THE DOORS ARE LOCKED.
WH...
...WHAT?! STOP JOKING. I WENT THROUGH HELL TO GET THIS RANK!!
ANY INFORMATION ON THE KABBALAH IS CLASSIFIED. ONLY HIGH-RANKING MEMBERS OF THE GOVERNMENT KNOW IT.
I AM *NOT* GOING TO *DIE* HERE!!
YOU'RE THE IDIOT WHO USED YOUR HIGH RANK TO NOSE AROUND THIS PROJECT.
YOU THERE! *DO* SOMETHING!!
SHP
LIEUTENANT GENERAL MISHIMA!! I, KAZU YAMAYA...
...AM HONORED TO HAVE WORKED UNDER YOU.

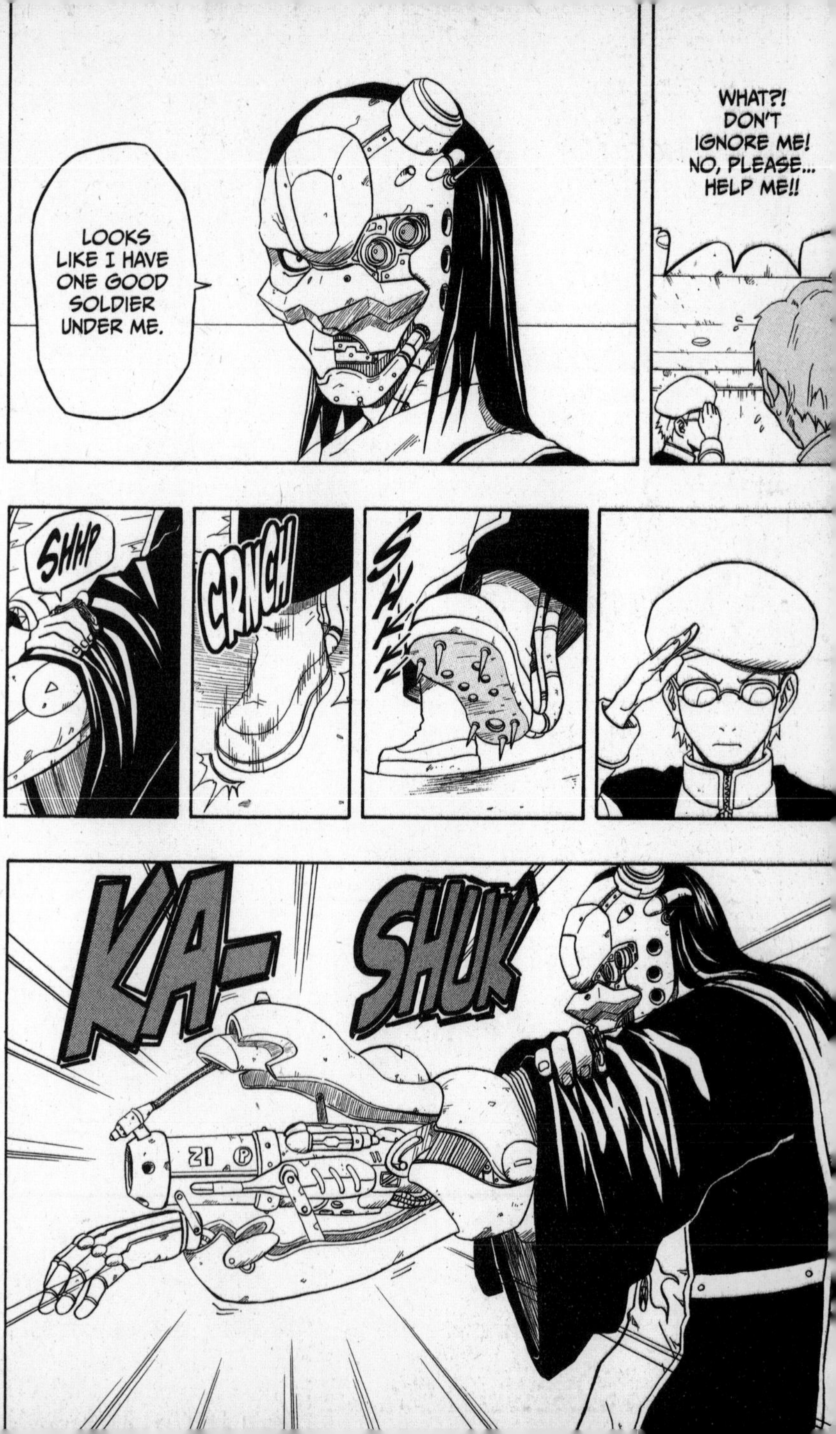
WHAT?! DON'T IGNORE ME! NO, PLEASE... HELP ME!!
LOOKS LIKE I HAVE ONE GOOD SOLDIER UNDER ME.
SHKKK
CRNCH
SHHP
KA-
SHUK

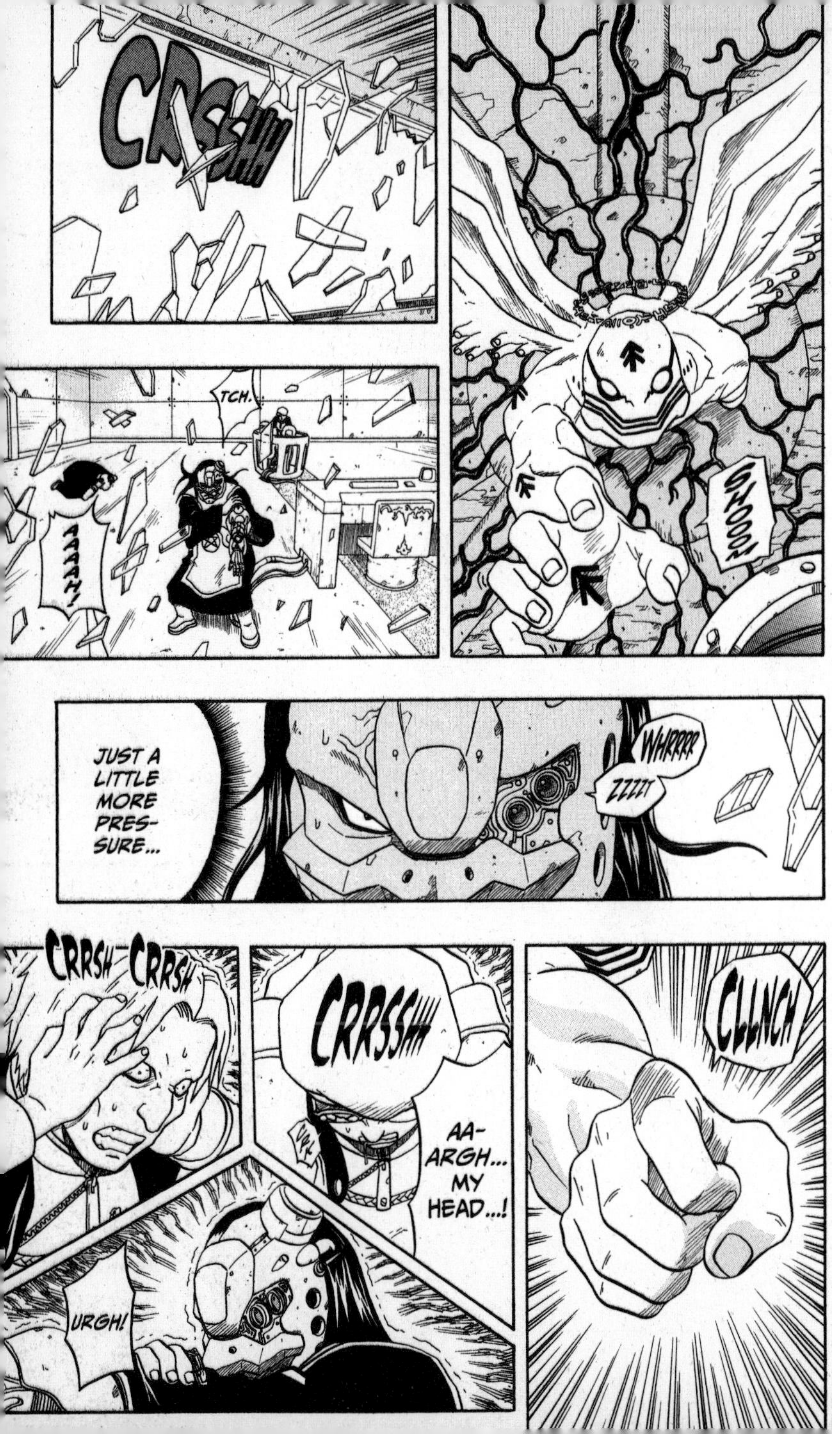
SHOOOM
CRSSHH
TCH.
AAAAH!
WHRRRR
ZZZZT
JUST A LITTLE MORE PRES-SURE...
CLLNCH
CRRSSHH
AA-ARGH... MY HEAD...!
CRRSH CRRSH
URGH!

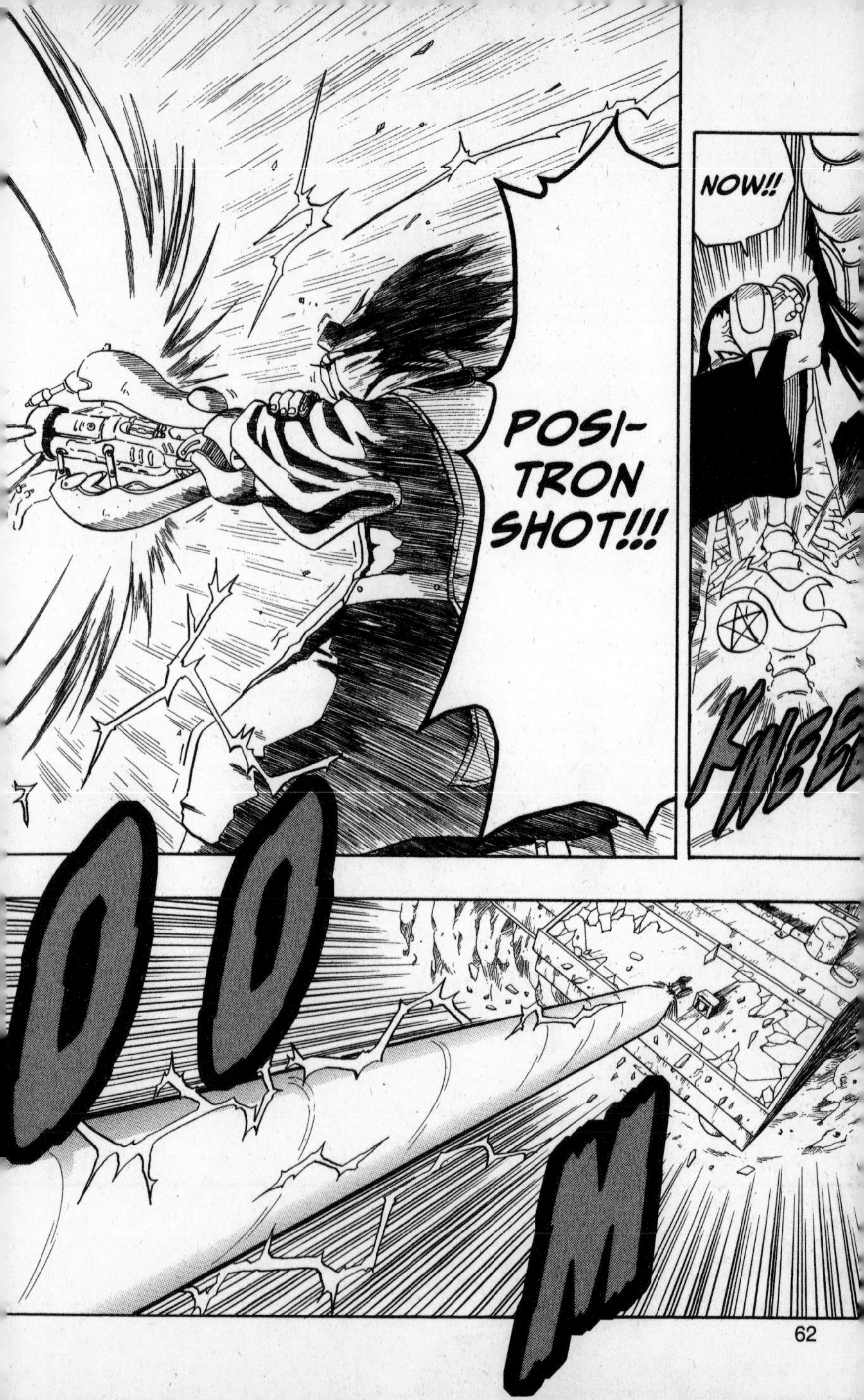
NOW!!
KNEE
POSI-
TRON
SHOT!!!
DOOM

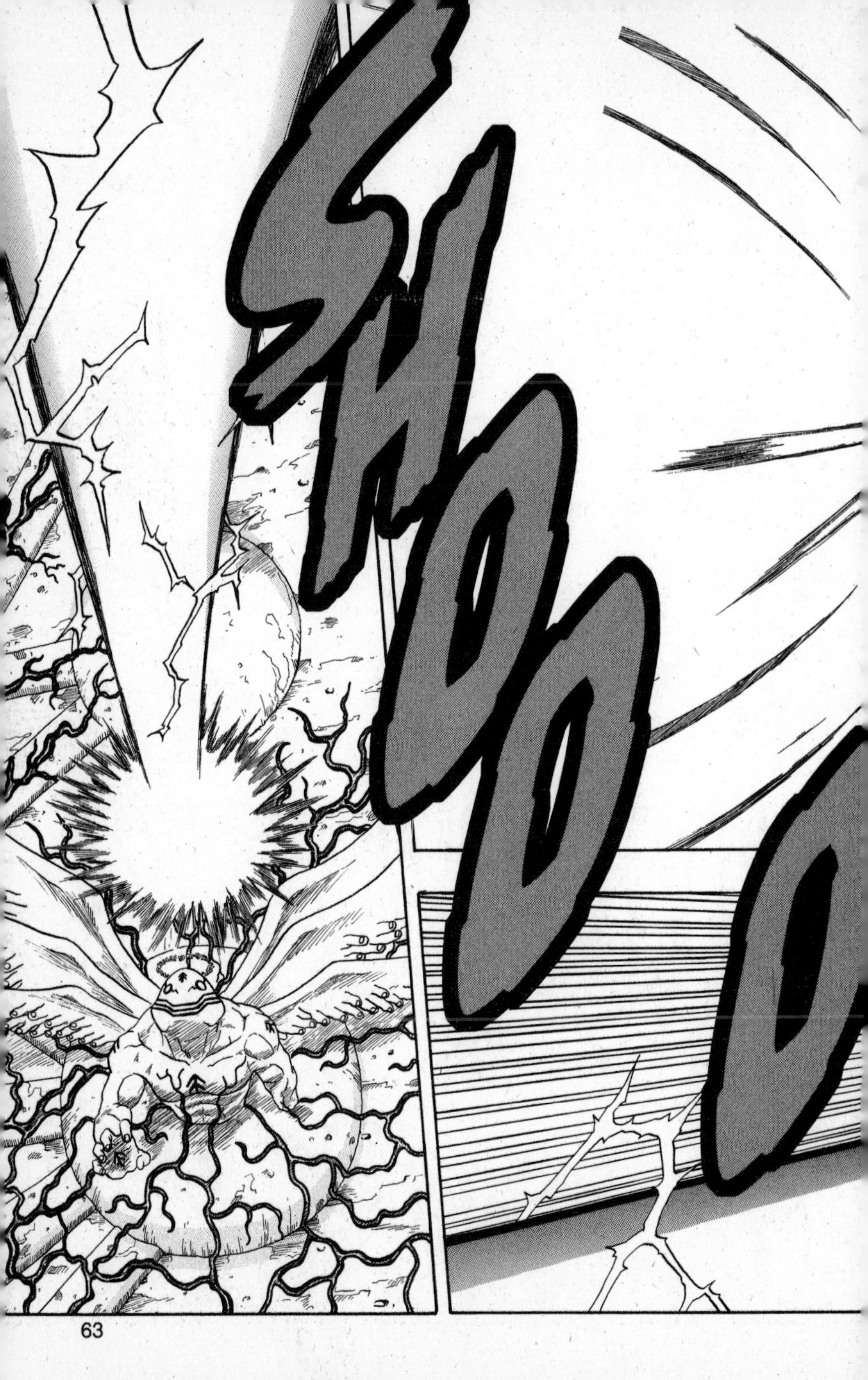
SHOOOO

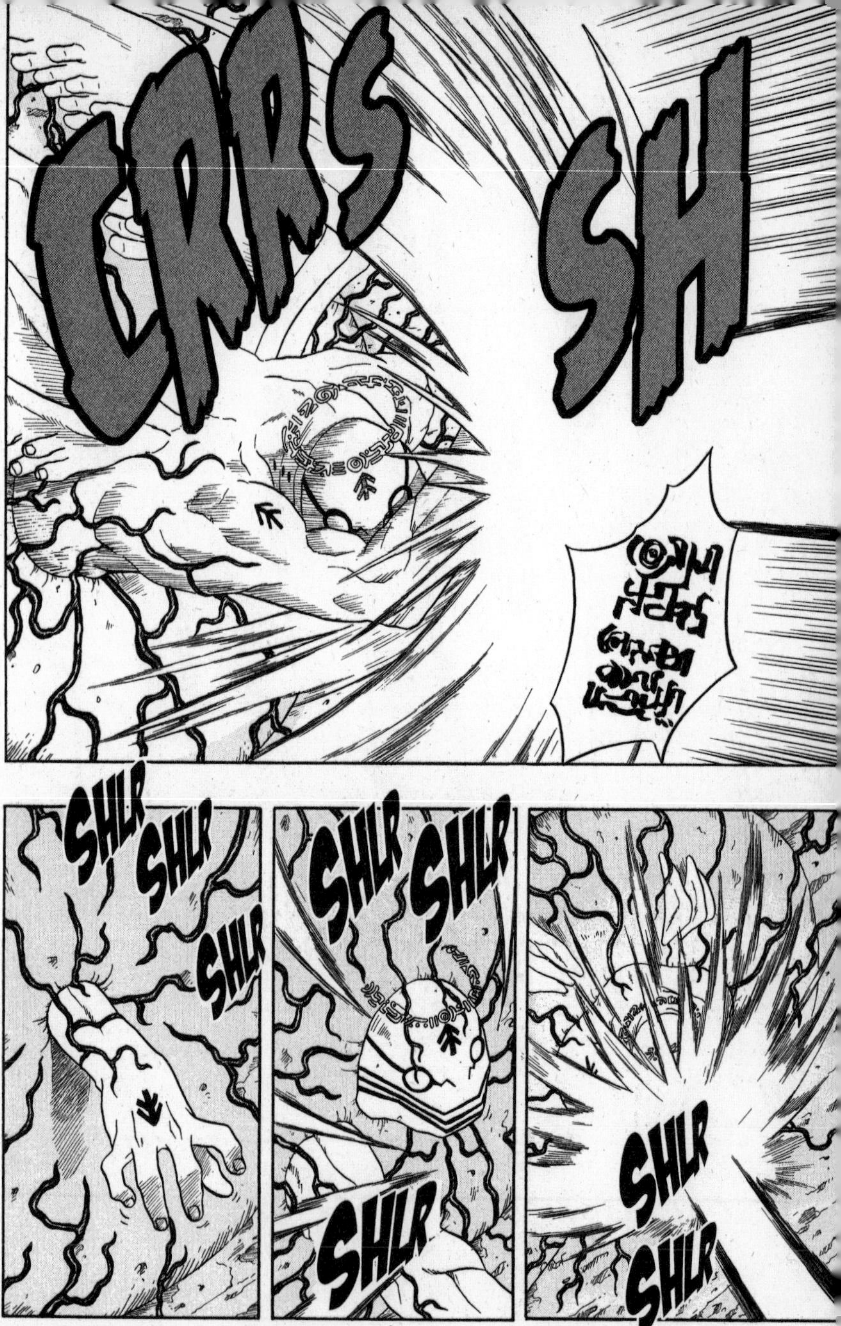
CRAS
SH
SHLR
SHLR
SHLR
SHLR
SHLR
SHLR
SHLR
SHLR

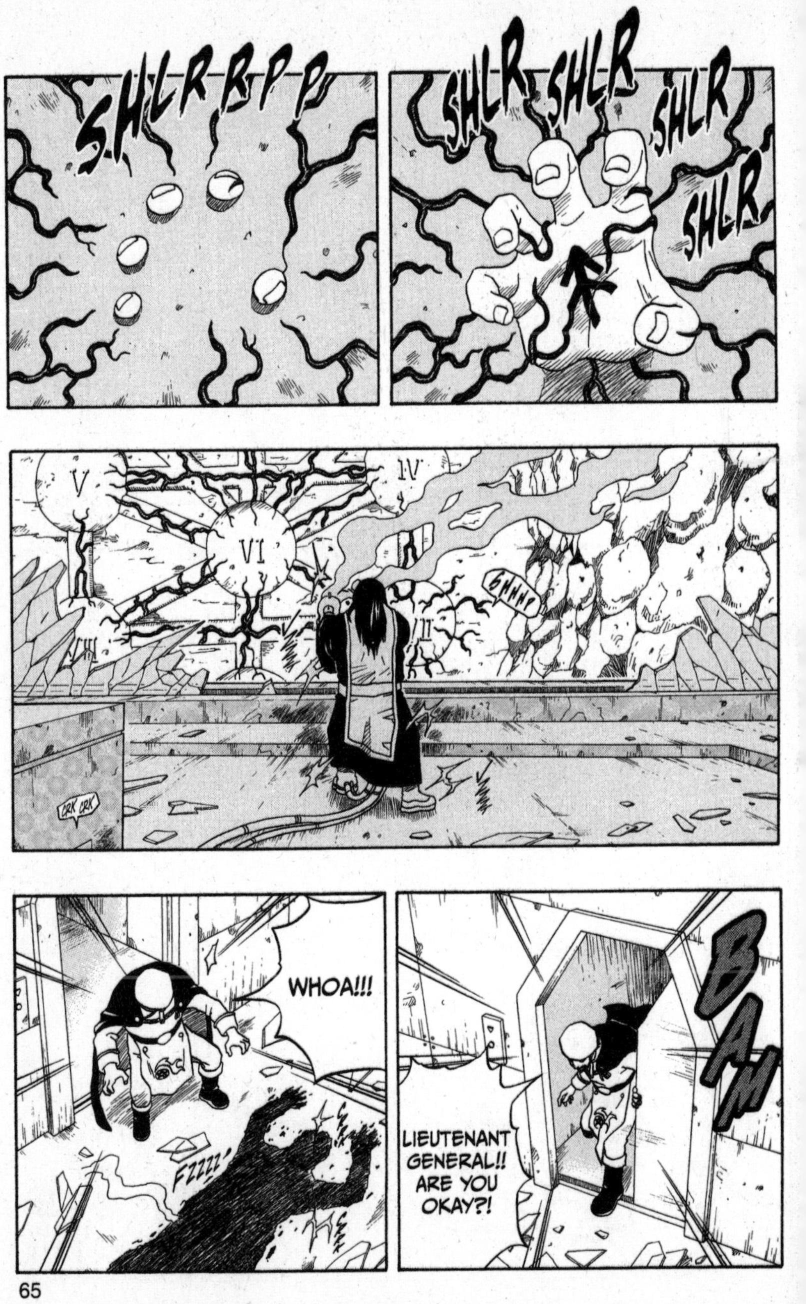
SHLR SHLR SHLR SHLR
SHLRRPP
GHNNP
CRK CRK
BAM
LIEUTENANT GENERAL!! ARE YOU OKAY?!
WHOA!!!
FZZZZ

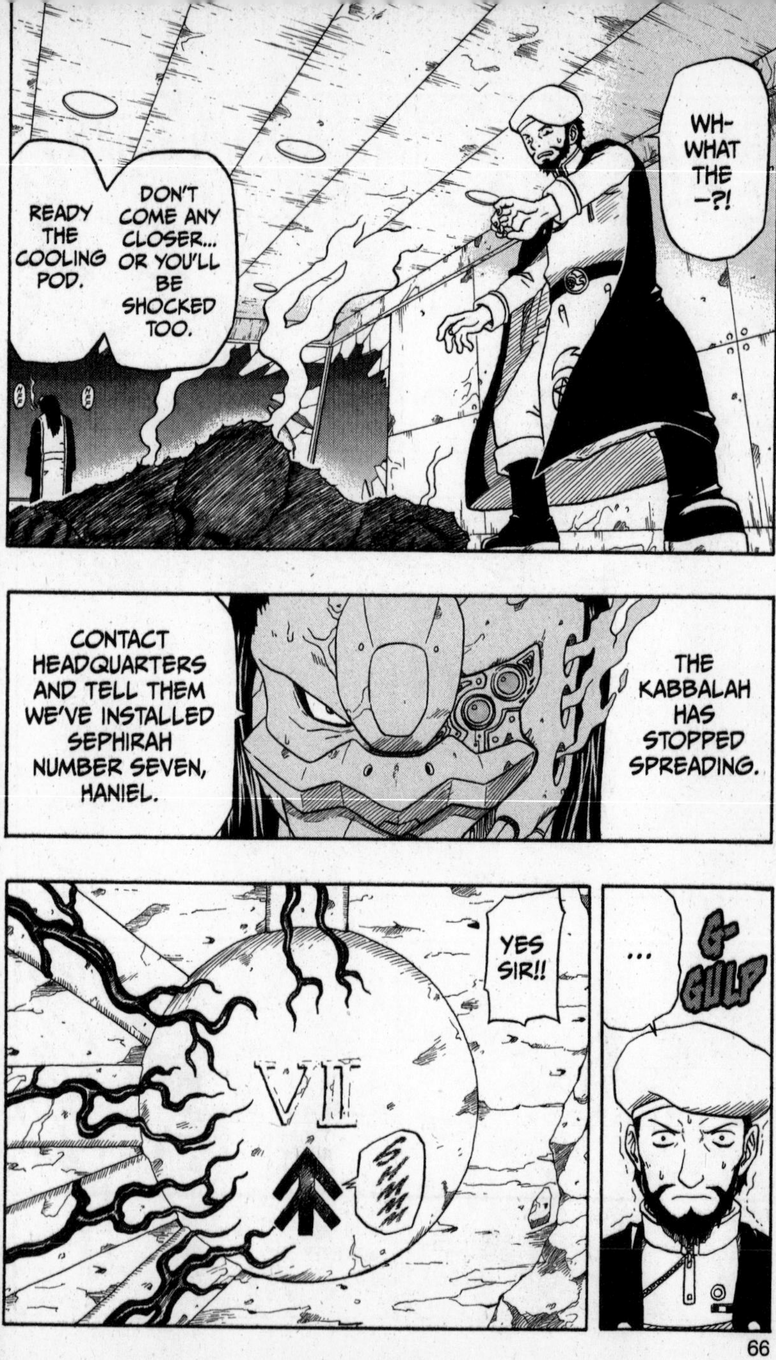
WH-WHAT THE—?!
DON'T COME ANY CLOSER... OR YOU'LL BE SHOCKED TOO.
READY THE COOLING POD.
THE KABBALAH HAS STOPPED SPREADING.
CONTACT HEADQUARTERS AND TELL THEM WE'VE INSTALLED SEPHIRAH NUMBER SEVEN, HANIEL.
...
G-GULP
YES SIR!!
VII
SHMM

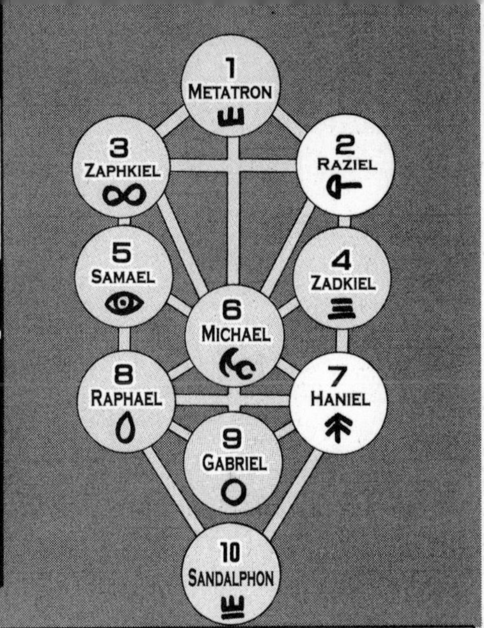
1
METATRON
2
RAZIEL
3
ZAPHKIEL
4
ZADKIEL
5
SAMAEL
6
MICHAEL
7
HANIEL
8
RAPHAEL
9
GABRIEL
10
SANDALPHON

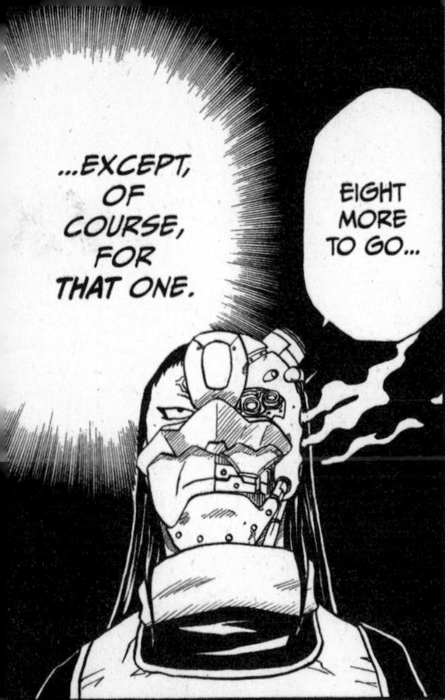
EIGHT MORE TO GO...
...EXCEPT, OF COURSE, FOR THAT ONE.

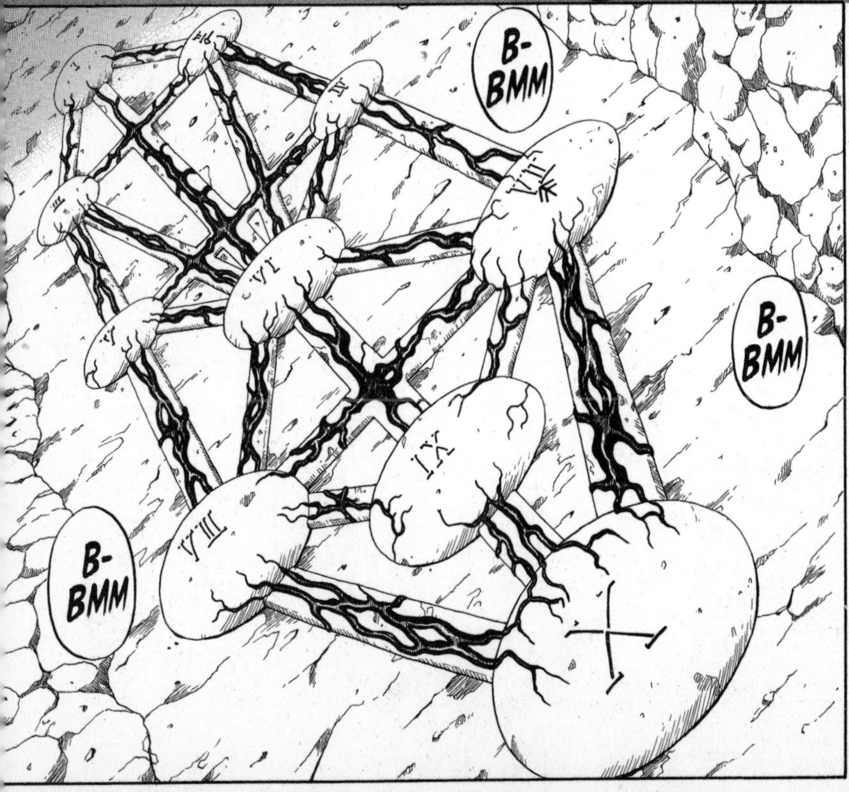
B-BMM
B-BMM
B-BMM

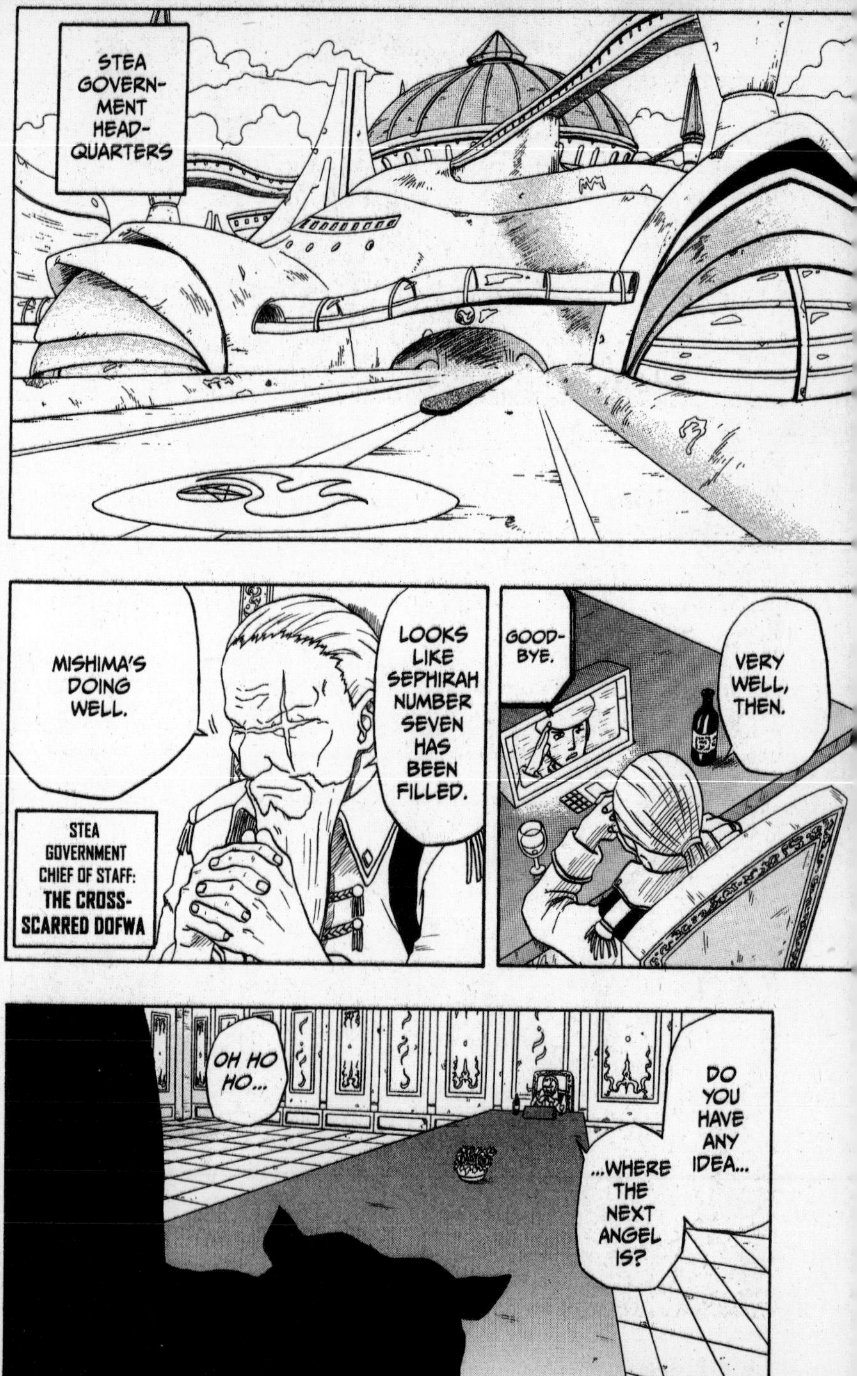
STEA GOVERNMENT HEADQUARTERS
VERY WELL, THEN.
GOOD-BYE.
LOOKS LIKE SEPHIRAH NUMBER SEVEN HAS BEEN FILLED.
MISHIMA'S DOING WELL.
STEA GOVERNMENT CHIEF OF STAFF: THE CROSS-SCARRED DOFWA
DO YOU HAVE ANY IDEA...
...WHERE THE NEXT ANGEL IS?
OH HO HO...

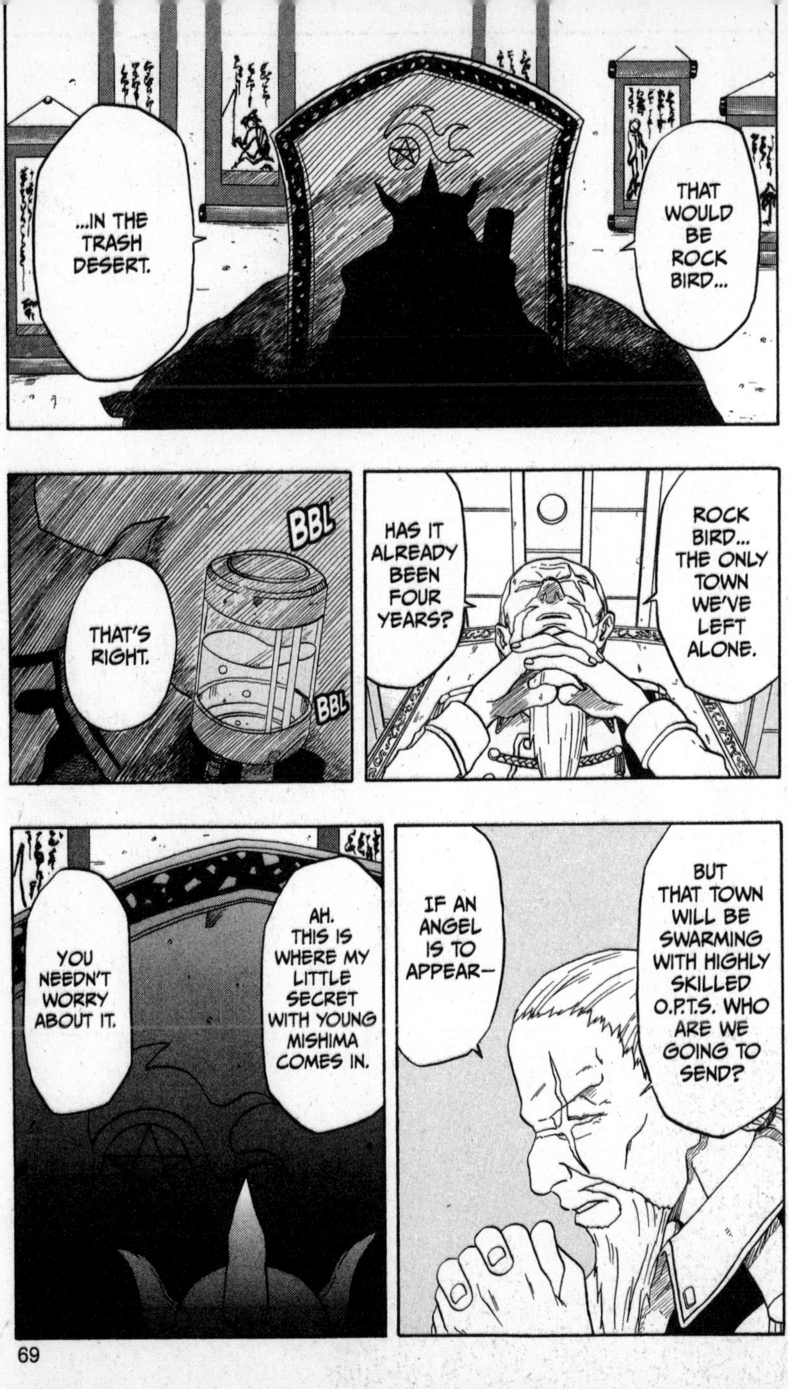
THAT WOULD BE ROCK BIRD...
...IN THE TRASH DESERT.
ROCK BIRD... THE ONLY TOWN WE'VE LEFT ALONE.
HAS IT ALREADY BEEN FOUR YEARS?
BBL
THAT'S RIGHT.
BBL
BUT THAT TOWN WILL BE SWARMING WITH HIGHLY SKILLED O.P.T.S. WHO ARE WE GOING TO SEND?
IF AN ANGEL IS TO APPEAR—
AH. THIS IS WHERE MY LITTLE SECRET WITH YOUNG MISHIMA COMES IN.
YOU NEEDN'T WORRY ABOUT IT.

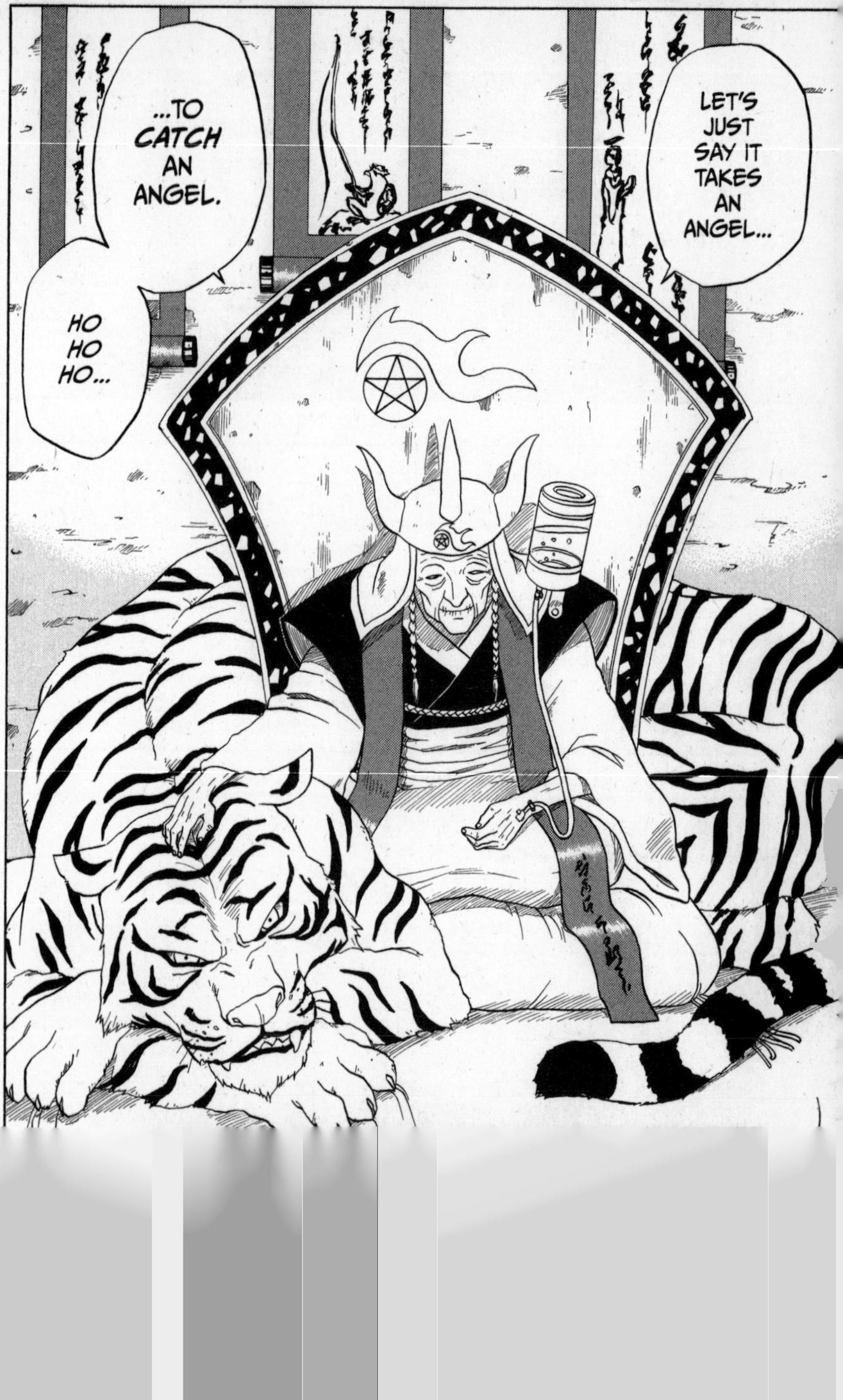
LET'S JUST SAY IT TAKES AN ANGEL...
...TO CATCH AN ANGEL.
HO HO HO...

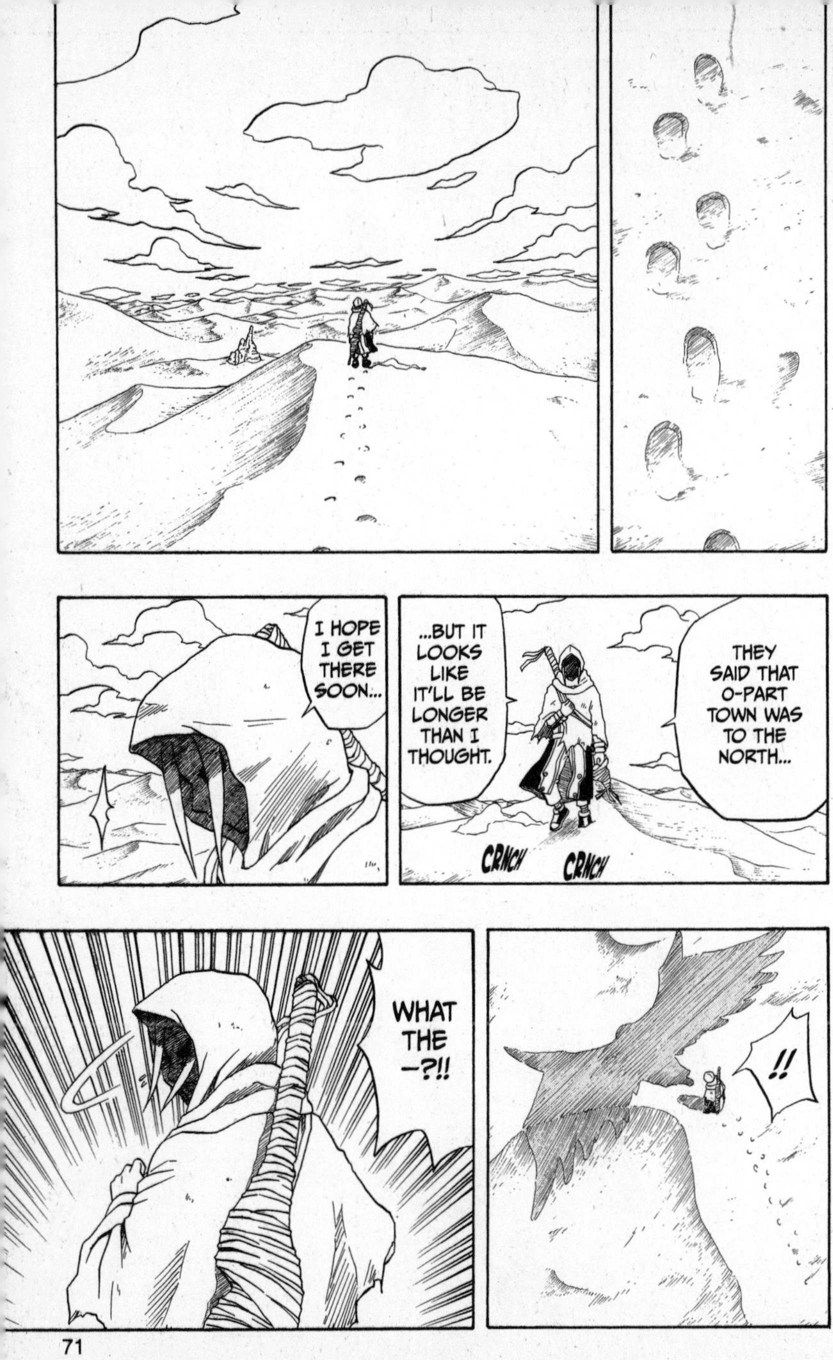
THEY SAID THAT O-PART TOWN WAS TO THE NORTH...
...BUT IT LOOKS LIKE IT'LL BE LONGER THAN I THOUGHT.
CRNCH
CRNCH
I HOPE I GET THERE SOON...
!!
WHAT THE —?!!

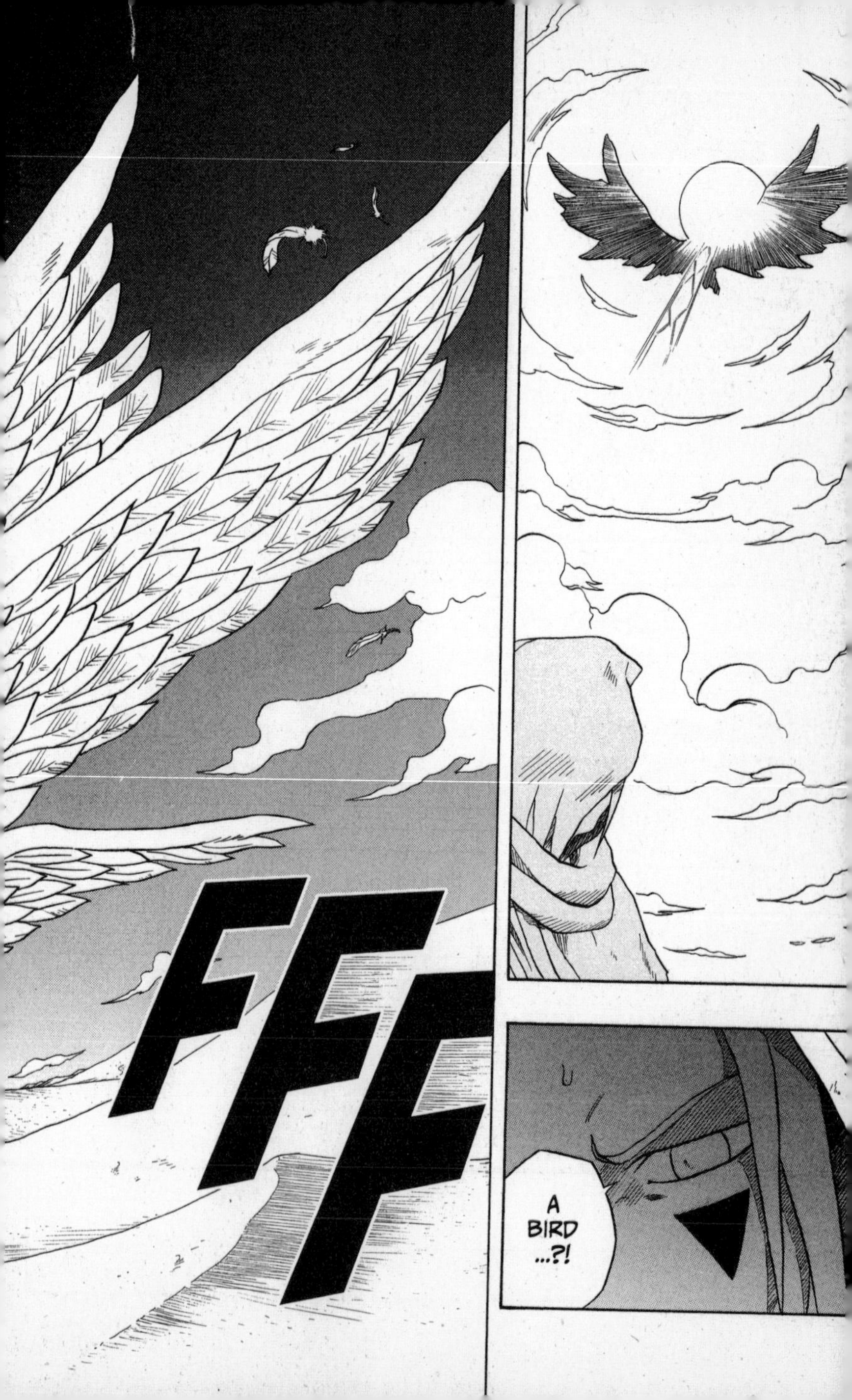
A BIRD ...?!
FFF

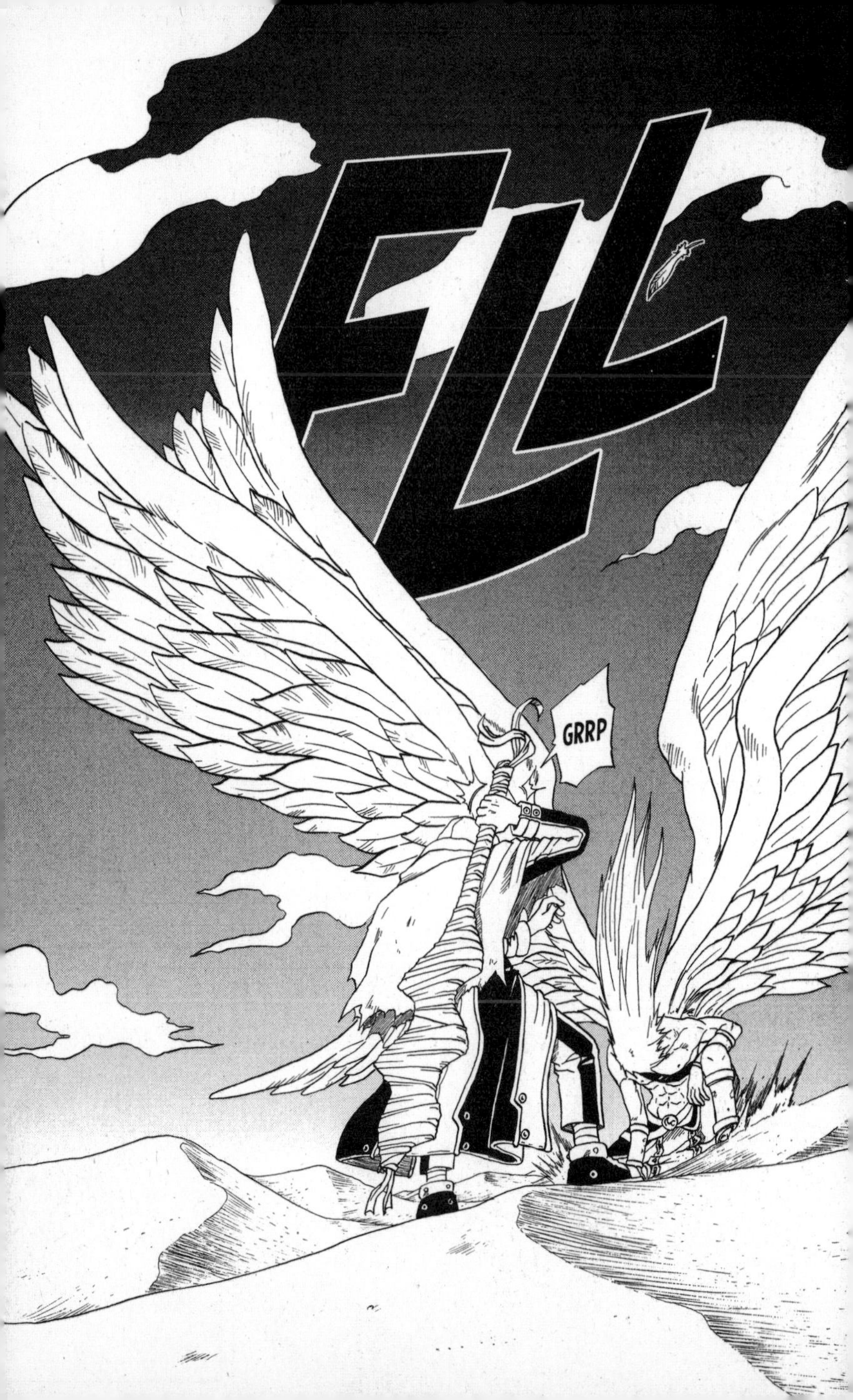
GRRP

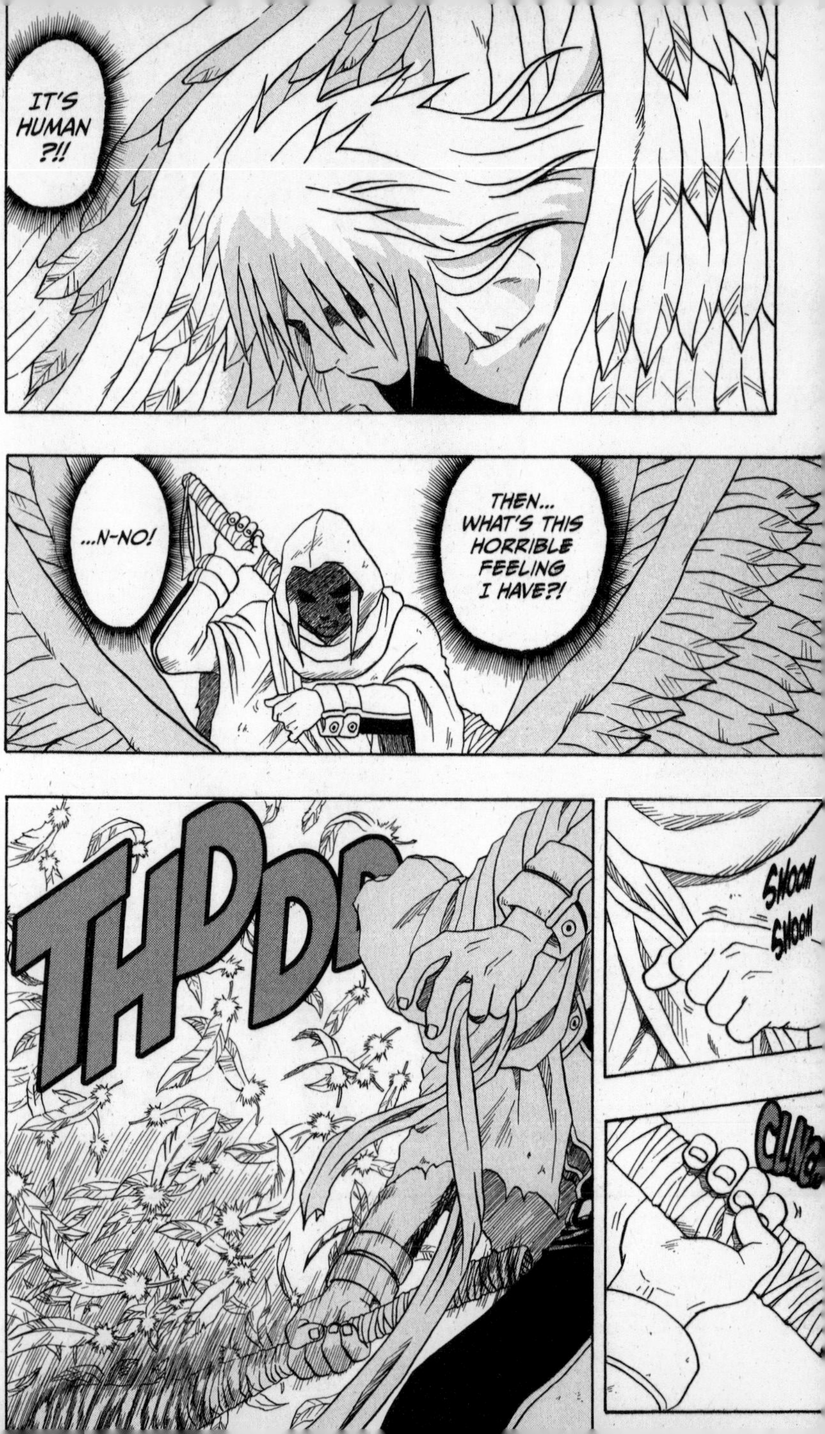
IT'S HUMAN ?!!
THEN... WHAT'S THIS HORRIBLE FEELING I HAVE?!
...N-NO!
SMOOM SMOOM
CLING
THDD

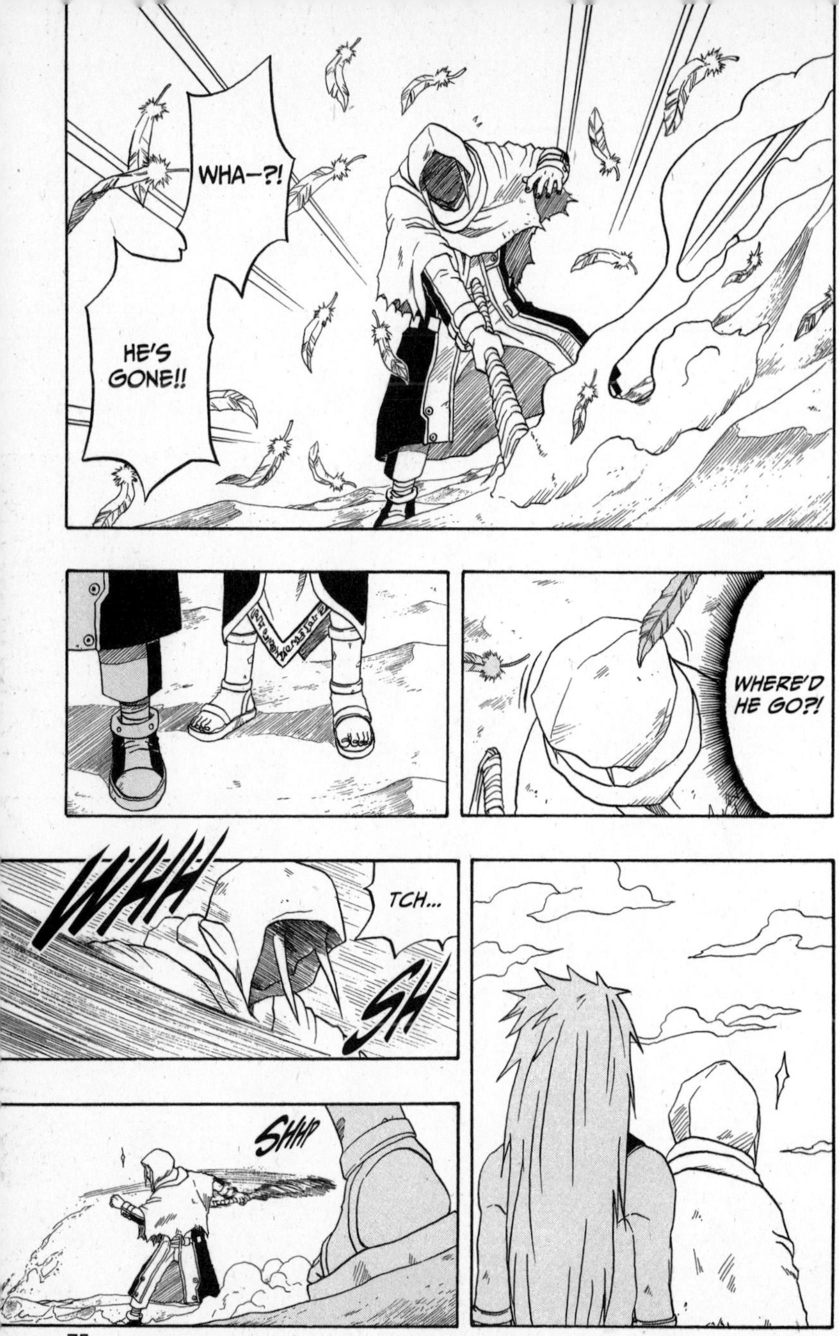
WHA-?!
HE'S GONE!!
WHERE'D HE GO?!
TCH...
WHH
SH
SHHP

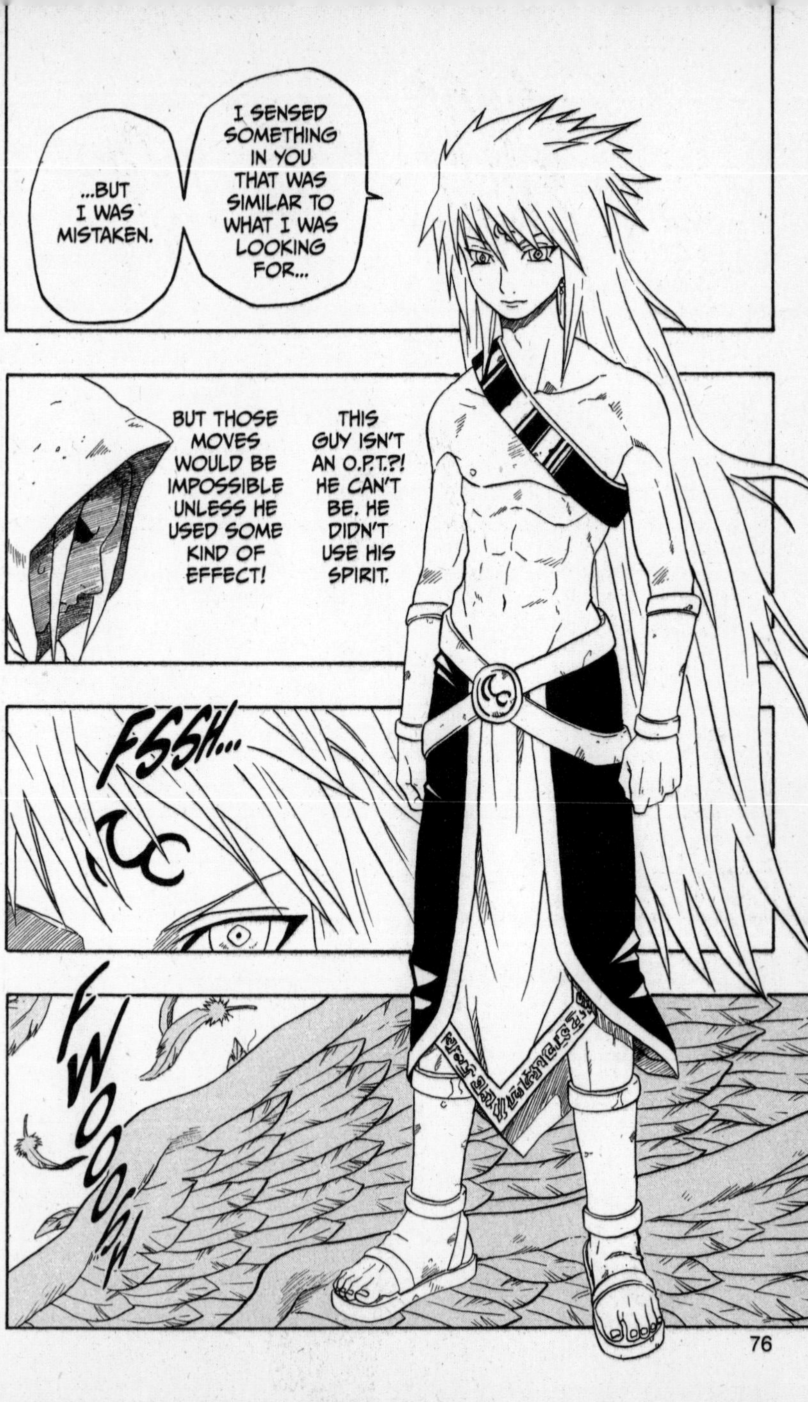
I SENSED SOMETHING IN YOU THAT WAS SIMILAR TO WHAT I WAS LOOKING FOR...
...BUT I WAS MISTAKEN.
THIS GUY ISN'T AN O.P.T.?! HE CAN'T BE. HE DIDN'T USE HIS SPIRIT.
BUT THOSE MOVES WOULD BE IMPOSSIBLE UNLESS HE USED SOME KIND OF EFFECT!
FSSH...
FWOOOSH

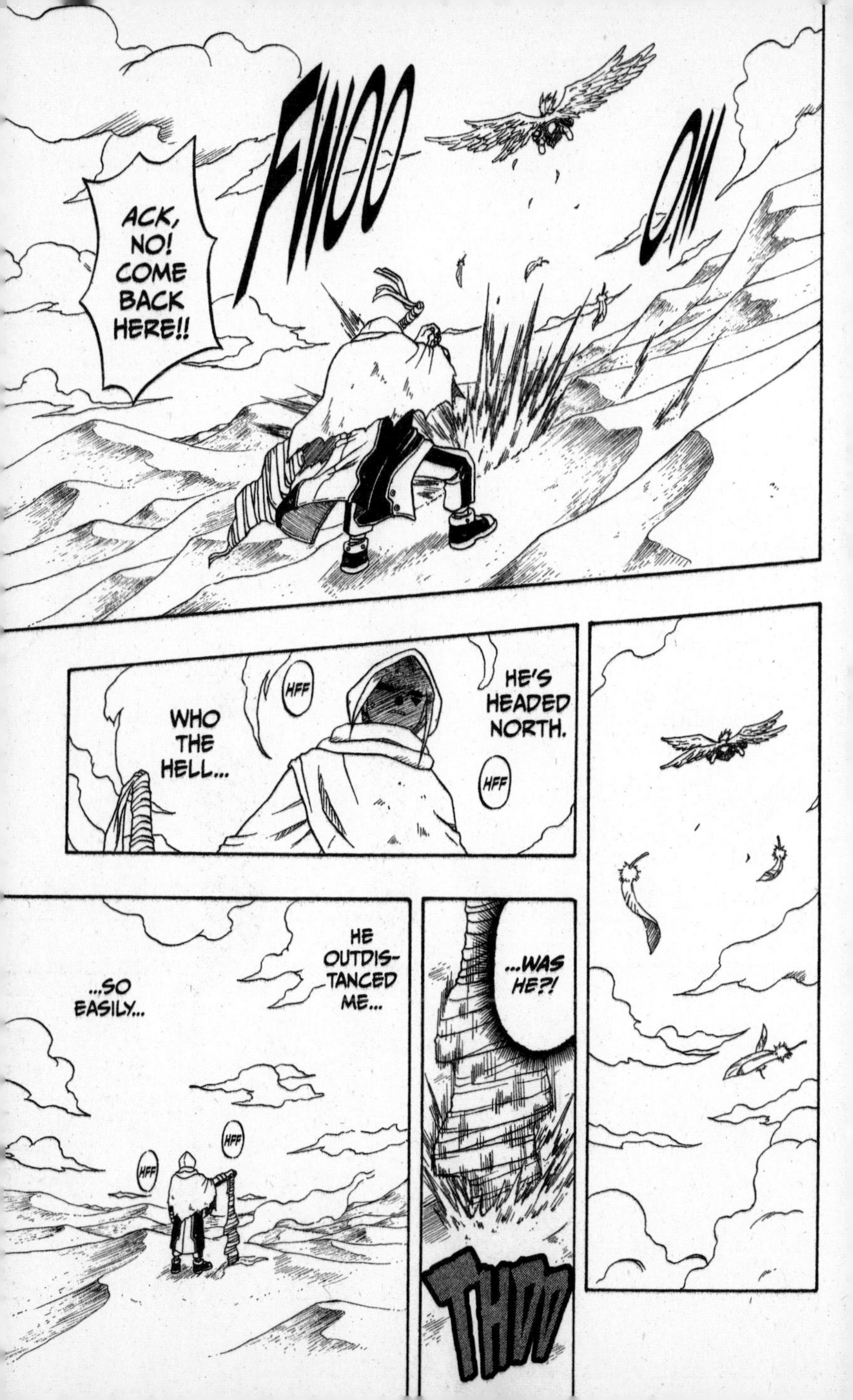
FWOO
OM
ACK, NO! COME BACK HERE!!
HE'S HEADED NORTH.
HFF
WHO THE HELL...
HFF
...WAS HE?!
THUD
HE OUTDIS-TANCED ME...
...SO EASILY...
HFF
HFF

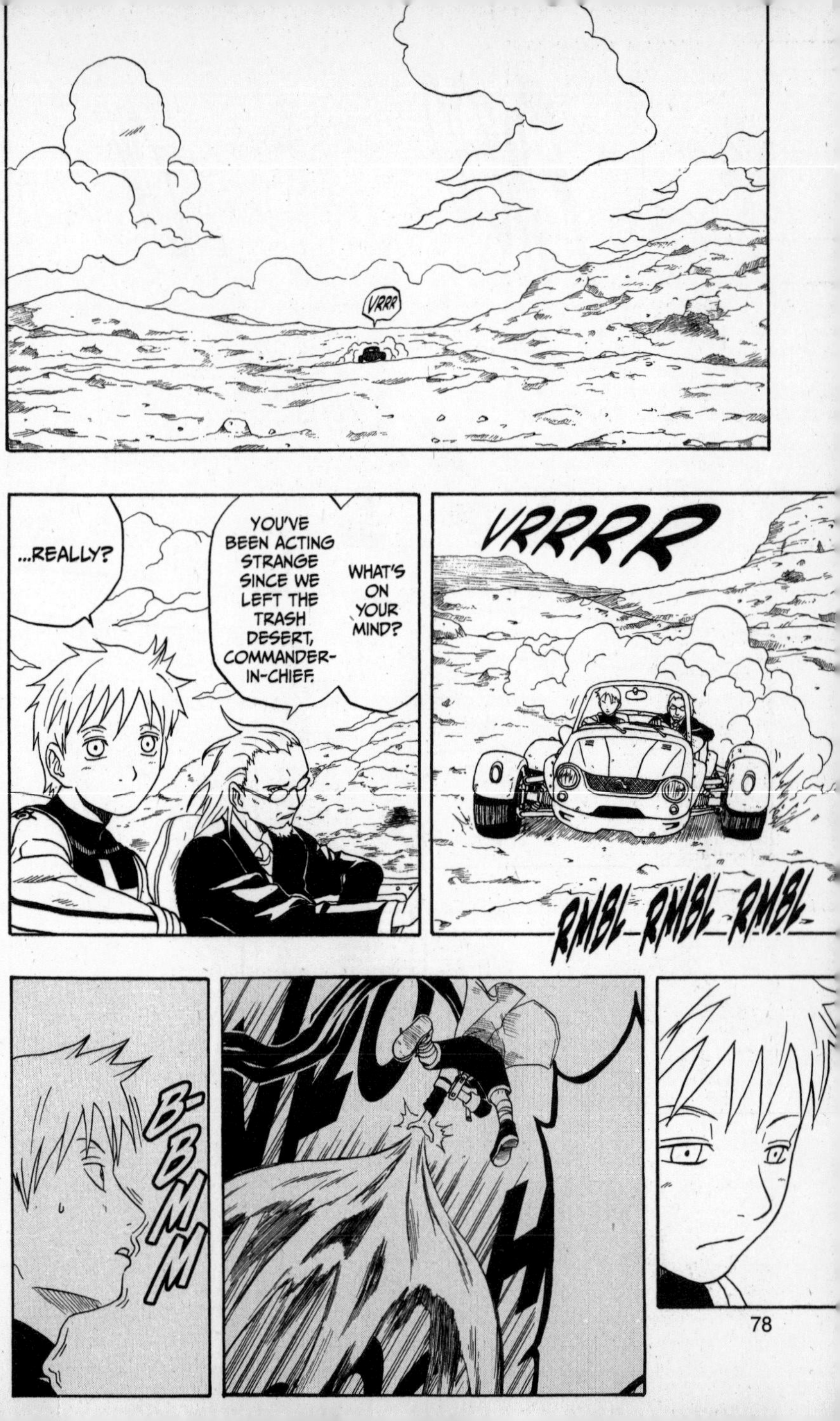
VRRR
VRRRR
RMBL RMBL RMBL
YOU'VE BEEN ACTING STRANGE SINCE WE LEFT THE TRASH DESERT, COMMANDER-IN-CHIEF.
WHAT'S ON YOUR MIND?
...REALLY?
B-BMM

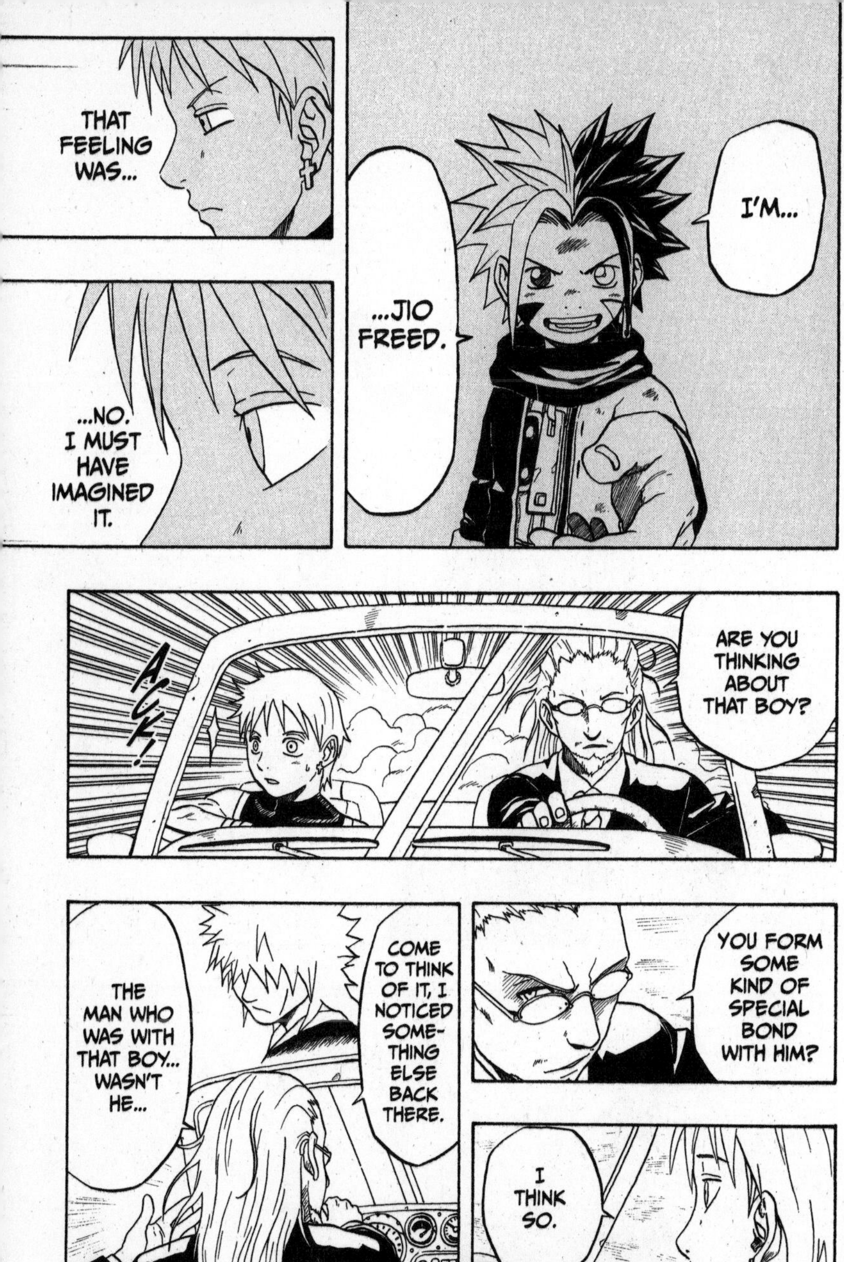
I'M...
...JIO FREED.
THAT FEELING WAS...
...NO. I MUST HAVE IMAGINED IT.
ARE YOU THINKING ABOUT THAT BOY?
ACK!
YOU FORM SOME KIND OF SPECIAL BOND WITH HIM?
I THINK SO.
COME TO THINK OF IT, I NOTICED SOME-THING ELSE BACK THERE.
THE MAN WHO WAS WITH THAT BOY... WASN'T HE...

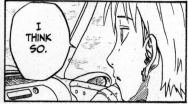

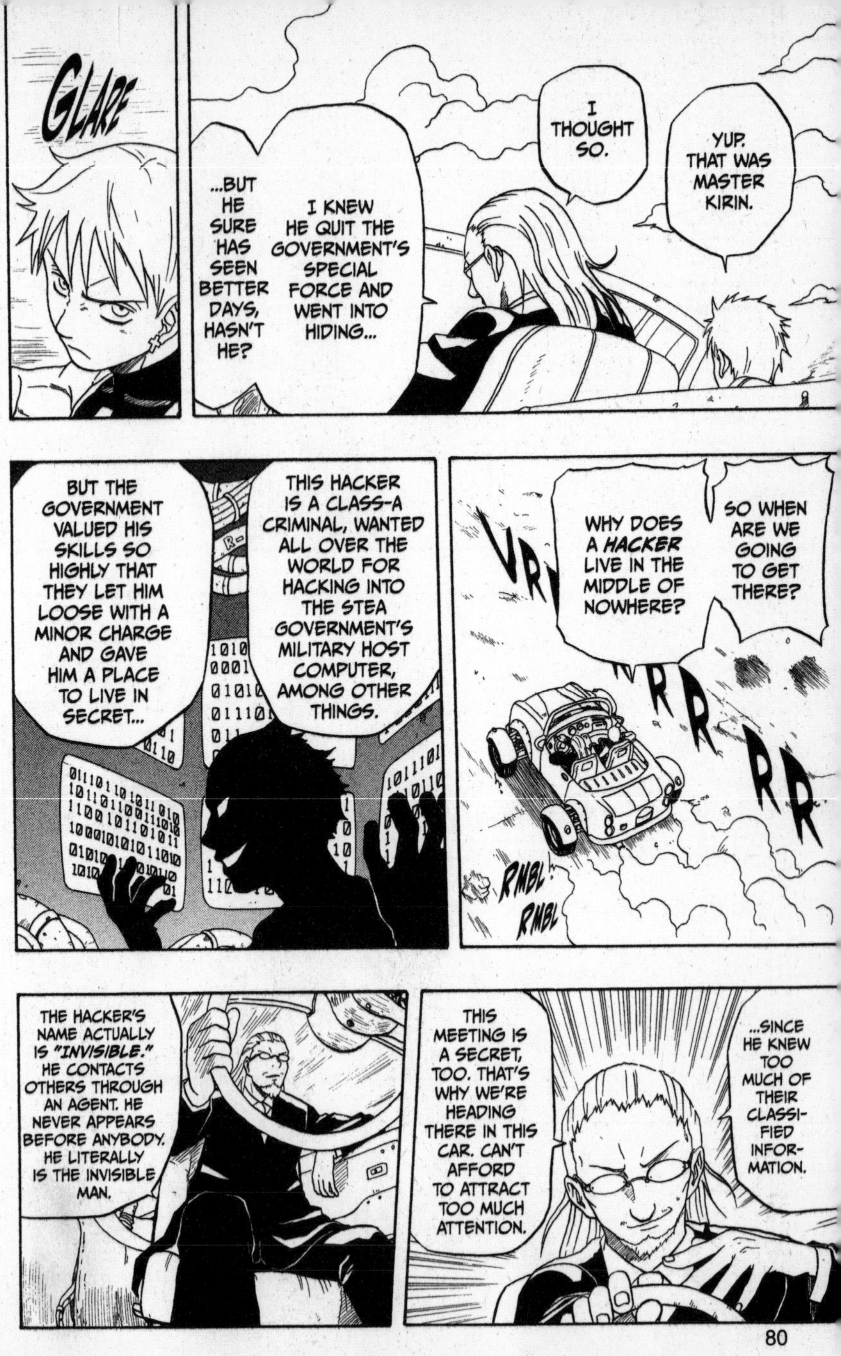

YUP. THAT WAS MASTER KIRIN.
I THOUGHT SO.
I KNEW HE QUIT THE GOVERNMENT'S SPECIAL FORCE AND WENT INTO HIDING...
...BUT HE SURE HAS SEEN BETTER DAYS, HASN'T HE?
GLARE
SO WHEN ARE WE GOING TO GET THERE?
WHY DOES A *HACKER* LIVE IN THE MIDDLE OF NOWHERE?
VRRRRRR
RMBL RMBL
THIS HACKER IS A CLASS-A CRIMINAL, WANTED ALL OVER THE WORLD FOR HACKING INTO THE STEA GOVERNMENT'S MILITARY HOST COMPUTER, AMONG OTHER THINGS.
BUT THE GOVERNMENT VALUED HIS SKILLS SO HIGHLY THAT THEY LET HIM LOOSE WITH A MINOR CHARGE AND GAVE HIM A PLACE TO LIVE IN SECRET...
...SINCE HE KNEW TOO MUCH OF THEIR CLASSI-FIED INFOR-MATION.
THIS MEETING IS A SECRET, TOO. THAT'S WHY WE'RE HEADING THERE IN THIS CAR. CAN'T AFFORD TO ATTRACT TOO MUCH ATTENTION.
THE HACKER'S NAME ACTUALLY IS *"INVISIBLE."* HE CONTACTS OTHERS THROUGH AN AGENT. HE NEVER APPEARS BEFORE ANYBODY. HE LITERALLY IS THE INVISIBLE MAN.

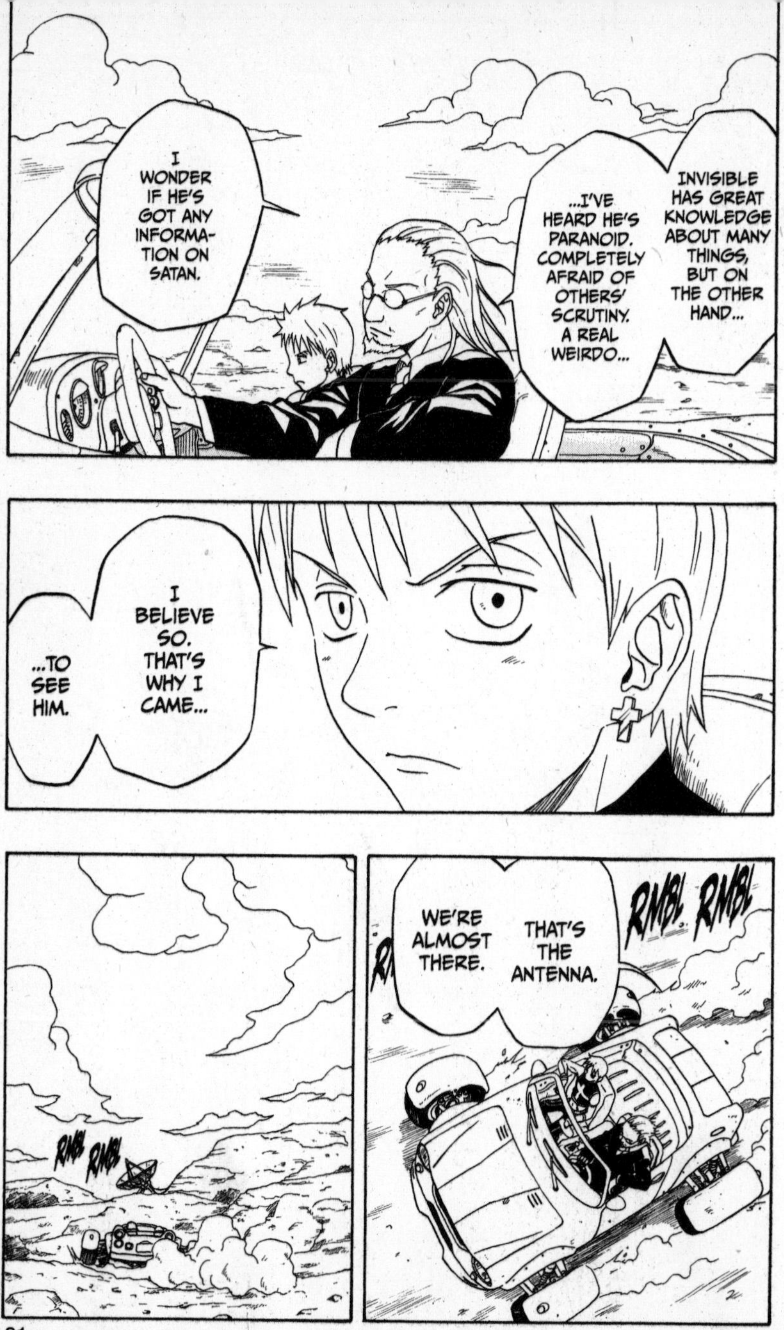
INVISIBLE HAS GREAT KNOWLEDGE ABOUT MANY THINGS, BUT ON THE OTHER HAND...
...I'VE HEARD HE'S PARANOID. COMPLETELY AFRAID OF OTHERS' SCRUTINY. A REAL WEIRDO...
I WONDER IF HE'S GOT ANY INFORMATION ON SATAN.
I BELIEVE SO. THAT'S WHY I CAME...
...TO SEE HIM.
RMBL RMBL
THAT'S THE ANTENNA.
WE'RE ALMOST THERE.
RMBL RMBL

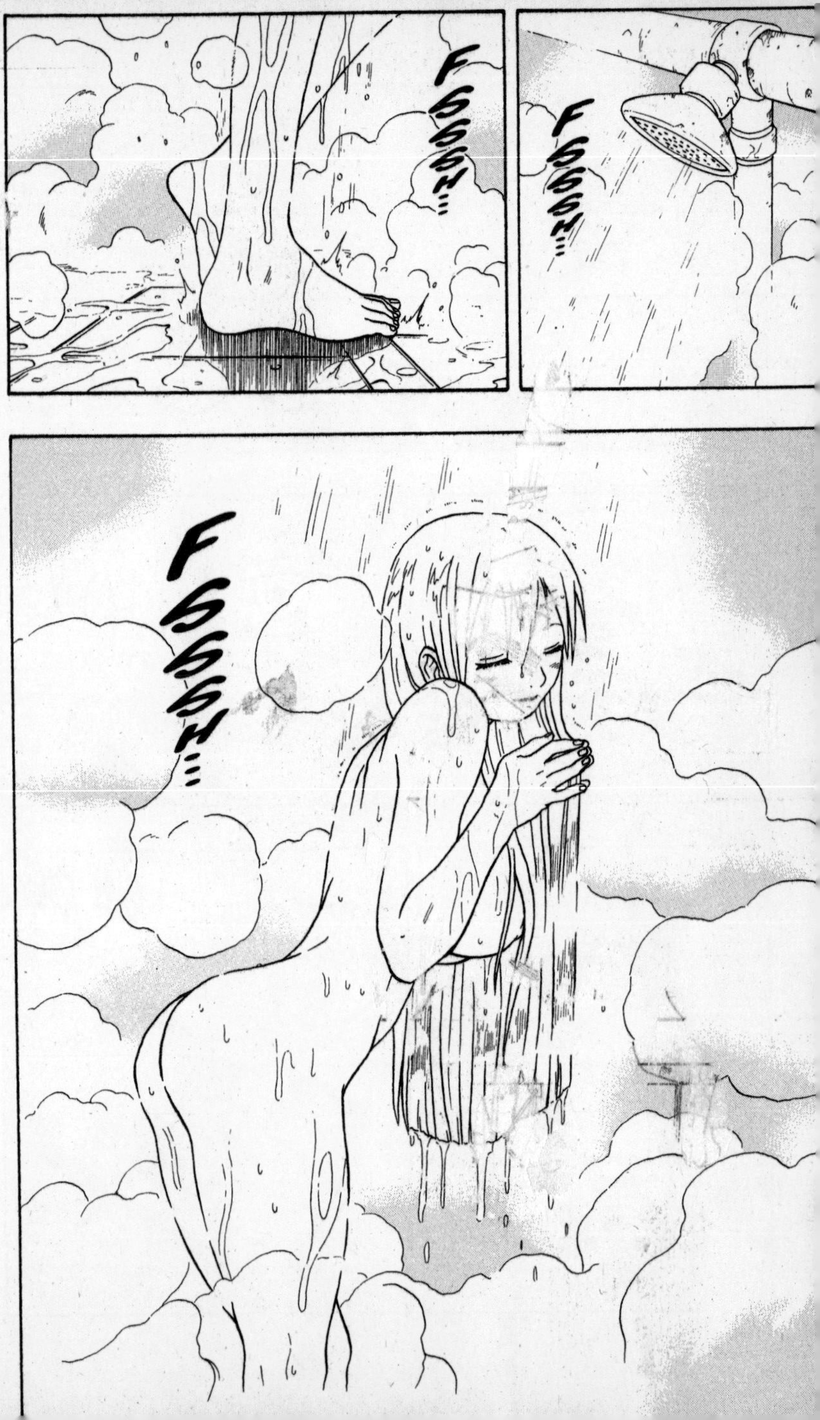
FSSSH!!
FSSSH!!
FSSSH!!

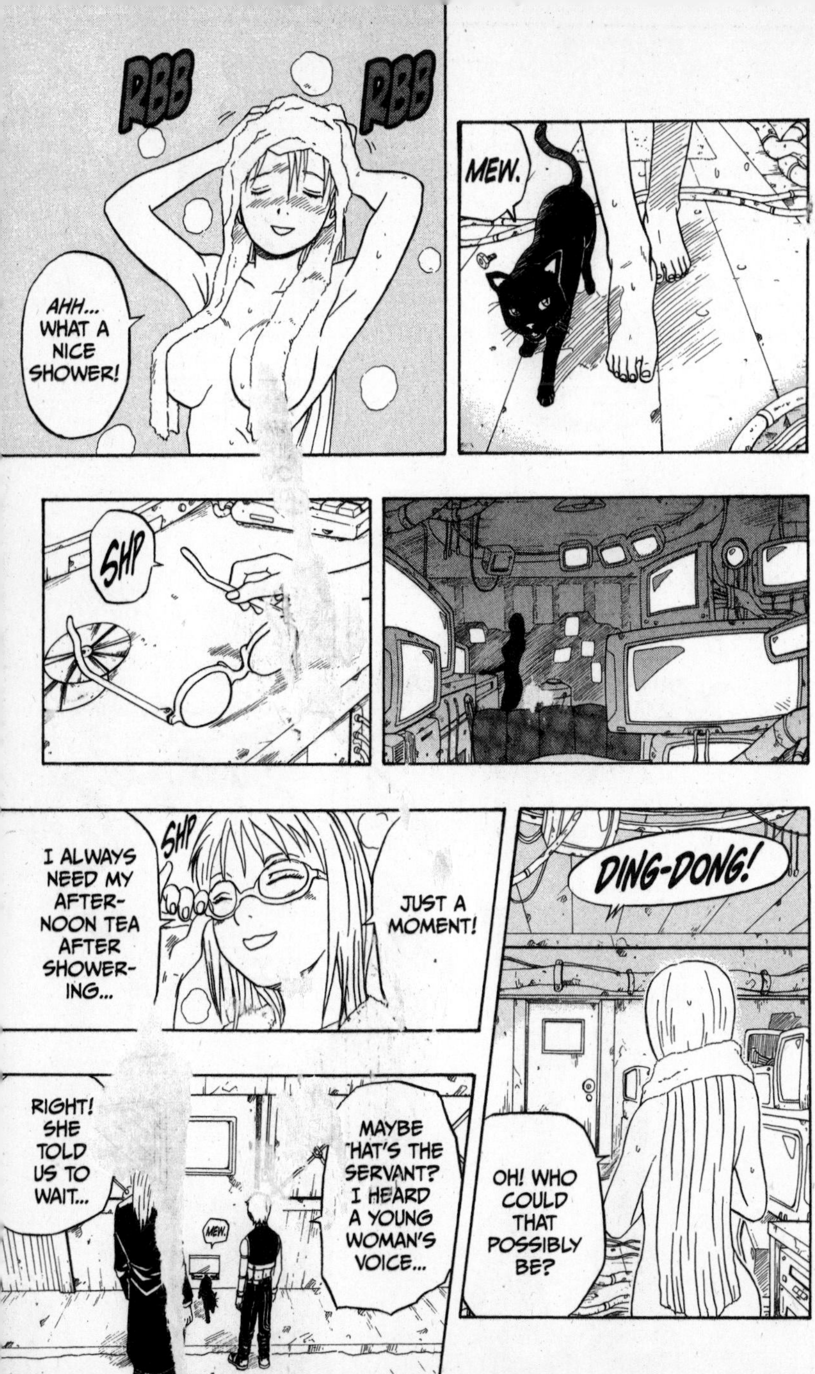
MEW.
RBB
RBB
AHH... WHAT A NICE SHOWER!
SHP
DING-DONG!
OH! WHO COULD THAT POSSIBLY BE?
SHP
JUST A MOMENT!
I ALWAYS NEED MY AFTER-NOON TEA AFTER SHOWER-ING...
MAYBE THAT'S THE SERVANT? I HEARD A YOUNG WOMAN'S VOICE...
MEW.
RIGHT! SHE TOLD US TO WAIT...

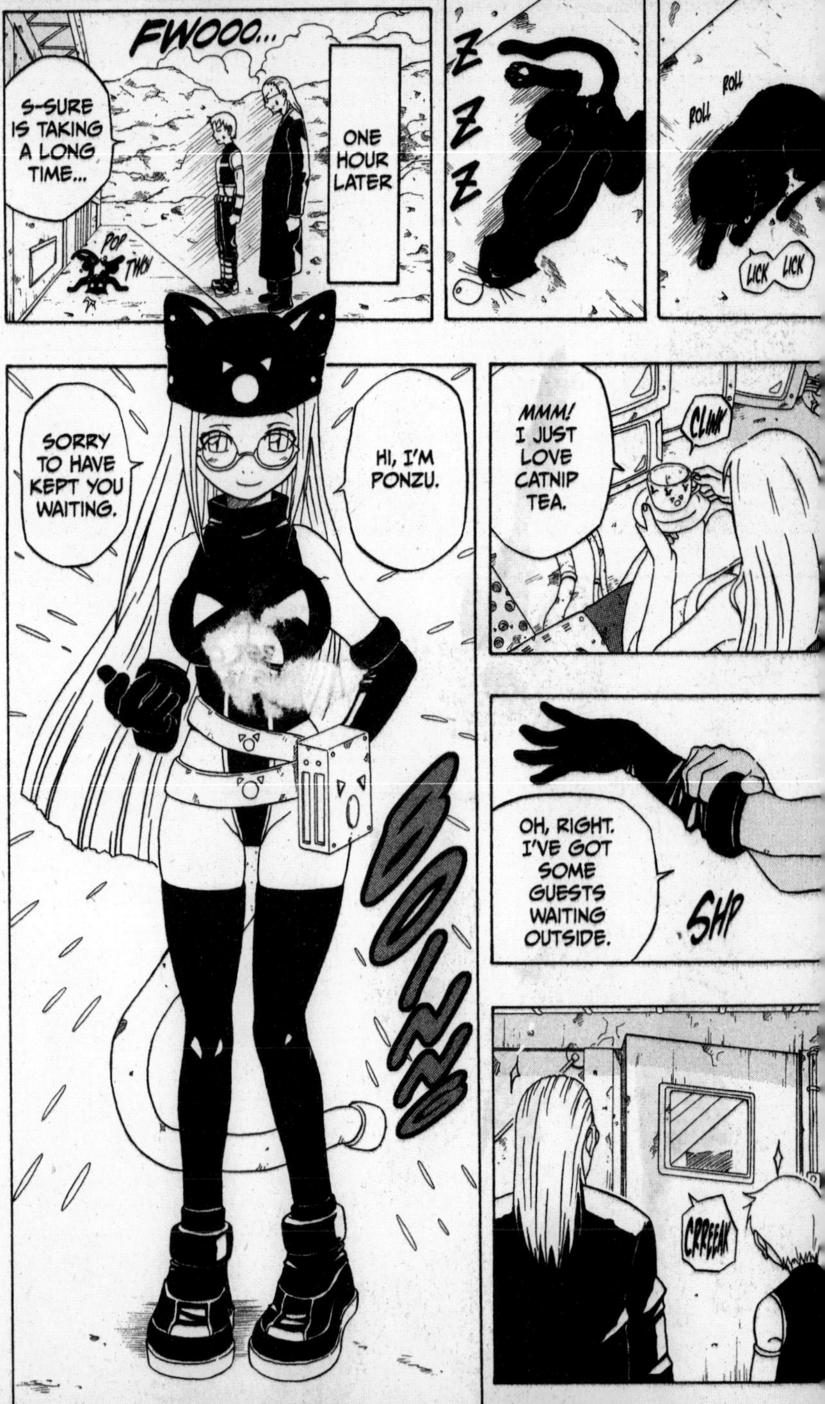
ROLL ROLL
LICK LICK
Z Z Z
ONE HOUR LATER
FWOOO...
S-SURE IS TAKING A LONG TIME...
POP THWK
CLINK
MMM! I JUST LOVE CATNIP TEA.
OH, RIGHT. I'VE GOT SOME GUESTS WAITING OUTSIDE.
SHP
CRREEAK
HI, I'M PONZU.
SORRY TO HAVE KEPT YOU WAITING.

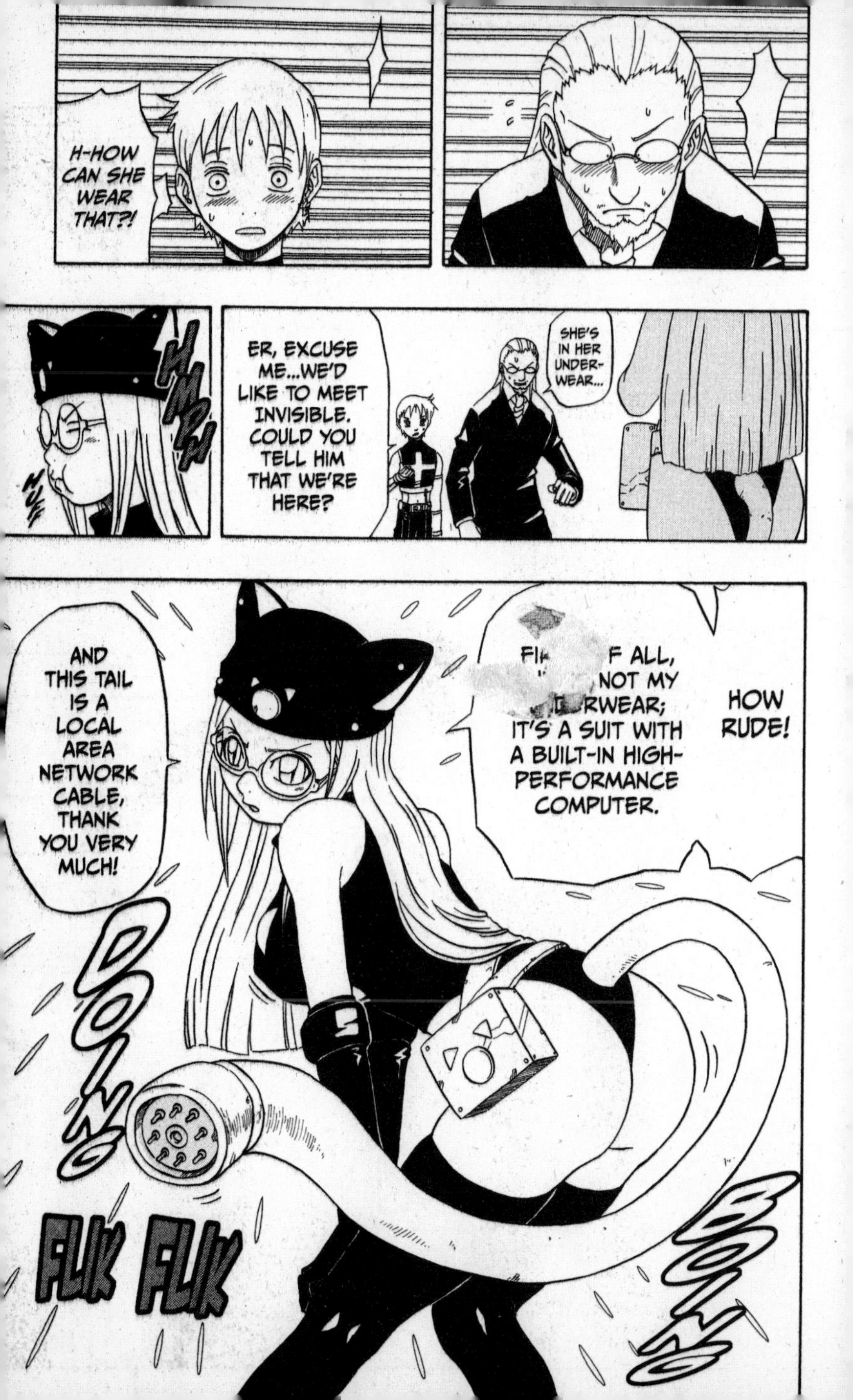
H-HOW CAN SHE WEAR THAT?!
SHE'S IN HER UNDER-WEAR...
ER, EXCUSE ME...WE'D LIKE TO MEET INVISIBLE. COULD YOU TELL HIM THAT WE'RE HERE?
HMPH
HUFF
HOW RUDE!
FI F ALL, NOT MY RWEAR; IT'S A SUIT WITH A BUILT-IN HIGH-PERFORMANCE COMPUTER.
AND THIS TAIL IS A LOCAL AREA NETWORK CABLE, THANK YOU VERY MUCH!
DOING
FLIK FLIK
DOING

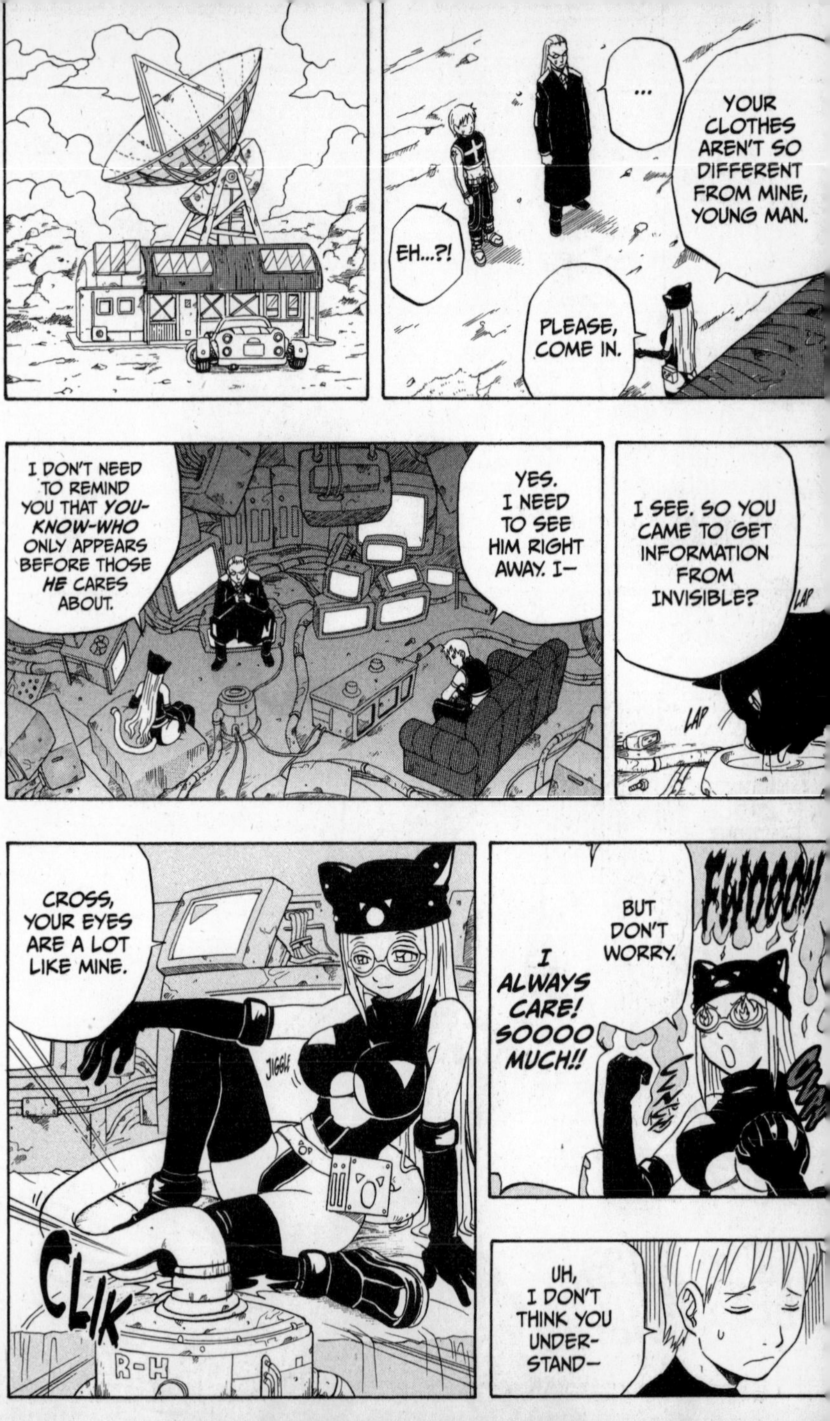
YOUR CLOTHES AREN'T SO DIFFERENT FROM MINE, YOUNG MAN.
...
EH...?!
PLEASE, COME IN.
I SEE. SO YOU CAME TO GET INFORMATION FROM INVISIBLE?
LAP
LAP
YES. I NEED TO SEE HIM RIGHT AWAY. I—
I DON'T NEED TO REMIND YOU THAT *YOU-KNOW-WHO* ONLY APPEARS BEFORE THOSE *HE* CARES ABOUT.
FWOOOM
BUT DON'T WORRY.
I ALWAYS CARE! SOOOO MUCH!!
UH, I DON'T THINK YOU UNDER-STAND—
CROSS, YOUR EYES ARE A LOT LIKE MINE.
JIGGLE
CLIK
R-H

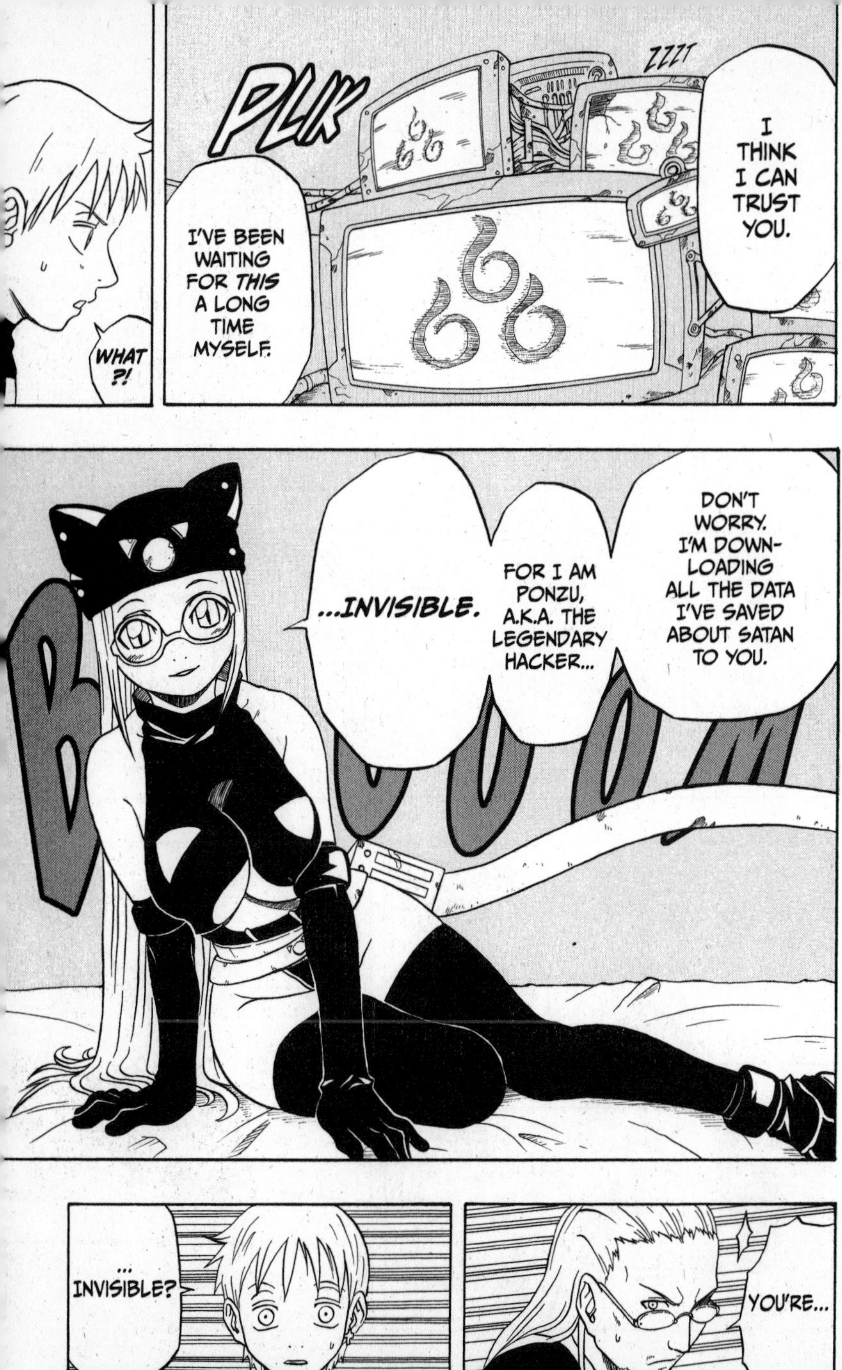
ZZZT
I THINK I CAN TRUST YOU.
PLIK
I'VE BEEN WAITING FOR *THIS* A LONG TIME MYSELF.
WHAT?!
DON'T WORRY. I'M DOWN-LOADING ALL THE DATA I'VE SAVED ABOUT SATAN TO YOU.
FOR I AM PONZU, A.K.A. THE LEGENDARY HACKER...
...INVISIBLE.
BOOOM
YOU'RE...
...INVISIBLE?

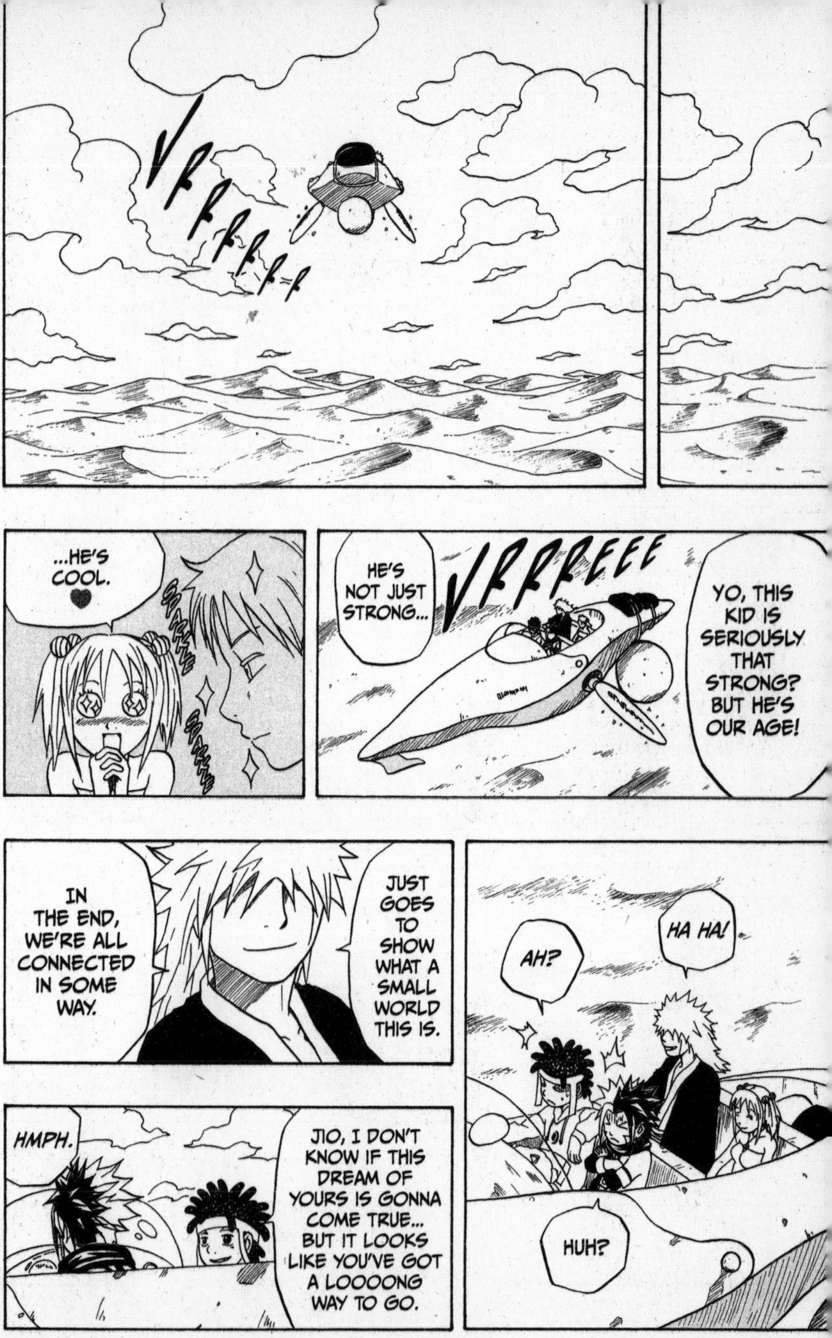
VRRRRRRR
YO, THIS KID IS SERIOUSLY THAT STRONG? BUT HE'S OUR AGE!
VRRREEE
HE'S NOT JUST STRONG...
...HE'S COOL. ♥
HA HA!
AH?
HUH?
JUST GOES TO SHOW WHAT A SMALL WORLD THIS IS.
IN THE END, WE'RE ALL CONNECTED IN SOME WAY.
JIO, I DON'T KNOW IF THIS DREAM OF YOURS IS GONNA COME TRUE... BUT IT LOOKS LIKE YOU'VE GOT A LOOOONG WAY TO GO.
HMPH.

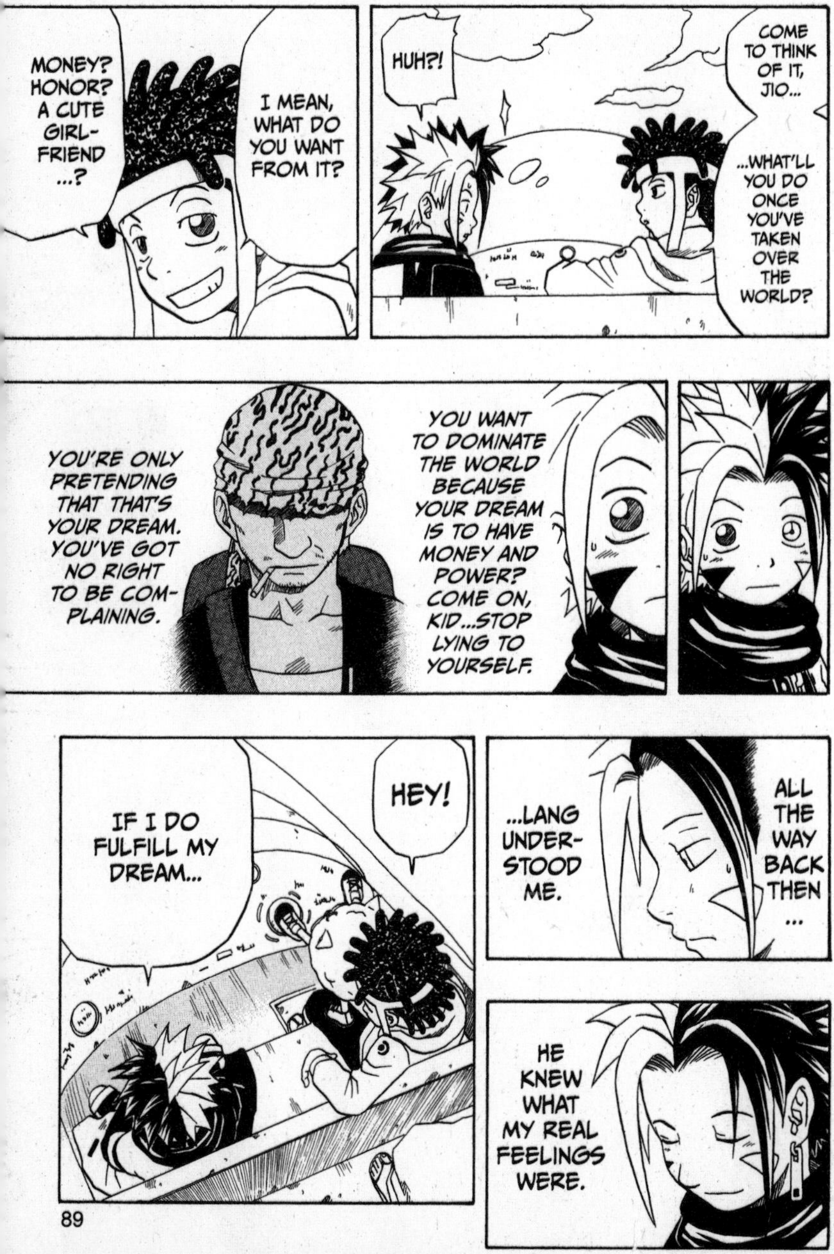
COME TO THINK OF IT, JIO...
...WHAT'LL YOU DO ONCE YOU'VE TAKEN OVER THE WORLD?
HUH?!
I MEAN, WHAT DO YOU WANT FROM IT?
MONEY? HONOR? A CUTE GIRL-FRIEND ...?
YOU WANT TO DOMINATE THE WORLD BECAUSE YOUR DREAM IS TO HAVE MONEY AND POWER? COME ON, KID...STOP LYING TO YOURSELF.
YOU'RE ONLY PRETENDING THAT THAT'S YOUR DREAM. YOU'VE GOT NO RIGHT TO BE COM-PLAINING.
ALL THE WAY BACK THEN ...
...LANG UNDER-STOOD ME.
HE KNEW WHAT MY REAL FEELINGS WERE.
HEY!
IF I DO FULFILL MY DREAM...

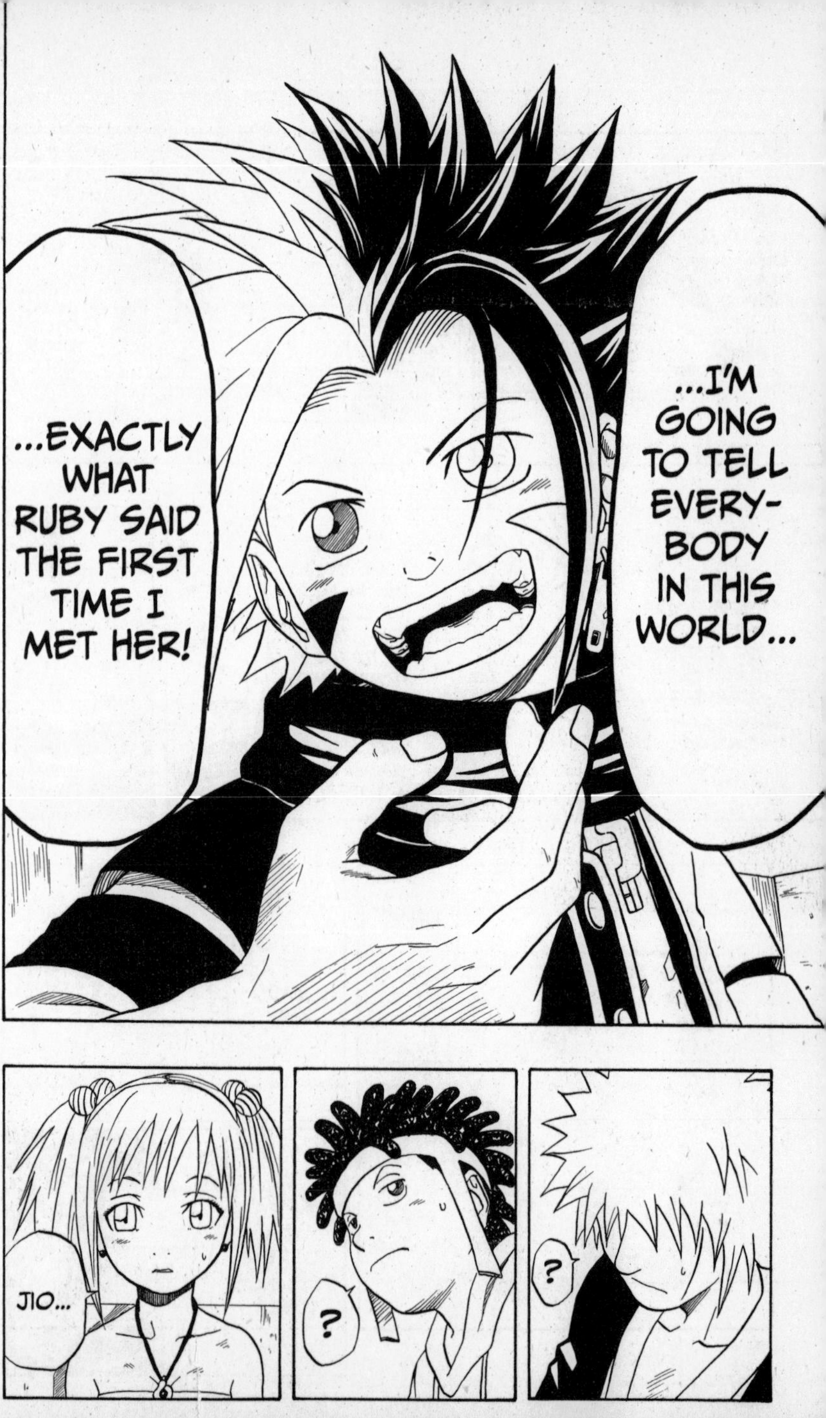
...I'M GOING TO TELL EVERY-BODY IN THIS WORLD...
...EXACTLY WHAT RUBY SAID THE FIRST TIME I MET HER!
?
?
JIO...

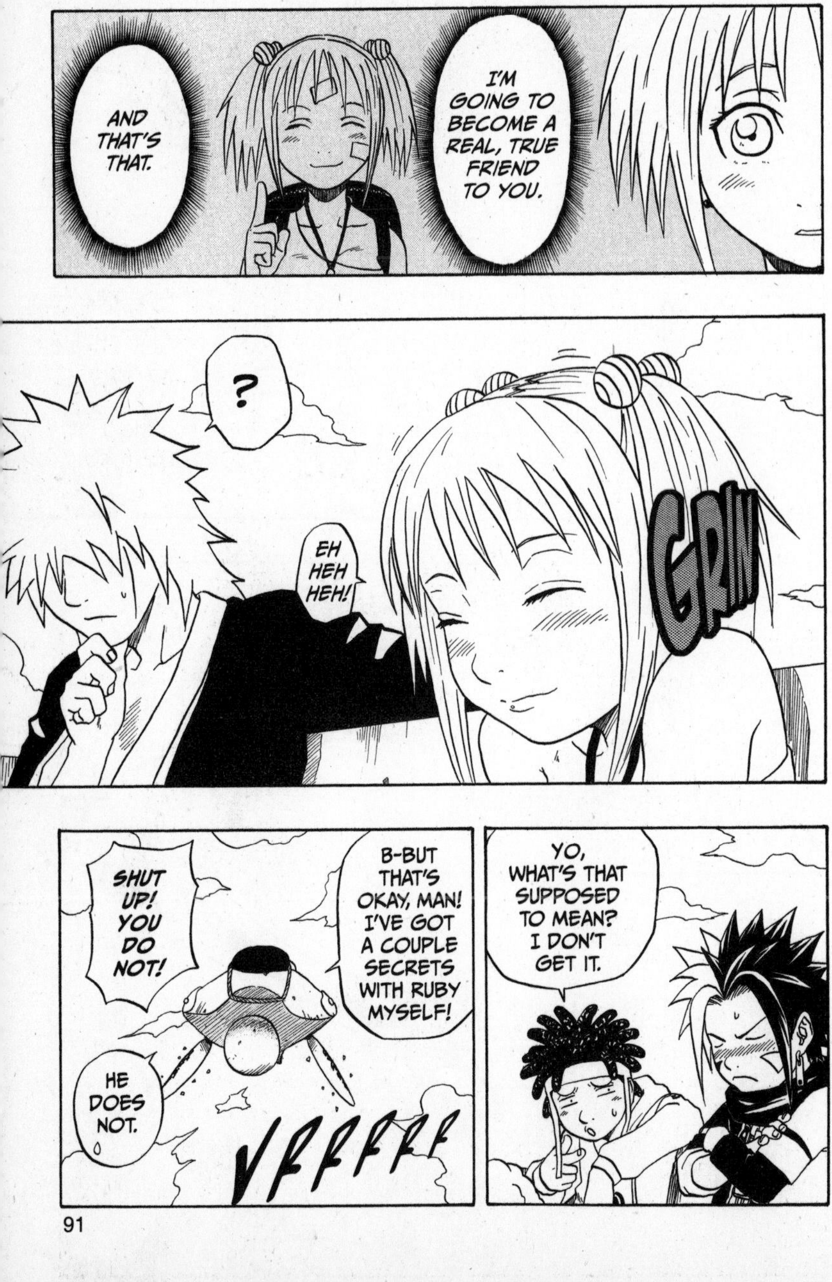
I'M GOING TO BECOME A REAL, TRUE FRIEND TO YOU.
AND THAT'S THAT.
GRIN
?
EH HEH HEH!
YO, WHAT'S THAT SUPPOSED TO MEAN? I DON'T GET IT.
B-BUT THAT'S OKAY, MAN! I'VE GOT A COUPLE SECRETS WITH RUBY MYSELF!
SHUT UP! YOU DO NOT!
HE DOES NOT.
VFFFFF

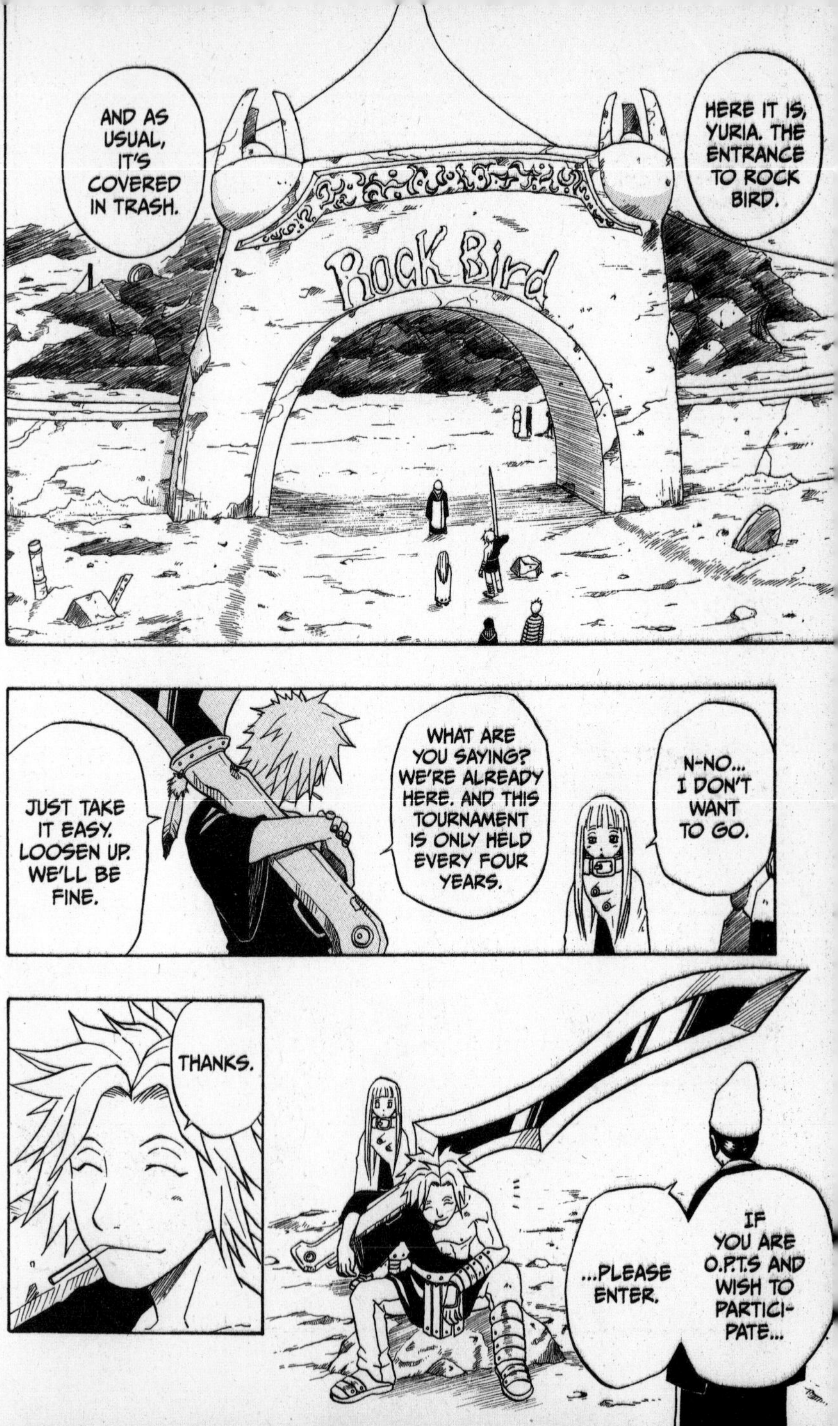
HERE IT IS, YURIA. THE ENTRANCE TO ROCK BIRD.
AND AS USUAL, IT'S COVERED IN TRASH.
Rock Bird
N-NO... I DON'T WANT TO GO.
WHAT ARE YOU SAYING? WE'RE ALREADY HERE. AND THIS TOURNAMENT IS ONLY HELD EVERY FOUR YEARS.
JUST TAKE IT EASY. LOOSEN UP. WE'LL BE FINE.
IF YOU ARE O.P.T.S AND WISH TO PARTICI-PATE...
...PLEASE ENTER.
THANKS.

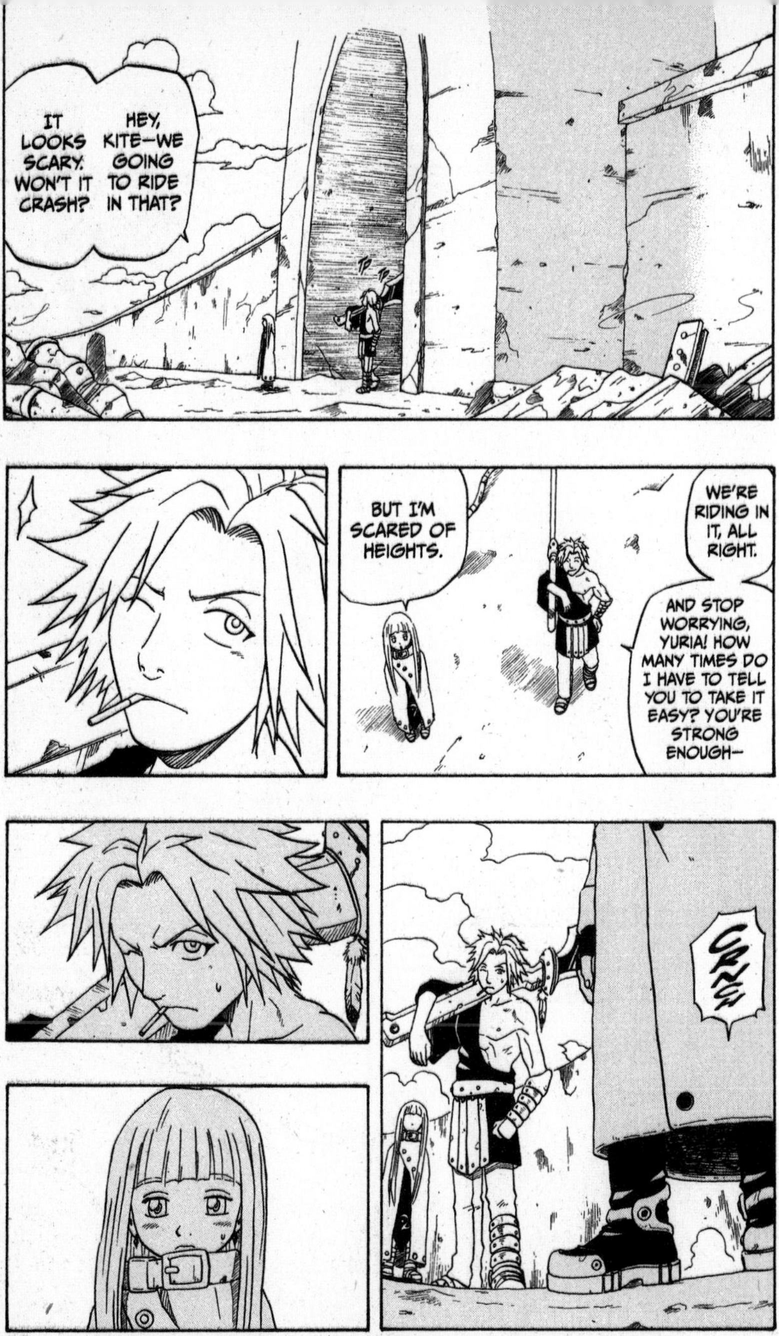
HEY, KITE—WE GOING TO RIDE IN THAT?
IT LOOKS SCARY. WON'T IT CRASH?
WE'RE RIDING IN IT, ALL RIGHT.
AND STOP WORRYING, YURIA! HOW MANY TIMES DO I HAVE TO TELL YOU TO TAKE IT EASY? YOU'RE STRONG ENOUGH—
BUT I'M SCARED OF HEIGHTS.
CRNCH

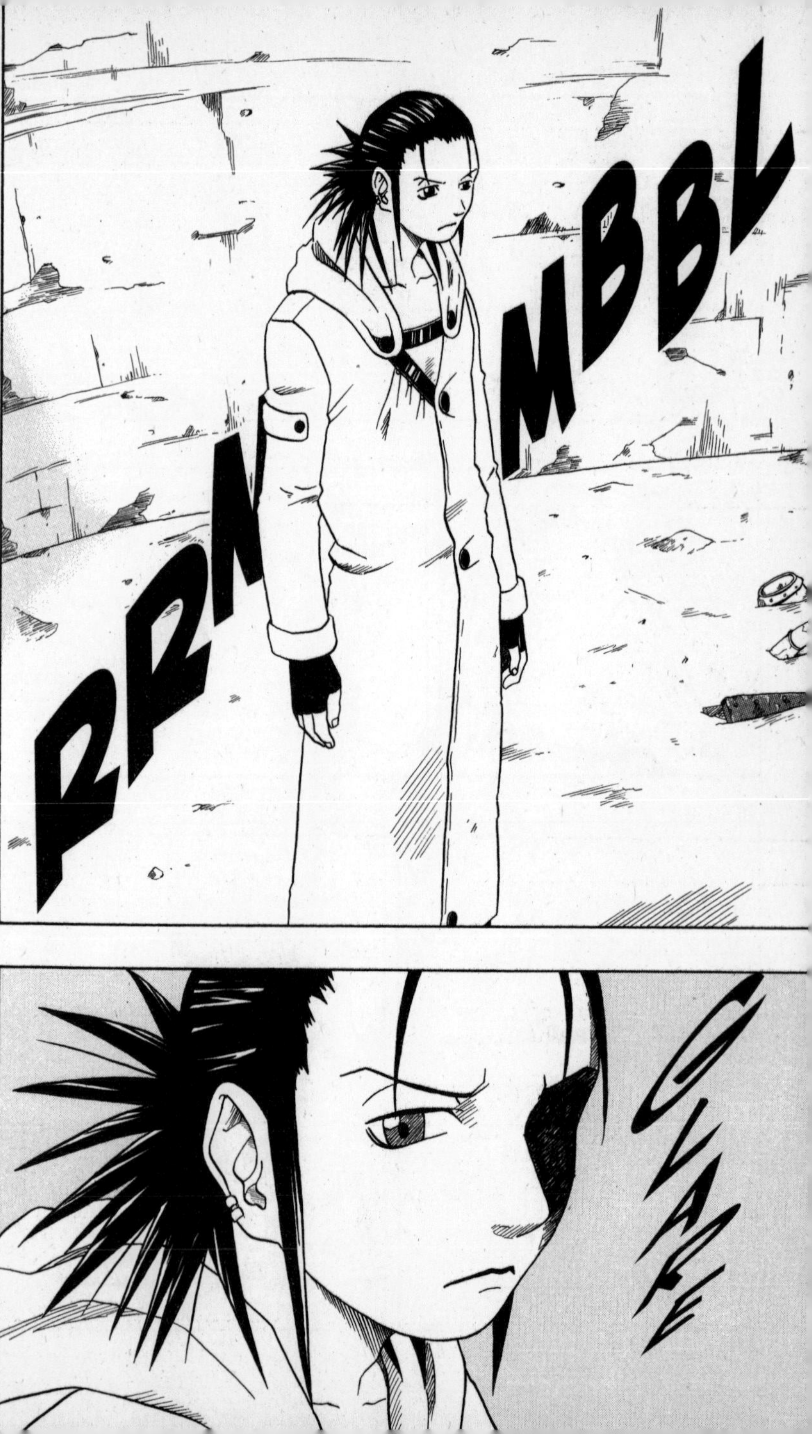
RRMMBBL
GLARE

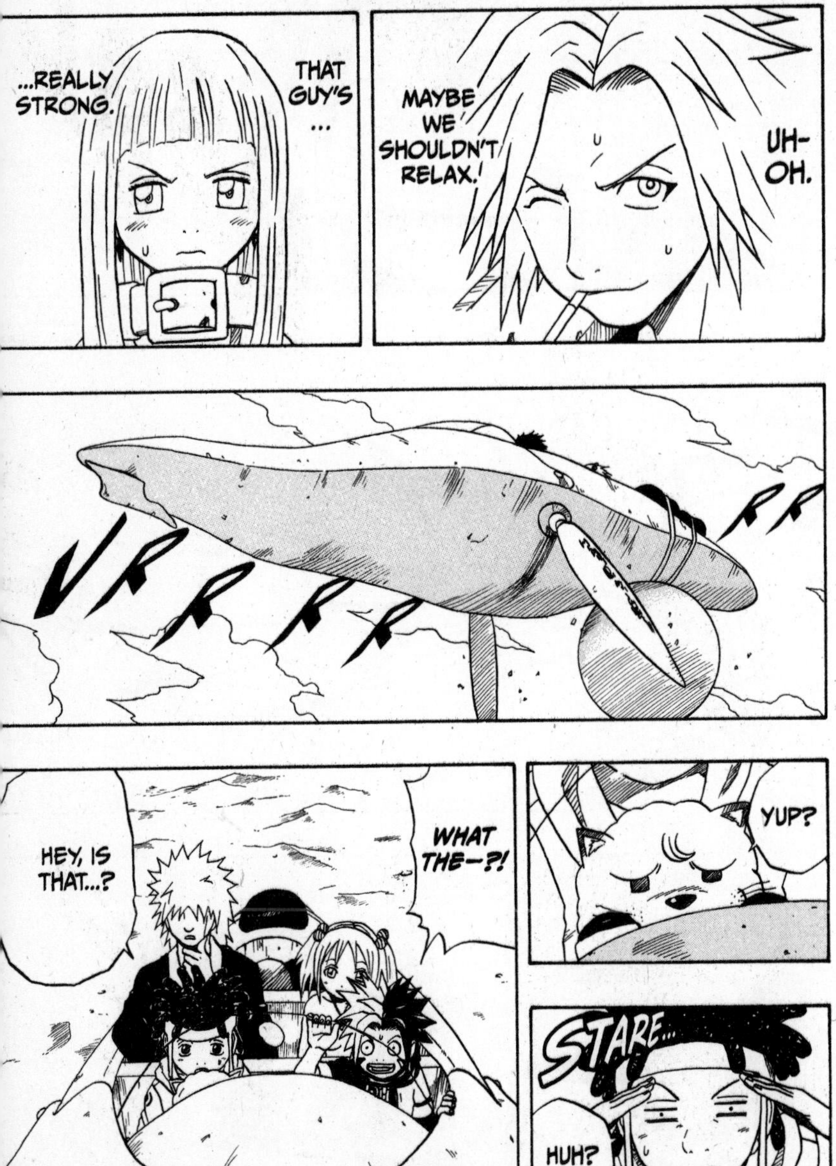
UH-OH.
MAYBE WE SHOULDN'T RELAX.
THAT GUY'S...
...REALLY STRONG.
VRRRRR
RR
YUP?
STARE...
HUH?
WHAT THE-?!
HEY, IS THAT...?

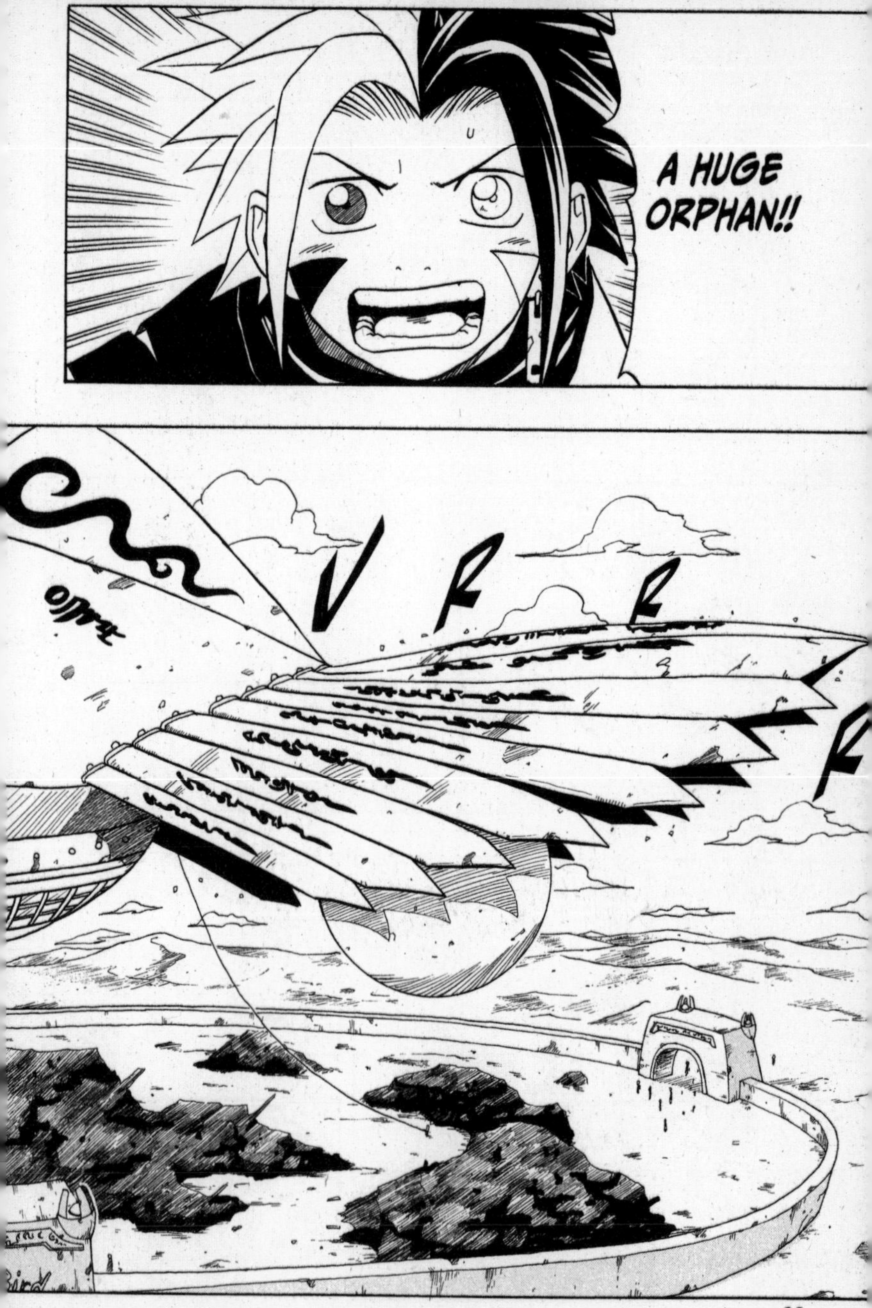
A HUGE ORPHAN!!
VRRR

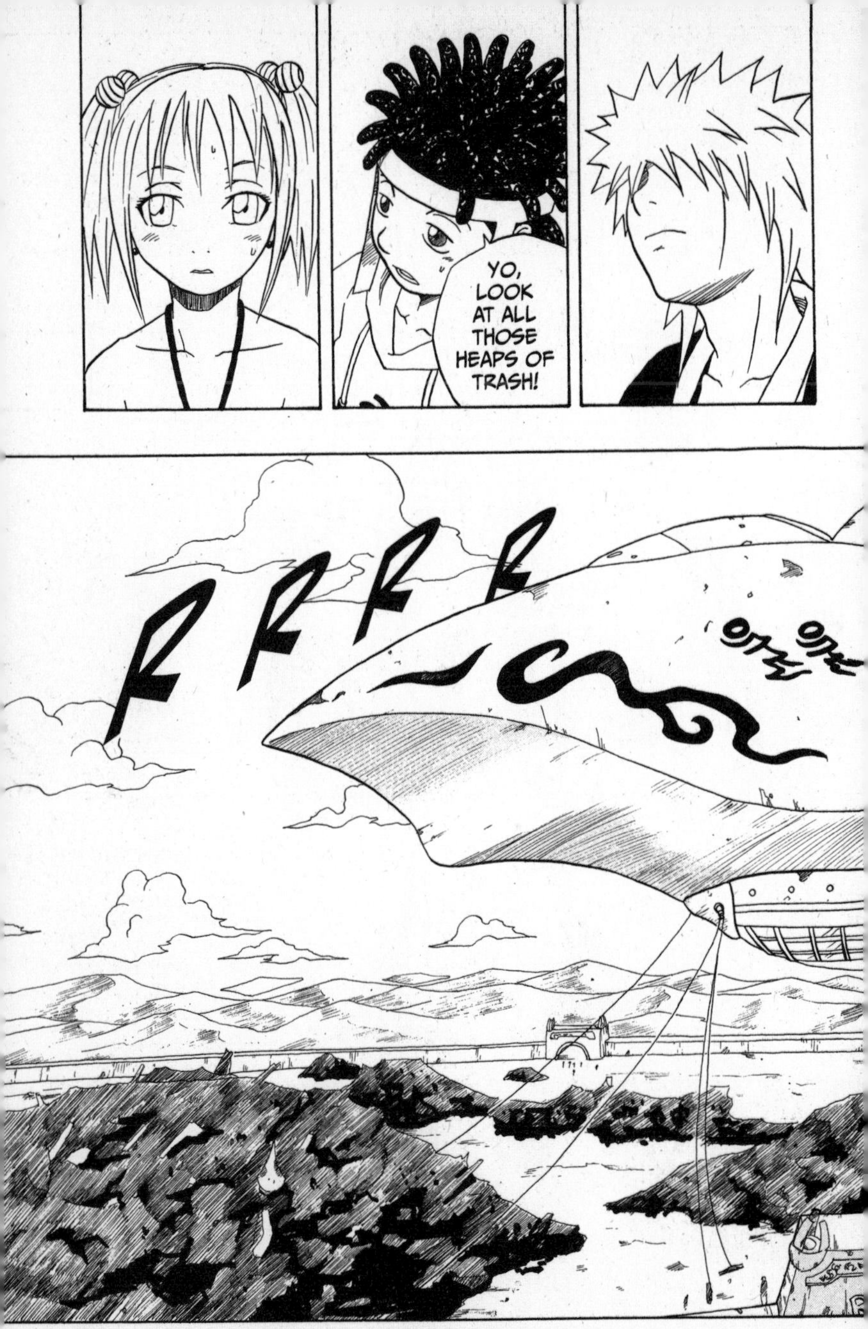
YO, LOOK AT ALL THOSE HEAPS OF TRASH!
RRRR

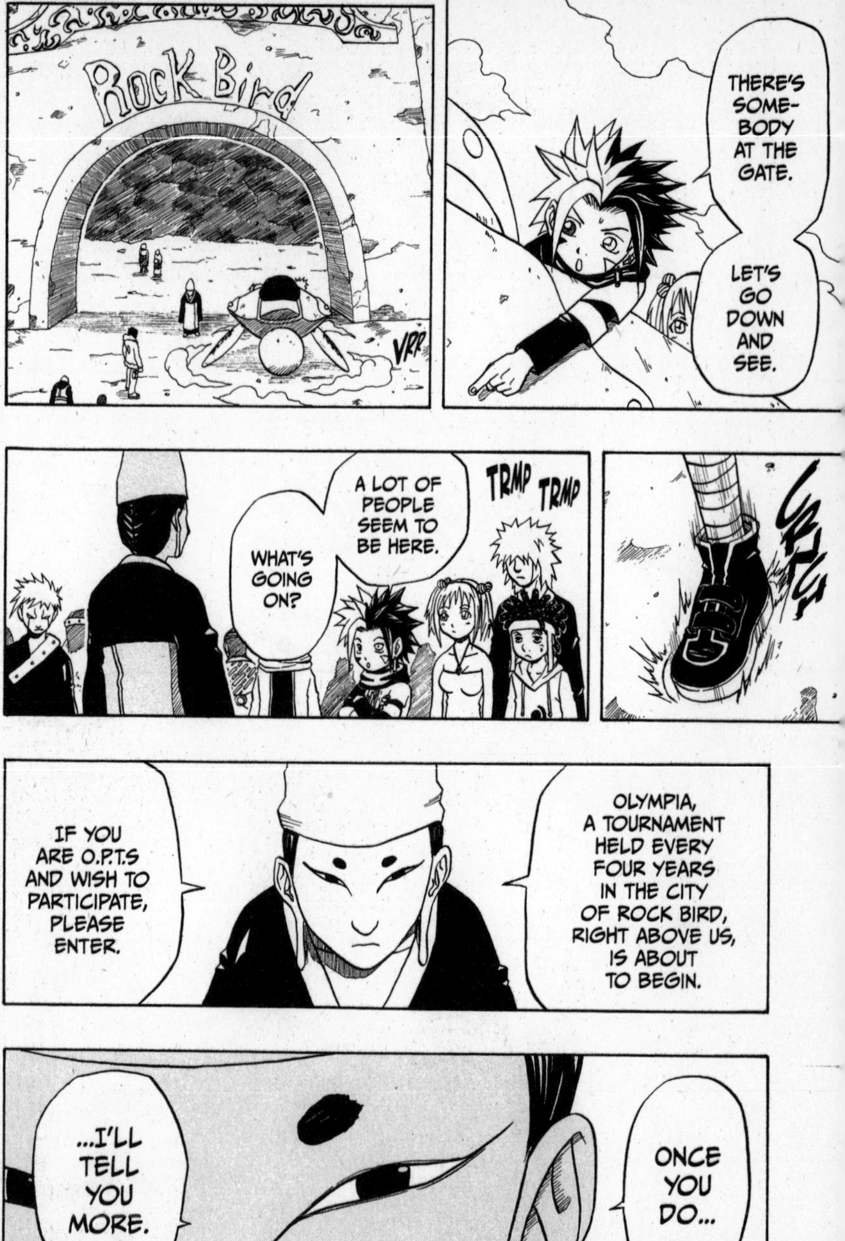
THERE'S SOMEBODY AT THE GATE.
LET'S GO DOWN AND SEE.
Rock Bird
VRR
TRMP TRMP
A LOT OF PEOPLE SEEM TO BE HERE.
WHAT'S GOING ON?
OLYMPIA, A TOURNAMENT HELD EVERY FOUR YEARS IN THE CITY OF ROCK BIRD, RIGHT ABOVE US, IS ABOUT TO BEGIN.
IF YOU ARE O.P.T.S AND WISH TO PARTICIPATE, PLEASE ENTER.
ONCE YOU DO...
...I'LL TELL YOU MORE.

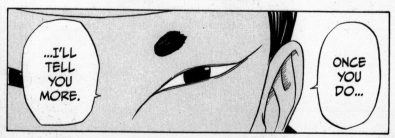

CHAPTER 31
OLYMPIA'S PRELIM ROUND

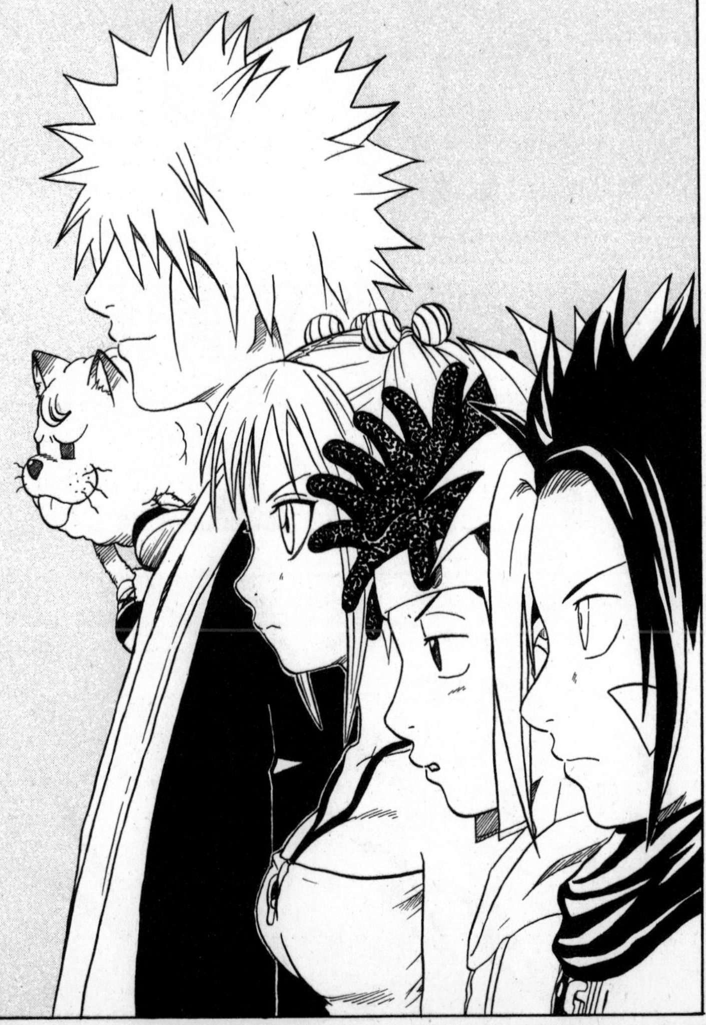

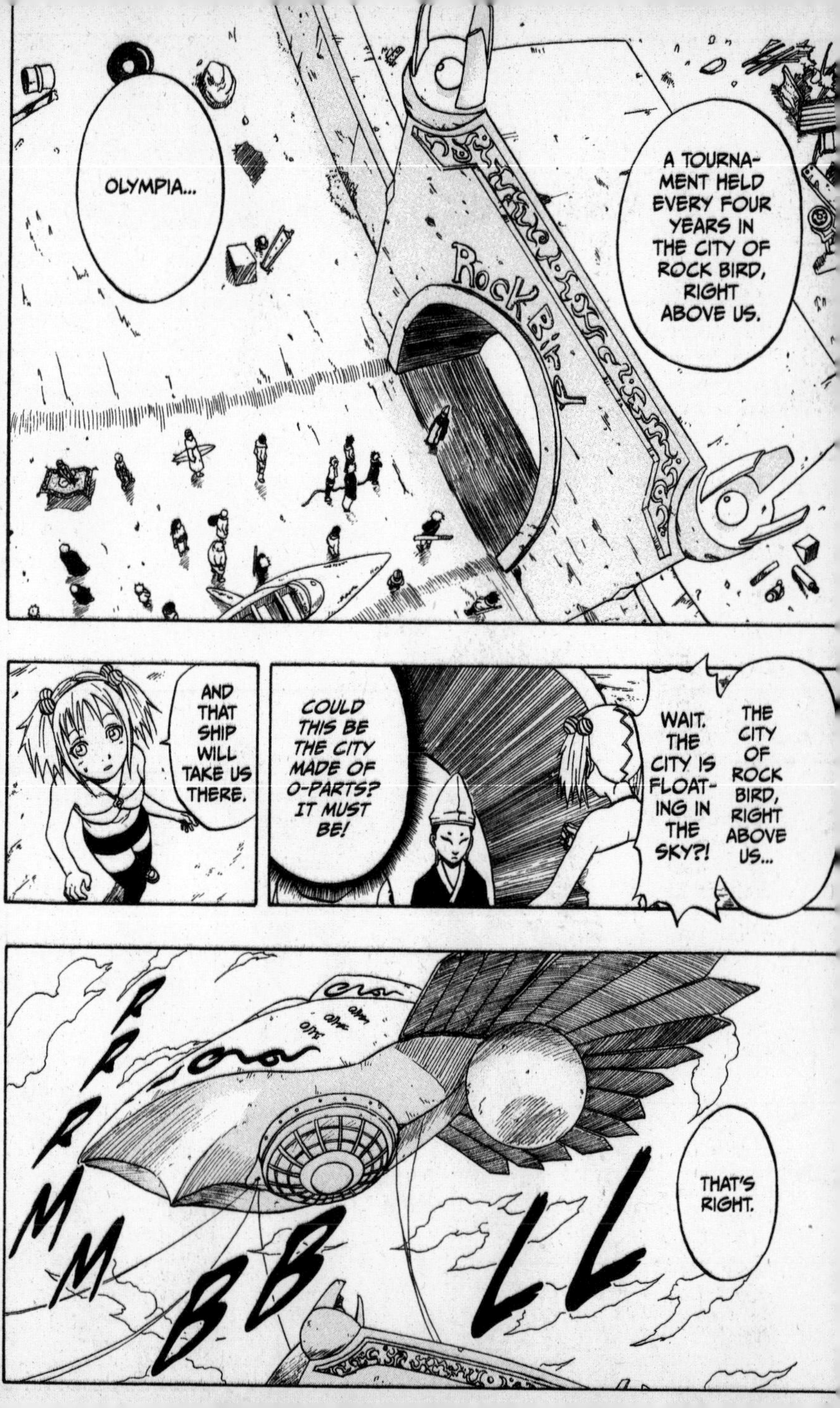
A TOURNAMENT HELD EVERY FOUR YEARS IN THE CITY OF ROCK BIRD, RIGHT ABOVE US.
OLYMPIA...
THE CITY OF ROCK BIRD, RIGHT ABOVE US...
WAIT. THE CITY IS FLOATING IN THE SKY?!
COULD THIS BE THE CITY MADE OF O-PARTS? IT MUST BE!
AND THAT SHIP WILL TAKE US THERE.
THAT'S RIGHT.

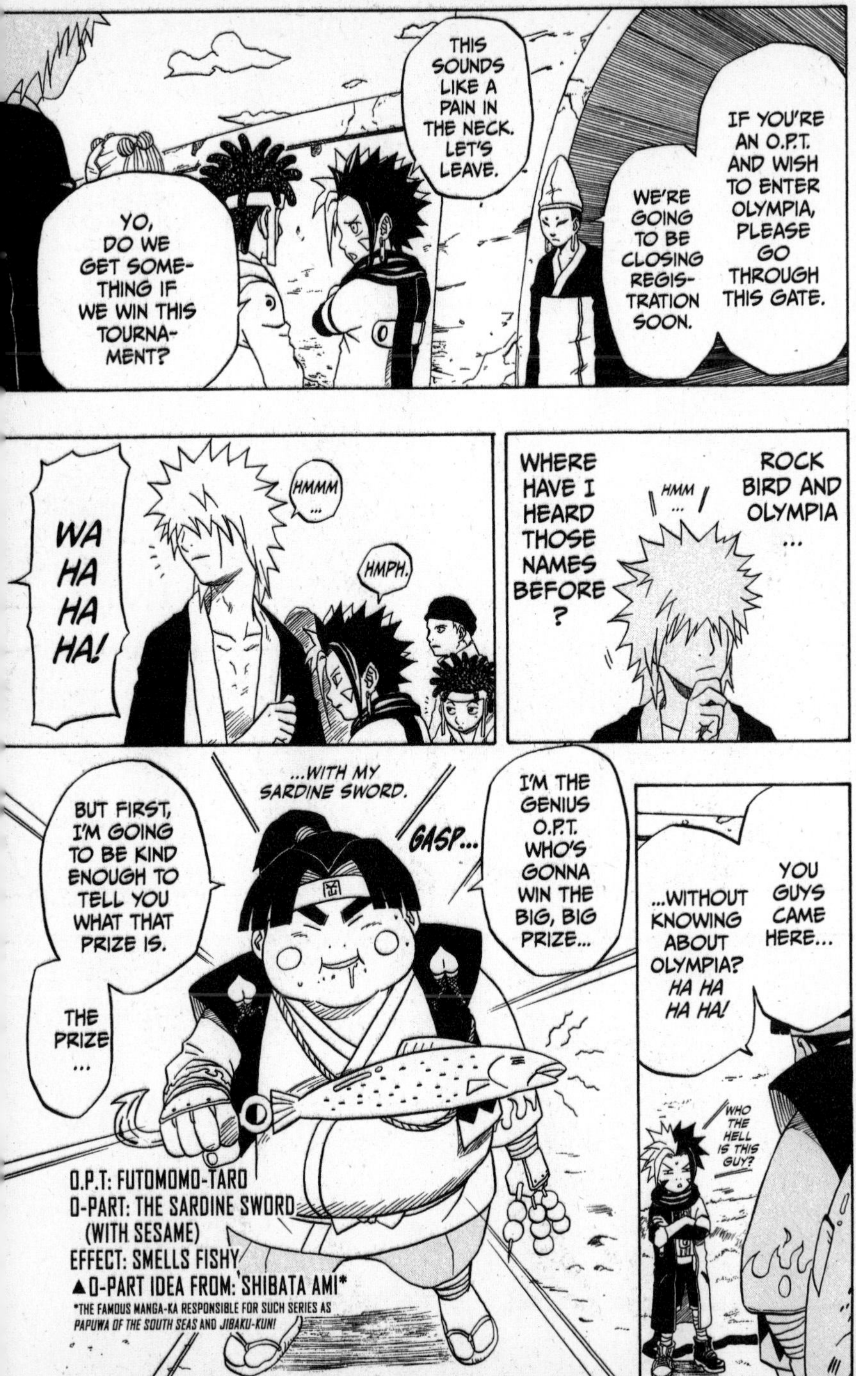
IF YOU'RE AN O.P.T. AND WISH TO ENTER OLYMPIA, PLEASE GO THROUGH THIS GATE.
WE'RE GOING TO BE CLOSING REGIS-TRATION SOON.
THIS SOUNDS LIKE A PAIN IN THE NECK. LET'S LEAVE.
YO, DO WE GET SOME-THING IF WE WIN THIS TOURNA-MENT?
ROCK BIRD AND OLYMPIA ...
HMM ...
WHERE HAVE I HEARD THOSE NAMES BEFORE ?
HMMM ...
HMPH.
WA HA HA HA!
YOU GUYS CAME HERE...
...WITHOUT KNOWING ABOUT OLYMPIA? HA HA HA HA!
WHO THE HELL IS THIS GUY?
I'M THE GENIUS O.P.T. WHO'S GONNA WIN THE BIG, BIG PRIZE...
GASP...
...WITH MY SARDINE SWORD.
BUT FIRST, I'M GOING TO BE KIND ENOUGH TO TELL YOU WHAT THAT PRIZE IS.
THE PRIZE ...
O.P.T: FUTOMOMO-TARO
O-PART: THE SARDINE SWORD (WITH SESAME)
EFFECT: SMELLS FISHY
▲O-PART IDEA FROM: SHIBATA AMI*
*THE FAMOUS MANGA-KA RESPONSIBLE FOR SUCH SERIES AS PAPUWA OF THE SOUTH SEAS AND JIBAKU-KUN!

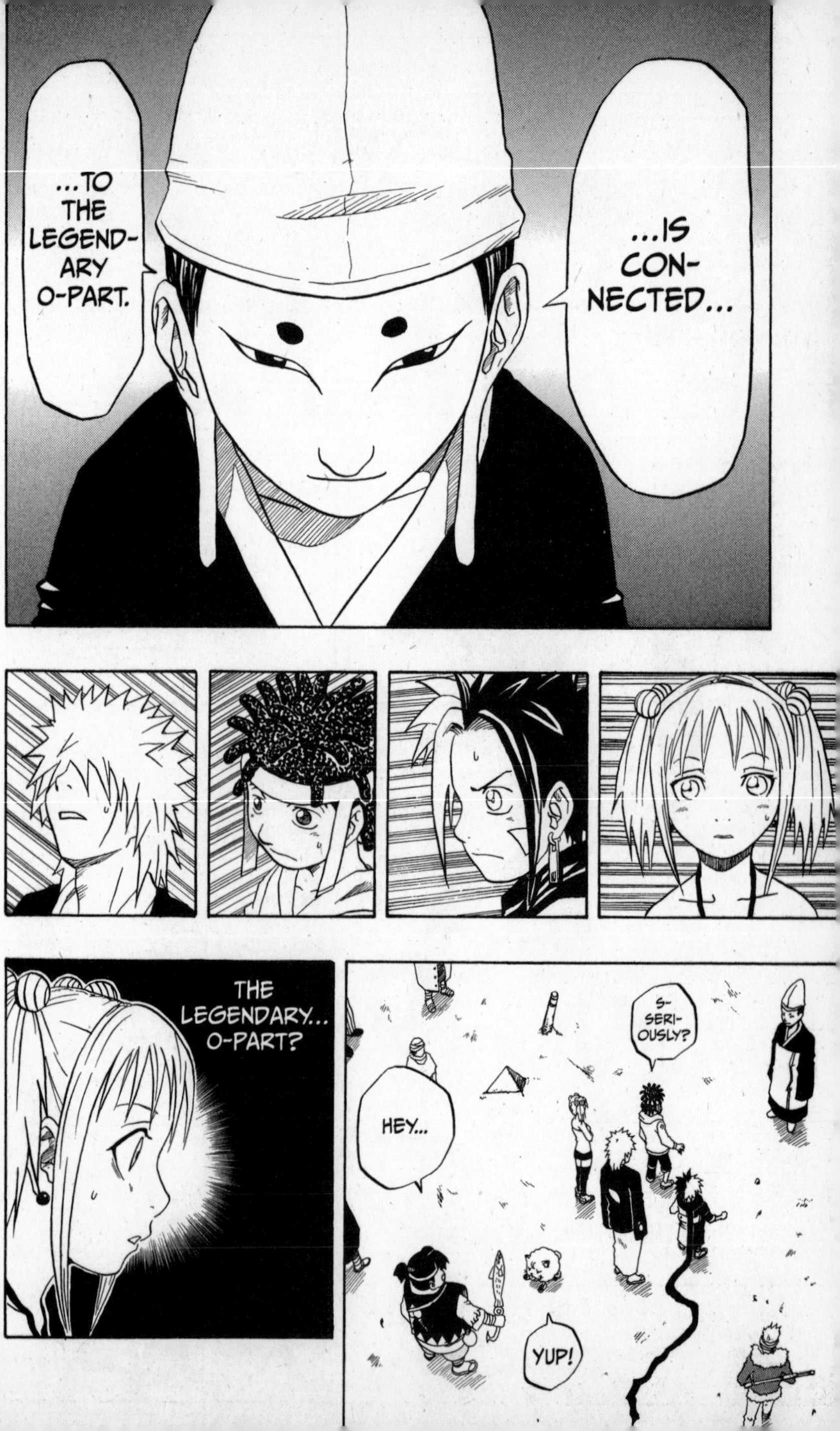
...IS CON-NECTED...
...TO THE LEGEND-ARY O-PART.
S-SERI-OUSLY?
HEY...
YUP!
THE LEGENDARY... O-PART?

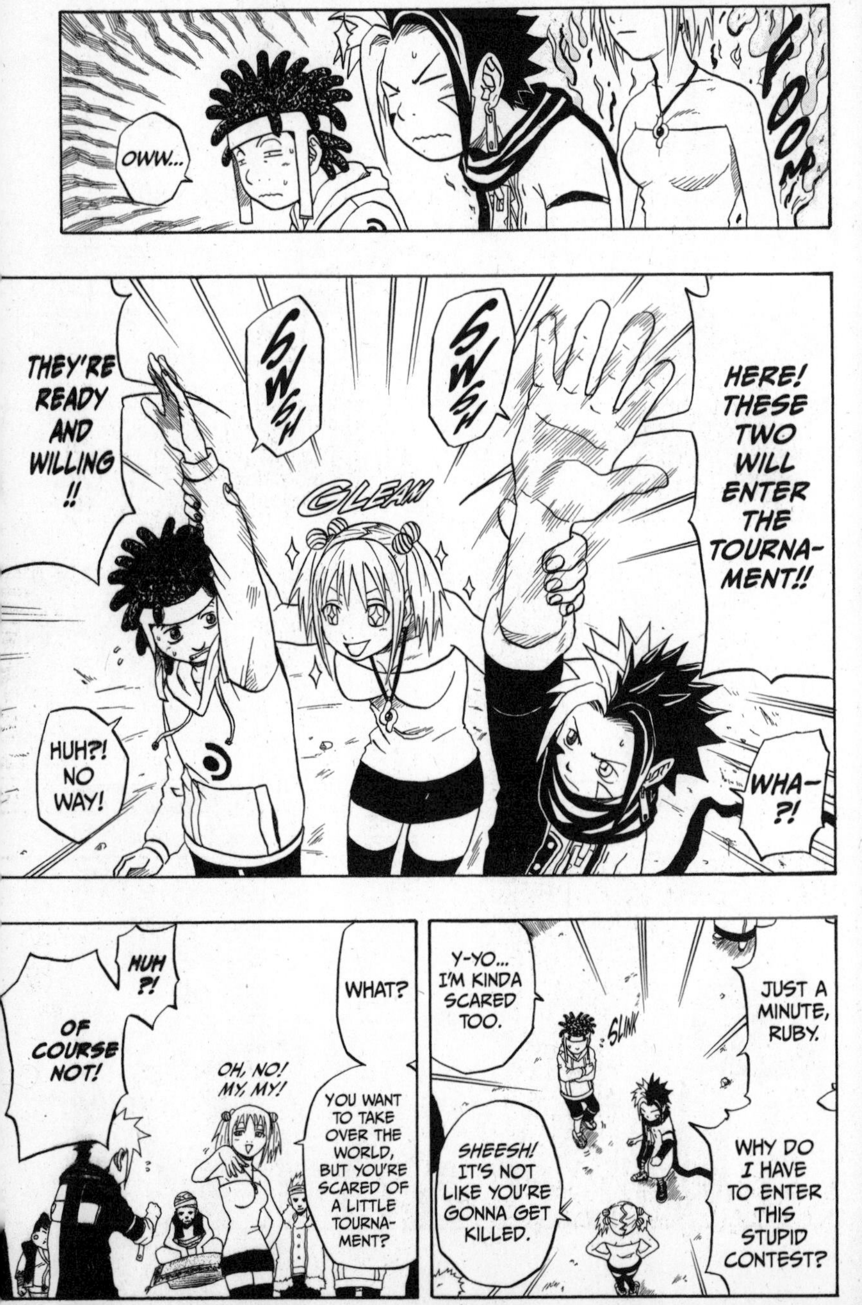
FOOM
OWW...
HERE! THESE TWO WILL ENTER THE TOURNAMENT!!
SWSH
SWSH
GLEAM
THEY'RE READY AND WILLING!!
WHA-?!
HUH?! NO WAY!
JUST A MINUTE, RUBY.
WHY DO I HAVE TO ENTER THIS STUPID CONTEST?
SLINK
Y-YO... I'M KINDA SCARED TOO.
SHEESH! IT'S NOT LIKE YOU'RE GONNA GET KILLED.
WHAT?
YOU WANT TO TAKE OVER THE WORLD, BUT YOU'RE SCARED OF A LITTLE TOURNAMENT?
OH, NO! MY, MY!
HUH?!
OF COURSE NOT!

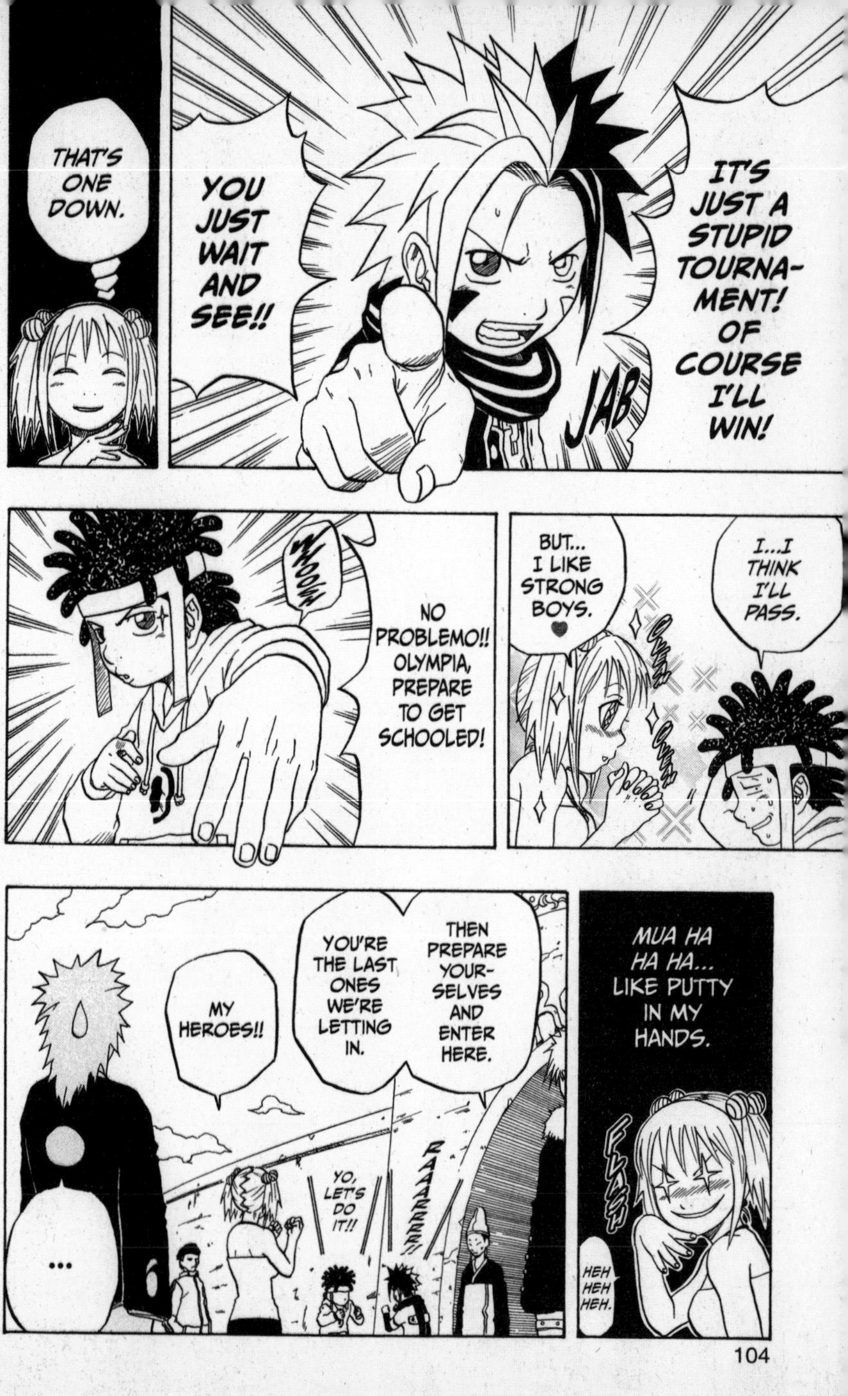
IT'S JUST A STUPID TOURNAMENT! OF COURSE I'LL WIN!
JAB
YOU JUST WAIT AND SEE!!
THAT'S ONE DOWN.
I...I THINK I'LL PASS.
BUT... I LIKE STRONG BOYS. ♥
NO PROBLEMO!! OLYMPIA, PREPARE TO GET SCHOOLED!
MUA HA HA HA... LIKE PUTTY IN MY HANDS.
HEH HEH HEH.
THEN PREPARE YOUR-SELVES AND ENTER HERE.
YOU'RE THE LAST ONES WE'RE LETTING IN.
YO, LET'S DO IT!!
MY HEROES!!
...

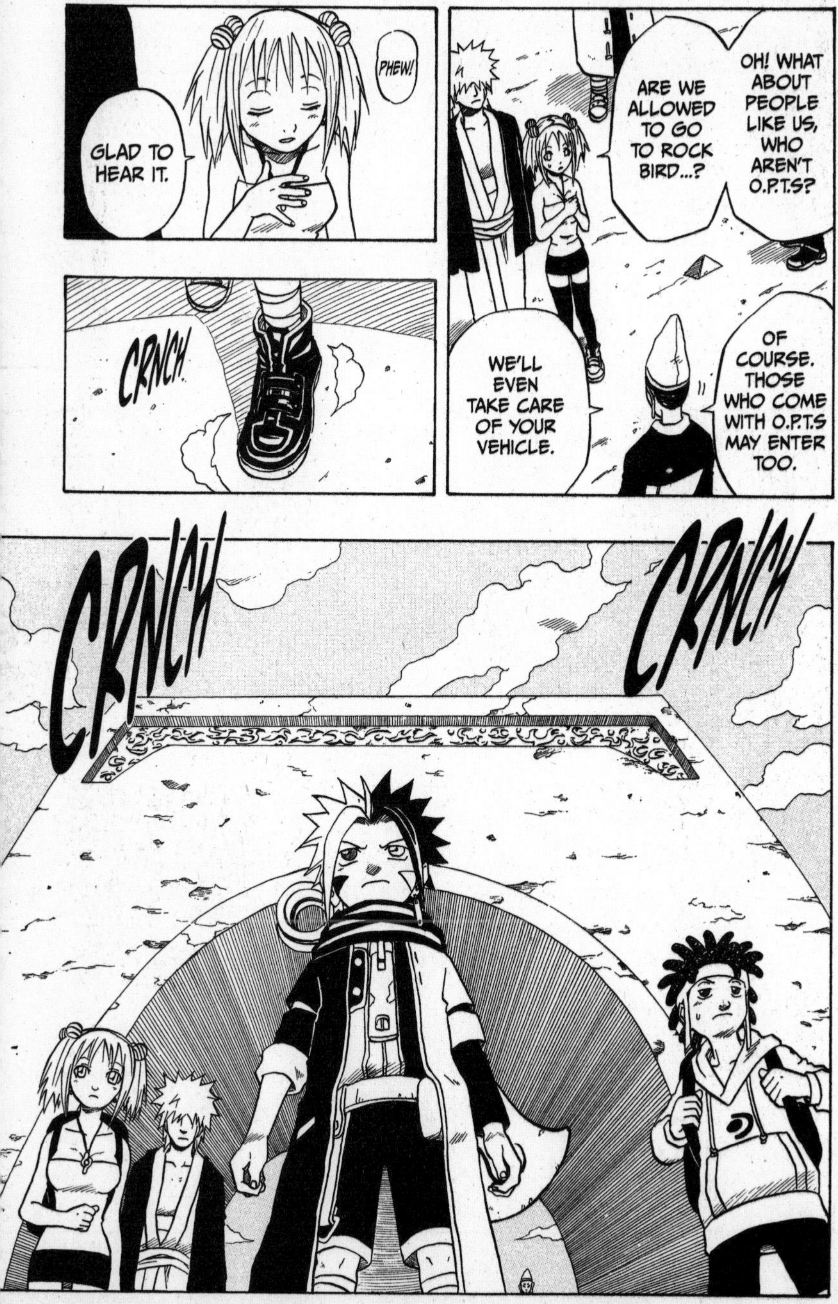
OH! WHAT ABOUT PEOPLE LIKE US, WHO AREN'T O.P.T.S?
ARE WE ALLOWED TO GO TO ROCK BIRD...?
OF COURSE. THOSE WHO COME WITH O.P.T.S MAY ENTER TOO.
WE'LL EVEN TAKE CARE OF YOUR VEHICLE.
PHEW!
GLAD TO HEAR IT.
CRNCH.
CRNCH
CRNCH

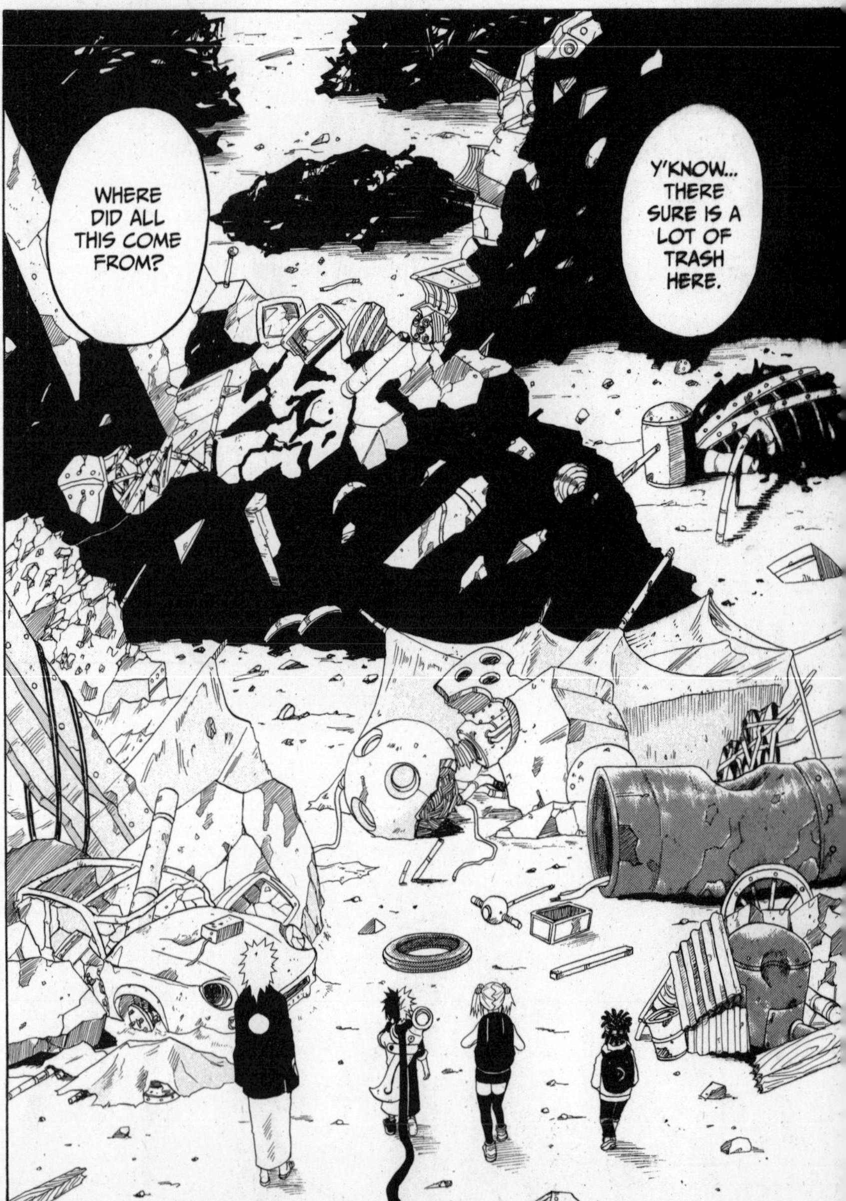
Y'KNOW... THERE SURE IS A LOT OF TRASH HERE.
WHERE DID ALL THIS COME FROM?

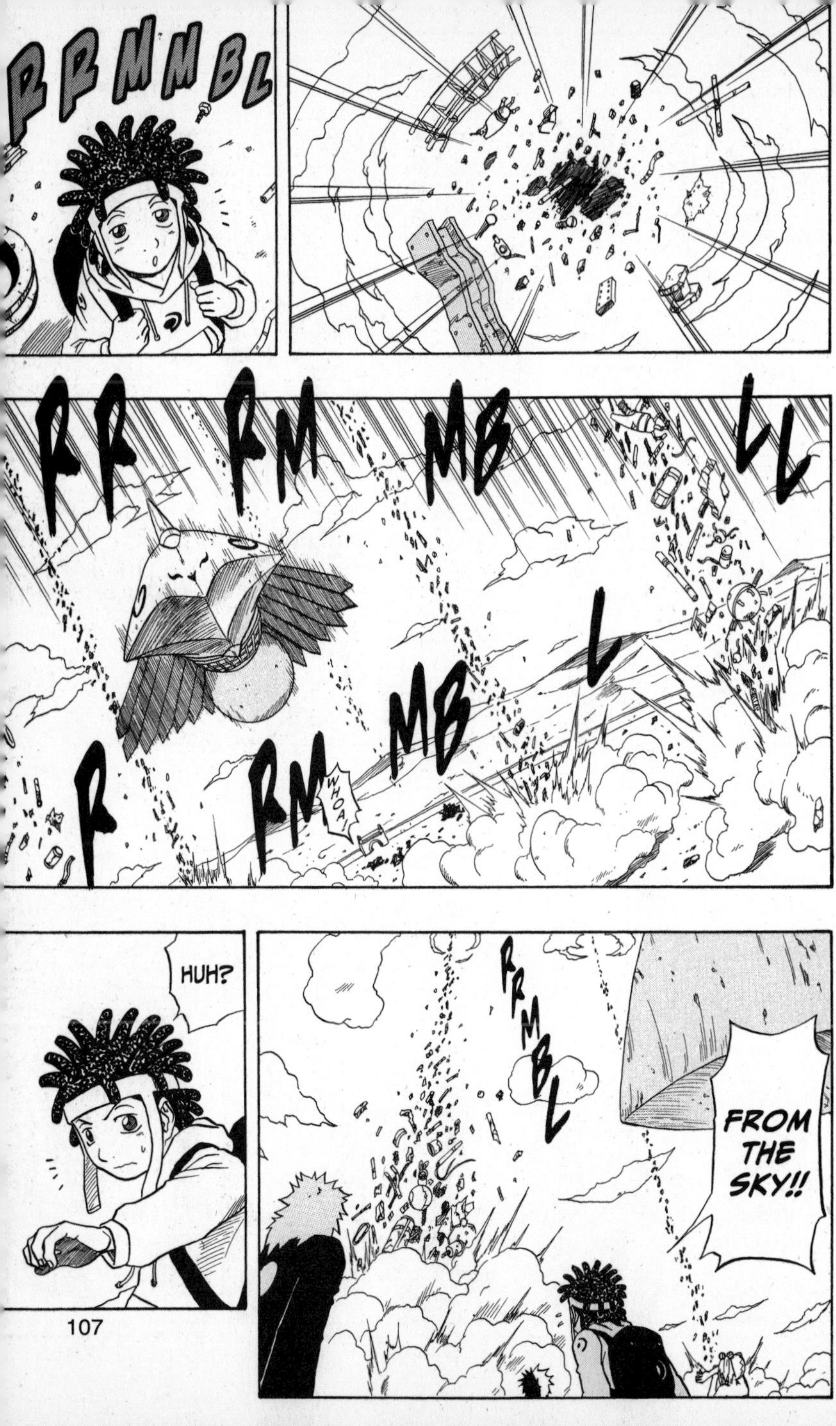
RRMMBL
RR RM MB LL
R RM MB L
WHOA!
FROM THE SKY!!
RRMBL
HUH?

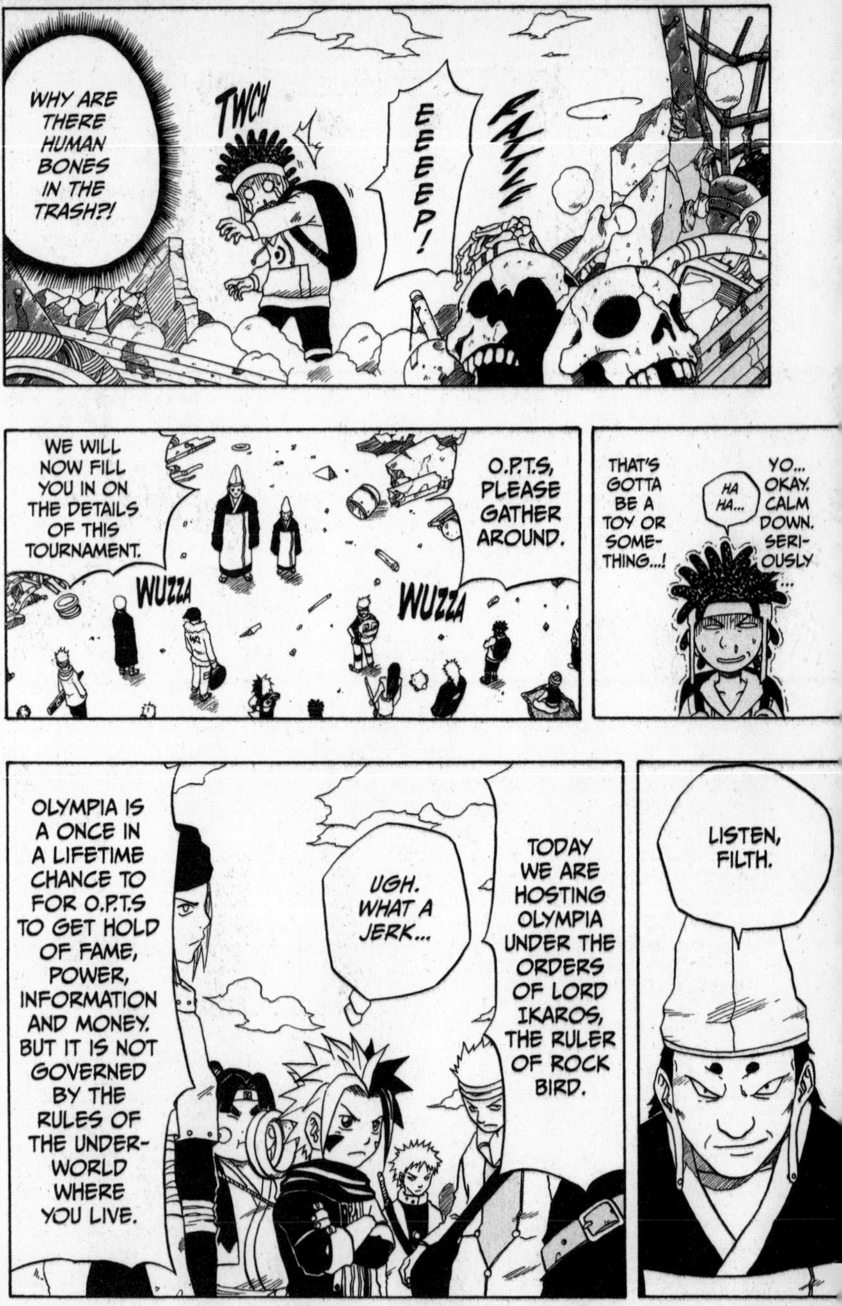
EEEEP!
TWCH
WHY ARE THERE HUMAN BONES IN THE TRASH?!
YO... OKAY. CALM DOWN. SERIOUSLY...
HA HA...
THAT'S GOTTA BE A TOY OR SOME-THING...!
O.P.T.S, PLEASE GATHER AROUND.
WE WILL NOW FILL YOU IN ON THE DETAILS OF THIS TOURNAMENT.
WUZZA
WUZZA
LISTEN, FILTH.
TODAY WE ARE HOSTING OLYMPIA UNDER THE ORDERS OF LORD IKAROS, THE RULER OF ROCK BIRD.
UGH. WHAT A JERK...
OLYMPIA IS A ONCE IN A LIFETIME CHANCE TO FOR O.P.T.S TO GET HOLD OF FAME, POWER, INFORMATION AND MONEY. BUT IT IS NOT GOVERNED BY THE RULES OF THE UNDER-WORLD WHERE YOU LIVE.

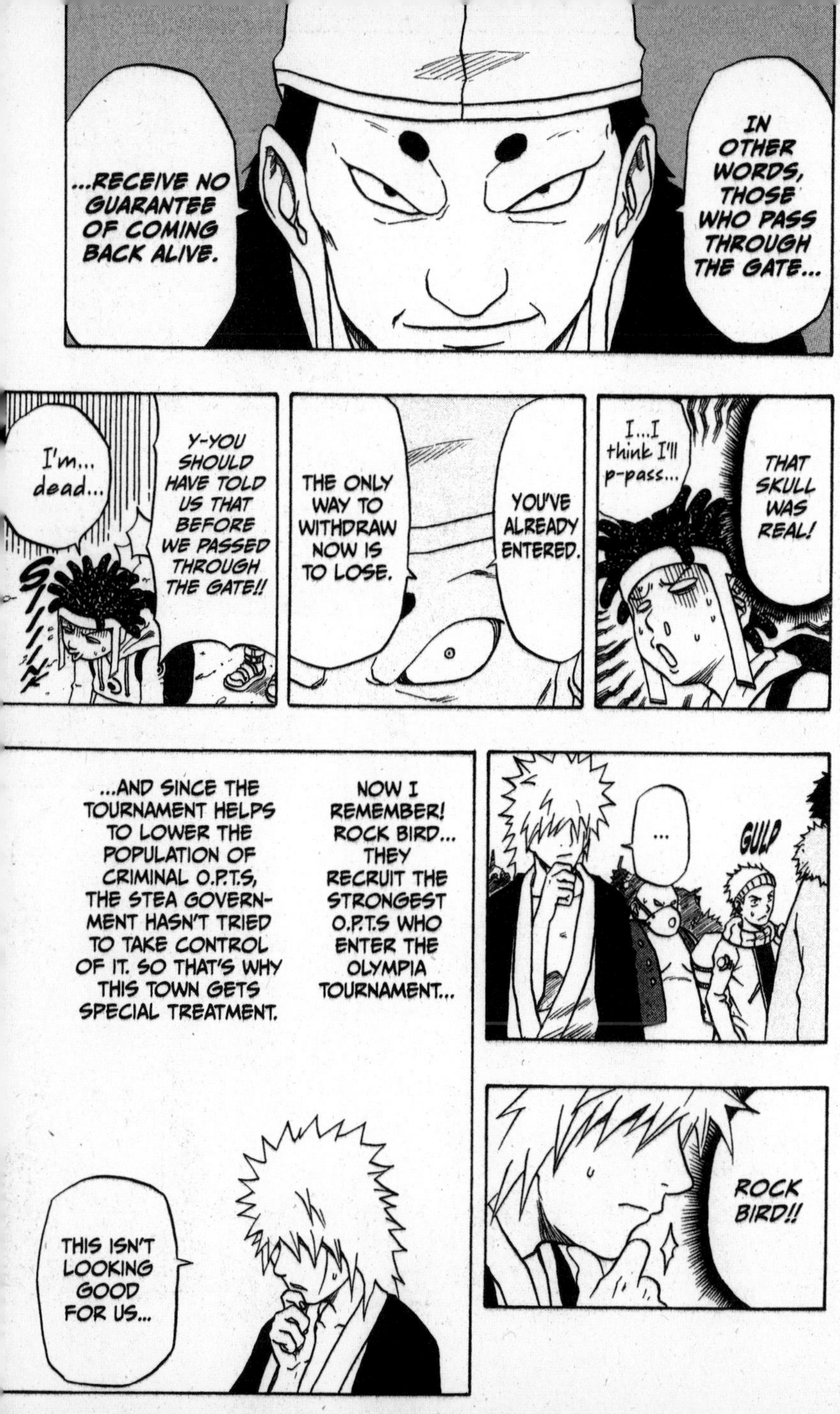
IN OTHER WORDS, THOSE WHO PASS THROUGH THE GATE...
...RECEIVE NO GUARANTEE OF COMING BACK ALIVE.
THAT SKULL WAS REAL!
I...I think I'll p-pass...
YOU'VE ALREADY ENTERED.
THE ONLY WAY TO WITHDRAW NOW IS TO LOSE.
Y-YOU SHOULD HAVE TOLD US THAT BEFORE WE PASSED THROUGH THE GATE!!
I'm... dead...
...
GULP
ROCK BIRD!!
NOW I REMEMBER! ROCK BIRD... THEY RECRUIT THE STRONGEST O.P.T.S WHO ENTER THE OLYMPIA TOURNAMENT...
...AND SINCE THE TOURNAMENT HELPS TO LOWER THE POPULATION OF CRIMINAL O.P.T.S, THE STEA GOVERNMENT HASN'T TRIED TO TAKE CONTROL OF IT. SO THAT'S WHY THIS TOWN GETS SPECIAL TREATMENT.
THIS ISN'T LOOKING GOOD FOR US...

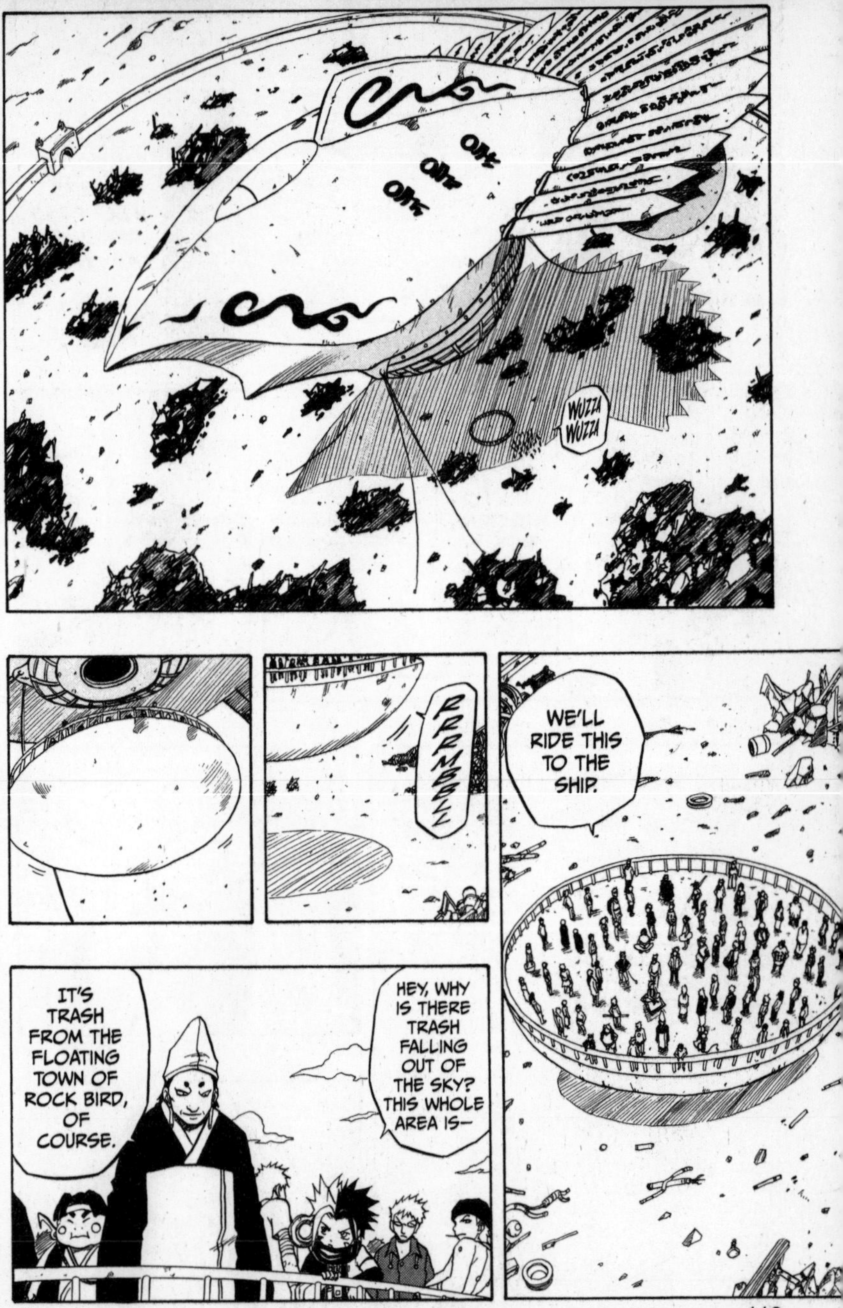
WUZZA WUZZA
WE'LL RIDE THIS TO THE SHIP.
RRRMBBLL
HEY, WHY IS THERE TRASH FALLING OUT OF THE SKY? THIS WHOLE AREA IS—
IT'S TRASH FROM THE FLOATING TOWN OF ROCK BIRD, OF COURSE.

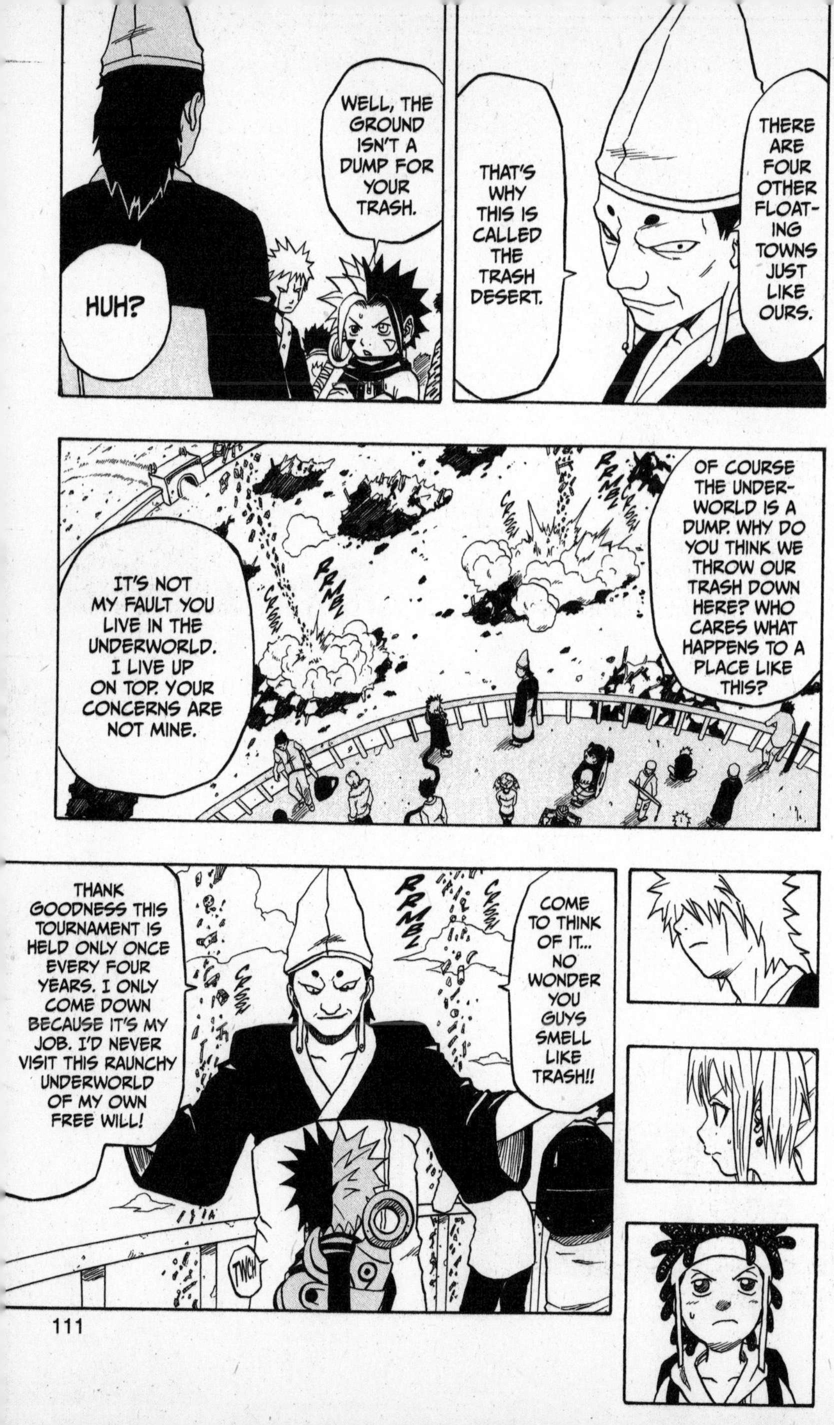
THERE ARE FOUR OTHER FLOATING TOWNS JUST LIKE OURS.
THAT'S WHY THIS IS CALLED THE TRASH DESERT.
WELL, THE GROUND ISN'T A DUMP FOR YOUR TRASH.
HUH?
RRMBL
CRSSH
OF COURSE THE UNDERWORLD IS A DUMP. WHY DO YOU THINK WE THROW OUR TRASH DOWN HERE? WHO CARES WHAT HAPPENS TO A PLACE LIKE THIS?
IT'S NOT MY FAULT YOU LIVE IN THE UNDERWORLD. I LIVE UP ON TOP. YOUR CONCERNS ARE NOT MINE.
COME TO THINK OF IT... NO WONDER YOU GUYS SMELL LIKE TRASH!!
RRMBL
CRSSH
THANK GOODNESS THIS TOURNAMENT IS HELD ONLY ONCE EVERY FOUR YEARS. I ONLY COME DOWN BECAUSE IT'S MY JOB. I'D NEVER VISIT THIS RAUNCHY UNDERWORLD OF MY OWN FREE WILL!
TWCH

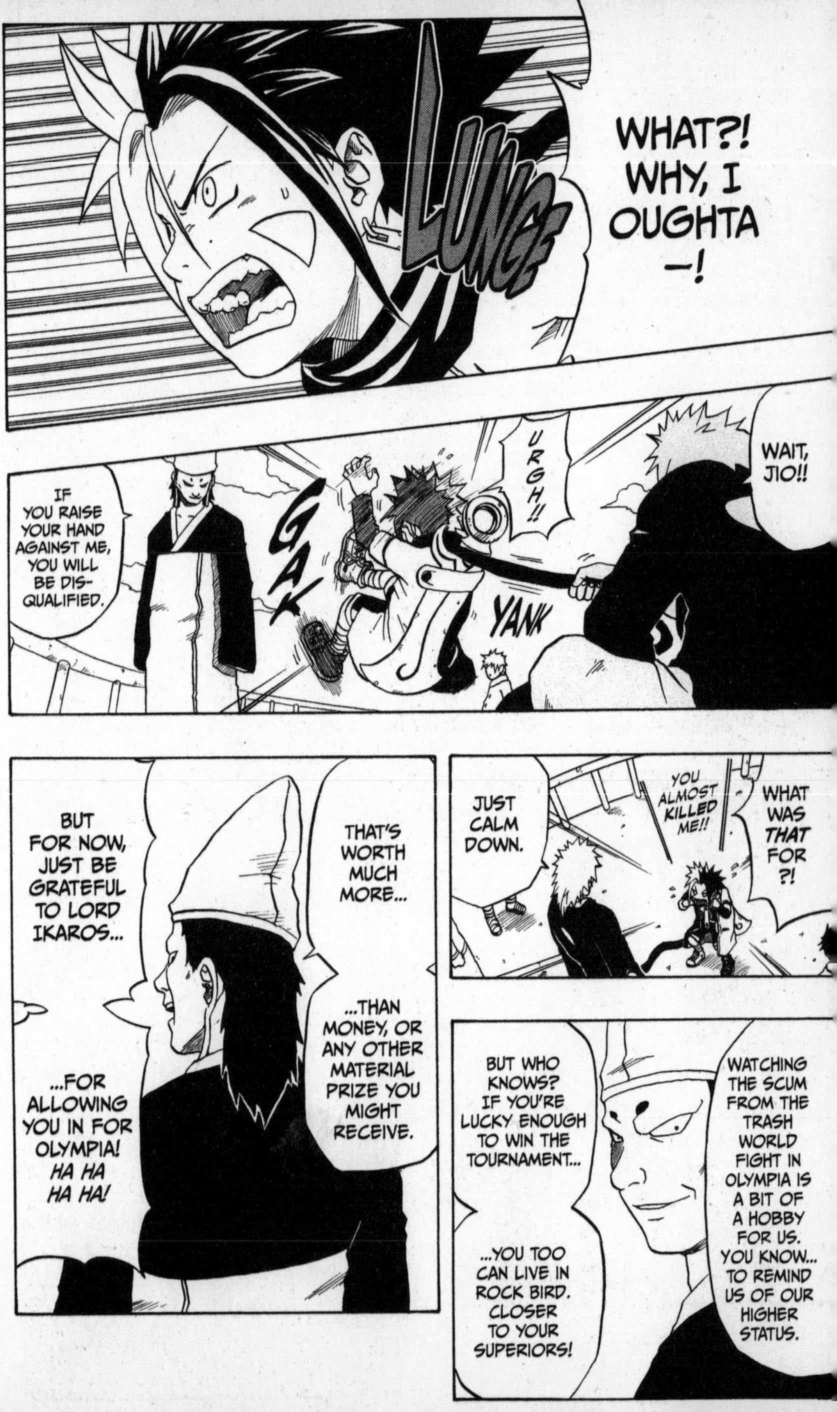
LUNGE
WHAT?! WHY, I OUGHTA —!
WAIT, JIO!!
URGH!!
YANK
GAK
IF YOU RAISE YOUR HAND AGAINST ME, YOU WILL BE DIS-QUALIFIED.
WHAT WAS THAT FOR?!
YOU ALMOST KILLED ME!!
JUST CALM DOWN.
WATCHING THE SCUM FROM THE TRASH WORLD FIGHT IN OLYMPIA IS A BIT OF A HOBBY FOR US. YOU KNOW... TO REMIND US OF OUR HIGHER STATUS.
BUT WHO KNOWS? IF YOU'RE LUCKY ENOUGH TO WIN THE TOURNAMENT...
...YOU TOO CAN LIVE IN ROCK BIRD. CLOSER TO YOUR SUPERIORS!
THAT'S WORTH MUCH MORE...
...THAN MONEY, OR ANY OTHER MATERIAL PRIZE YOU MIGHT RECEIVE.
BUT FOR NOW, JUST BE GRATEFUL TO LORD IKAROS...
...FOR ALLOWING YOU IN FOR OLYMPIA! HA HA HA HA!

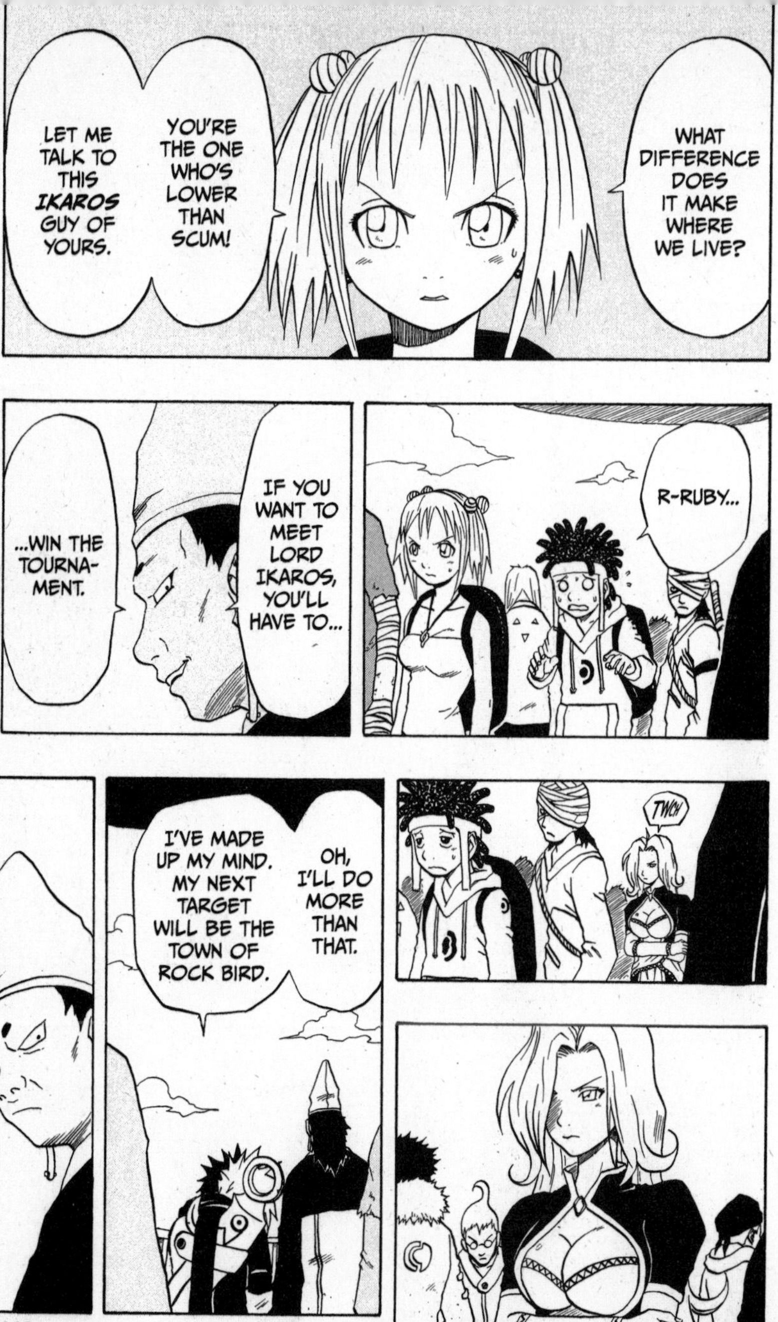
WHAT DIFFERENCE DOES IT MAKE WHERE WE LIVE?
YOU'RE THE ONE WHO'S LOWER THAN SCUM!
LET ME TALK TO THIS *IKAROS* GUY OF YOURS.
R-RUBY...
IF YOU WANT TO MEET LORD IKAROS, YOU'LL HAVE TO...
...WIN THE TOURNA-MENT.
TWCH
OH, I'LL DO MORE THAN THAT.
I'VE MADE UP MY MIND. MY NEXT TARGET WILL BE THE TOWN OF ROCK BIRD.
...

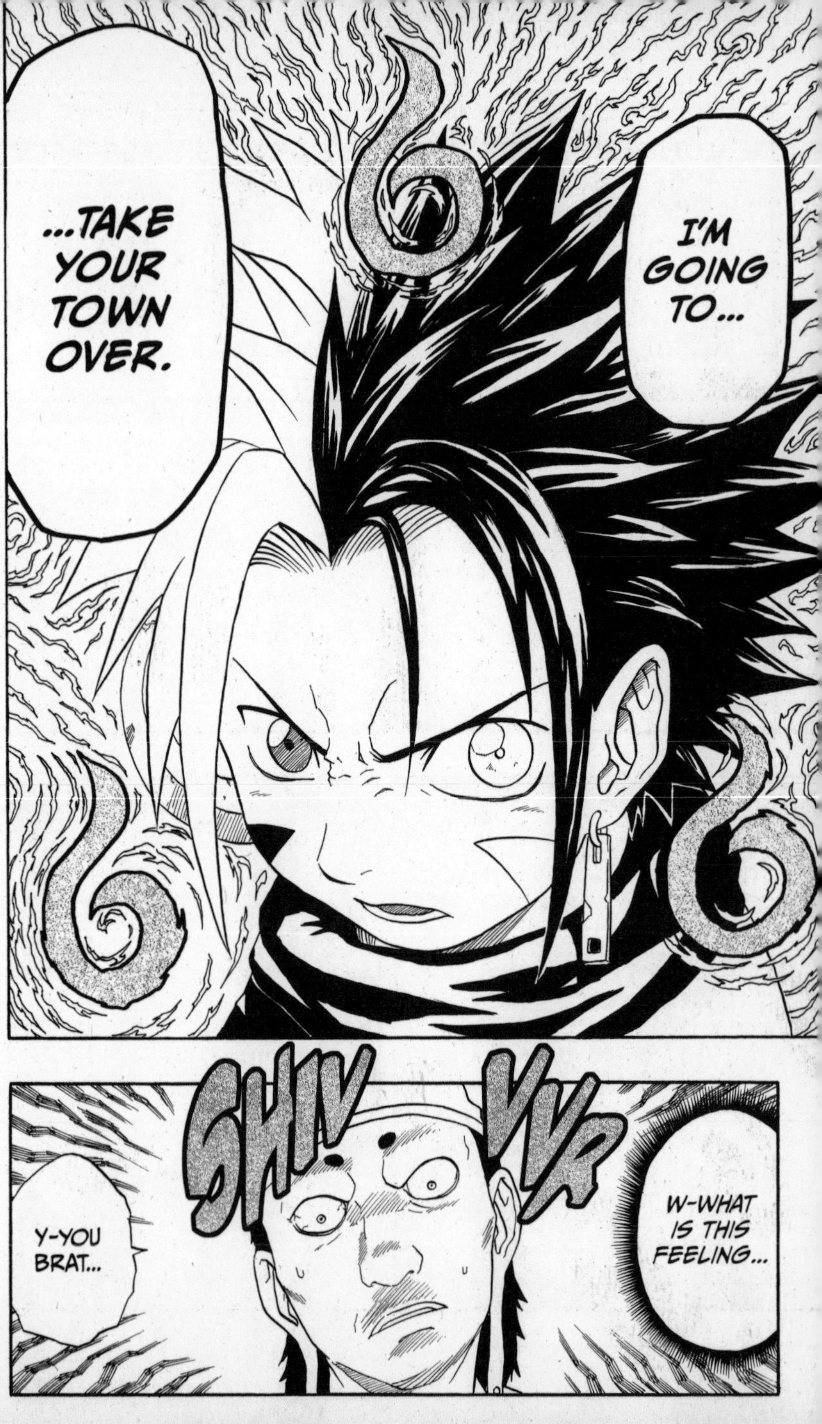
I'M GOING TO...
...TAKE YOUR TOWN OVER.
SHIVVVR
W-WHAT IS THIS FEELING...
Y-YOU BRAT...

WEEEN

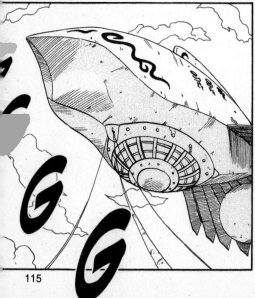

G
G
G

KA-KLANK

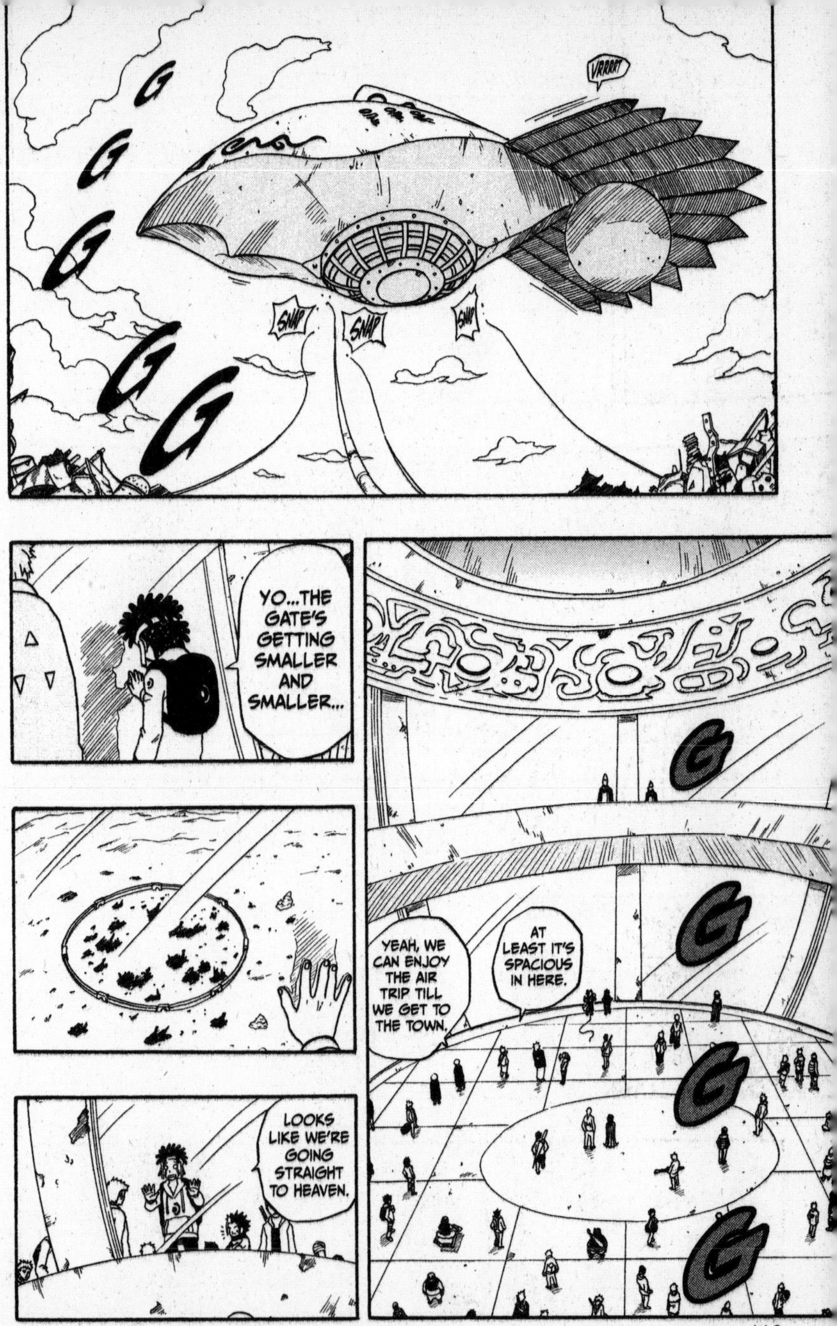
VRRRRT
SNAP
SNAP
SNAP
GGGGGG
G
G
G
G
AT LEAST IT'S SPACIOUS IN HERE.
YEAH, WE CAN ENJOY THE AIR TRIP TILL WE GET TO THE TOWN.
YO...THE GATE'S GETTING SMALLER AND SMALLER...
LOOKS LIKE WE'RE GOING STRAIGHT TO HEAVEN.

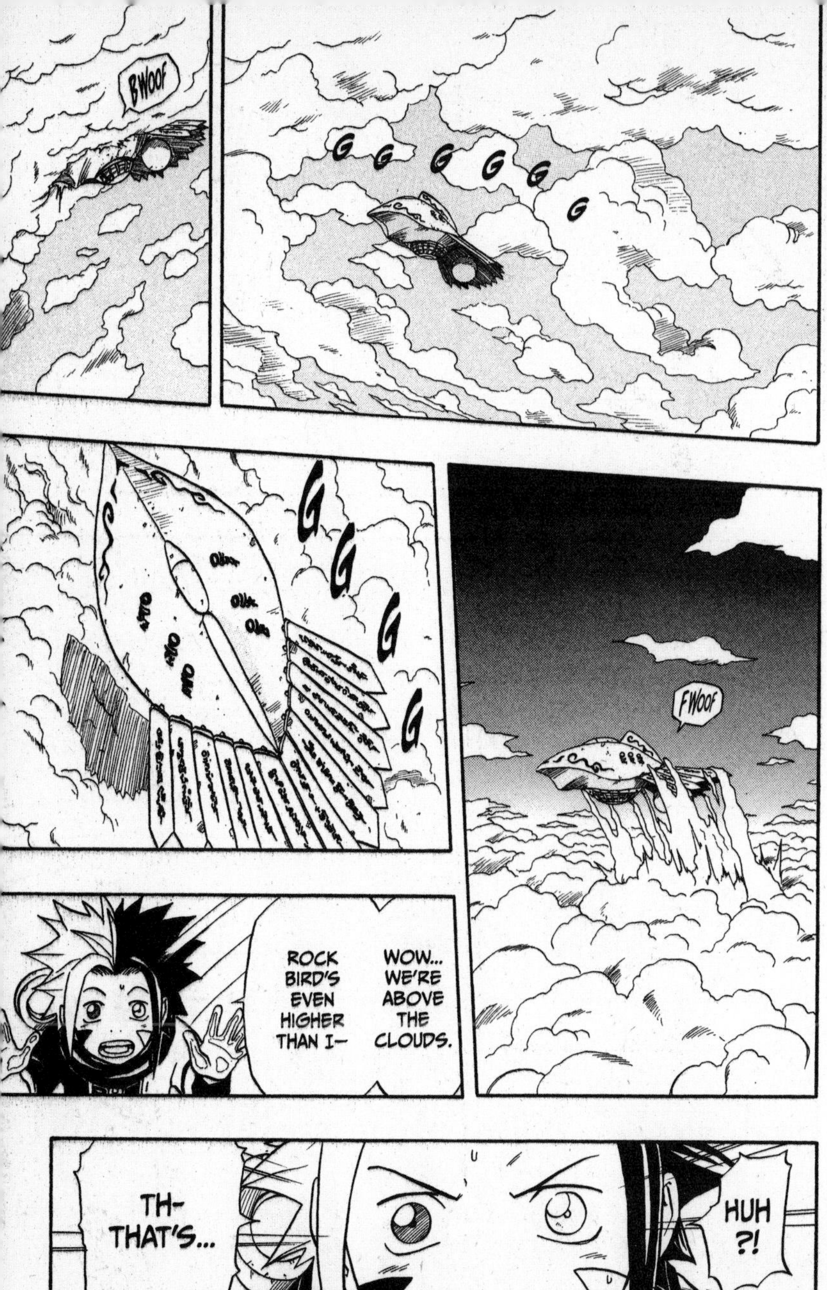
GGGGGG
BWOOF
FWOOF
GGGGG
WOW... WE'RE ABOVE THE CLOUDS.
ROCK BIRD'S EVEN HIGHER THAN I—
HUH ?!
TH- THAT'S...

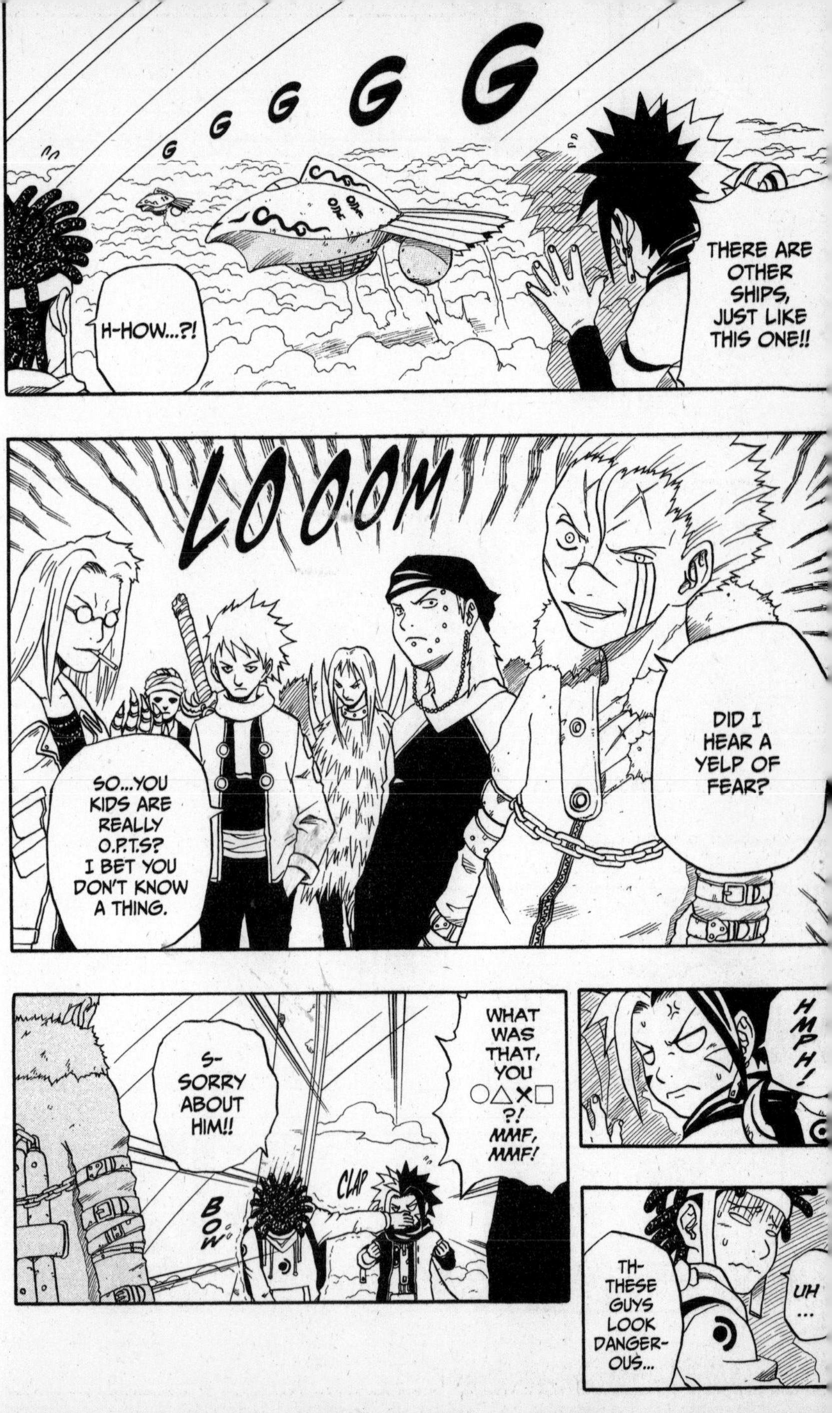
GGGGGG
THERE ARE OTHER SHIPS, JUST LIKE THIS ONE!!
H-HOW...?!
LOOOM
DID I HEAR A YELP OF FEAR?
SO...YOU KIDS ARE REALLY O.P.T.S? I BET YOU DON'T KNOW A THING.
HMPH!
UH...
TH-THESE GUYS LOOK DANGER-OUS...
WHAT WAS THAT, YOU ○△×□?! MMF, MMF!
CLAP
S-SORRY ABOUT HIM!!
BOW

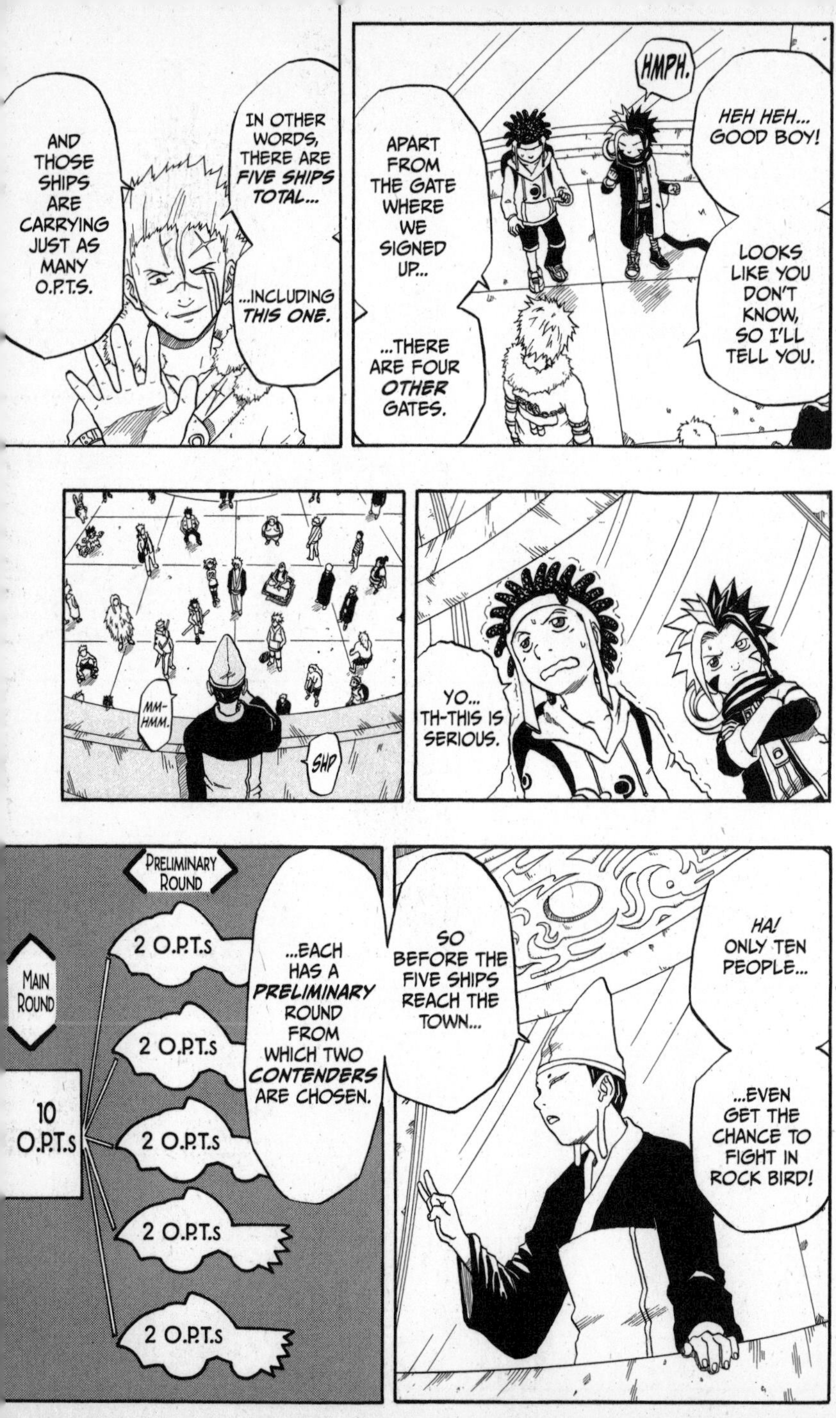
HMPH.
HEH HEH... GOOD BOY!
LOOKS LIKE YOU DON'T KNOW, SO I'LL TELL YOU.
APART FROM THE GATE WHERE WE SIGNED UP...
...THERE ARE FOUR OTHER GATES.
IN OTHER WORDS, THERE ARE FIVE SHIPS TOTAL...
...INCLUDING THIS ONE.
AND THOSE SHIPS ARE CARRYING JUST AS MANY O.P.T.S.
YO... TH-THIS IS SERIOUS.
MM-HMM.
SHP
HA! ONLY TEN PEOPLE...
...EVEN GET THE CHANCE TO FIGHT IN ROCK BIRD!
SO BEFORE THE FIVE SHIPS REACH THE TOWN...
...EACH HAS A PRELIMINARY ROUND FROM WHICH TWO CONTENDERS ARE CHOSEN.
PRELIMINARY ROUND
MAIN ROUND
10 O.P.T.s
2 O.P.T.s
2 O.P.T.s
2 O.P.T.s
2 O.P.T.s
2 O.P.T.s

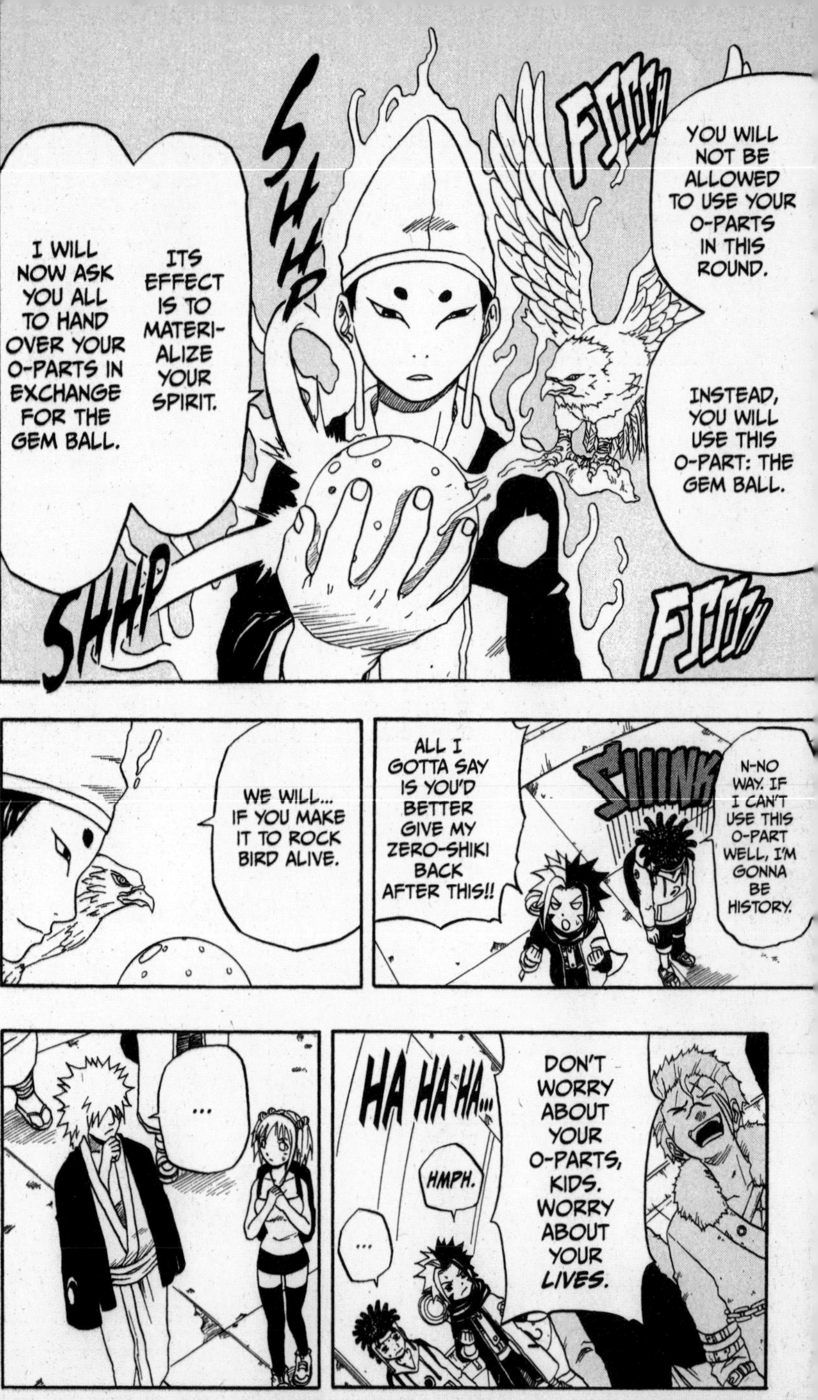
YOU WILL NOT BE ALLOWED TO USE YOUR O-PARTS IN THIS ROUND.
INSTEAD, YOU WILL USE THIS O-PART: THE GEM BALL.
SHHP
ITS EFFECT IS TO MATERIALIZE YOUR SPIRIT.
I WILL NOW ASK YOU ALL TO HAND OVER YOUR O-PARTS IN EXCHANGE FOR THE GEM BALL.
SHHP
N-NO WAY. IF I CAN'T USE THIS O-PART WELL, I'M GONNA BE HISTORY.
ALL I GOTTA SAY IS YOU'D BETTER GIVE MY ZERO-SHIKI BACK AFTER THIS!!
WE WILL... IF YOU MAKE IT TO ROCK BIRD ALIVE.
DON'T WORRY ABOUT YOUR O-PARTS, KIDS. WORRY ABOUT YOUR LIVES.
HA HA HA...
HMPH.
...
...

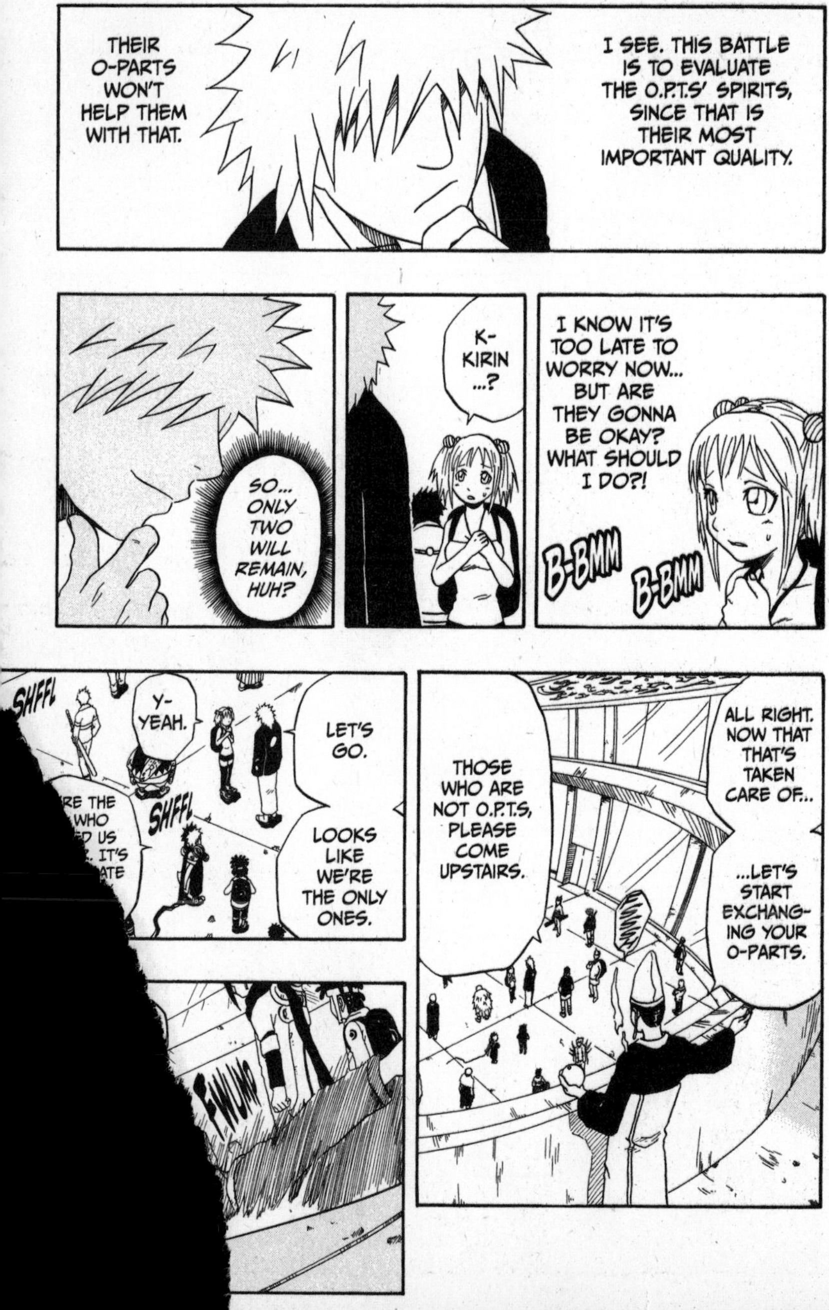
I SEE. THIS BATTLE IS TO EVALUATE THE O.P.T.S' SPIRITS, SINCE THAT IS THEIR MOST IMPORTANT QUALITY.
THEIR O-PARTS WON'T HELP THEM WITH THAT.
I KNOW IT'S TOO LATE TO WORRY NOW... BUT ARE THEY GONNA BE OKAY? WHAT SHOULD I DO?!
B-BMM
B-BMM
K-KIRIN ...?
SO... ONLY TWO WILL REMAIN, HUH?
ALL RIGHT. NOW THAT THAT'S TAKEN CARE OF...
...LET'S START EXCHANGING YOUR O-PARTS.
THOSE WHO ARE NOT O.P.T.S, PLEASE COME UPSTAIRS.
LET'S GO.
LOOKS LIKE WE'RE THE ONLY ONES.
Y-YEAH.
SHFFL
SHFFL
FWUMP

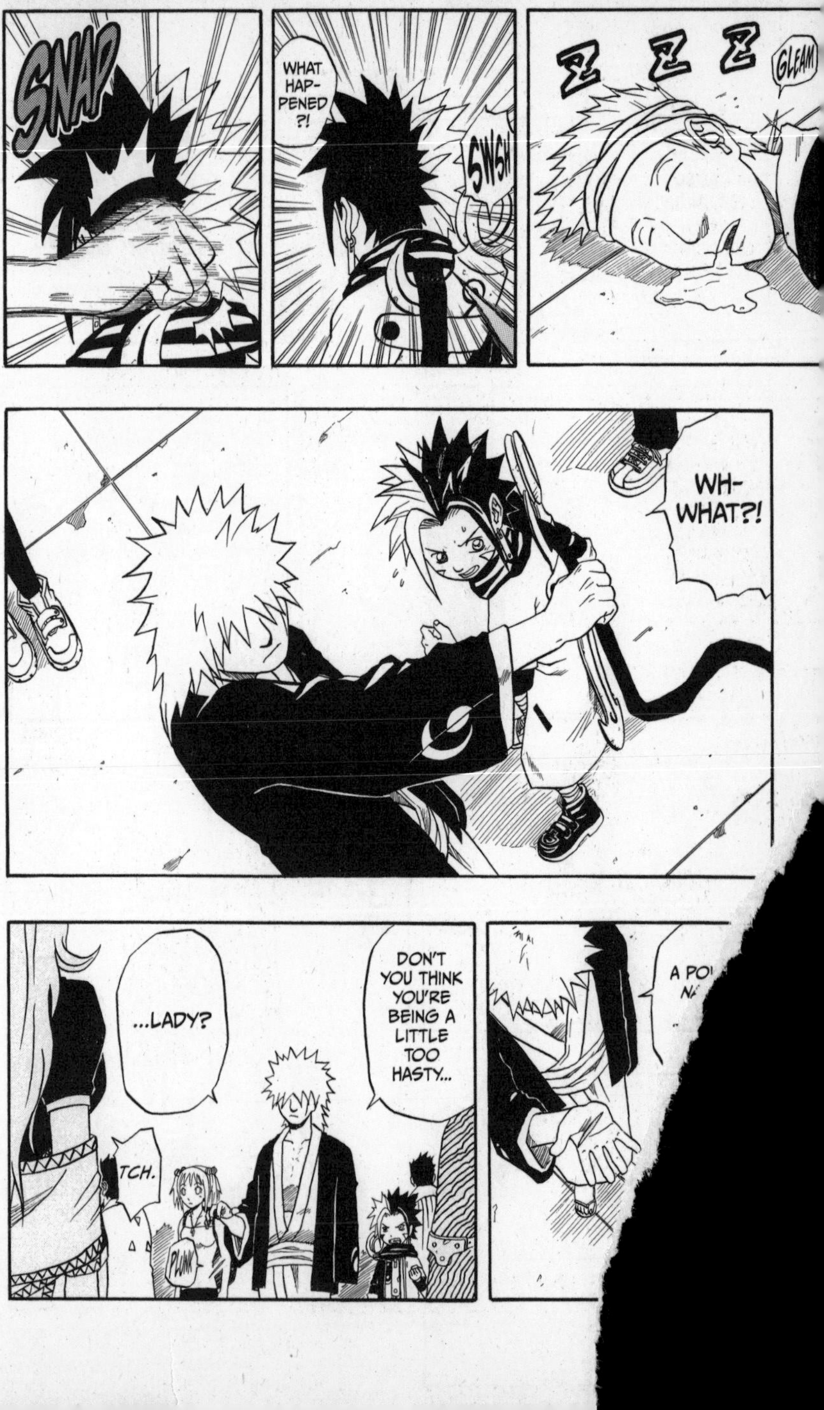
Z Z Z
GLEAM
WHAT HAP-PENED?!
SWSH
SNAP
WH-WHAT?!
A PO
DON'T YOU THINK YOU'RE BEING A LITTLE TOO HASTY...
...LADY?
TCH.
PLUNK

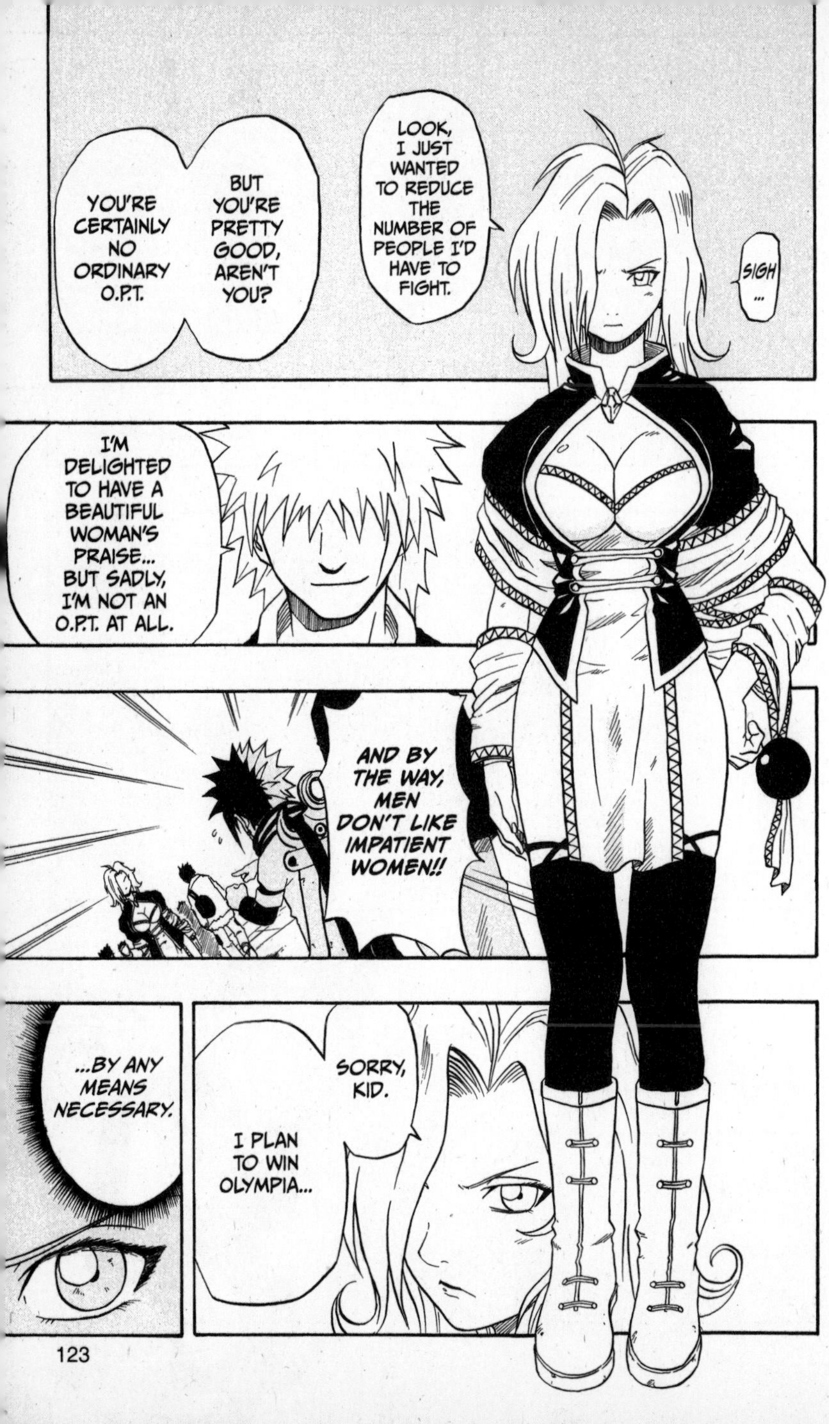
SIGH...
LOOK, I JUST WANTED TO REDUCE THE NUMBER OF PEOPLE I'D HAVE TO FIGHT.
BUT YOU'RE PRETTY GOOD, AREN'T YOU?
YOU'RE CERTAINLY NO ORDINARY O.P.T.
I'M DELIGHTED TO HAVE A BEAUTIFUL WOMAN'S PRAISE... BUT SADLY, I'M NOT AN O.P.T. AT ALL.
AND BY THE WAY, MEN DON'T LIKE IMPATIENT WOMEN!!
SORRY, KID.
I PLAN TO WIN OLYMPIA...
...BY ANY MEANS NECESSARY.

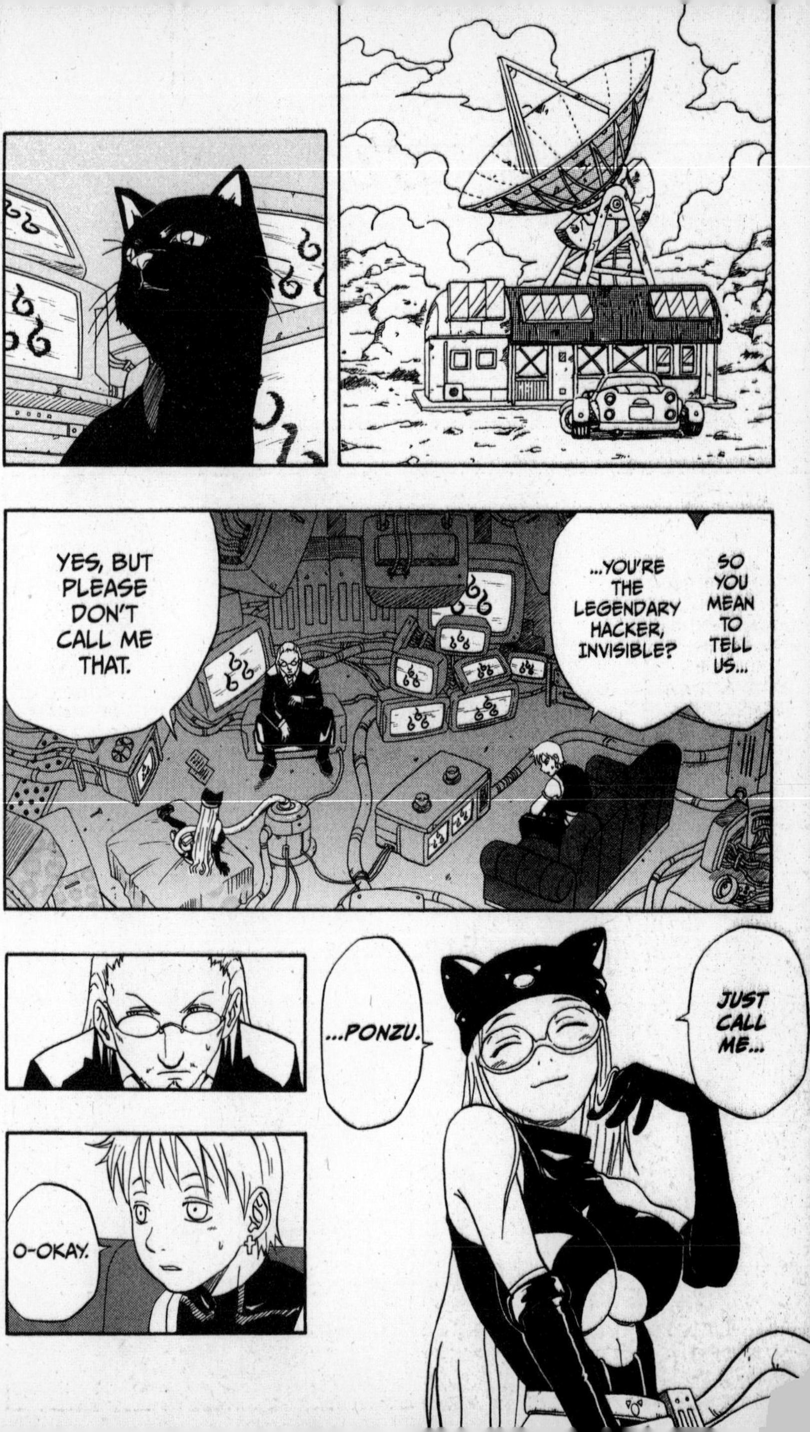
SO YOU MEAN TO TELL US...
...YOU'RE THE LEGENDARY HACKER, INVISIBLE?
YES, BUT PLEASE DON'T CALL ME THAT.
JUST CALL ME...
...PONZU.
O-OKAY.

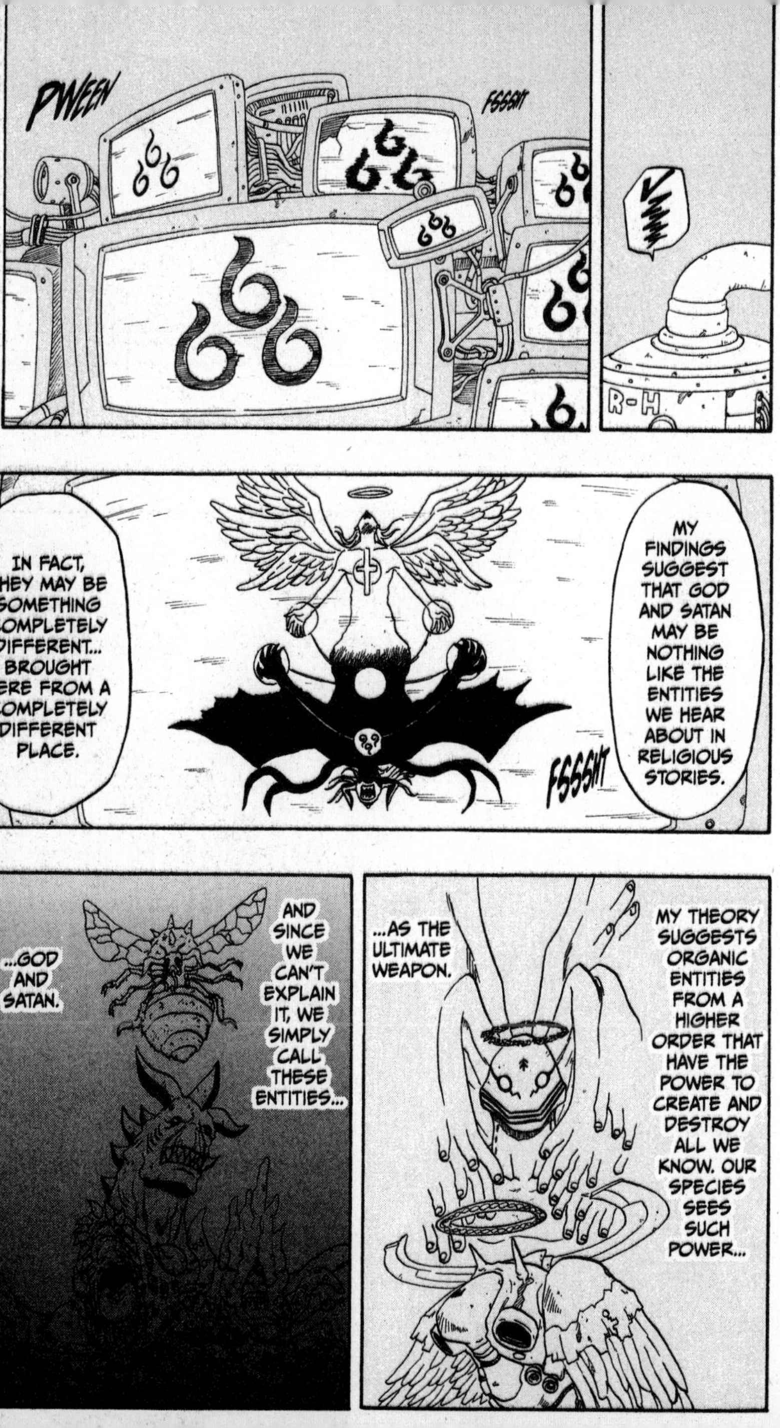
R-H
FSSSHT
PWEEN
MY FINDINGS SUGGEST THAT GOD AND SATAN MAY BE NOTHING LIKE THE ENTITIES WE HEAR ABOUT IN RELIGIOUS STORIES.
FSSSHT
IN FACT, THEY MAY BE SOMETHING COMPLETELY DIFFERENT... BROUGHT HERE FROM A COMPLETELY DIFFERENT PLACE.
MY THEORY SUGGESTS ORGANIC ENTITIES FROM A HIGHER ORDER THAT HAVE THE POWER TO CREATE AND DESTROY ALL WE KNOW. OUR SPECIES SEES SUCH POWER...
...AS THE ULTIMATE WEAPON.
AND SINCE WE CAN'T EXPLAIN IT, WE SIMPLY CALL THESE ENTITIES...
...GOD AND SATAN.

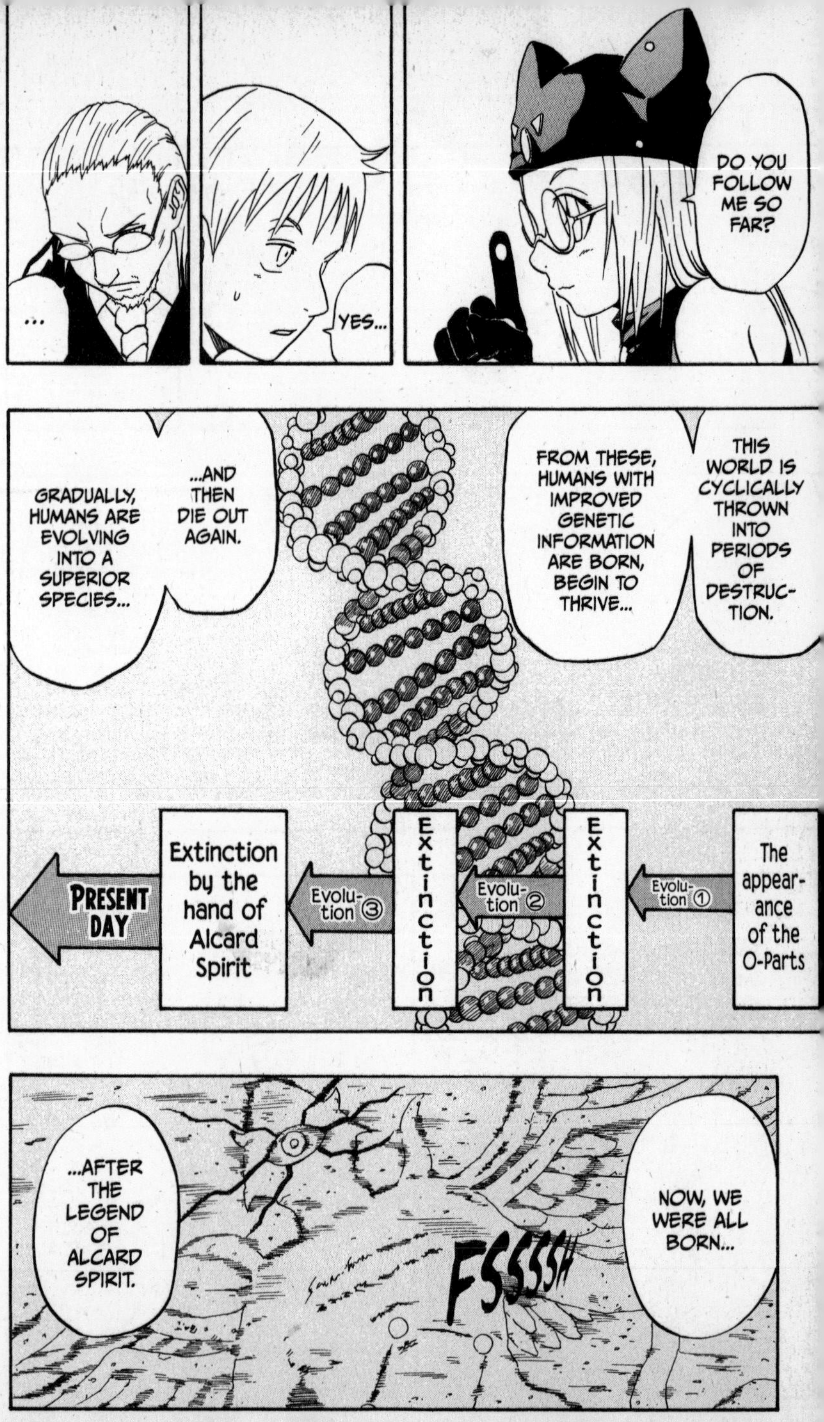
DO YOU FOLLOW ME SO FAR?
YES...
...
THIS WORLD IS CYCLICALLY THROWN INTO PERIODS OF DESTRUCTION.
FROM THESE, HUMANS WITH IMPROVED GENETIC INFORMATION ARE BORN, BEGIN TO THRIVE...
...AND THEN DIE OUT AGAIN.
GRADUALLY, HUMANS ARE EVOLVING INTO A SUPERIOR SPECIES...
The appearance of the O-Parts
Evolution ①
Extinction
Evolution ②
Extinction
Evolution ③
Extinction by the hand of Alcard Spirit
PRESENT DAY
NOW, WE WERE ALL BORN...
FSSSSH
...AFTER THE LEGEND OF ALCARD SPIRIT.

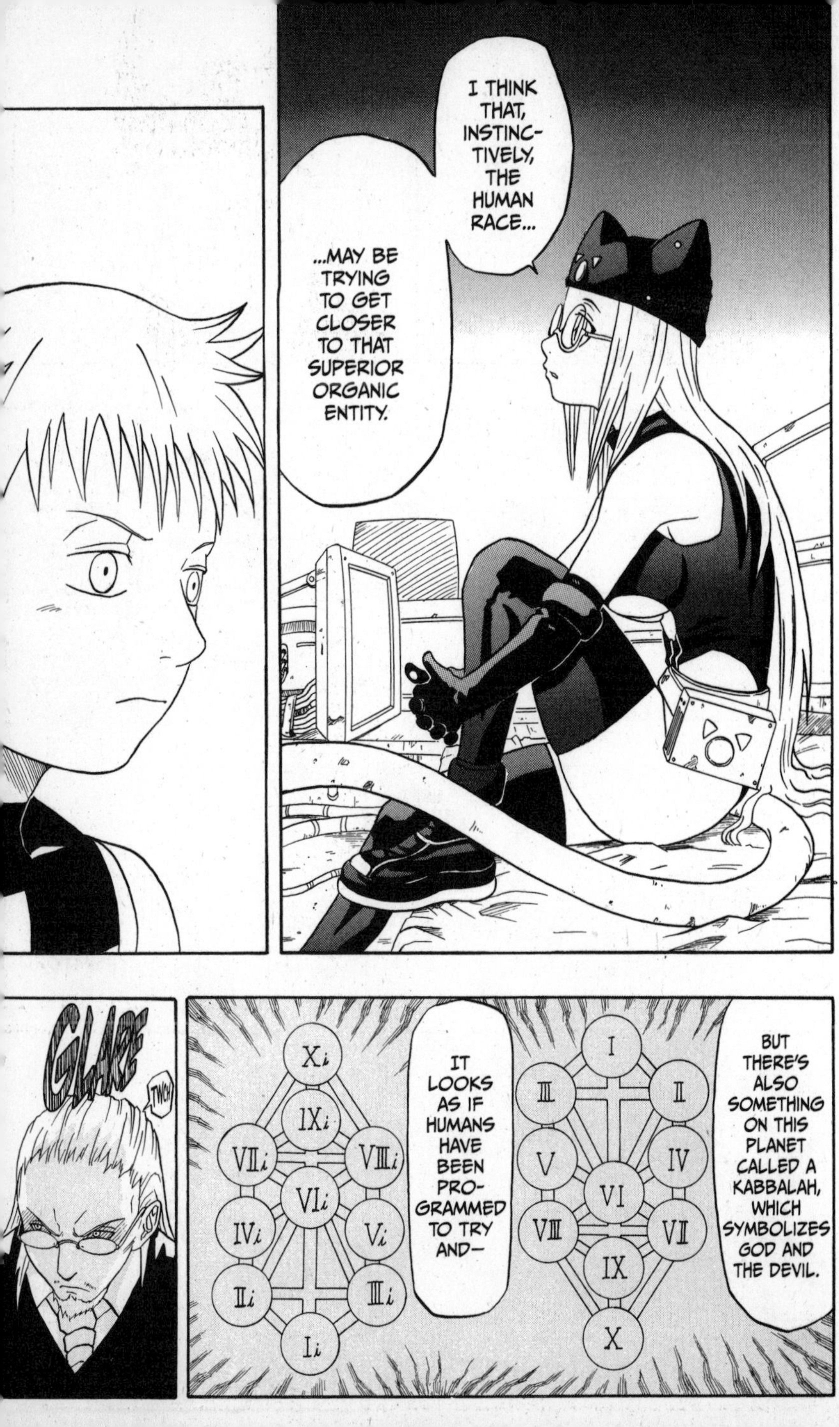
I THINK THAT, INSTINCTIVELY, THE HUMAN RACE...
...MAY BE TRYING TO GET CLOSER TO THAT SUPERIOR ORGANIC ENTITY.
BUT THERE'S ALSO SOMETHING ON THIS PLANET CALLED A KABBALAH, WHICH SYMBOLIZES GOD AND THE DEVIL.
IT LOOKS AS IF HUMANS HAVE BEEN PRO-GRAMMED TO TRY AND—
GLARE
TWCH

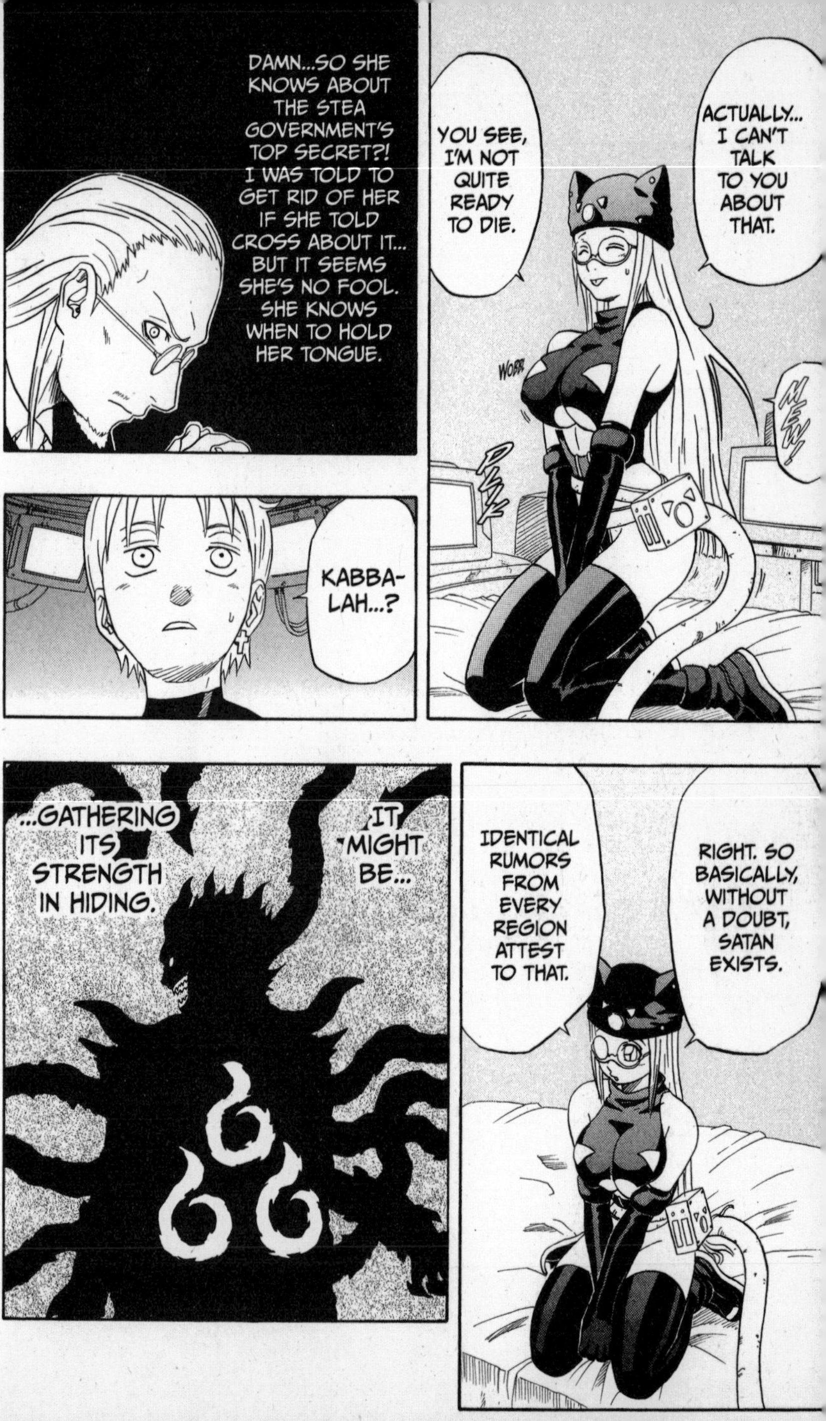
ACTUALLY... I CAN'T TALK TO YOU ABOUT THAT.
YOU SEE, I'M NOT QUITE READY TO DIE.
MEW!
DAMN...SO SHE KNOWS ABOUT THE STEA GOVERNMENT'S TOP SECRET?! I WAS TOLD TO GET RID OF HER IF SHE TOLD CROSS ABOUT IT... BUT IT SEEMS SHE'S NO FOOL. SHE KNOWS WHEN TO HOLD HER TONGUE.
KABBA-LAH...?
RIGHT. SO BASICALLY, WITHOUT A DOUBT, SATAN EXISTS.
IDENTICAL RUMORS FROM EVERY REGION ATTEST TO THAT.
IT MIGHT BE...
...GATHERING ITS STRENGTH IN HIDING.

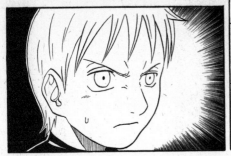

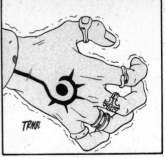

TRMBL
BUT THE CONDITIONS UNDER WHICH SATAN WILL APPEAR...
...OR DISAPPEAR... ARE STILL A MYSTERY.
WOBBL
IT'S POSSIBLE...
...THAT SATAN HAS THE POWER TO TAKE HUMAN FORM.
TIIING

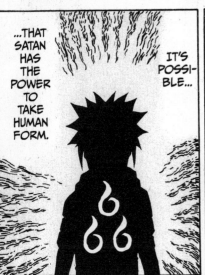

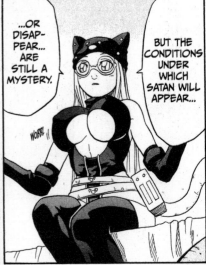

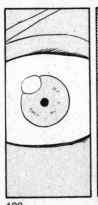

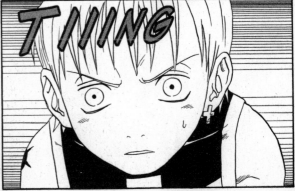

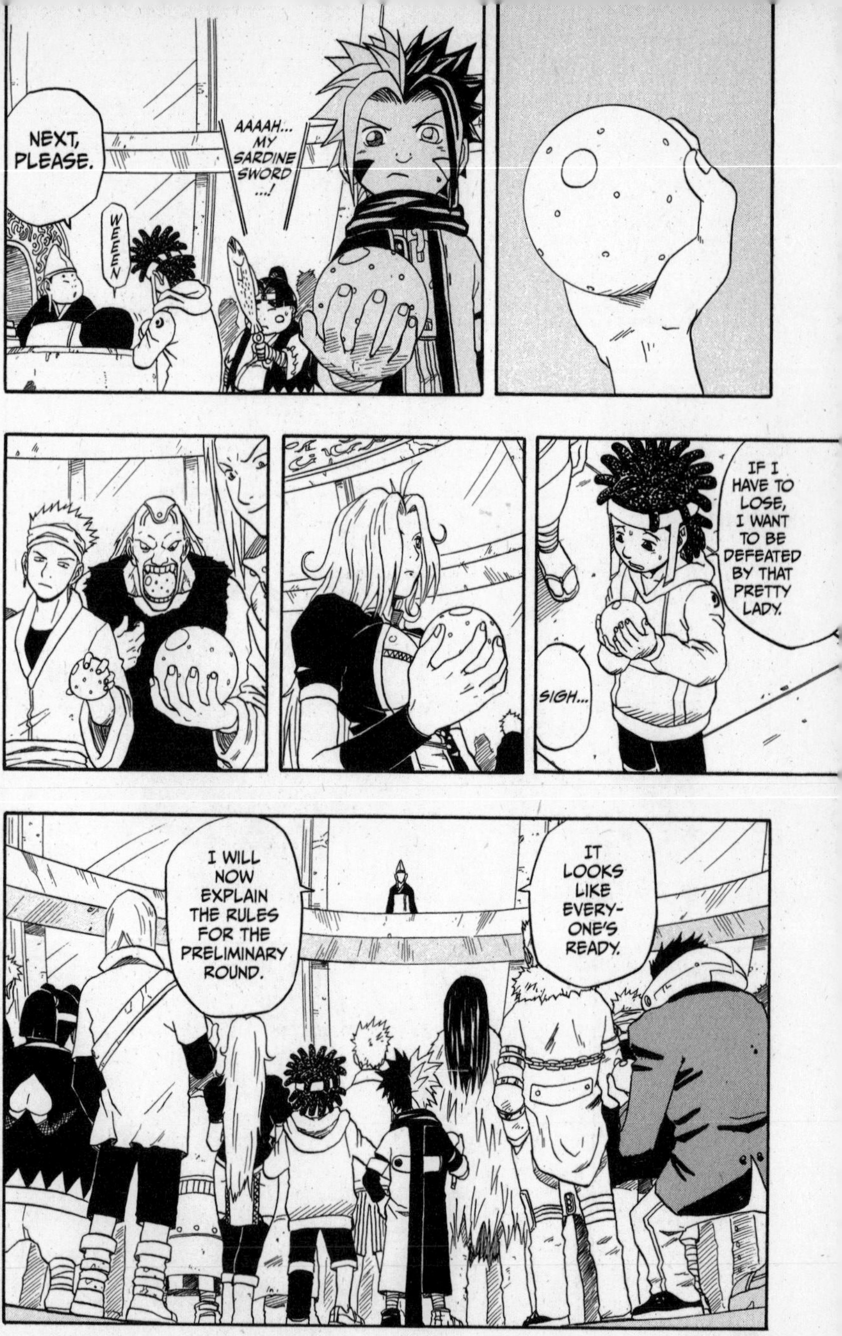
AAAAH... MY SARDINE SWORD ...!
NEXT, PLEASE.
WEEEEN
IF I HAVE TO LOSE, I WANT TO BE DEFEATED BY THAT PRETTY LADY.
SIGH...
IT LOOKS LIKE EVERY-ONE'S READY.
I WILL NOW EXPLAIN THE RULES FOR THE PRELIMINARY ROUND.

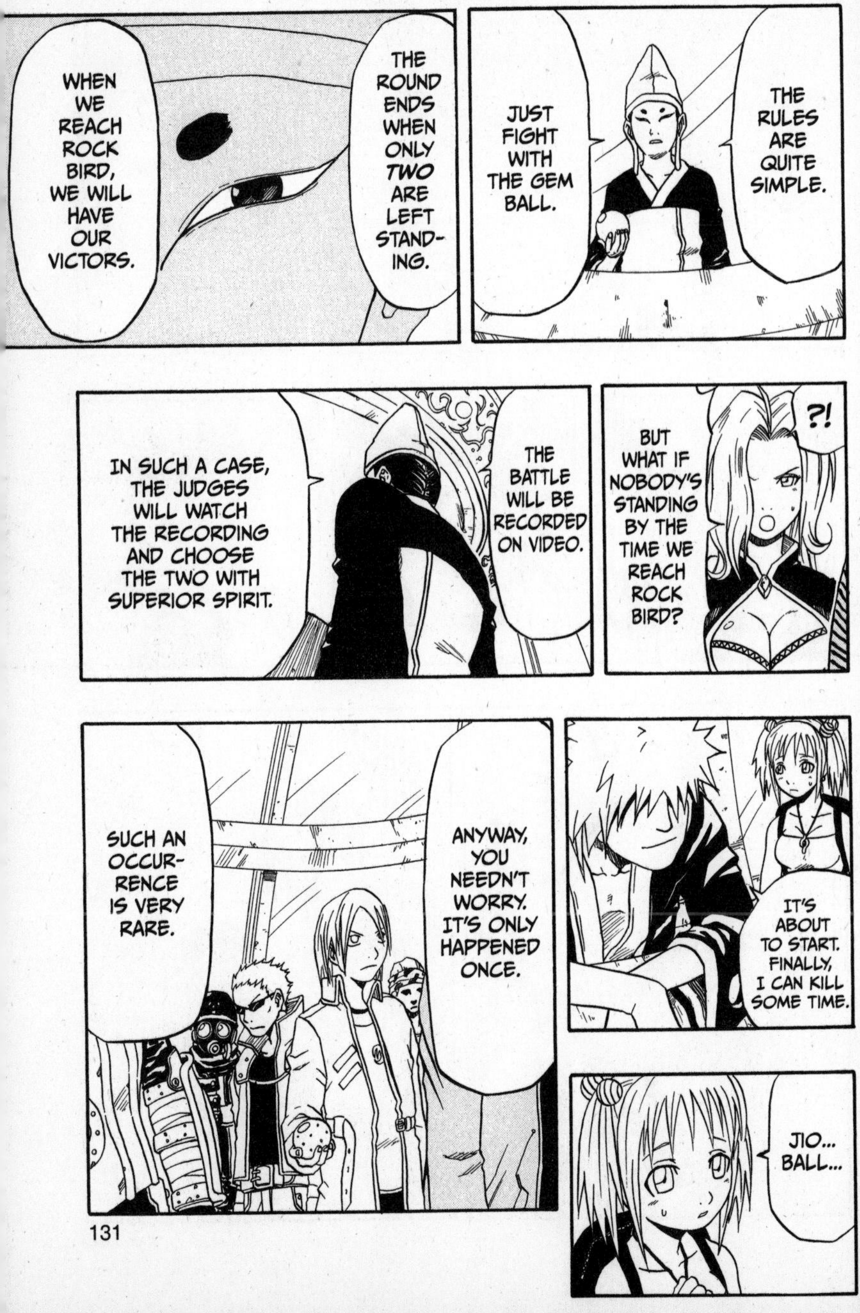
THE RULES ARE QUITE SIMPLE.
JUST FIGHT WITH THE GEM BALL.
THE ROUND ENDS WHEN ONLY *TWO* ARE LEFT STANDING.
WHEN WE REACH ROCK BIRD, WE WILL HAVE OUR VICTORS.
?!
BUT WHAT IF NOBODY'S STANDING BY THE TIME WE REACH ROCK BIRD?
THE BATTLE WILL BE RECORDED ON VIDEO.
IN SUCH A CASE, THE JUDGES WILL WATCH THE RECORDING AND CHOOSE THE TWO WITH SUPERIOR SPIRIT.
IT'S ABOUT TO START. FINALLY, I CAN KILL SOME TIME.
JIO... BALL...
ANYWAY, YOU NEEDN'T WORRY. IT'S ONLY HAPPENED ONCE.
SUCH AN OCCURRENCE IS VERY RARE.

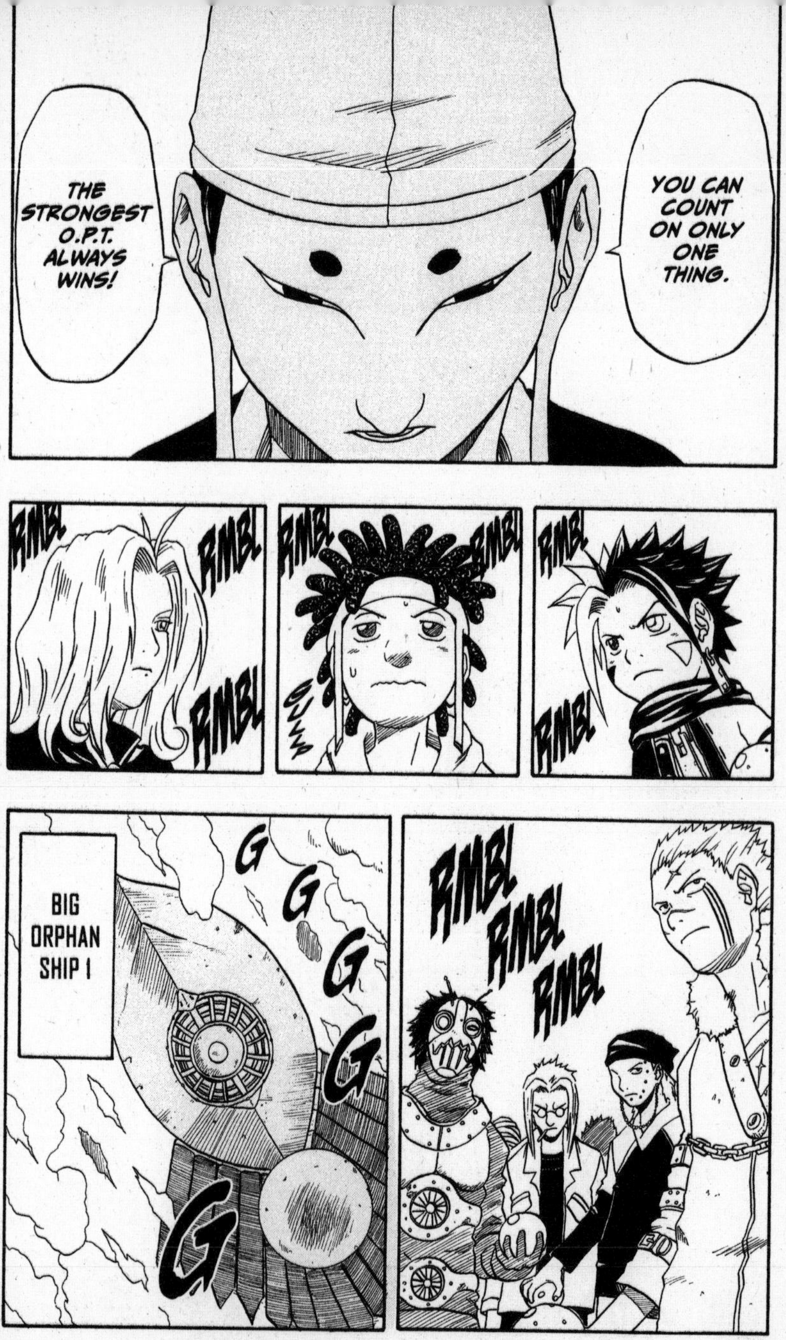
YOU CAN COUNT ON ONLY ONE THING.
THE STRONGEST O.P.T. ALWAYS WINS!
RMBL
RMBL
RMBL
RMBL
GULP
RMBL
RMBL
RMBL
RMBL
RMBL
RMBL
BIG ORPHAN SHIP 1
G
G
G
G
G
G

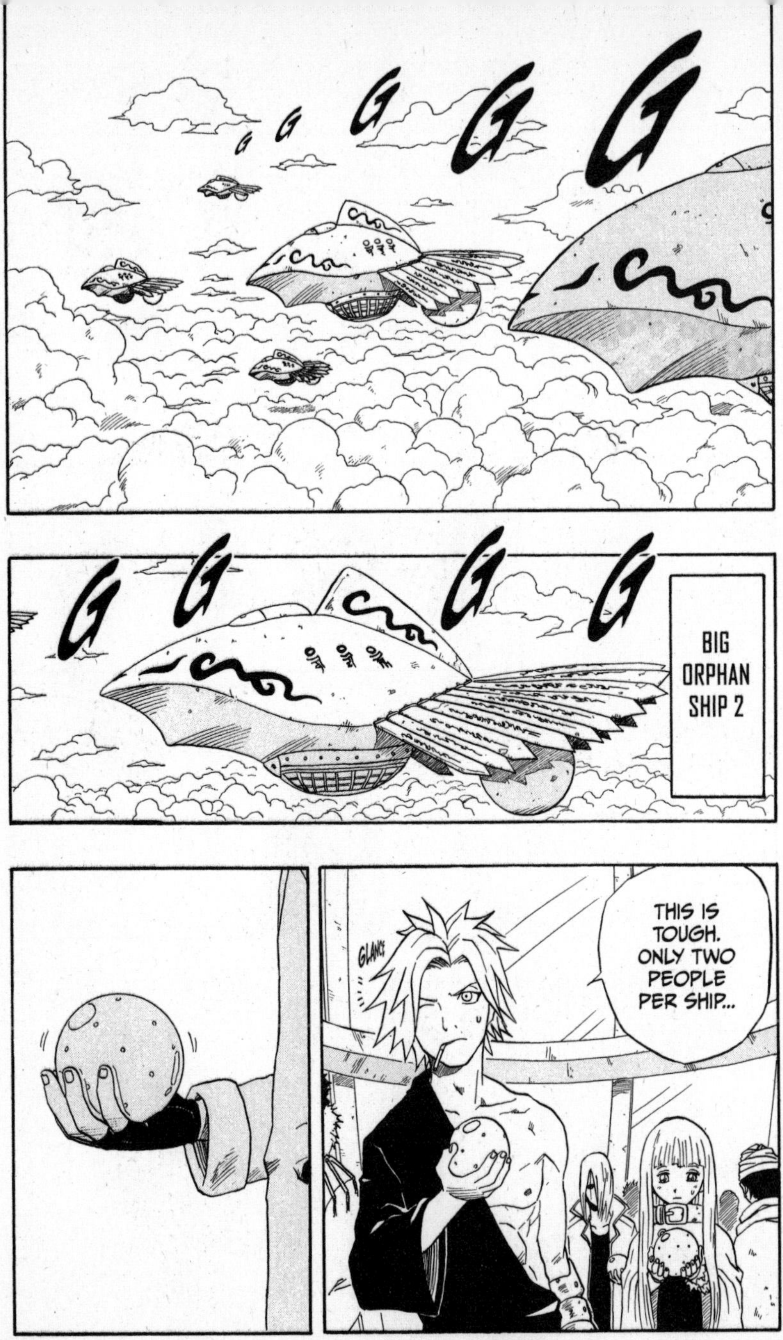
BIG ORPHAN SHIP 2
GLANCE
THIS IS TOUGH. ONLY TWO PEOPLE PER SHIP...

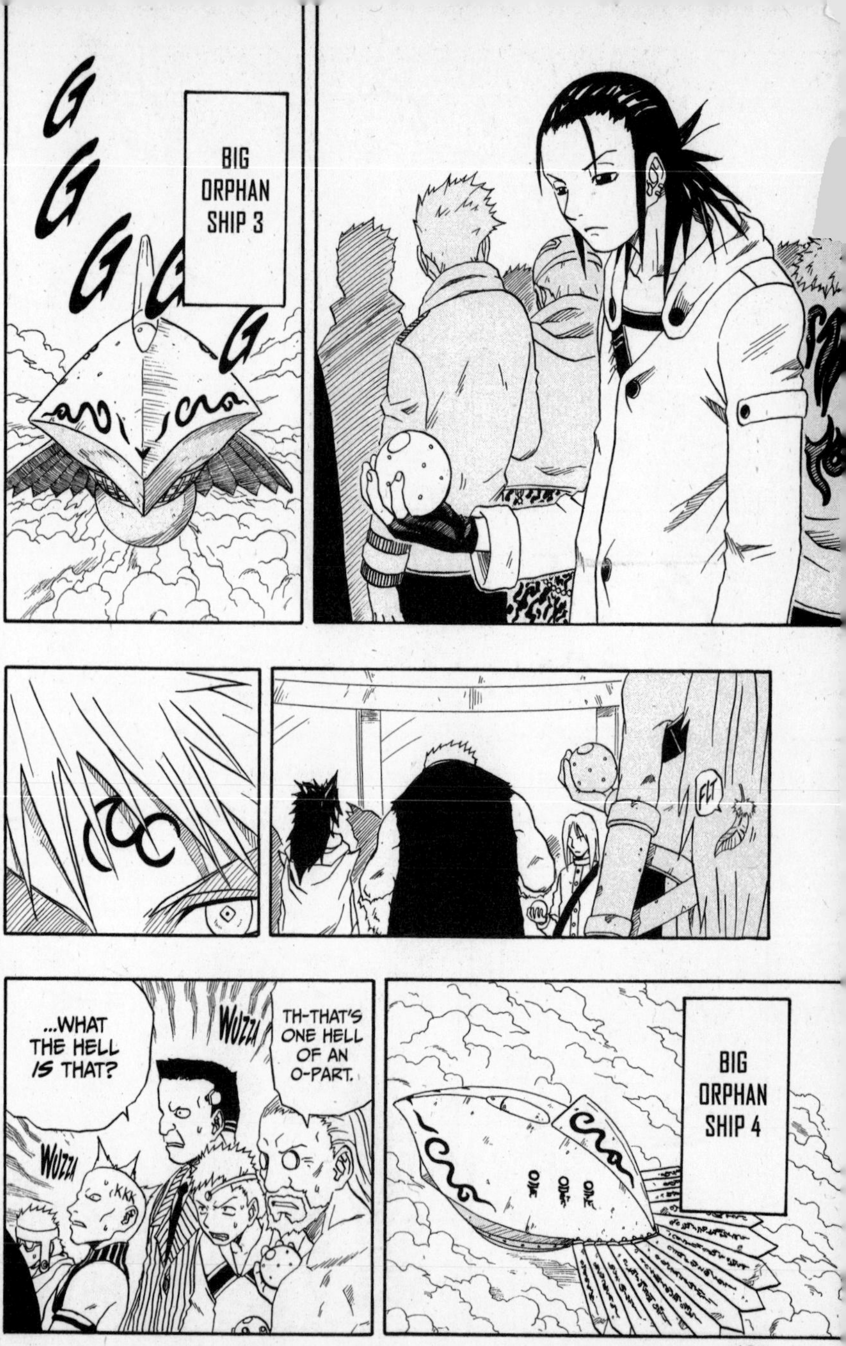
BIG ORPHAN SHIP 3
GGGGG
FLT
BIG ORPHAN SHIP 4
TH-THAT'S ONE HELL OF AN O-PART.
WUZZA
...WHAT THE HELL *IS* THAT?
WUZZA
KKK

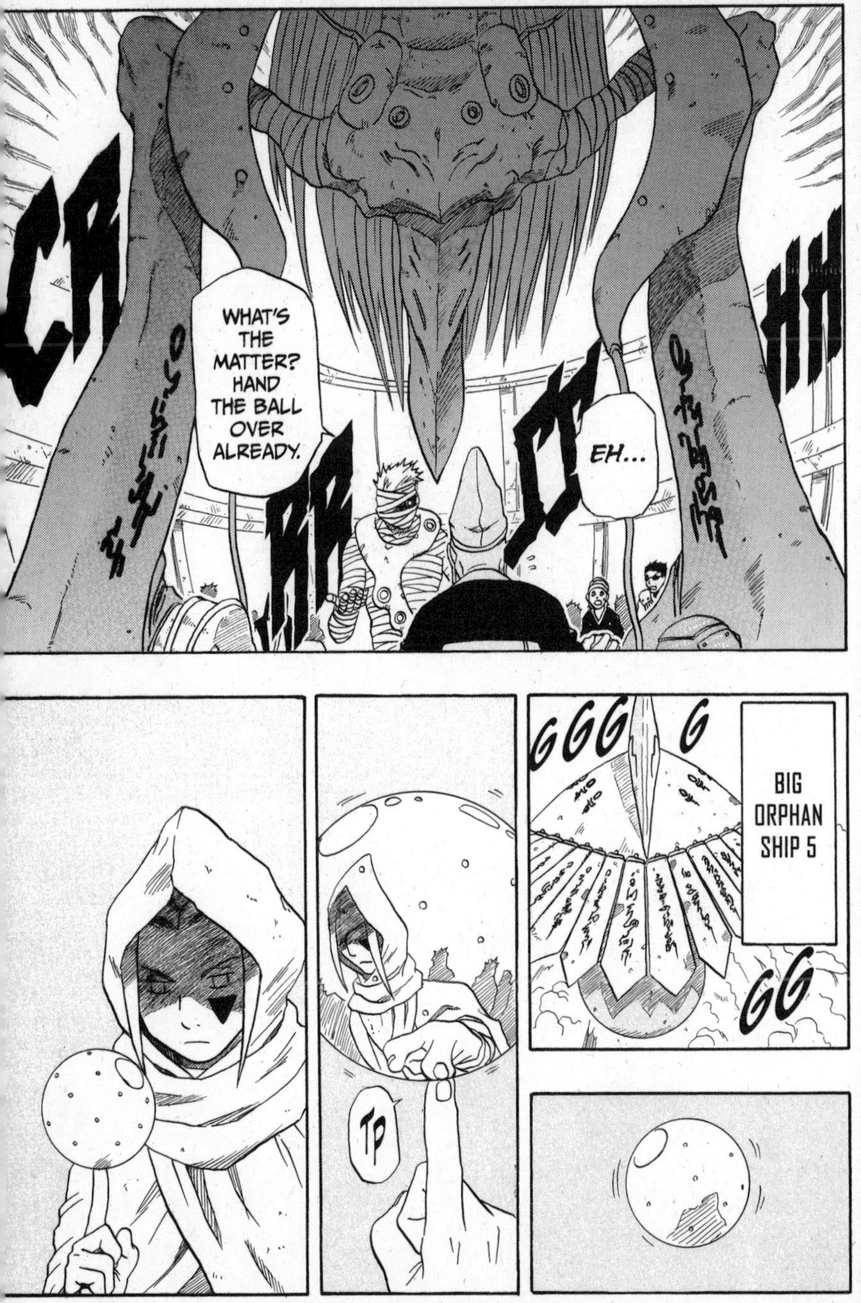
WHAT'S THE MATTER? HAND THE BALL OVER ALREADY.
EH...
BIG ORPHAN SHIP 5
GGG G
GG
TP

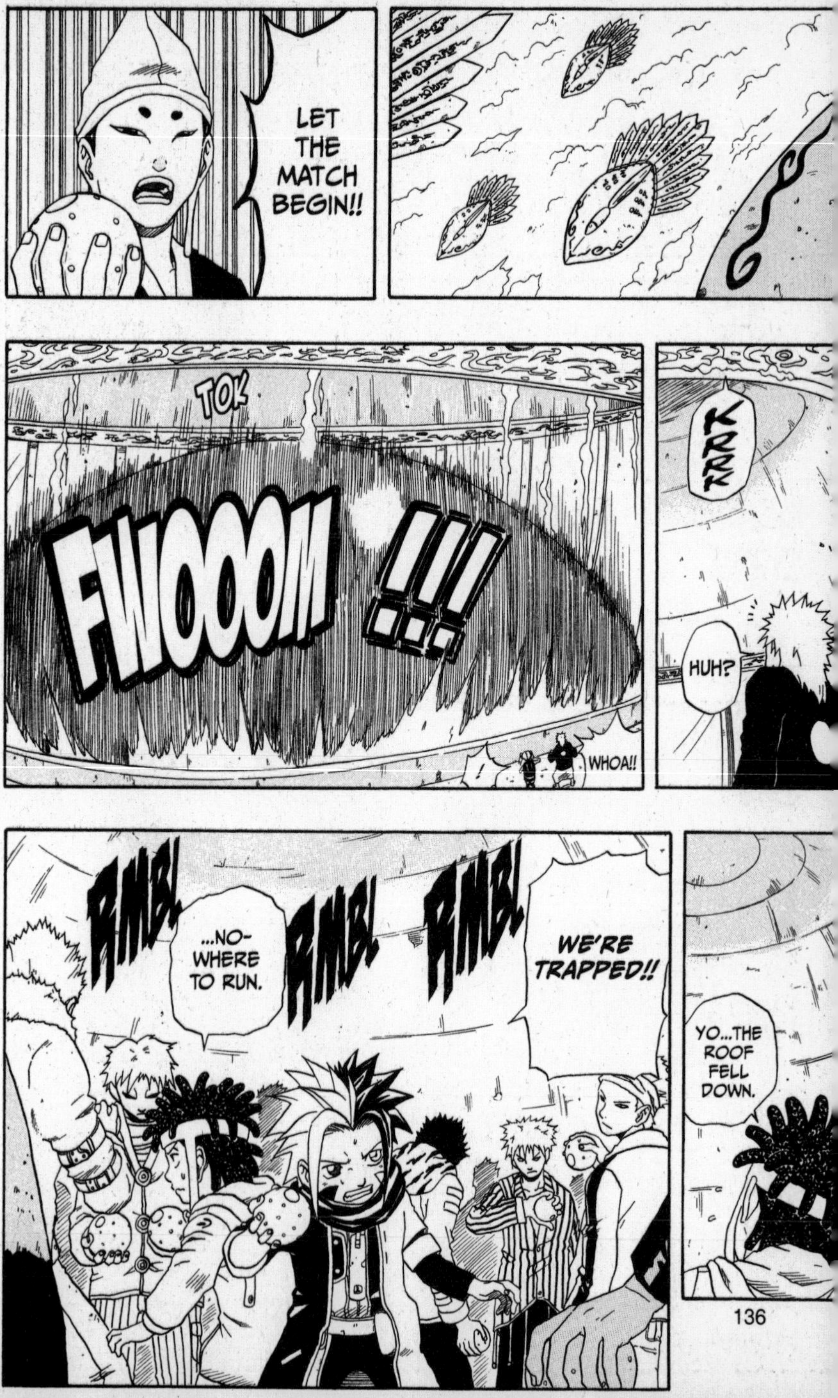
LET THE MATCH BEGIN!!
KRRK
HUH?
TOK
FWOOOM!!!
!
WHOA!!
YO...THE ROOF FELL DOWN.
WE'RE TRAPPED!!
RMBL
RMBL
...NO-WHERE TO RUN.
RMBL

CHAPTER 32: THE CHOSEN TWO

Only ten may move up to the main event. The preliminary round takes place on five ships. Two winners per ship are chosen for the main tournament.

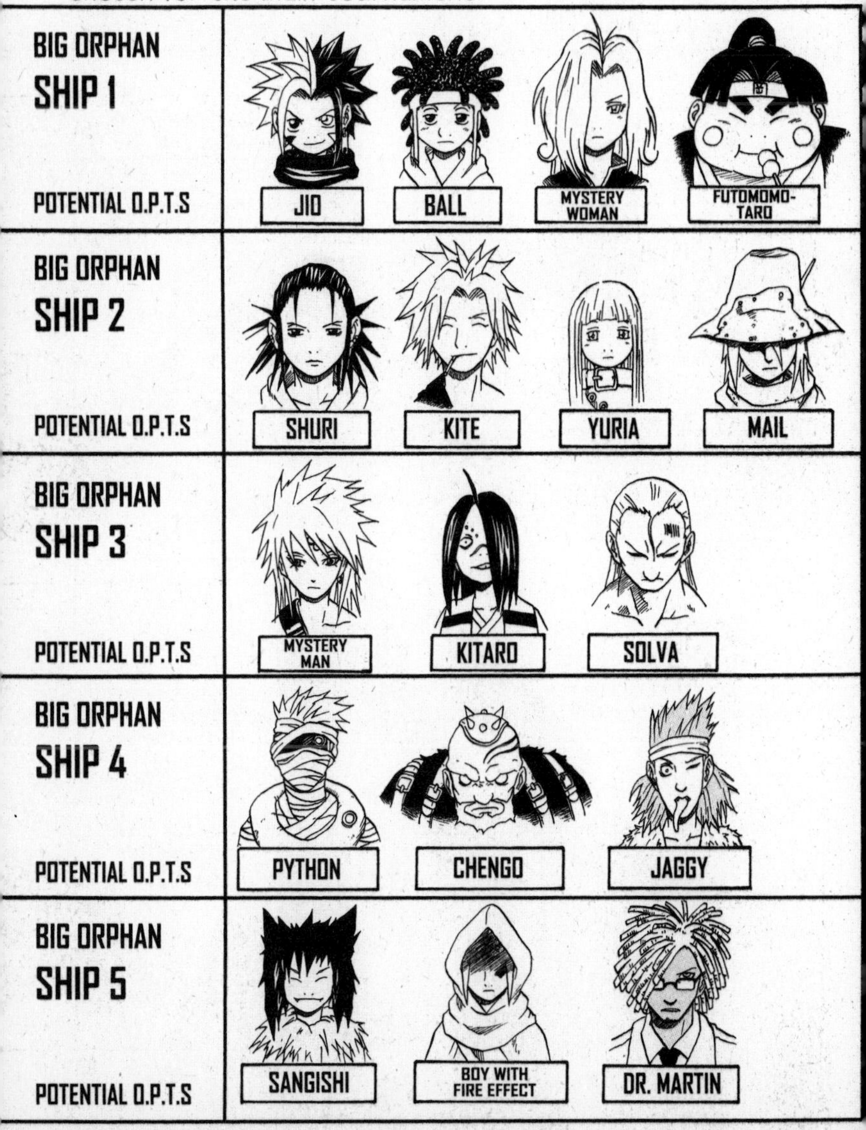

BIG ORPHAN SHIP 1
POTENTIAL O.P.T.S
JIO
BALL
MYSTERY WOMAN
FUTOMOMO-TARO
BIG ORPHAN SHIP 2
POTENTIAL O.P.T.S
SHURI
KITE
YURIA
MAIL
BIG ORPHAN SHIP 3
POTENTIAL O.P.T.S
MYSTERY MAN
KITARO
SOLVA
BIG ORPHAN SHIP 4
POTENTIAL O.P.T.S
PYTHON
CHENGO
JAGGY
BIG ORPHAN SHIP 5
POTENTIAL O.P.T.S
SANGISHI
BOY WITH FIRE EFFECT
DR. MARTIN

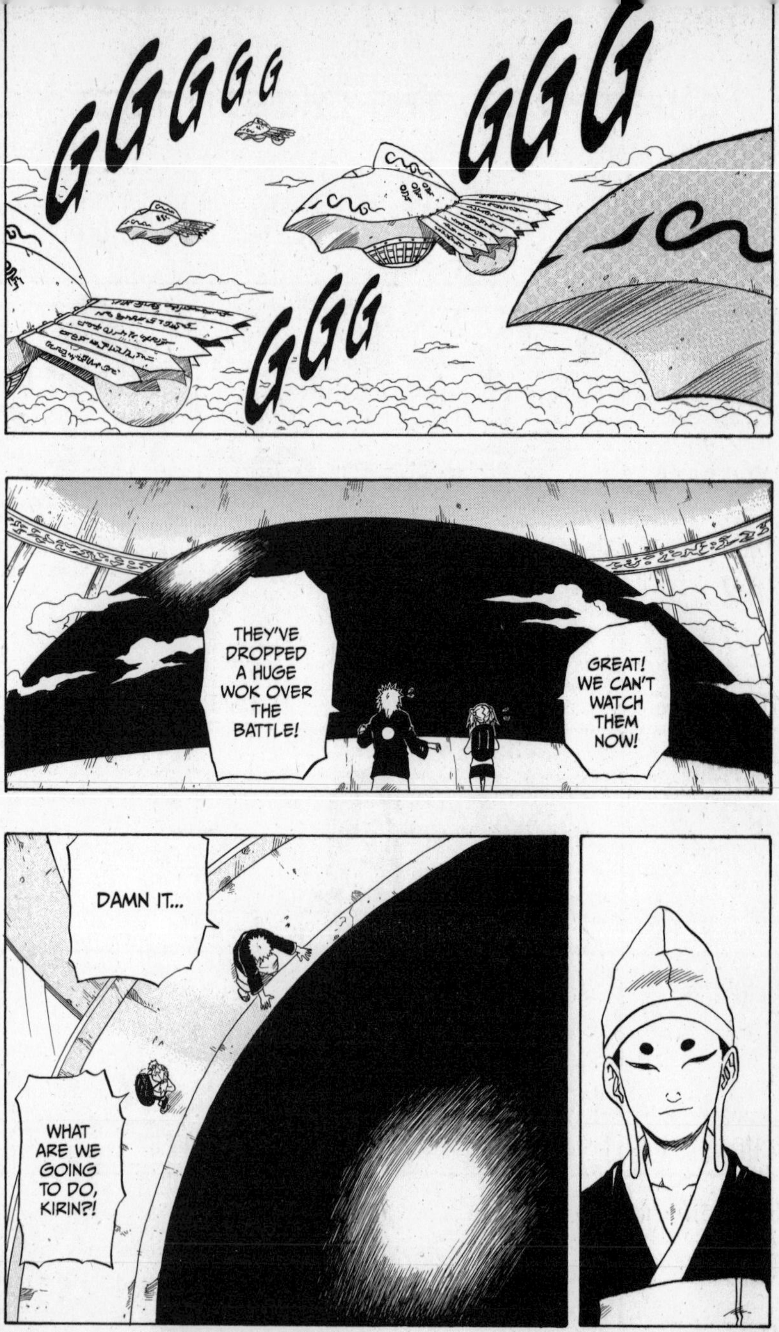
GGG
GGGGG
GGG
GREAT! WE CAN'T WATCH THEM NOW!
THEY'VE DROPPED A HUGE WOK OVER THE BATTLE!
DAMN IT...
WHAT ARE WE GOING TO DO, KIRIN?!

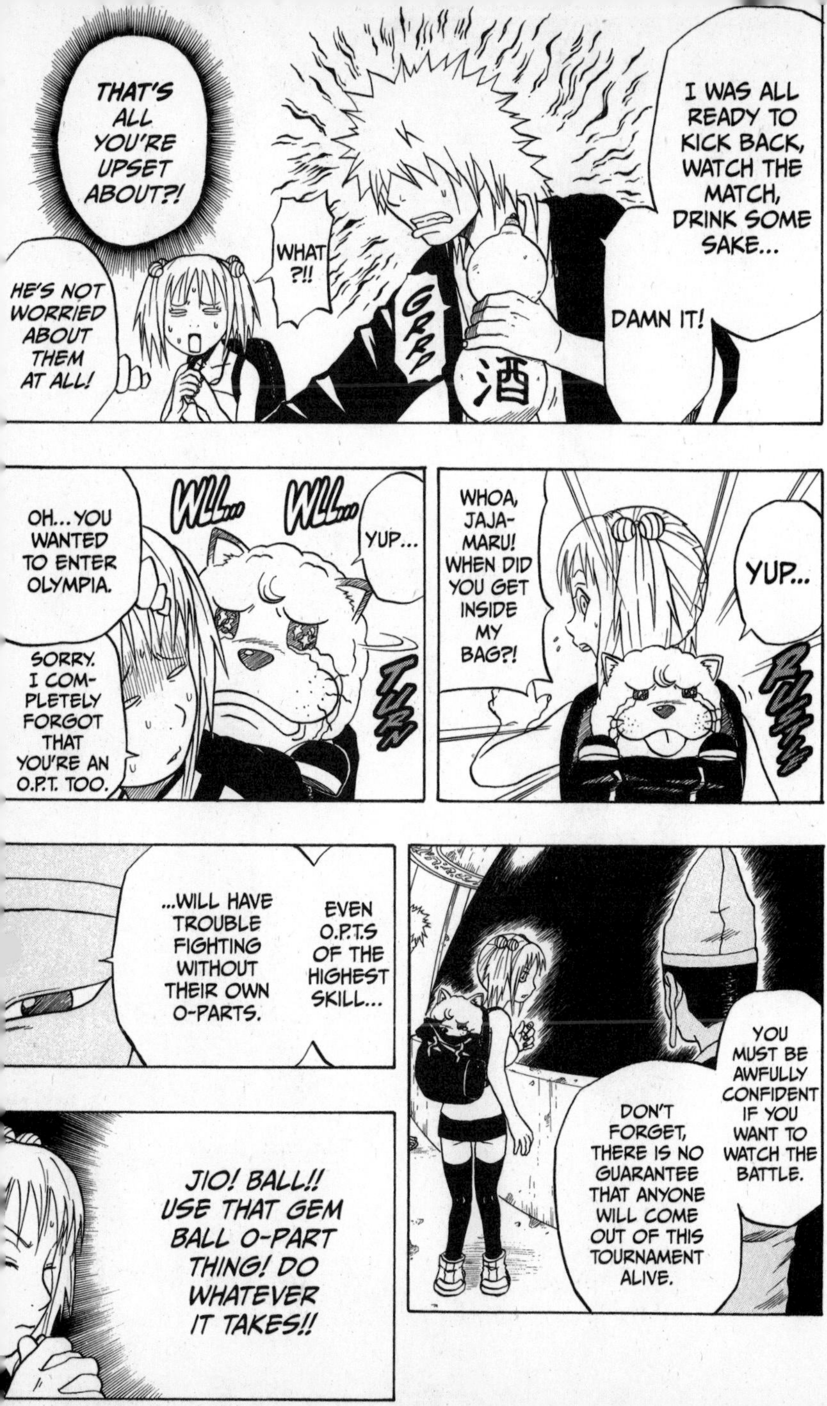
I WAS ALL READY TO KICK BACK, WATCH THE MATCH, DRINK SOME SAKE...
DAMN IT!
GRRR
酒
WHAT?!!
THAT'S ALL YOU'RE UPSET ABOUT?!
HE'S NOT WORRIED ABOUT THEM AT ALL!
YUP...
WHOA, JAJA-MARU! WHEN DID YOU GET INSIDE MY BAG?!
YUP...
WLL... WLL...
TURN
OH... YOU WANTED TO ENTER OLYMPIA.
SORRY. I COMPLETELY FORGOT THAT YOU'RE AN O.P.T. TOO.
YOU MUST BE AWFULLY CONFIDENT IF YOU WANT TO WATCH THE BATTLE.
DON'T FORGET, THERE IS NO GUARANTEE THAT ANYONE WILL COME OUT OF THIS TOURNAMENT ALIVE.
EVEN O.P.T.S OF THE HIGHEST SKILL...
...WILL HAVE TROUBLE FIGHTING WITHOUT THEIR OWN O-PARTS.
JIO! BALL!! USE THAT GEM BALL O-PART THING! DO WHATEVER IT TAKES!!

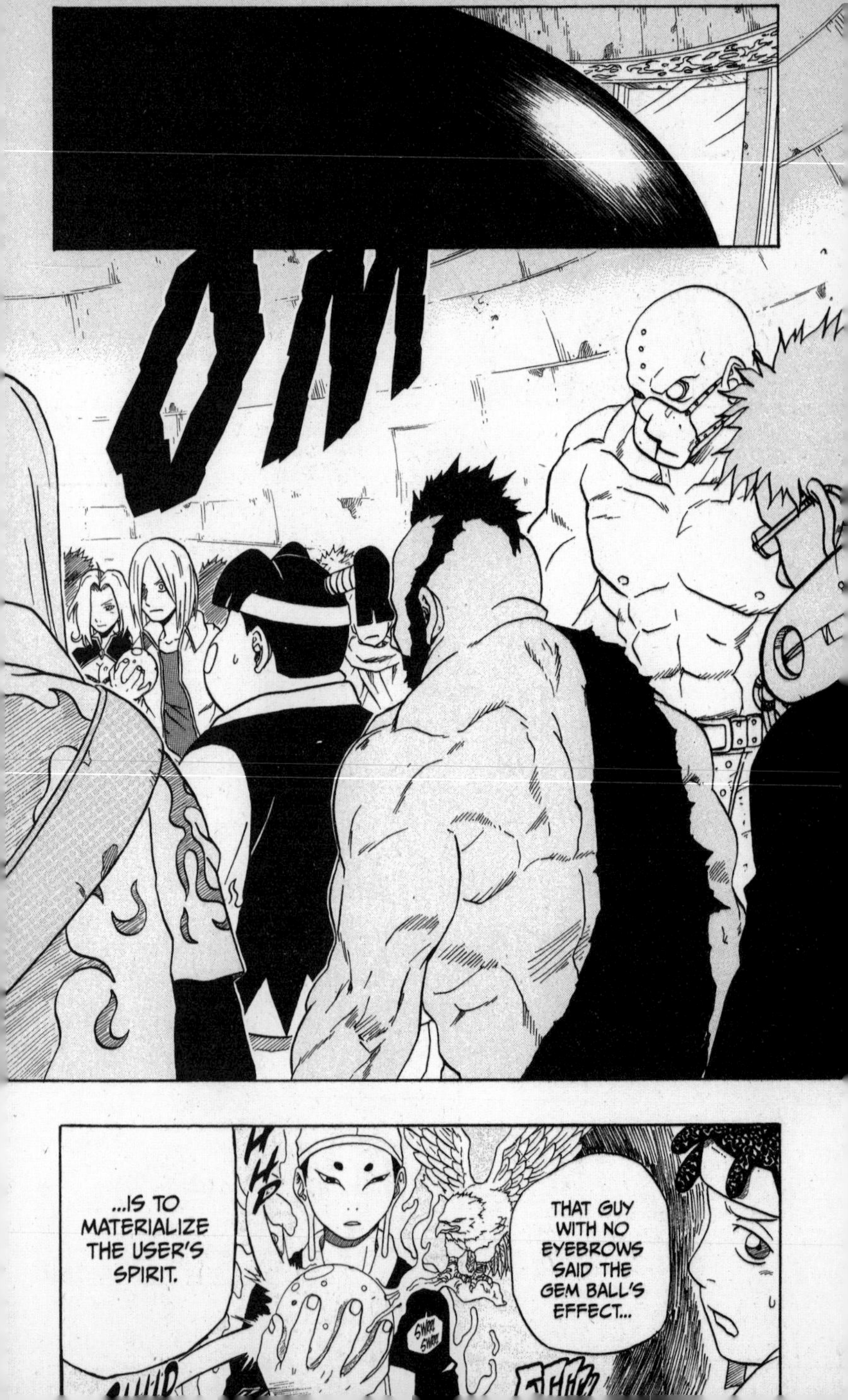
OM
THAT GUY WITH NO EYEBROWS SAID THE GEM BALL'S EFFECT...
...IS TO MATERIALIZE THE USER'S SPIRIT.

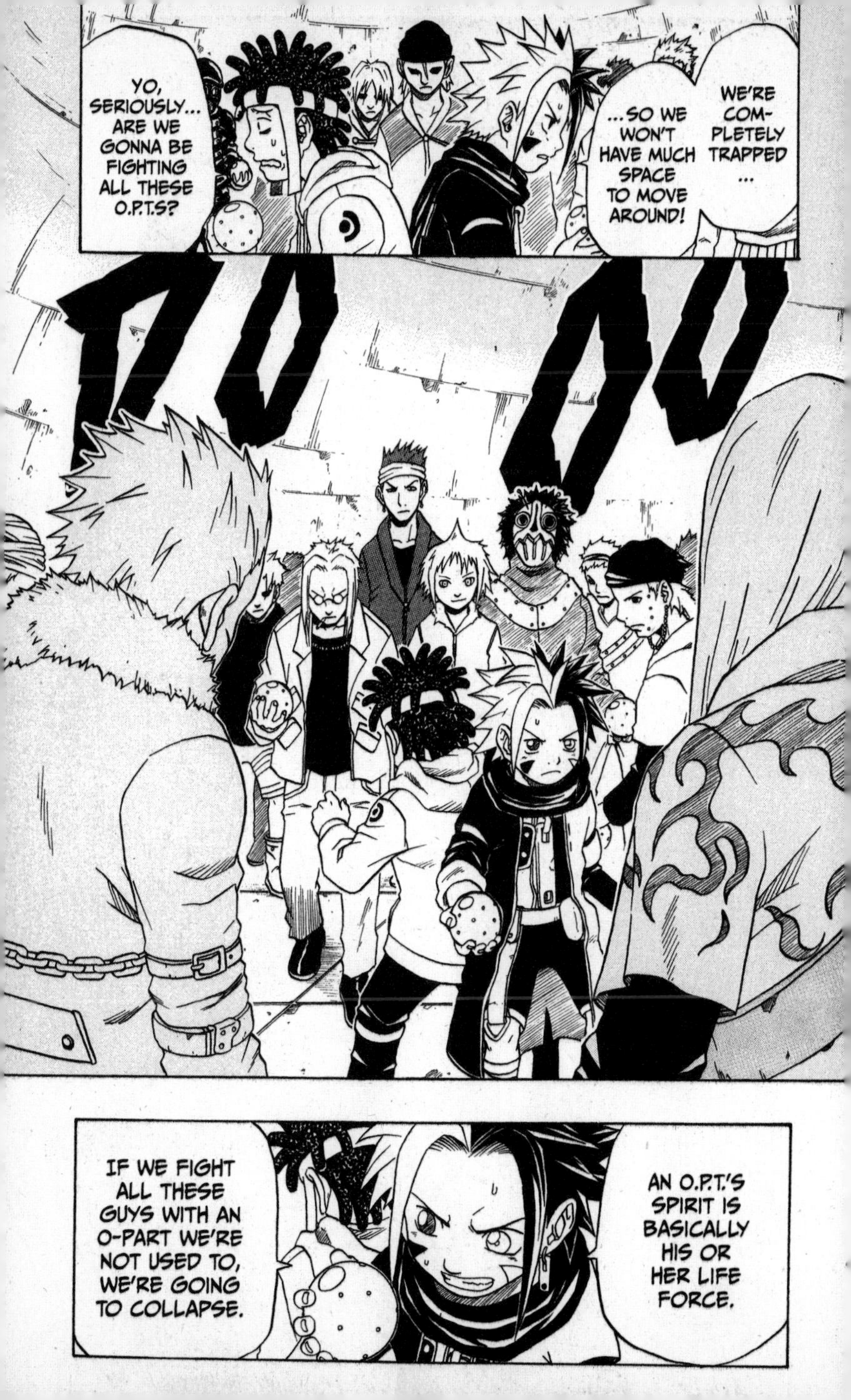
WE'RE COMPLETELY TRAPPED...
...SO WE WON'T HAVE MUCH SPACE TO MOVE AROUND!
YO, SERIOUSLY... ARE WE GONNA BE FIGHTING ALL THESE O.P.T.S?
AN O.P.T.'S SPIRIT IS BASICALLY HIS OR HER LIFE FORCE.
IF WE FIGHT ALL THESE GUYS WITH AN O-PART WE'RE NOT USED TO, WE'RE GOING TO COLLAPSE.

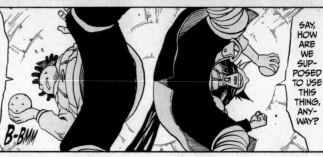

SAY, HOW ARE WE SUP-POSED TO USE THIS THING, ANY-WAY?
YO—WHAT IF OUR SPIRIT'S NOT COMPATIBLE WITH IT?! WE'LL HAVE TO FIGHT THEM EMPTY-HANDED!
B-BMM
GLARE
GLARE
GLARE
LOOKS LIKE WE WON'T TO HAVE TIME TO COMPLAIN.
WE SEEM TO BE THEIR FIRST TARGET.
YO, THEY'RE COM-PLETELY SIZING US UP!
SHO
OM
BAM
HOLD IT!!

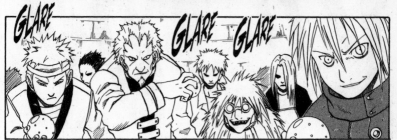

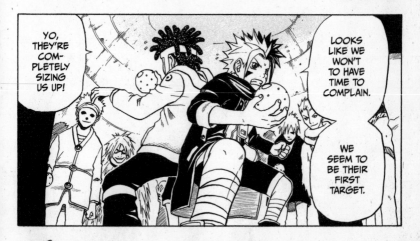

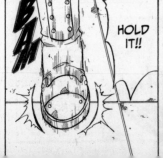

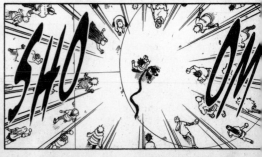

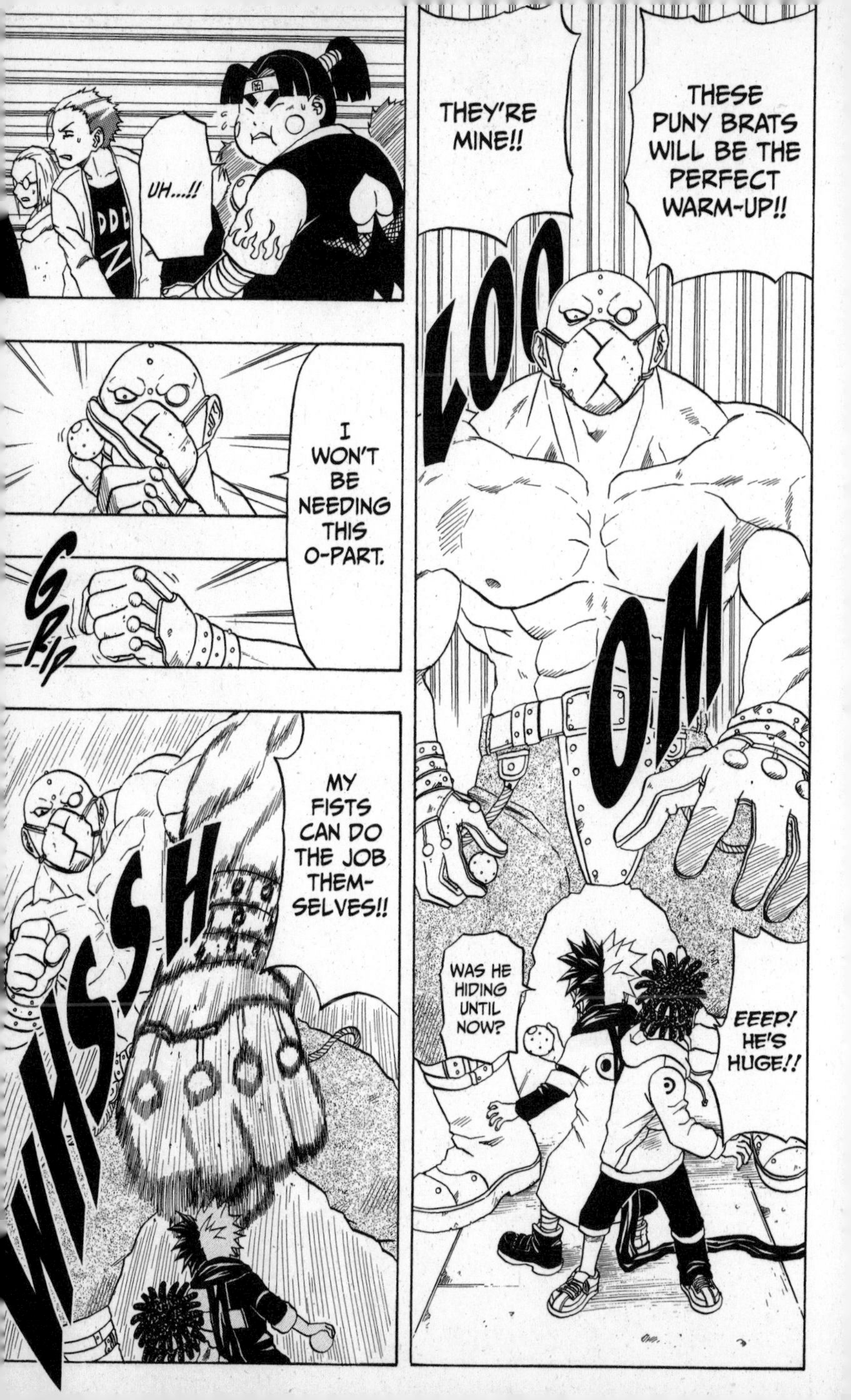
THESE PUNY BRATS WILL BE THE PERFECT WARM-UP!!
THEY'RE MINE!!
ZOOOM
EEEP! HE'S HUGE!!
WAS HE HIDING UNTIL NOW?
UH...!!
I WON'T BE NEEDING THIS O-PART.
GRIP
MY FISTS CAN DO THE JOB THEM-SELVES!!
WHSSH

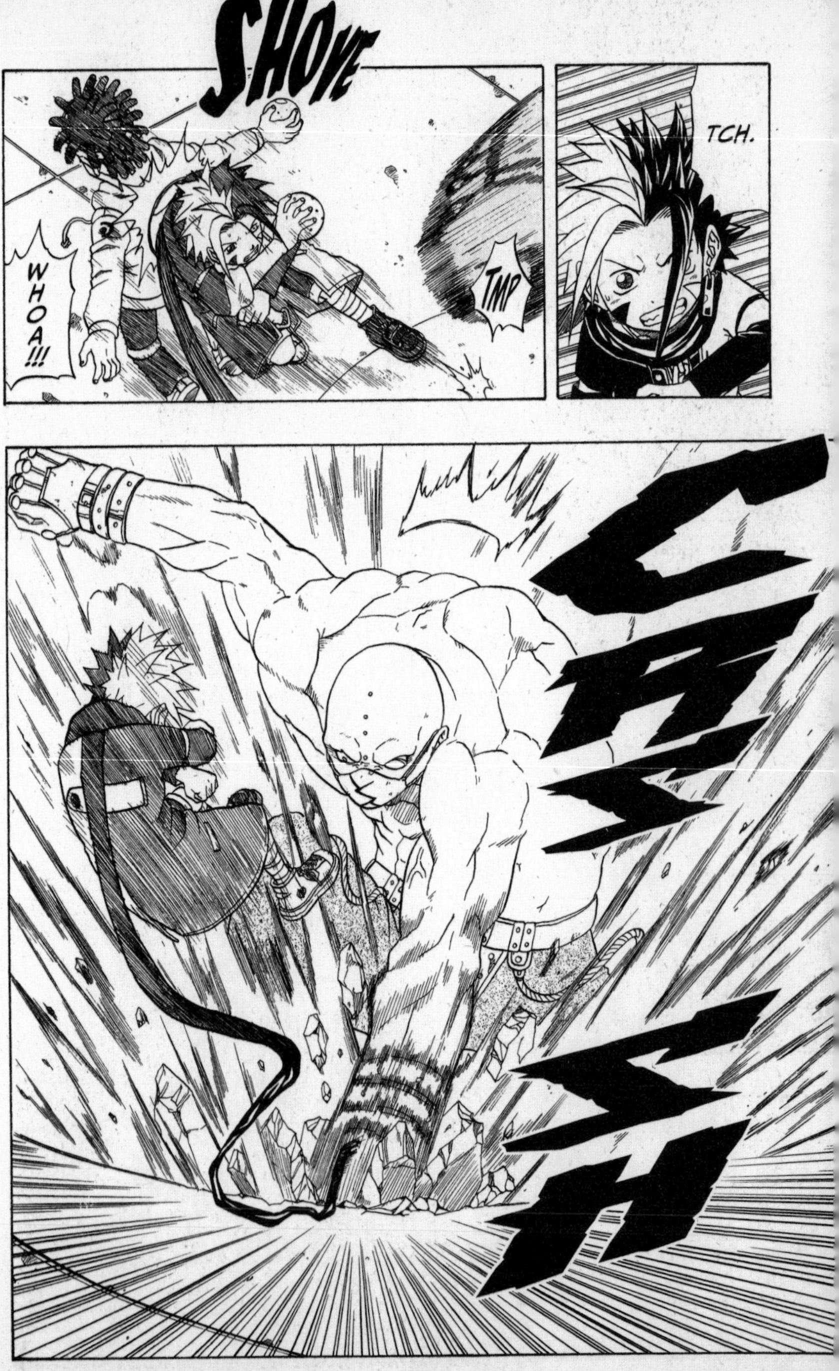
TCH.
SHOVE
TMP
WHOA!!!

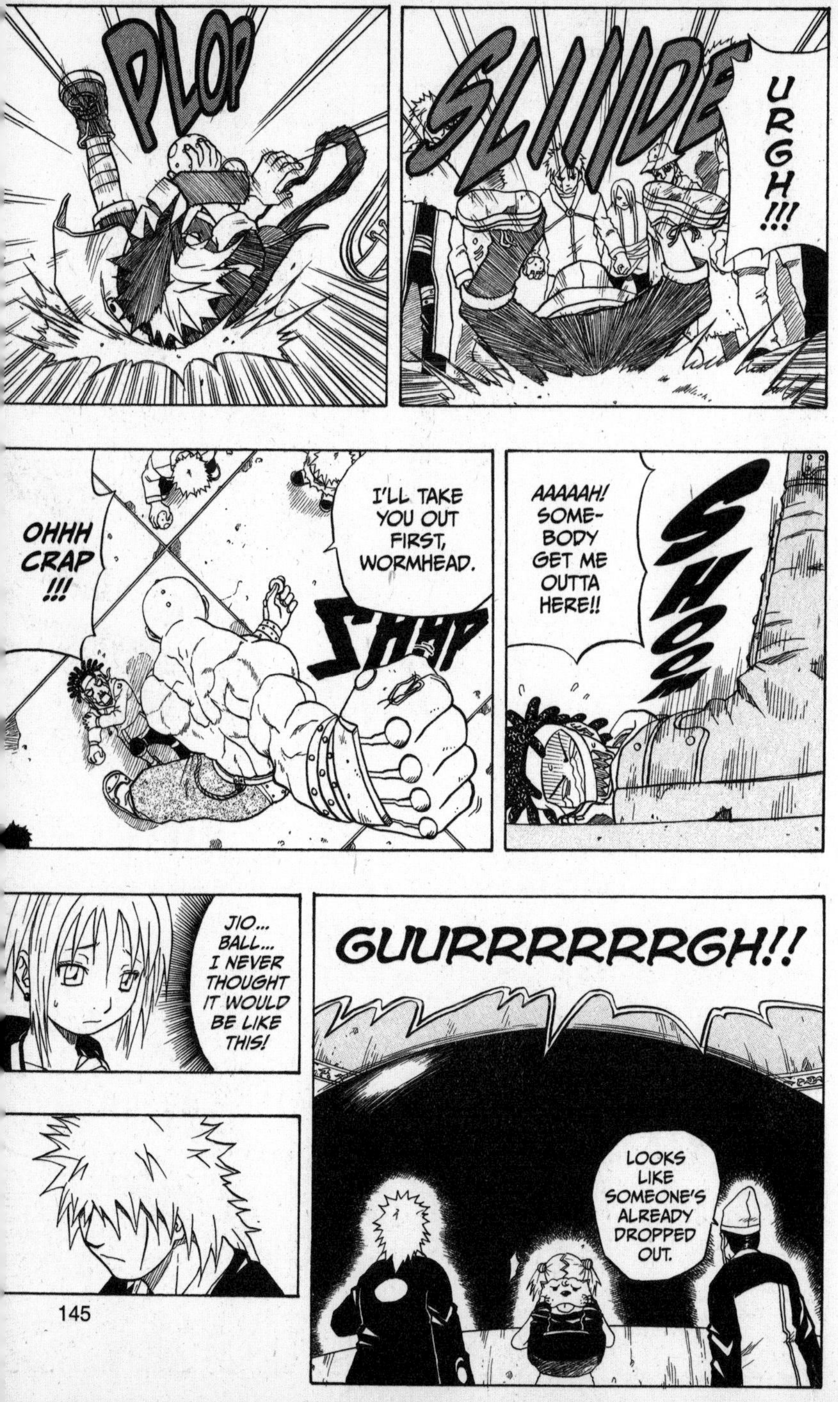
SLIIIDE
URGH!!!
PLOP
AAAAAH! SOME-BODY GET ME OUTTA HERE!!
SHOOM
I'LL TAKE YOU OUT FIRST, WORMHEAD.
SNAP
OHHH CRAP!!!
GUURRRRRRRGH!!
LOOKS LIKE SOMEONE'S ALREADY DROPPED OUT.
JIO... BALL... I NEVER THOUGHT IT WOULD BE LIKE THIS!

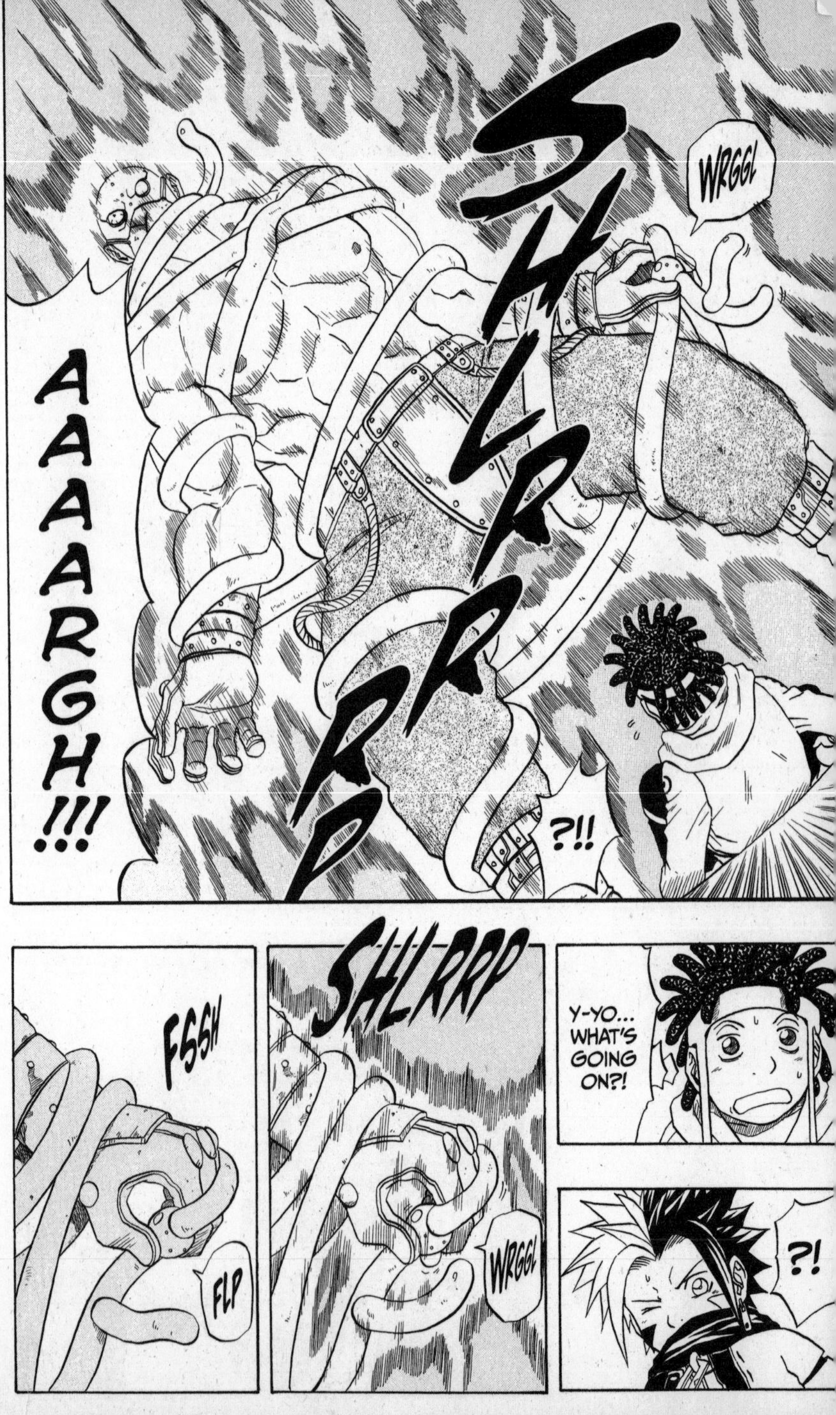
WRGGL
SHLRRRP
?!!
AAAARGH!!!
Y-YO... WHAT'S GOING ON?!
?!
SHLRRP
WRGGL
FSSH
FLP

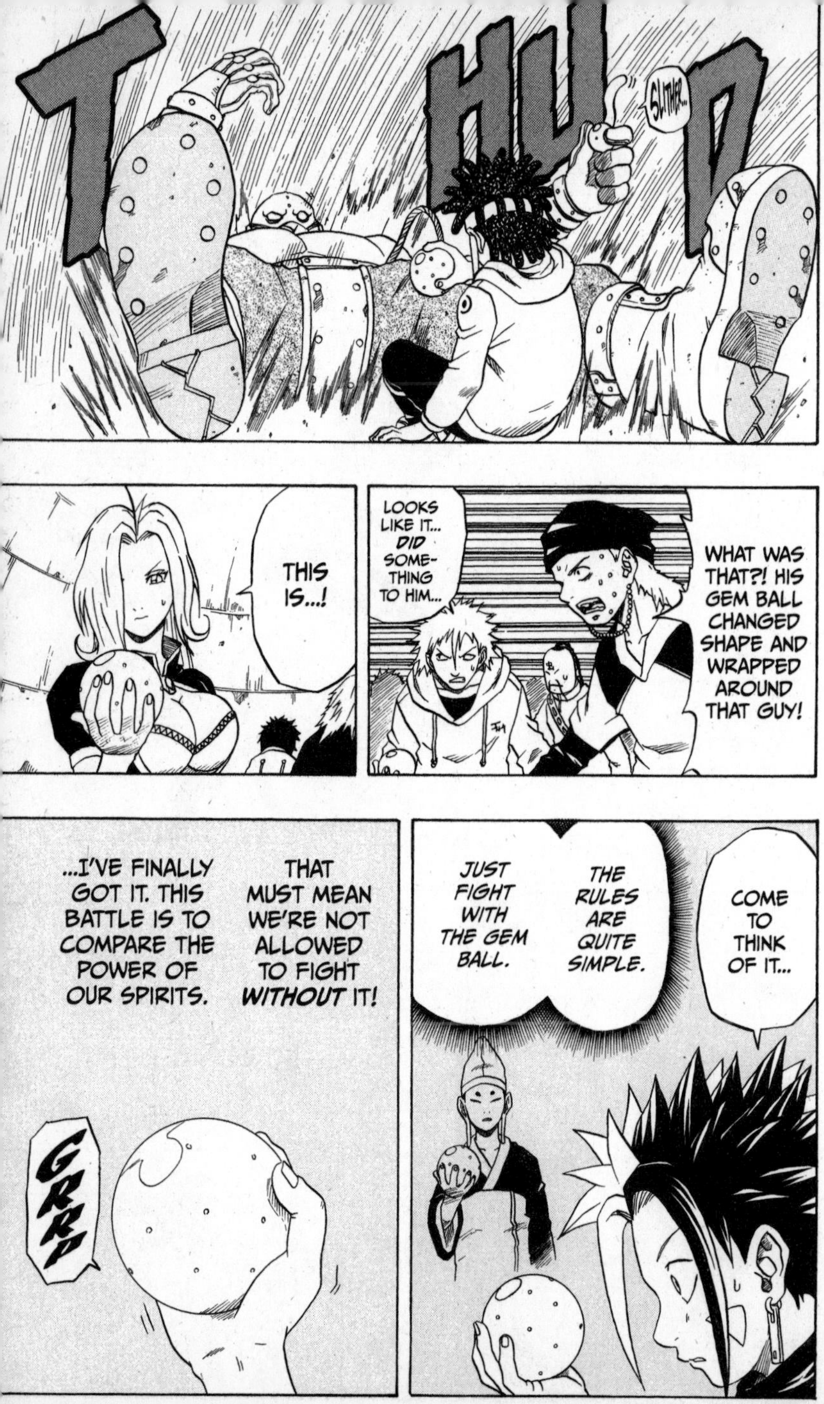
THUD
SLITHER...
WHAT WAS THAT?! HIS GEM BALL CHANGED SHAPE AND WRAPPED AROUND THAT GUY!
LOOKS LIKE IT... *DID* SOMETHING TO HIM...
THIS IS...!
COME TO THINK OF IT...
THE RULES ARE QUITE SIMPLE.
JUST FIGHT WITH THE GEM BALL.
THAT MUST MEAN WE'RE NOT ALLOWED TO FIGHT *WITHOUT* IT!
...I'VE FINALLY GOT IT. THIS BATTLE IS TO COMPARE THE POWER OF OUR SPIRITS.
GRRP

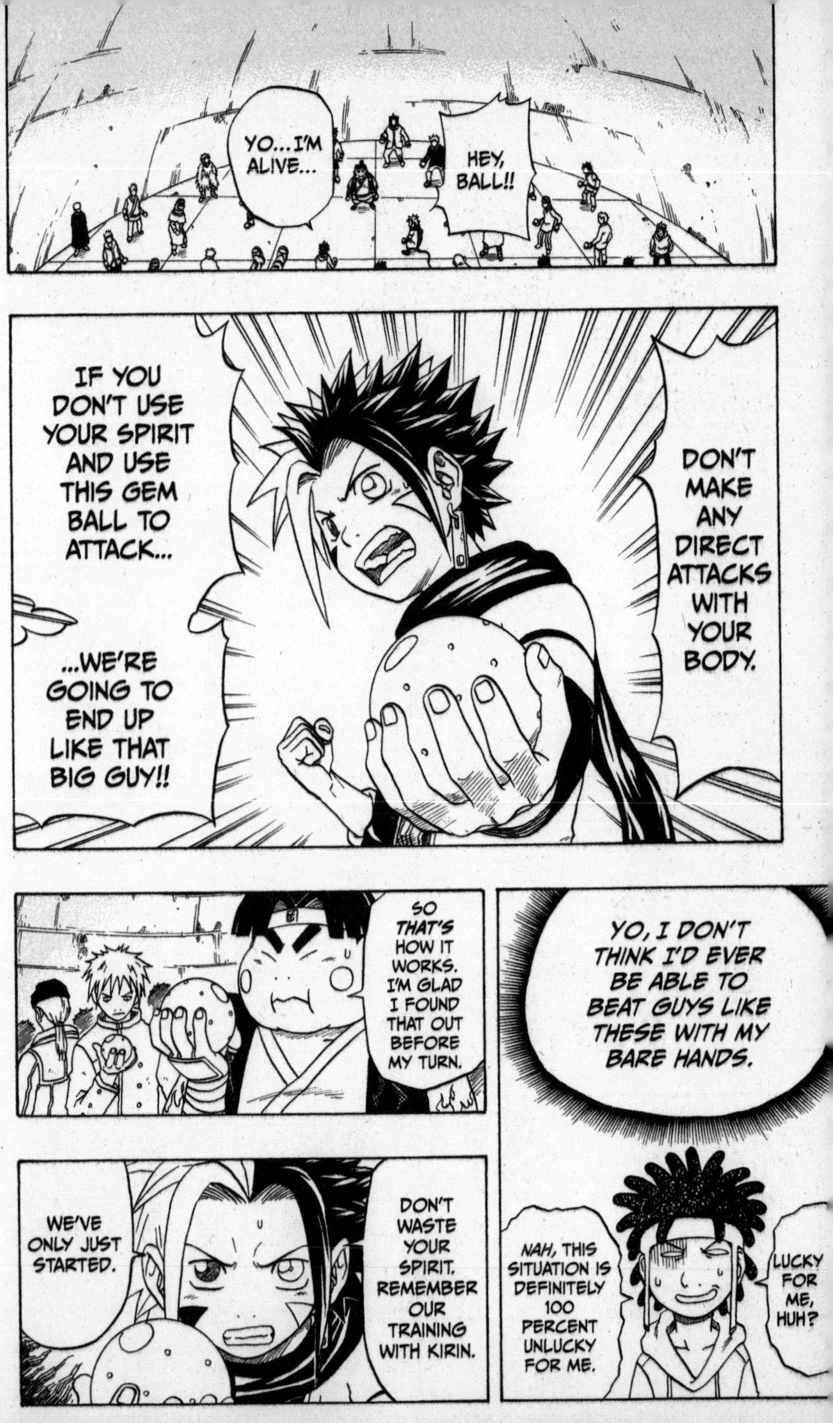
HEY, BALL!!
YO...I'M ALIVE...
DON'T MAKE ANY DIRECT ATTACKS WITH YOUR BODY.
IF YOU DON'T USE YOUR SPIRIT AND USE THIS GEM BALL TO ATTACK...
...WE'RE GOING TO END UP LIKE THAT BIG GUY!!
YO, I DON'T THINK I'D EVER BE ABLE TO BEAT GUYS LIKE THESE WITH MY BARE HANDS.
LUCKY FOR ME, HUH?
NAH, THIS SITUATION IS DEFINITELY 100 PERCENT UNLUCKY FOR ME.
SO THAT'S HOW IT WORKS. I'M GLAD I FOUND THAT OUT BEFORE MY TURN.
DON'T WASTE YOUR SPIRIT. REMEMBER OUR TRAINING WITH KIRIN.
WE'VE ONLY JUST STARTED.

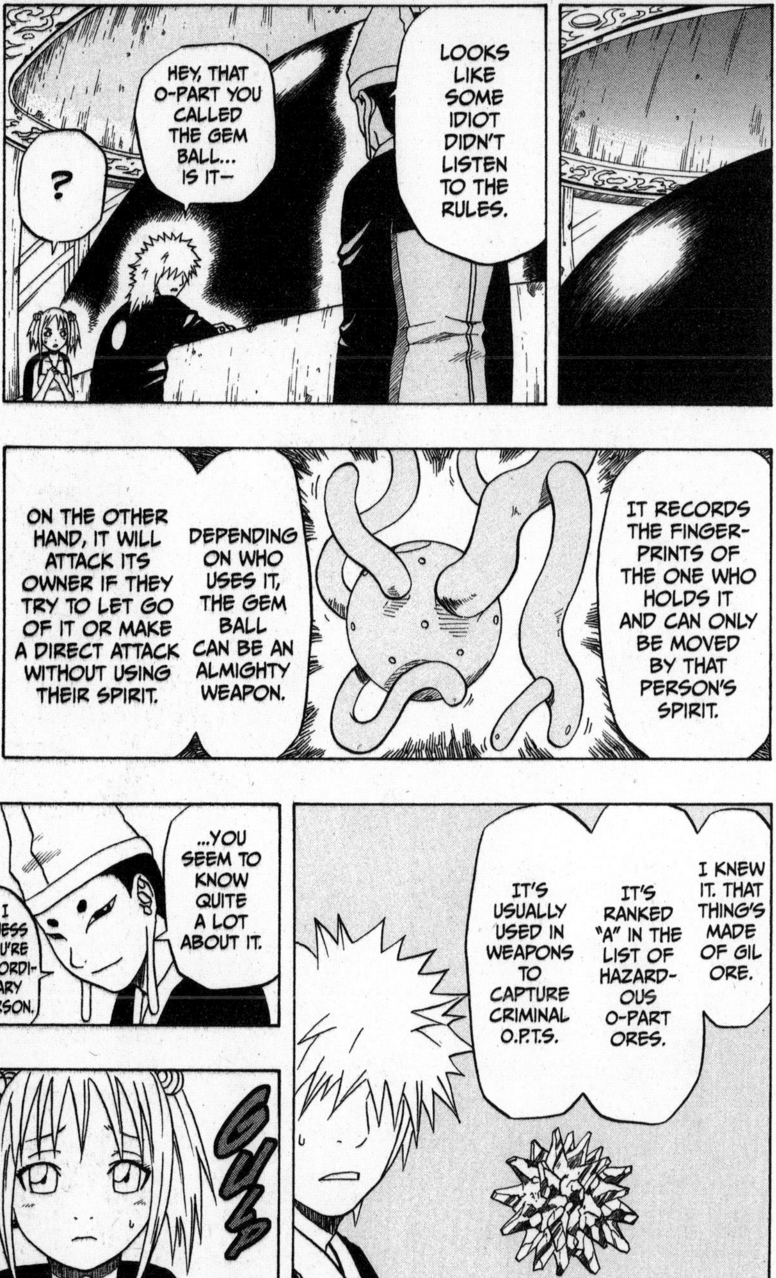

LOOKS LIKE SOME IDIOT DIDN'T LISTEN TO THE RULES.
HEY, THAT O-PART YOU CALLED THE GEM BALL... IS IT—
?
IT RECORDS THE FINGER-PRINTS OF THE ONE WHO HOLDS IT AND CAN ONLY BE MOVED BY THAT PERSON'S SPIRIT.
DEPENDING ON WHO USES IT, THE GEM BALL CAN BE AN ALMIGHTY WEAPON.
ON THE OTHER HAND, IT WILL ATTACK ITS OWNER IF THEY TRY TO LET GO OF IT OR MAKE A DIRECT ATTACK WITHOUT USING THEIR SPIRIT.
I KNEW IT. THAT THING'S MADE OF GIL ORE.
IT'S RANKED "A" IN THE LIST OF HAZARD-OUS O-PART ORES.
IT'S USUALLY USED IN WEAPONS TO CAPTURE CRIMINAL O.P.T.S.
...YOU SEEM TO KNOW QUITE A LOT ABOUT IT.
I GUESS YOU'RE NO ORDI-NARY PERSON.
GULP

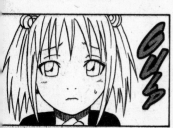

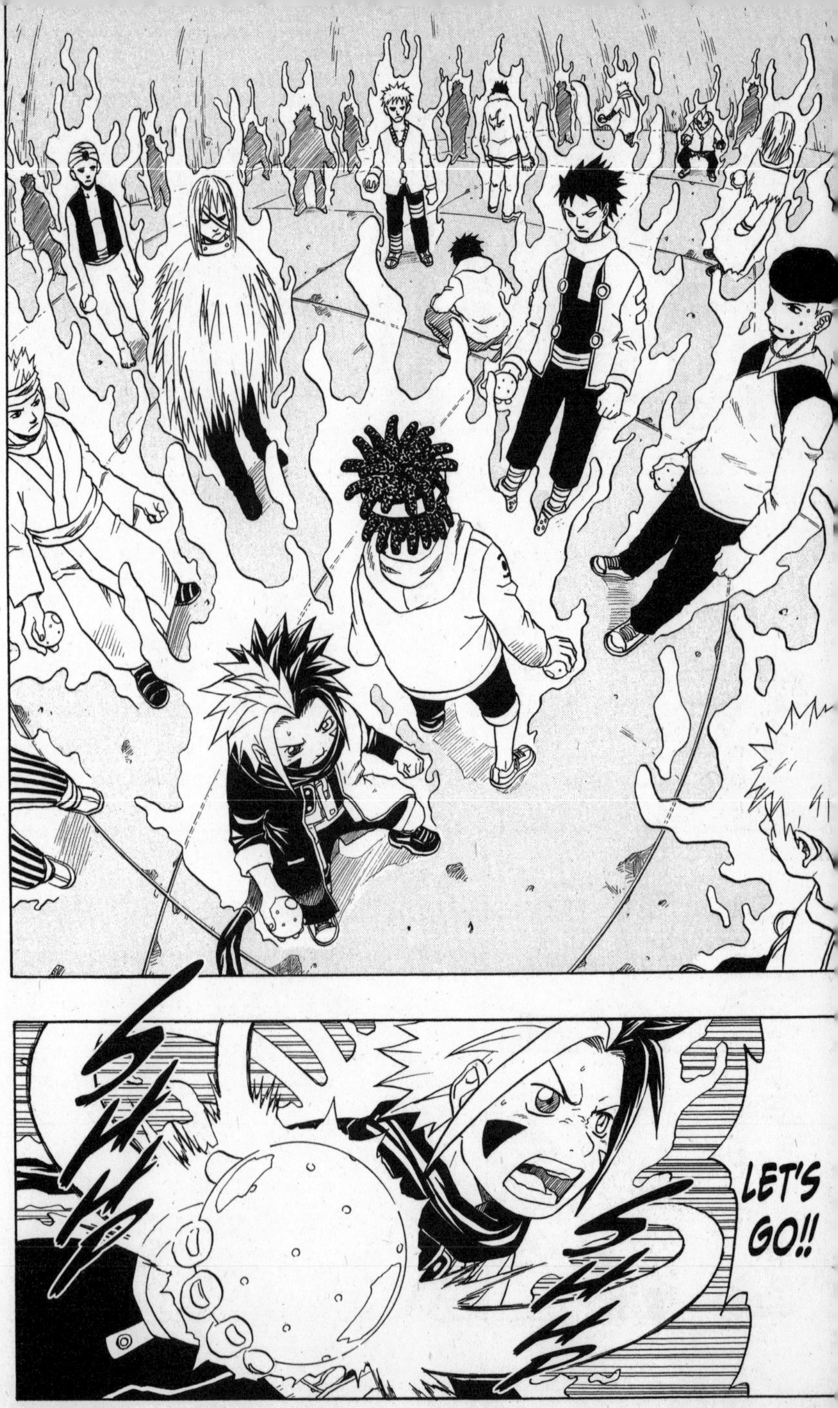
LET'S GO!!

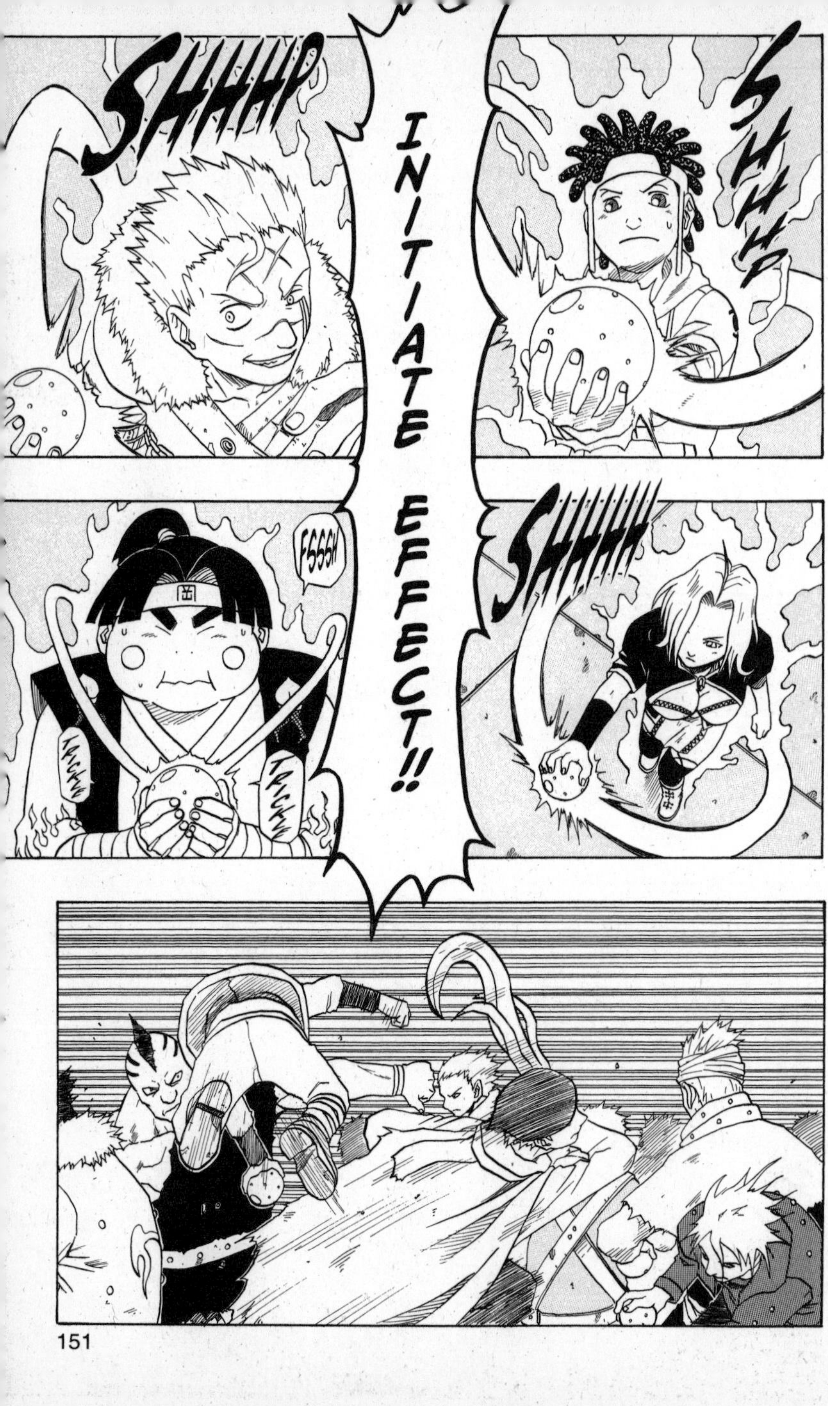
SHHHP
SHHHP
INITIATE EFFECT!!
SHHHH
FSSSH
TRICKLE
TRICKLE

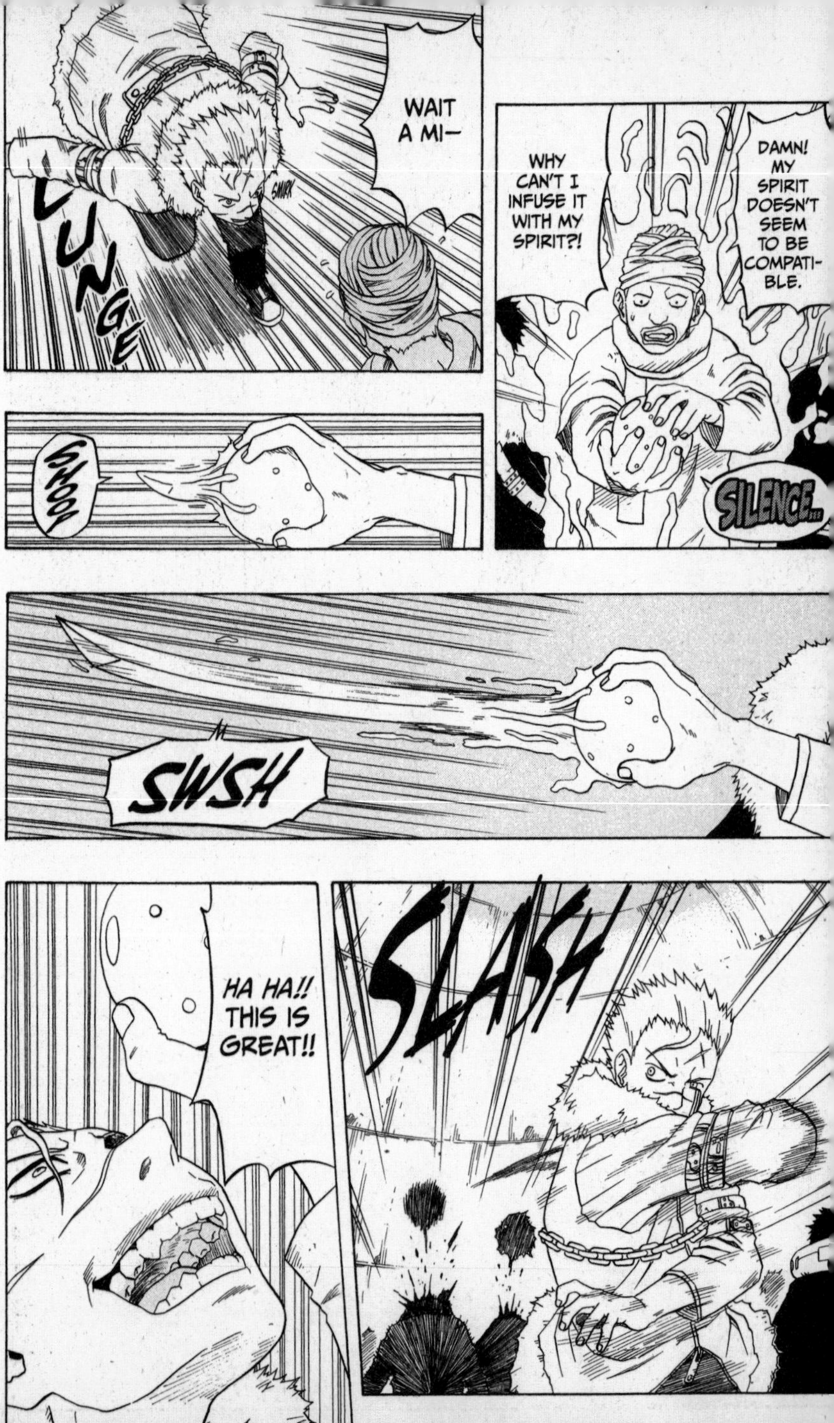
DAMN! MY SPIRIT DOESN'T SEEM TO BE COMPATI-BLE.
WHY CAN'T I INFUSE IT WITH MY SPIRIT?!
SILENCE...
WAIT A MI—
SMIRK
LUNGE
SHOOP
SWSH
SLASH
HA HA!! THIS IS GREAT!!

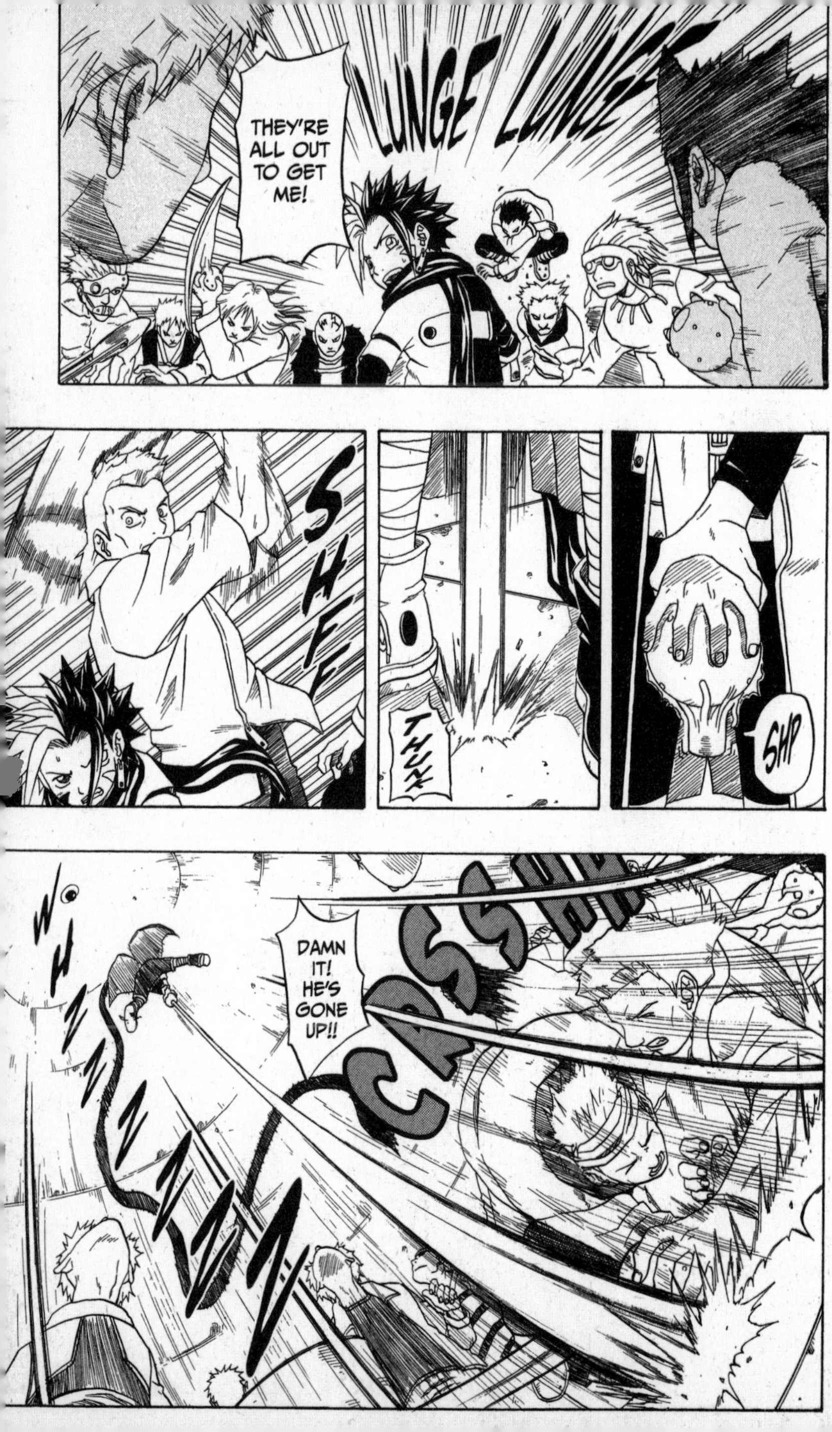
LUNGE LUNGE
THEY'RE ALL OUT TO GET ME!
SHP
THUNK
SHFF
CRSS
DAMN IT! HE'S GONE UP!!
WHNNNNNN

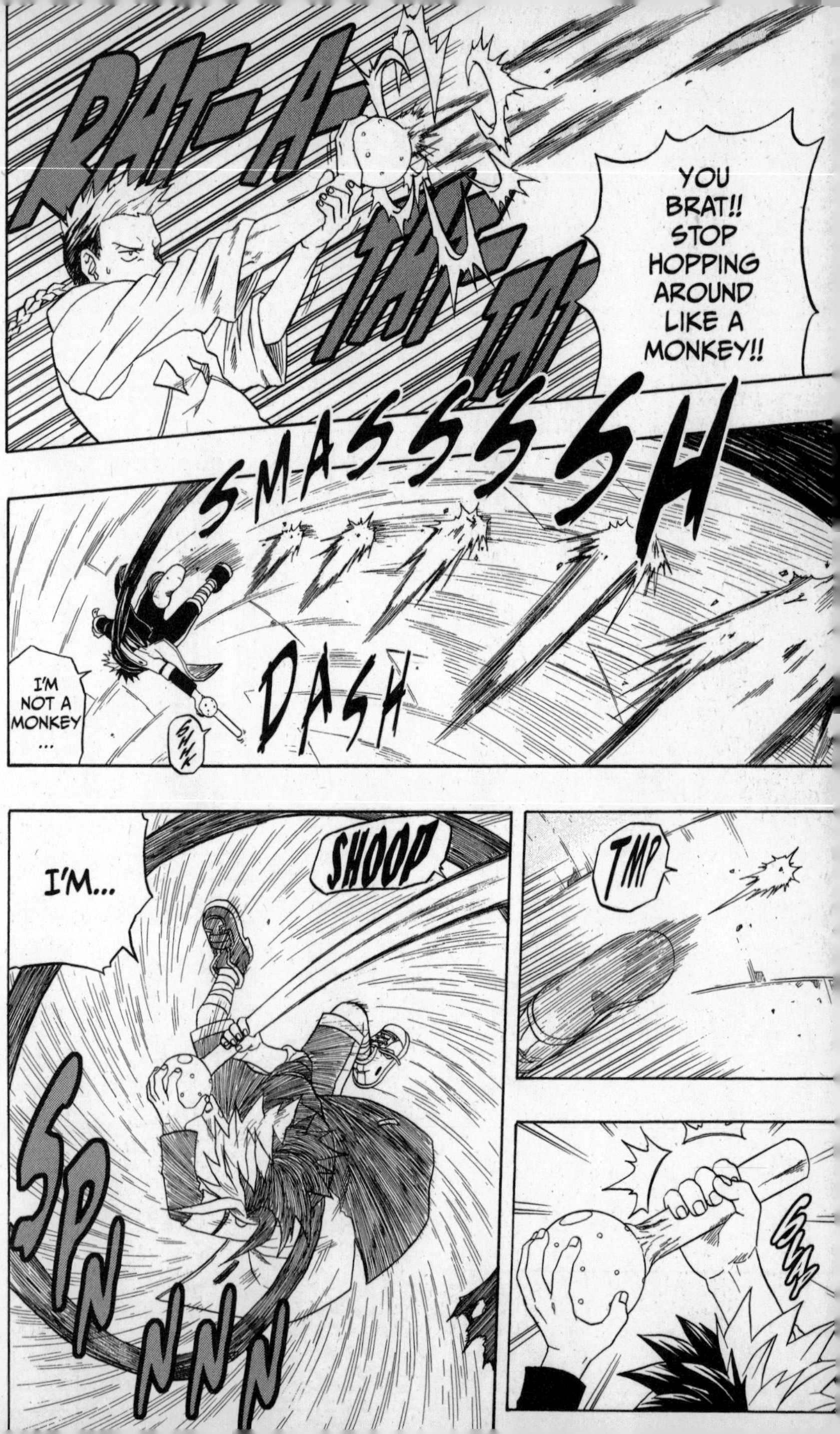
PAT-A-TAT-TA
YOU BRAT!! STOP HOPPING AROUND LIKE A MONKEY!!
SMASSSSH
DASH
I'M NOT A MONKEY ...
TMP
SHOOP
I'M...
SPNNNN

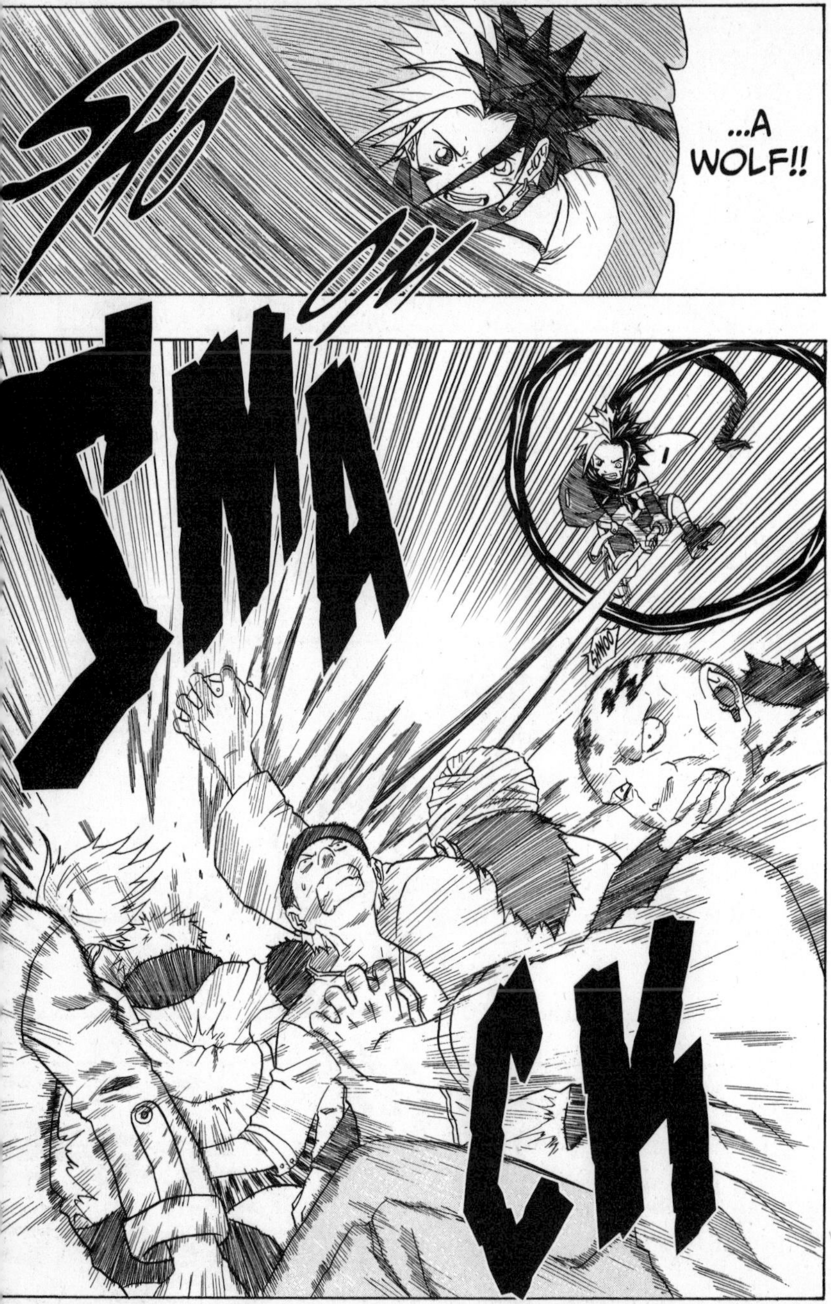
...A WOLF!!
SHOOM
SHWOO
SMACK

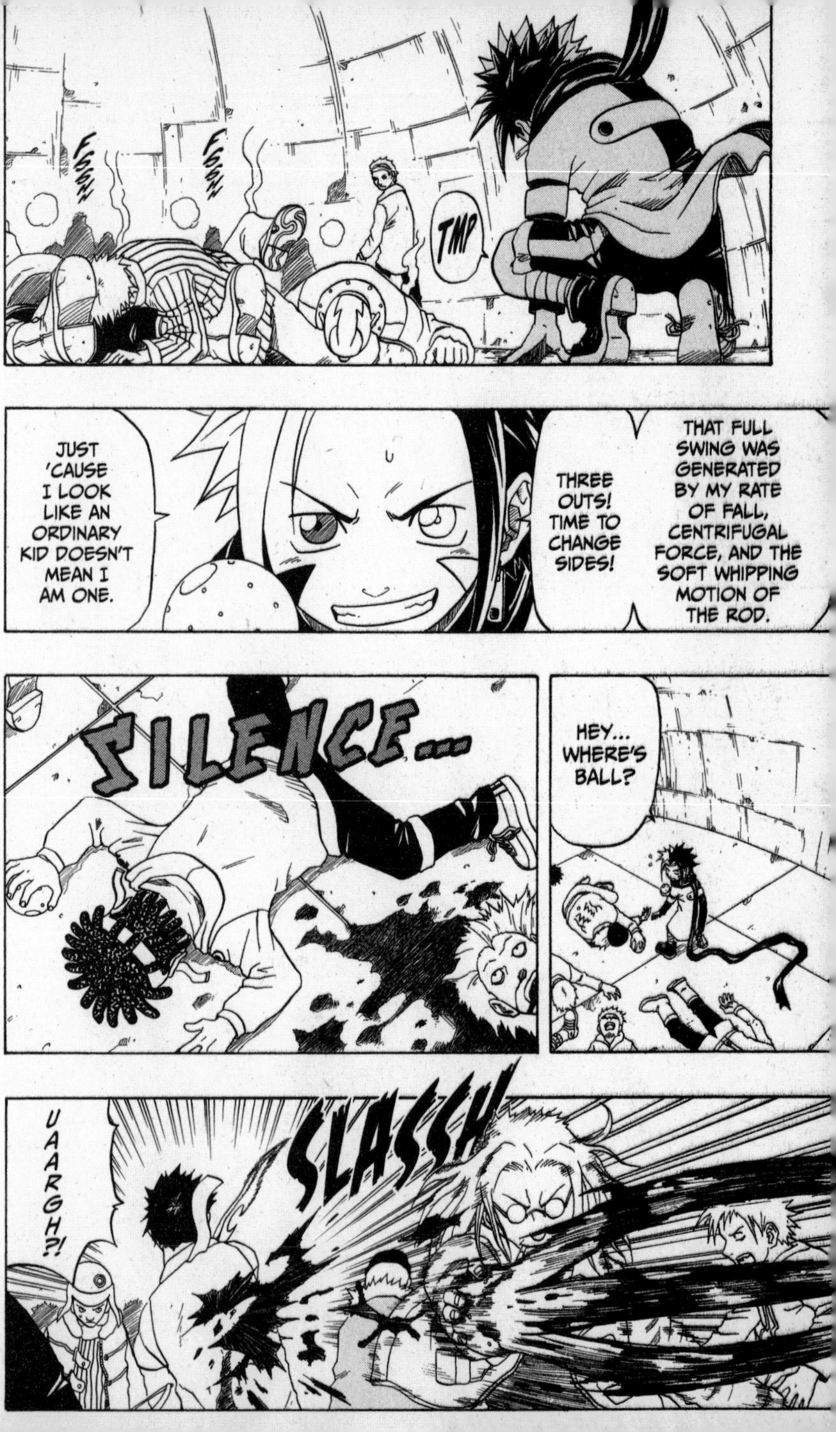
TMP
FSSSH
FSSSH
THAT FULL SWING WAS GENERATED BY MY RATE OF FALL, CENTRIFUGAL FORCE, AND THE SOFT WHIPPING MOTION OF THE ROD.
THREE OUTS! TIME TO CHANGE SIDES!
JUST 'CAUSE I LOOK LIKE AN ORDINARY KID DOESN'T MEAN I AM ONE.
HEY... WHERE'S BALL?
SILENCE...
SLASSH!
UAARGH?!

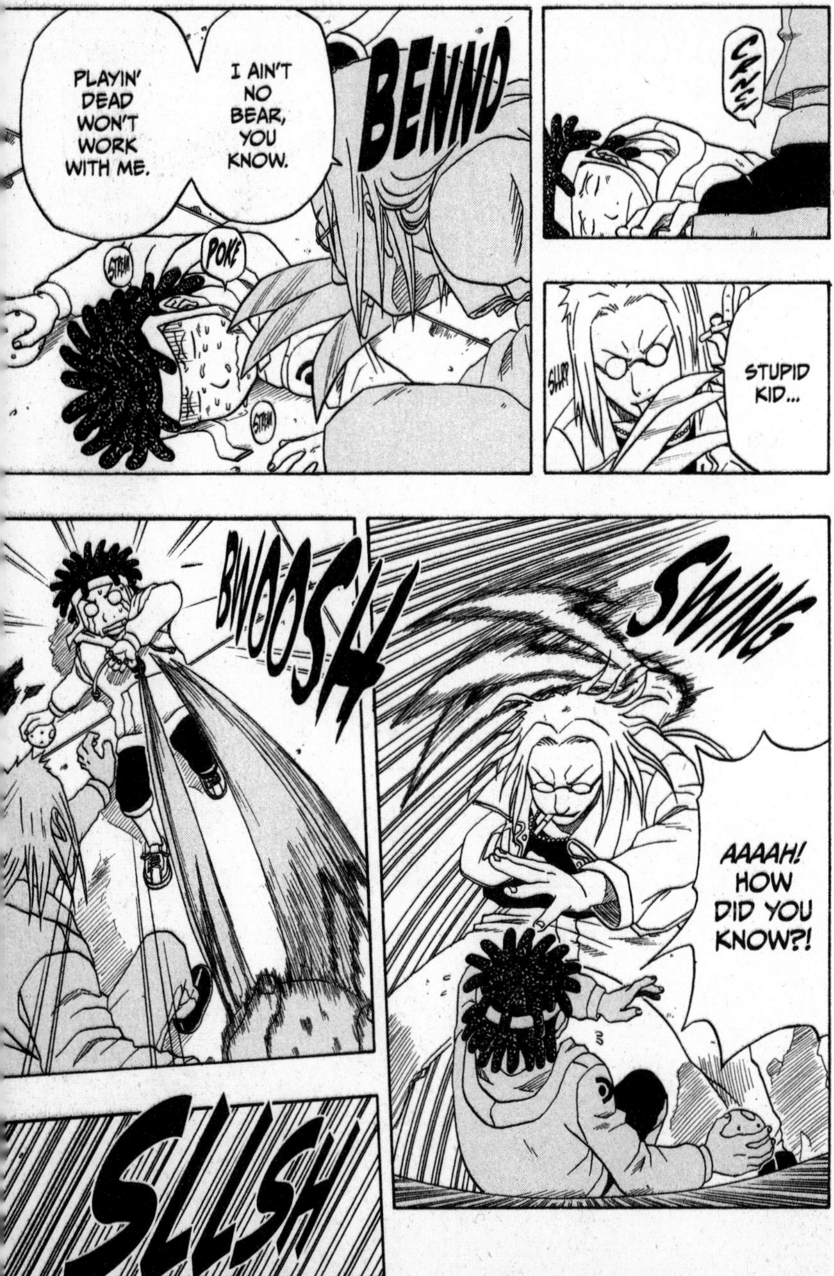
CANCH
SLURP
STUPID KID...
I AIN'T NO BEAR, YOU KNOW.
PLAYIN' DEAD WON'T WORK WITH ME.
BENND
POKE
STREAM
STREAM
SWING
AAAAH! HOW DID YOU KNOW?!
BWOOSH
SLLSH

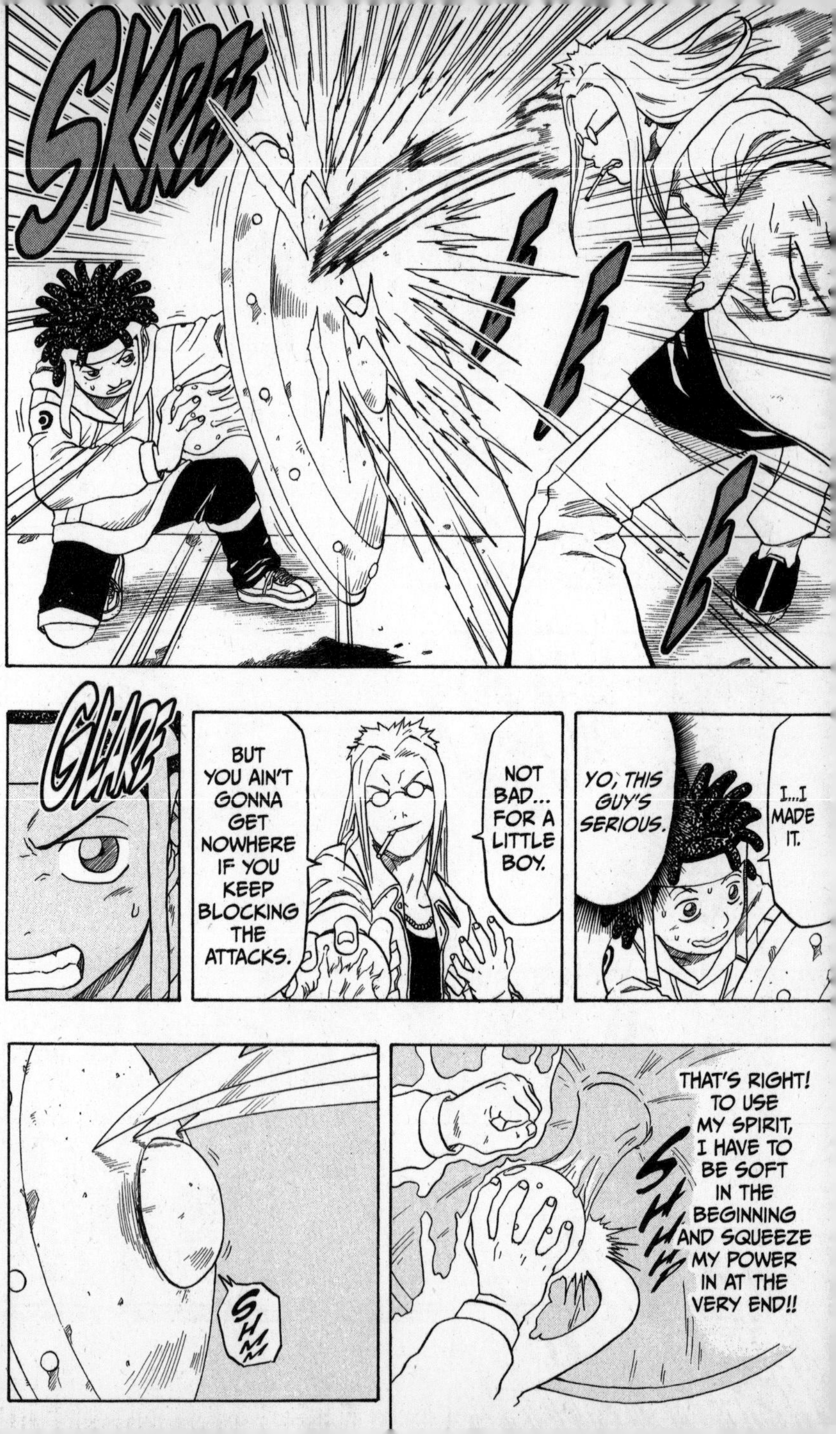
SKREE
I...I MADE IT.
YO, THIS GUY'S SERIOUS.
NOT BAD... FOR A LITTLE BOY.
BUT YOU AIN'T GONNA GET NOWHERE IF YOU KEEP BLOCKING THE ATTACKS.
GLARE
THAT'S RIGHT! TO USE MY SPIRIT, I HAVE TO BE SOFT IN THE BEGINNING AND SQUEEZE MY POWER IN AT THE VERY END!!
SHHH
SHM

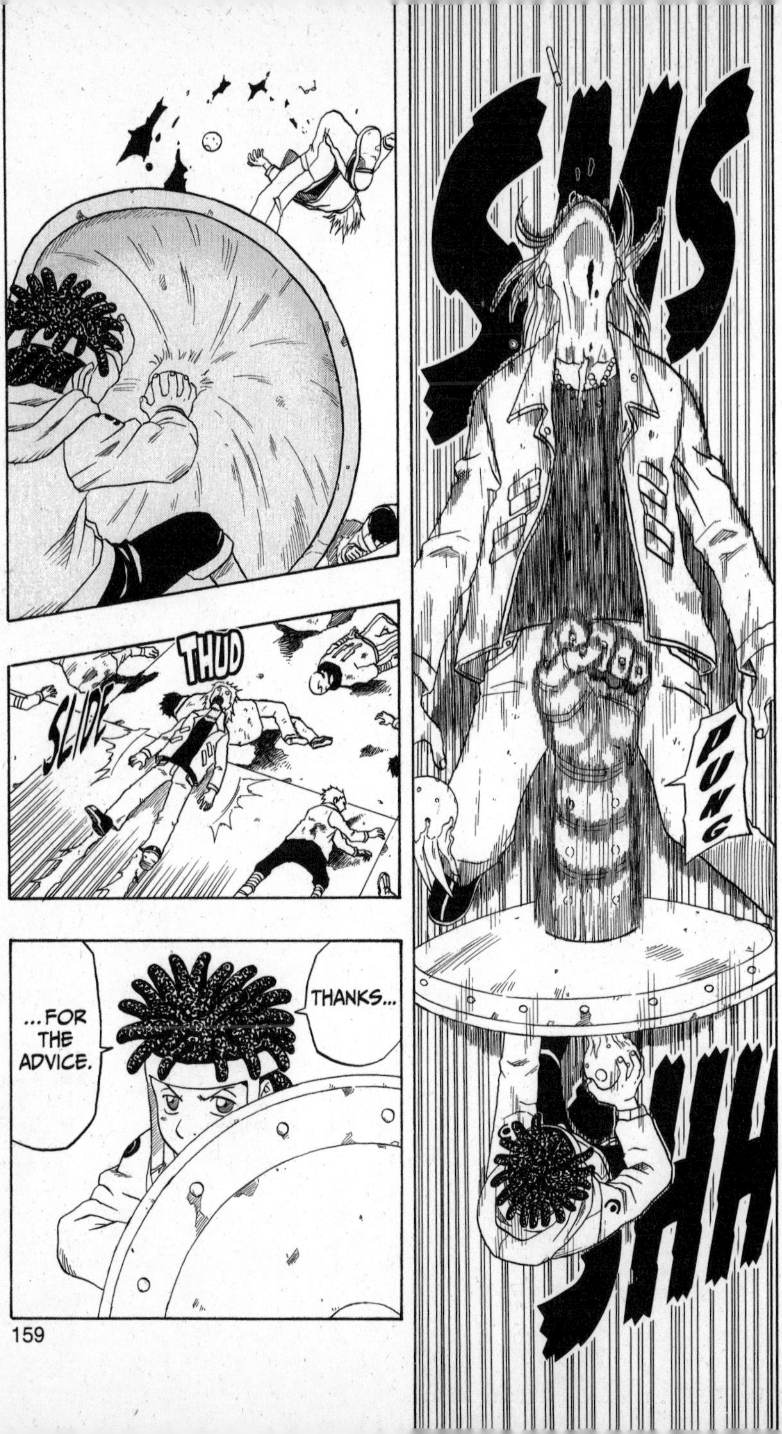
PUNG
THUD
SLIDE
THANKS...
...FOR THE ADVICE.

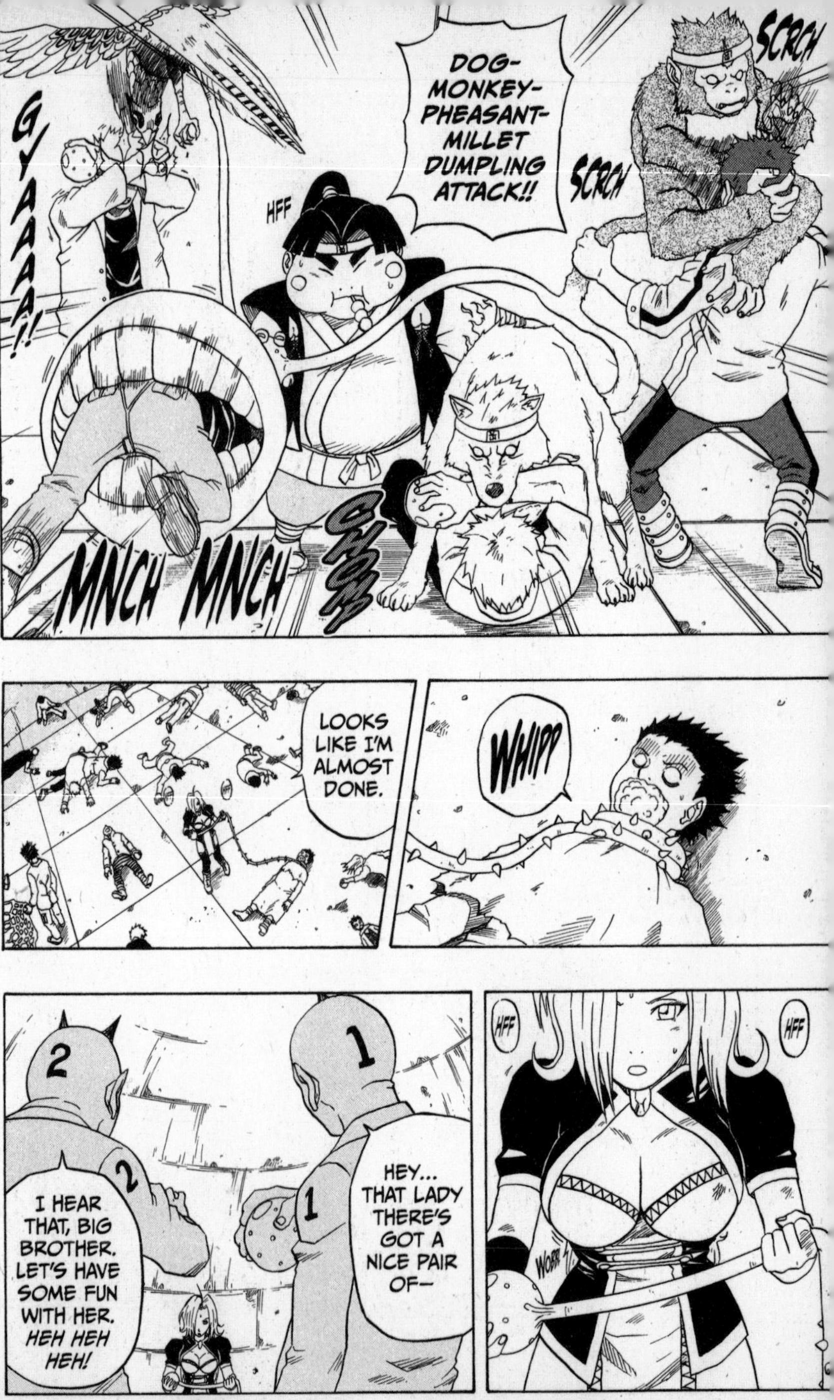
SCRCH
SCRCH
DOG-MONKEY-PHEASANT-MILLET DUMPLING ATTACK!!
HFF
GYAAAAA!!
CHOMP
MNCH MNCH
WHIP
LOOKS LIKE I'M ALMOST DONE.
HFF
HFF
WOBB
HEY... THAT LADY THERE'S GOT A NICE PAIR OF–
I HEAR THAT, BIG BROTHER. LET'S HAVE SOME FUN WITH HER. HEH HEH HEH!

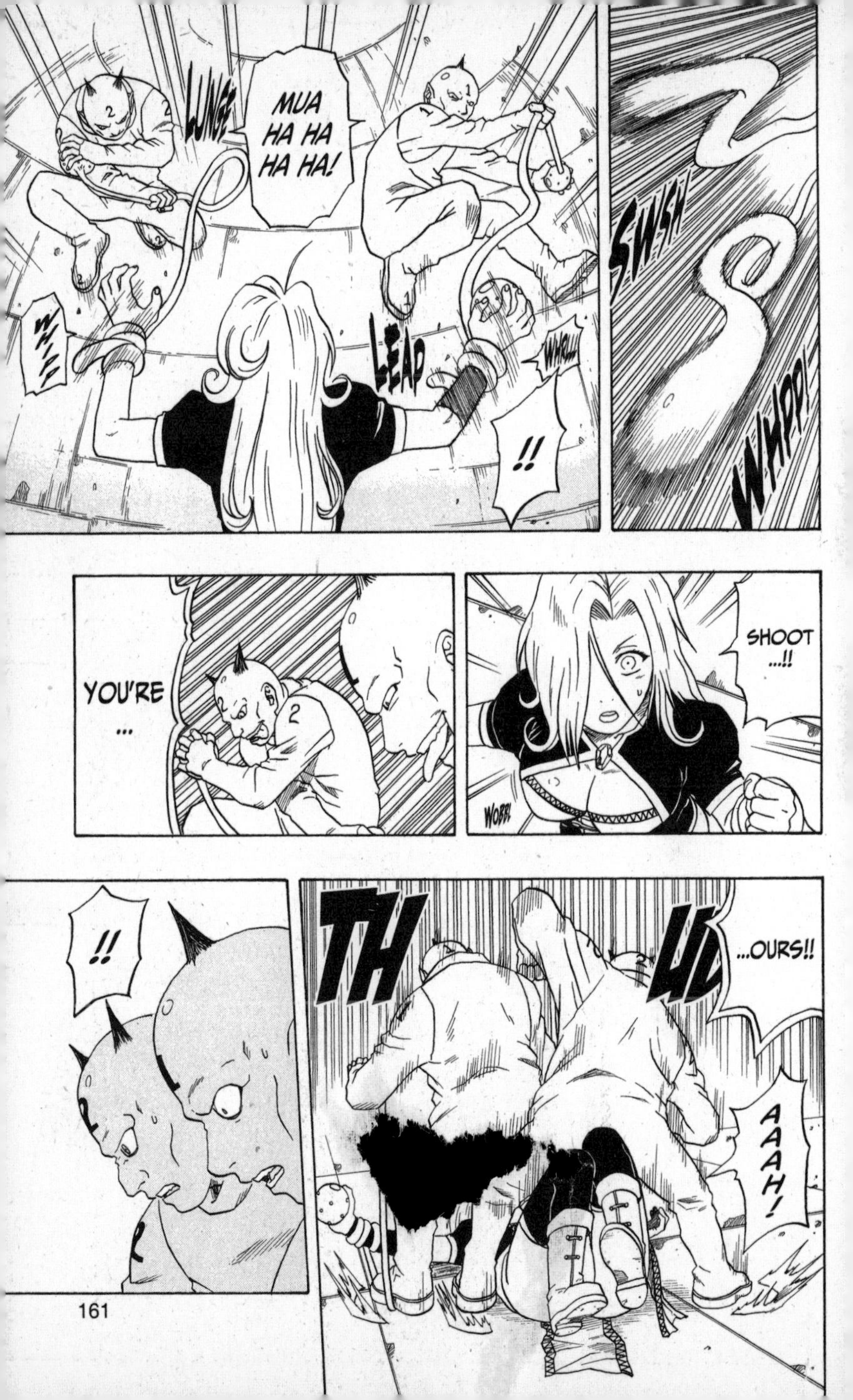
SWISH
WHPP!
MUA HA HA HA HA!
LUNGE
LEAP
!!
SHOOT ...!!
WOBBL
YOU'RE ...
TH
...OURS!!
AAAH!
!!

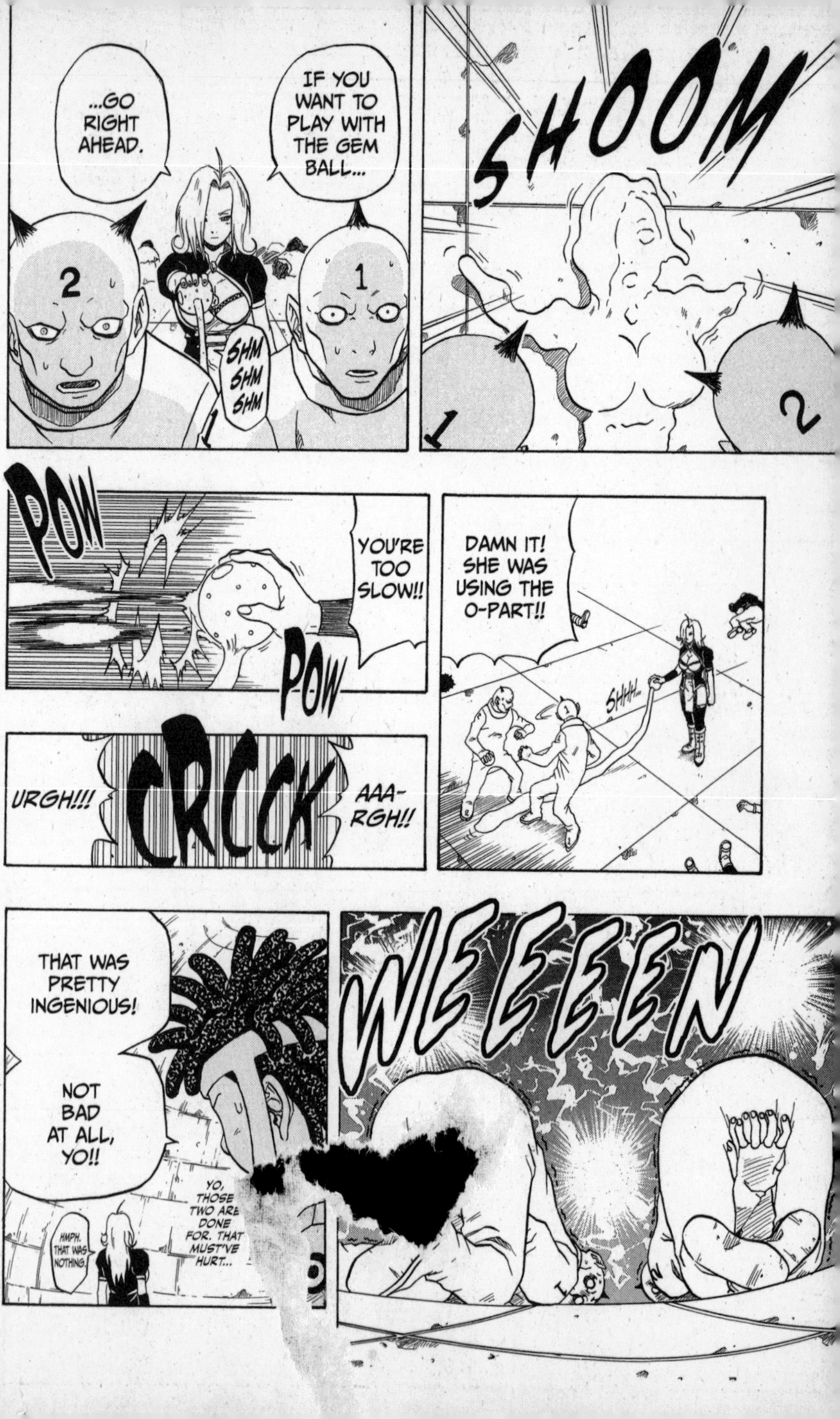
SHOOM
IF YOU WANT TO PLAY WITH THE GEM BALL...
...GO RIGHT AHEAD.
SHM SHM SHM
DAMN IT! SHE WAS USING THE O-PART!!
SHHH...
POW
YOU'RE TOO SLOW!!
POW
AAA-RGH!!
CRCCK
URGH!!!
WEEEEN
THAT WAS PRETTY INGENIOUS!
NOT BAD AT ALL, YO!!
YO, THOSE TWO ARE DONE FOR. THAT MUST'VE HURT...
HMPH. THAT WAS NOTHING.

WHOA!!

CHOMP

GOTCHA!!

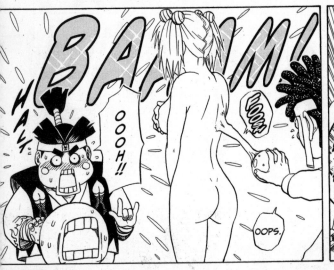

BAM!!

OOOH!!

OOPS.

DAMN YOU!

AH!!

GAPE

N-NICE THIGHS.

D-DANG IT! I COULDN'T HELP IMAGINING RUBY NAKED!!

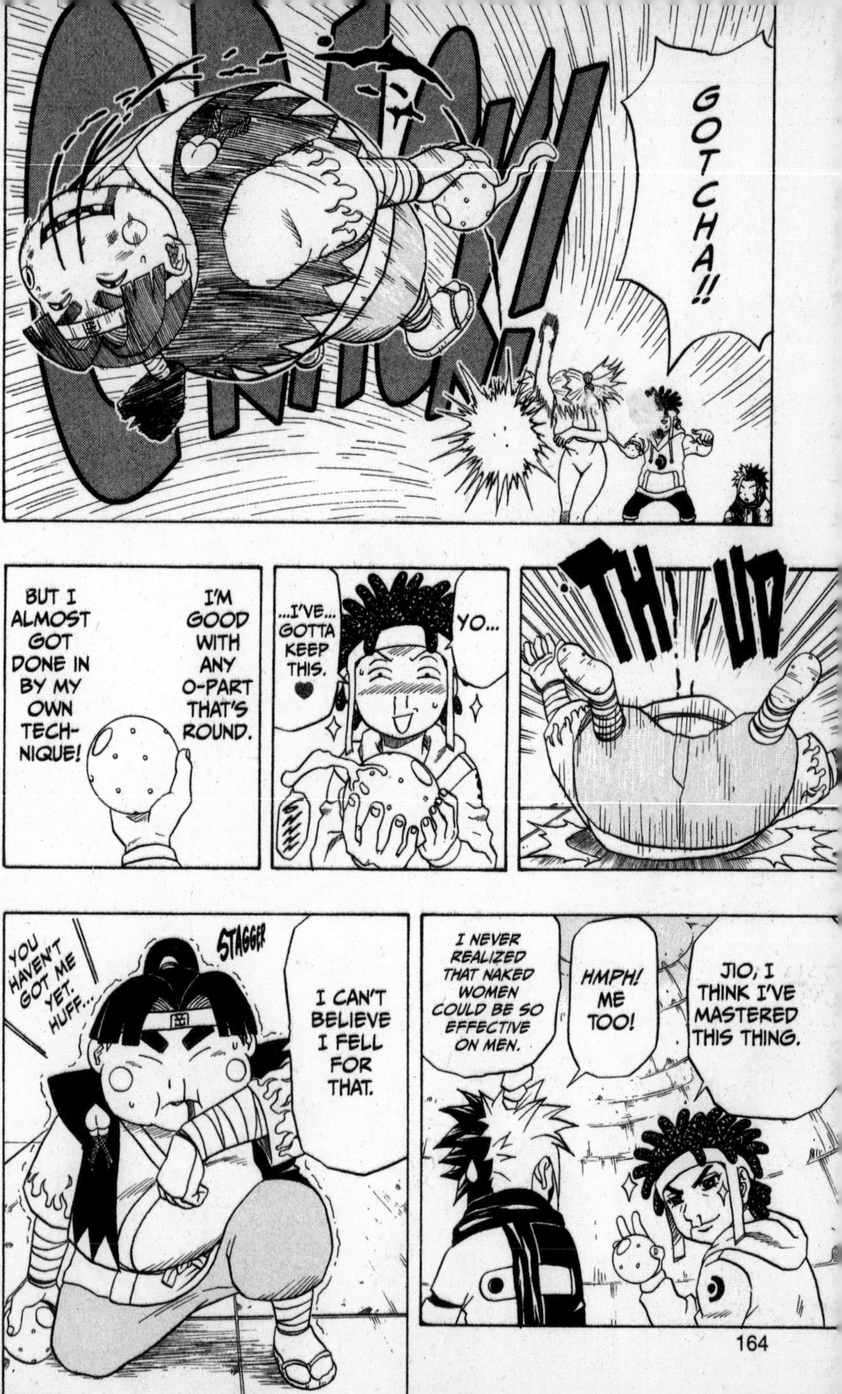
GOTCHA!!
THUD
YO...
...I'VE... GOTTA KEEP THIS. ♥
I'M GOOD WITH ANY O-PART THAT'S ROUND.
BUT I ALMOST GOT DONE IN BY MY OWN TECH-NIQUE!
JIO, I THINK I'VE MASTERED THIS THING.
HMPH! ME TOO!
I NEVER REALIZED THAT NAKED WOMEN COULD BE SO EFFECTIVE ON MEN.
I CAN'T BELIEVE I FELL FOR THAT.
STAGGER
YOU HAVEN'T GOT ME YET. HUFF...

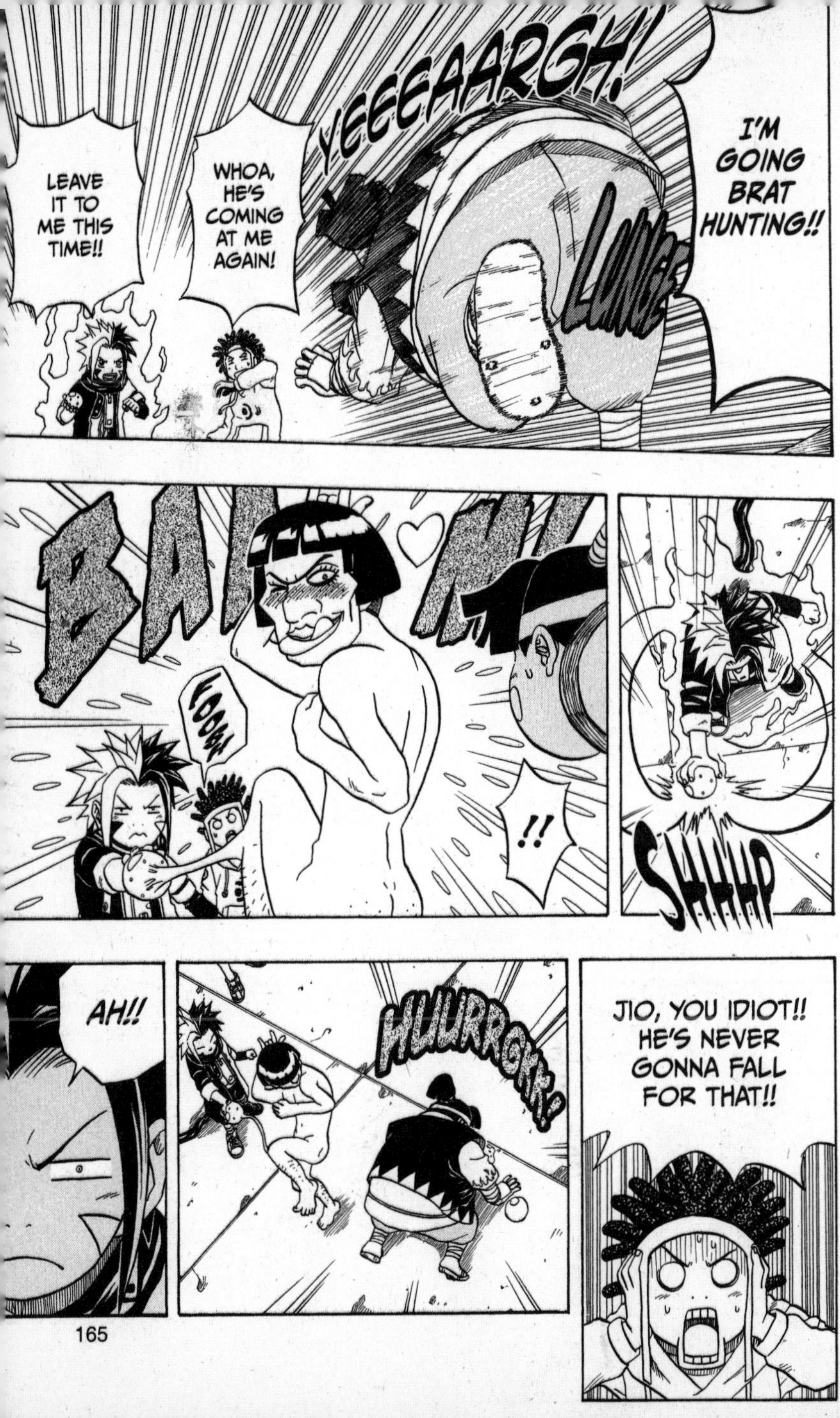
I'M GOING BRAT HUNTING!!
YEEEAARGH!
LUNGE
WHOA, HE'S COMING AT ME AGAIN!
LEAVE IT TO ME THIS TIME!!
SHHHP
!!
JIO, YOU IDIOT!! HE'S NEVER GONNA FALL FOR THAT!!
WUURRGKK!
AH!!

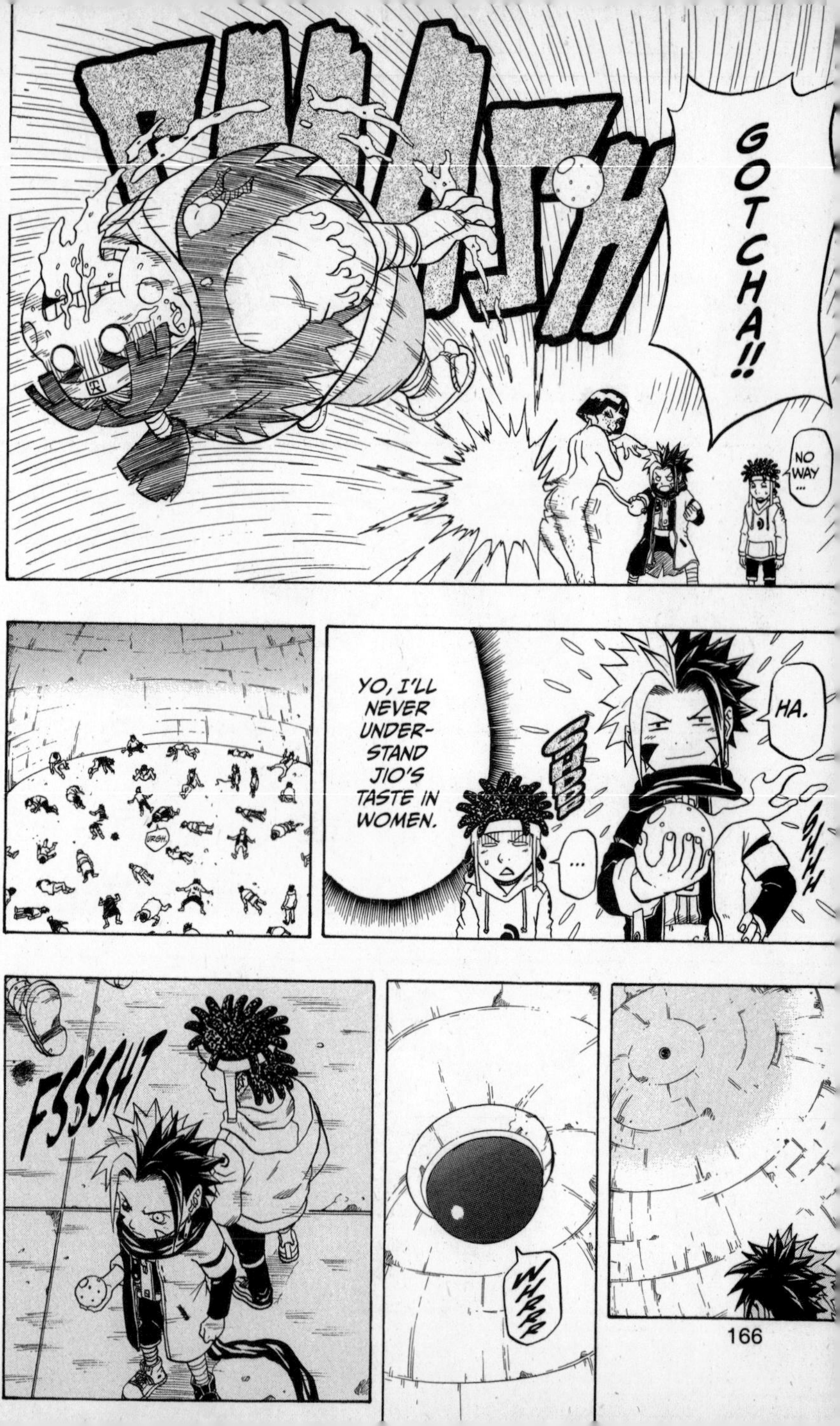
GOTCHA!!
NO WAY...
HA.
SHHH
YO, I'LL NEVER UNDER-STAND JIO'S TASTE IN WOMEN.
...
URGH.
WHRRR
FSSSHT

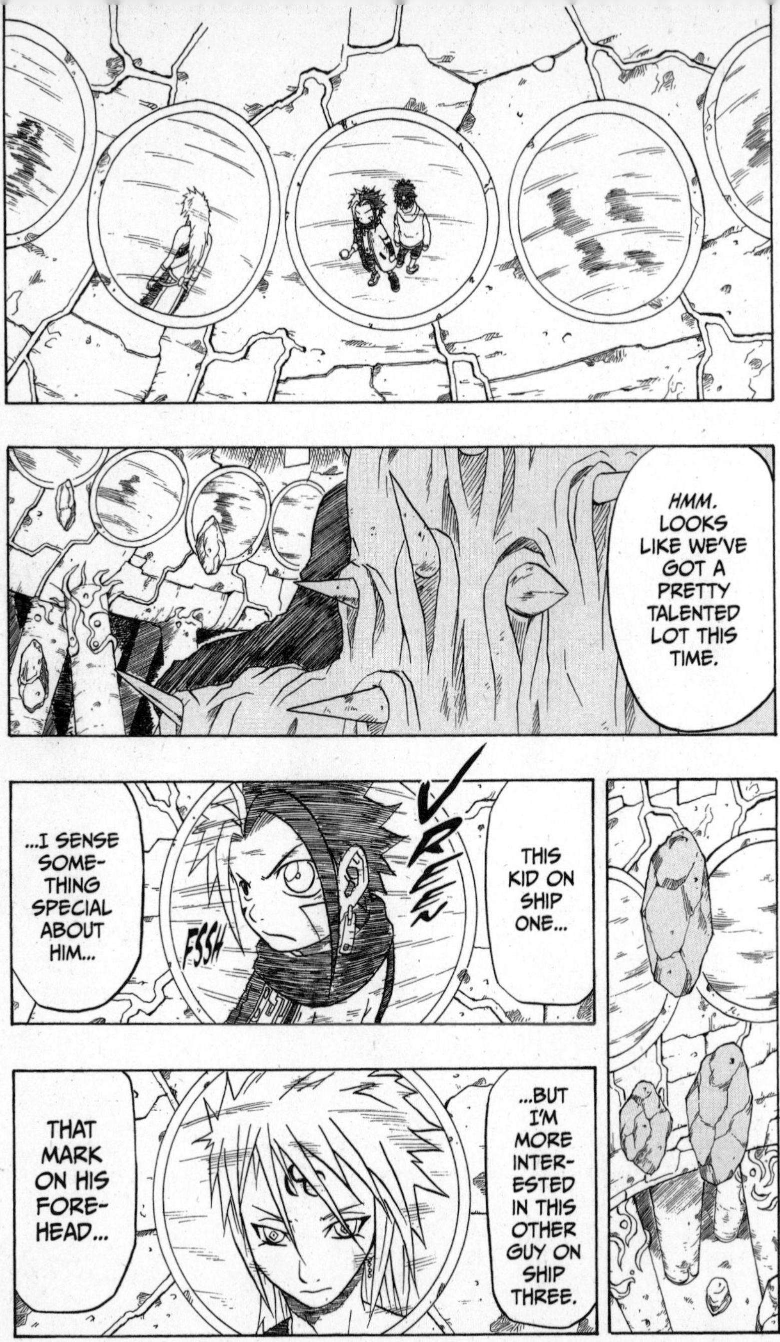
HMM. LOOKS LIKE WE'VE GOT A PRETTY TALENTED LOT THIS TIME.
THIS KID ON SHIP ONE...
VREEN
...I SENSE SOME-THING SPECIAL ABOUT HIM...
FSSH
...BUT I'M MORE INTER-ESTED IN THIS OTHER GUY ON SHIP THREE.
THAT MARK ON HIS FORE-HEAD...

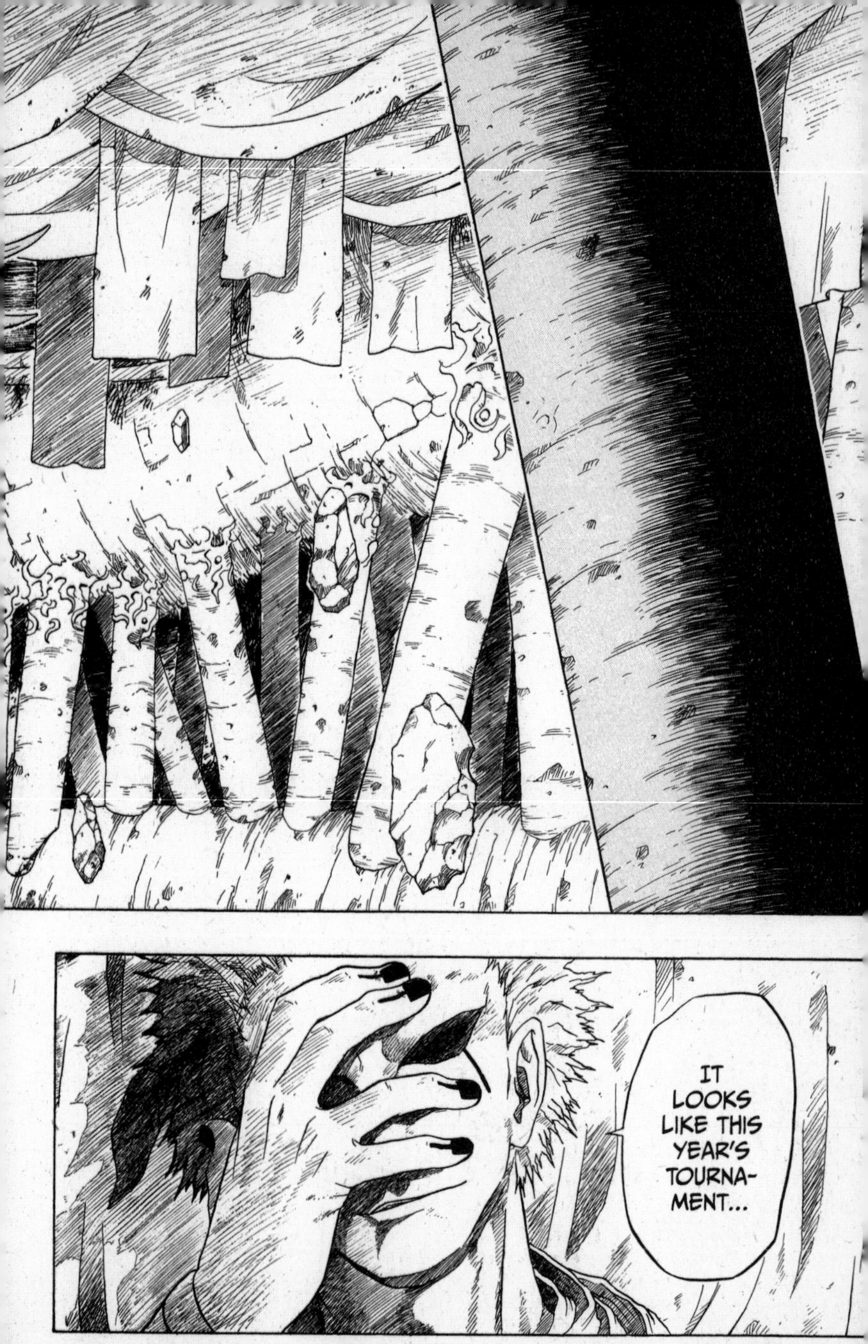
IT LOOKS LIKE THIS YEAR'S TOURNAMENT...

WELL, WHOEVER THEY ARE...

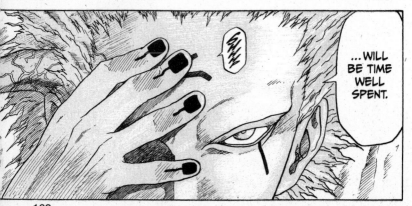

...WILL BE TIME WELL SPENT.

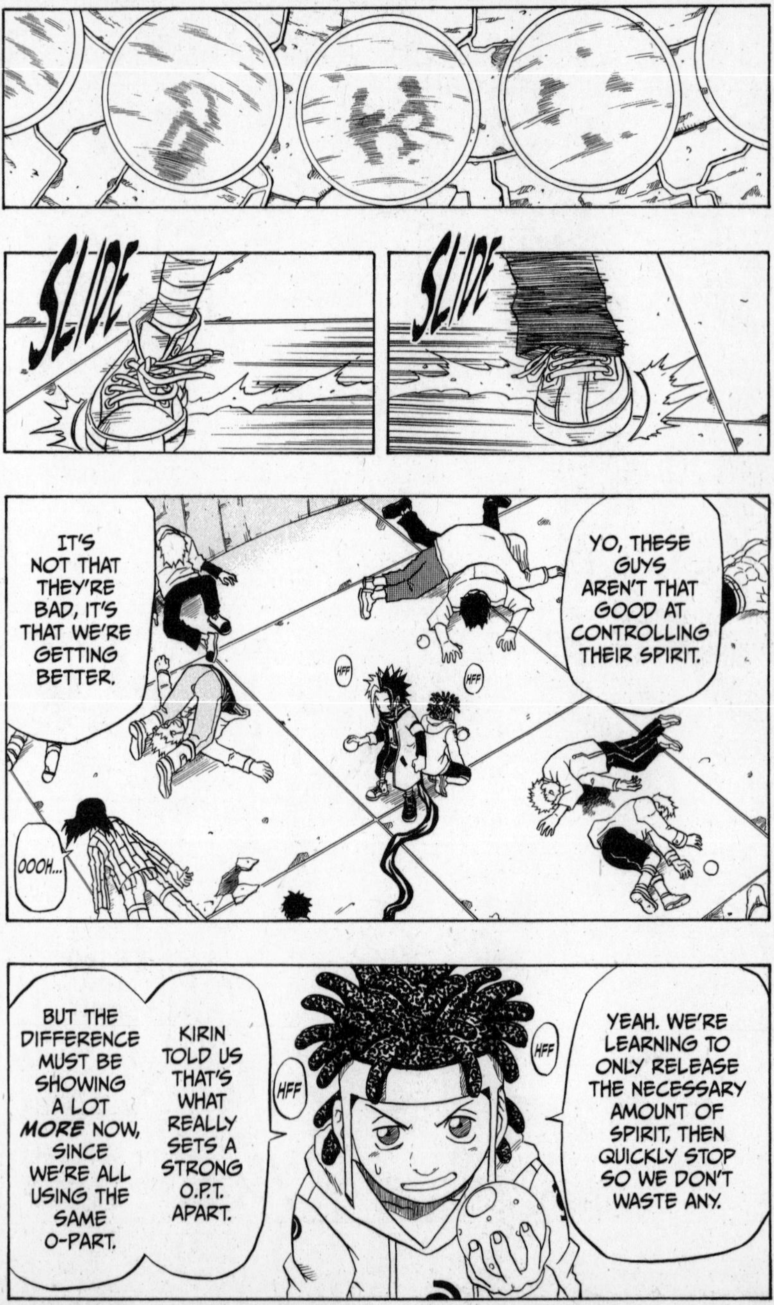

SLIDE
SLIDE
YO, THESE GUYS AREN'T THAT GOOD AT CONTROLLING THEIR SPIRIT.
IT'S NOT THAT THEY'RE BAD, IT'S THAT WE'RE GETTING BETTER.
HFF
HFF
OOOH...
YEAH. WE'RE LEARNING TO ONLY RELEASE THE NECESSARY AMOUNT OF SPIRIT, THEN QUICKLY STOP SO WE DON'T WASTE ANY.
HFF
HFF
KIRIN TOLD US THAT'S WHAT REALLY SETS A STRONG O.P.T. APART.
BUT THE DIFFERENCE MUST BE SHOWING A LOT *MORE* NOW, SINCE WE'RE ALL USING THE SAME O-PART.

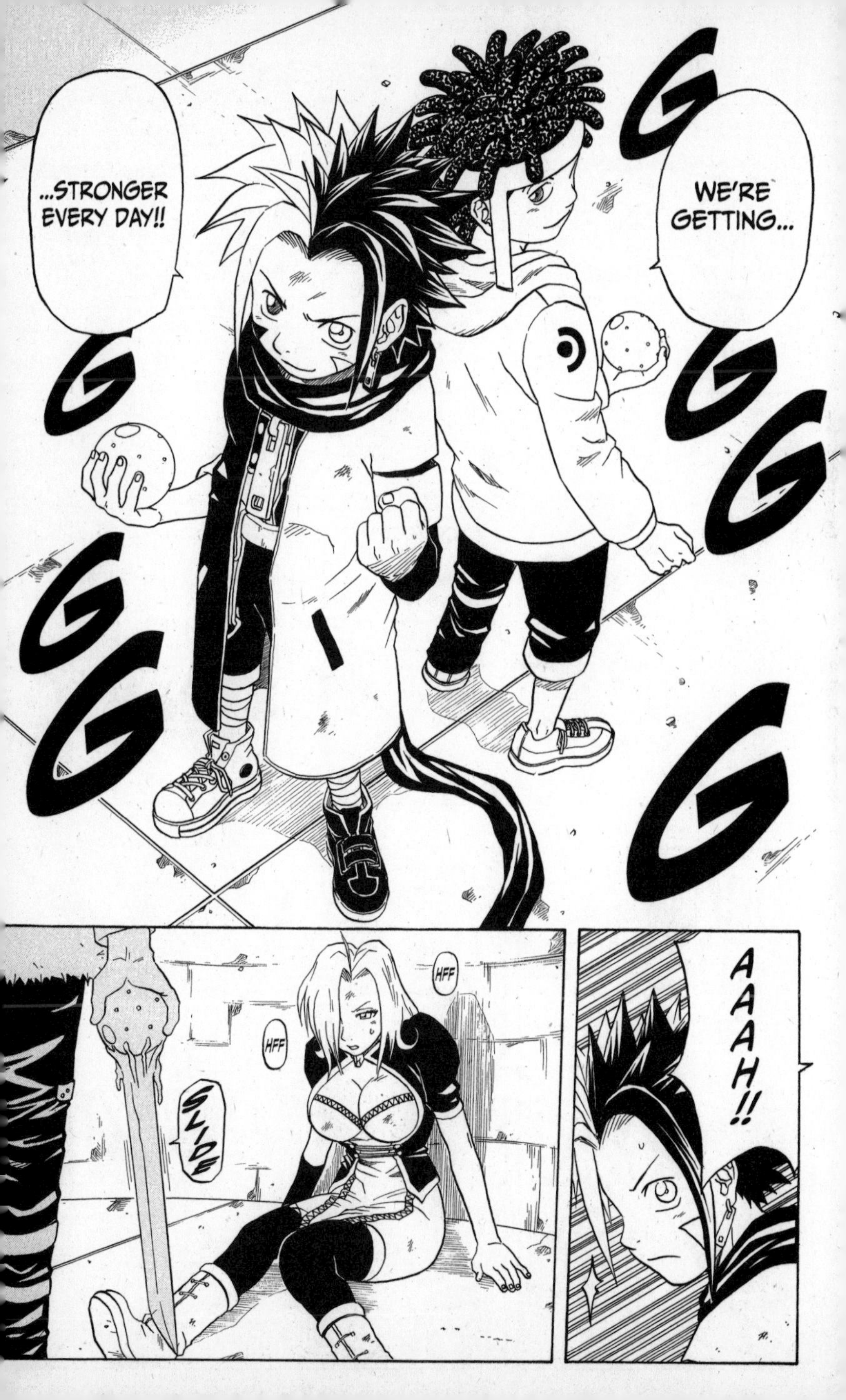
GGGGG
WE'RE GETTING...
...STRONGER EVERY DAY!!
GGG
AAAAH!!
HFF
HFF
SLIDE

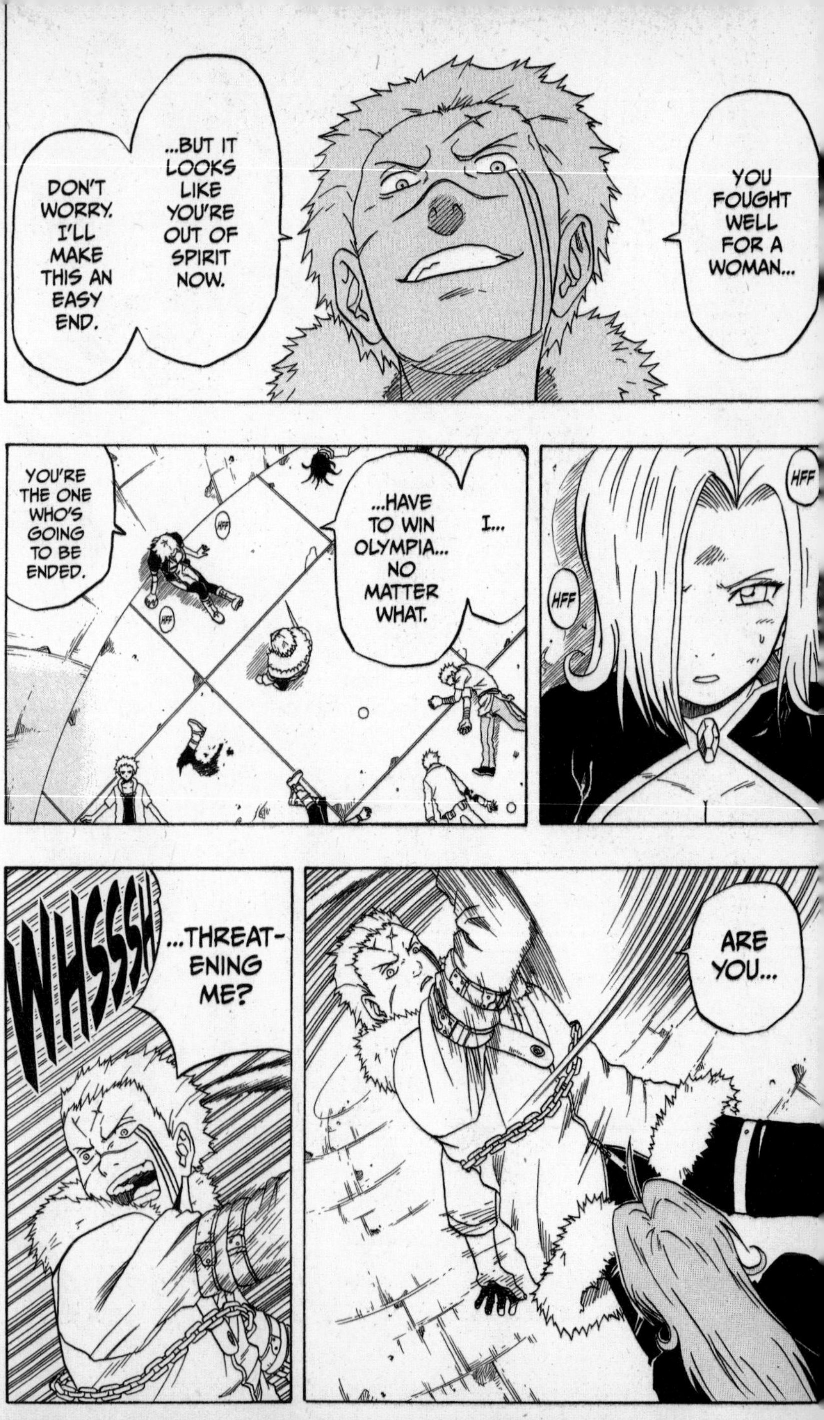
YOU FOUGHT WELL FOR A WOMAN...
...BUT IT LOOKS LIKE YOU'RE OUT OF SPIRIT NOW.
DON'T WORRY. I'LL MAKE THIS AN EASY END.
HFF
HFF
I...
...HAVE TO WIN OLYMPIA... NO MATTER WHAT.
HFF
HFF
YOU'RE THE ONE WHO'S GOING TO BE ENDED.
ARE YOU...
...THREAT-ENING ME?
WHSSSH

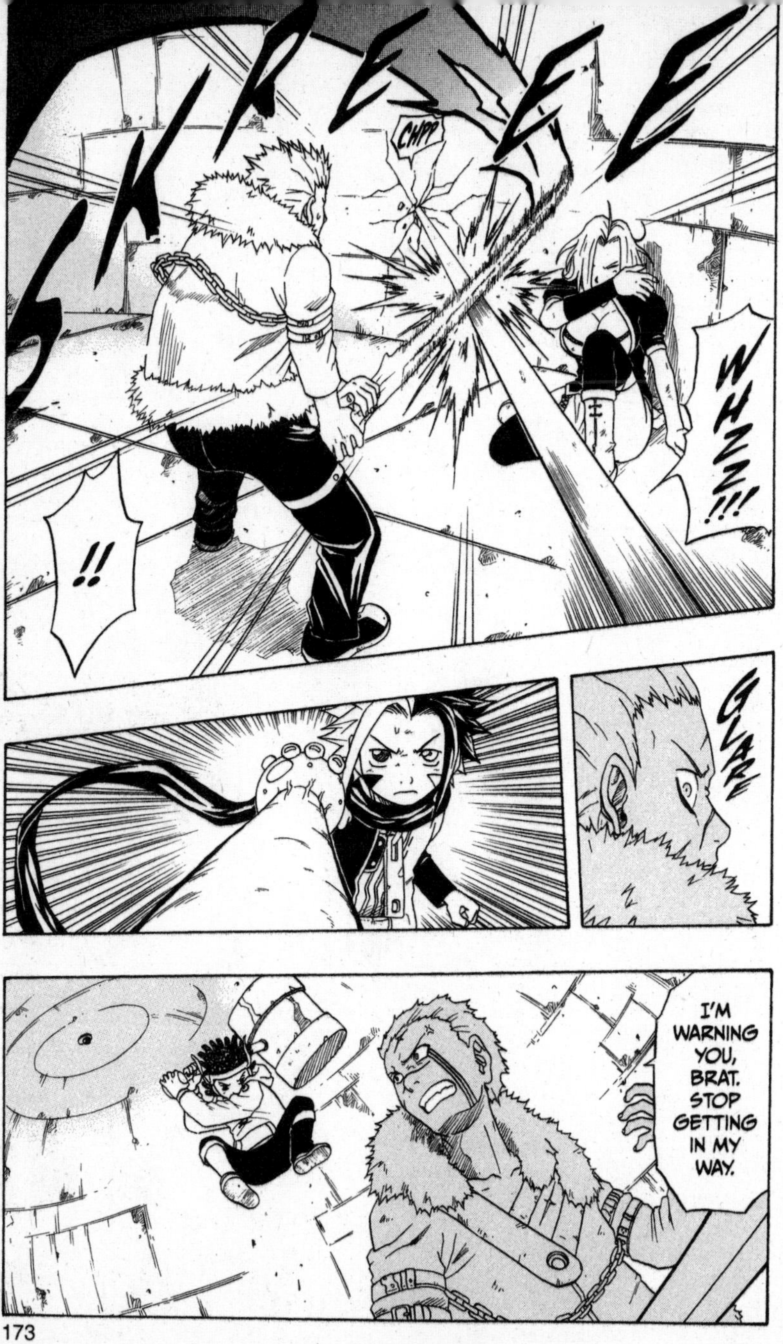
SKREEEE
CHPP
WHZZZ!!!
!!
GLARE
I'M WARNING YOU, BRAT. STOP GETTING IN MY WAY.

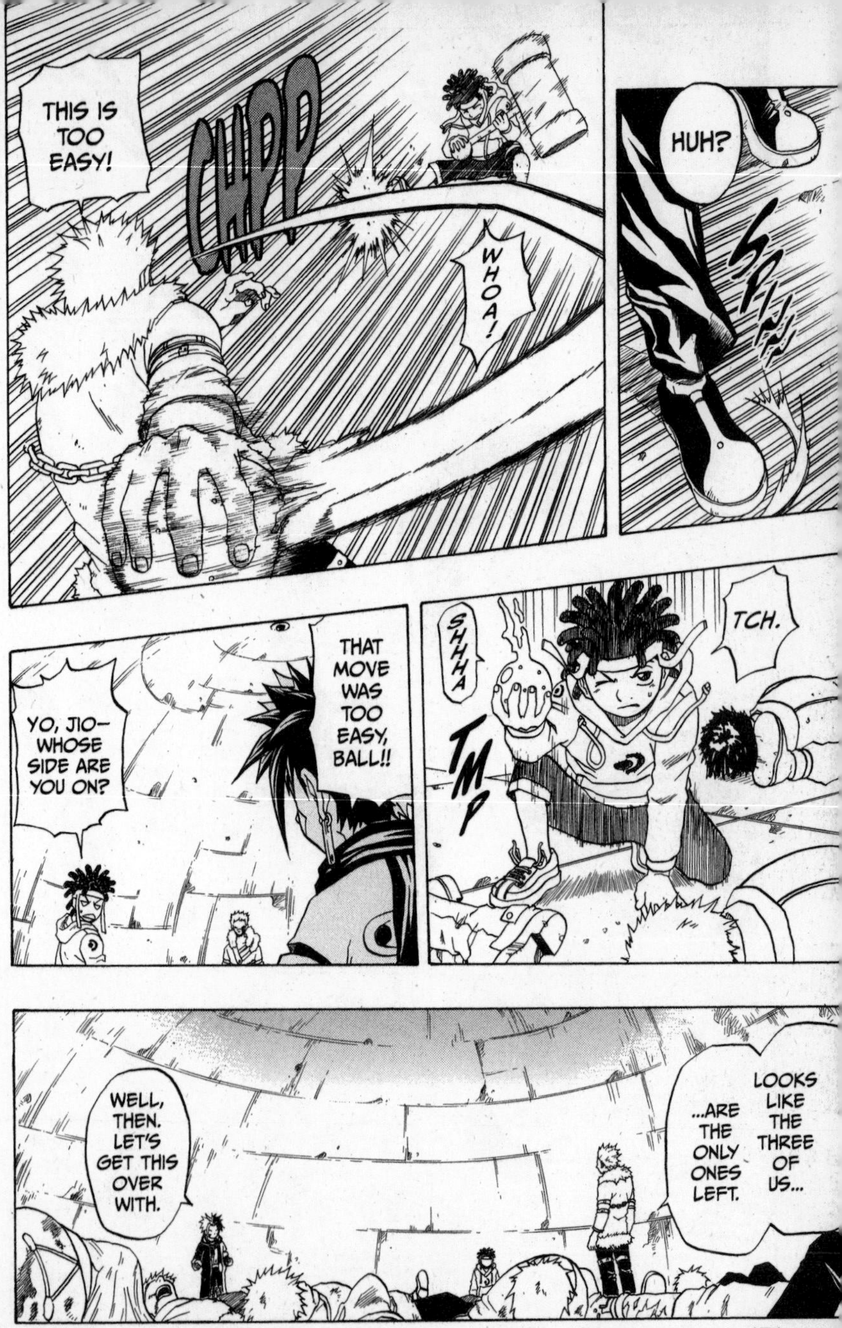

HUH?
SCHHH
WHOA!
CHPP
THIS IS TOO EASY!
TCH.
SHHHA
TMP
THAT MOVE WAS TOO EASY, BALL!!
YO, JIO— WHOSE SIDE ARE YOU ON?
LOOKS LIKE THE THREE OF US...
...ARE THE ONLY ONES LEFT.
WELL, THEN. LET'S GET THIS OVER WITH.

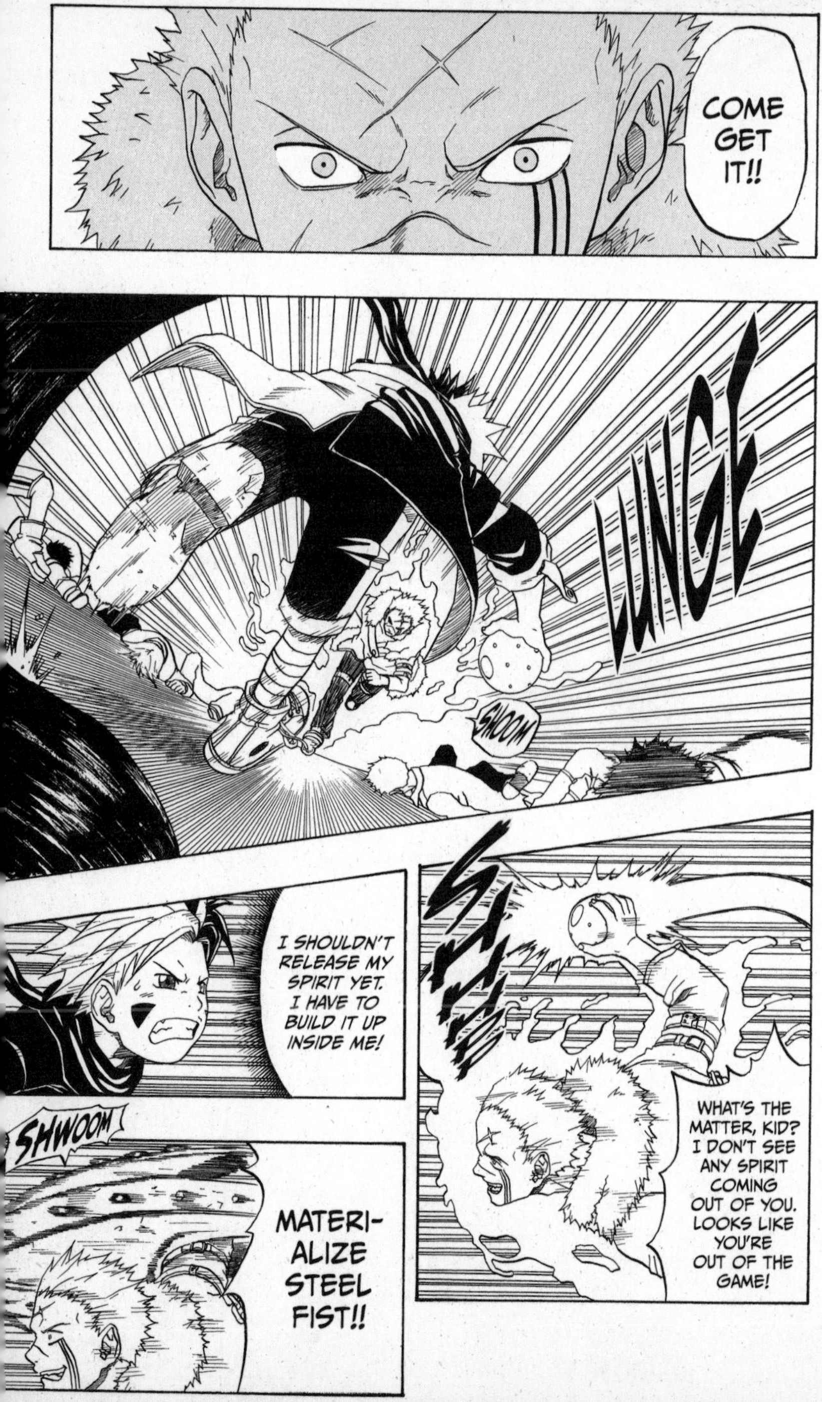
COME GET IT!!
LUNGE
SHOOM
WHAT'S THE MATTER, KID? I DON'T SEE ANY SPIRIT COMING OUT OF YOU. LOOKS LIKE YOU'RE OUT OF THE GAME!
I SHOULDN'T RELEASE MY SPIRIT YET. I HAVE TO BUILD IT UP INSIDE ME!
SHWOOM
MATERI-
ALIZE
STEEL
FIST!!

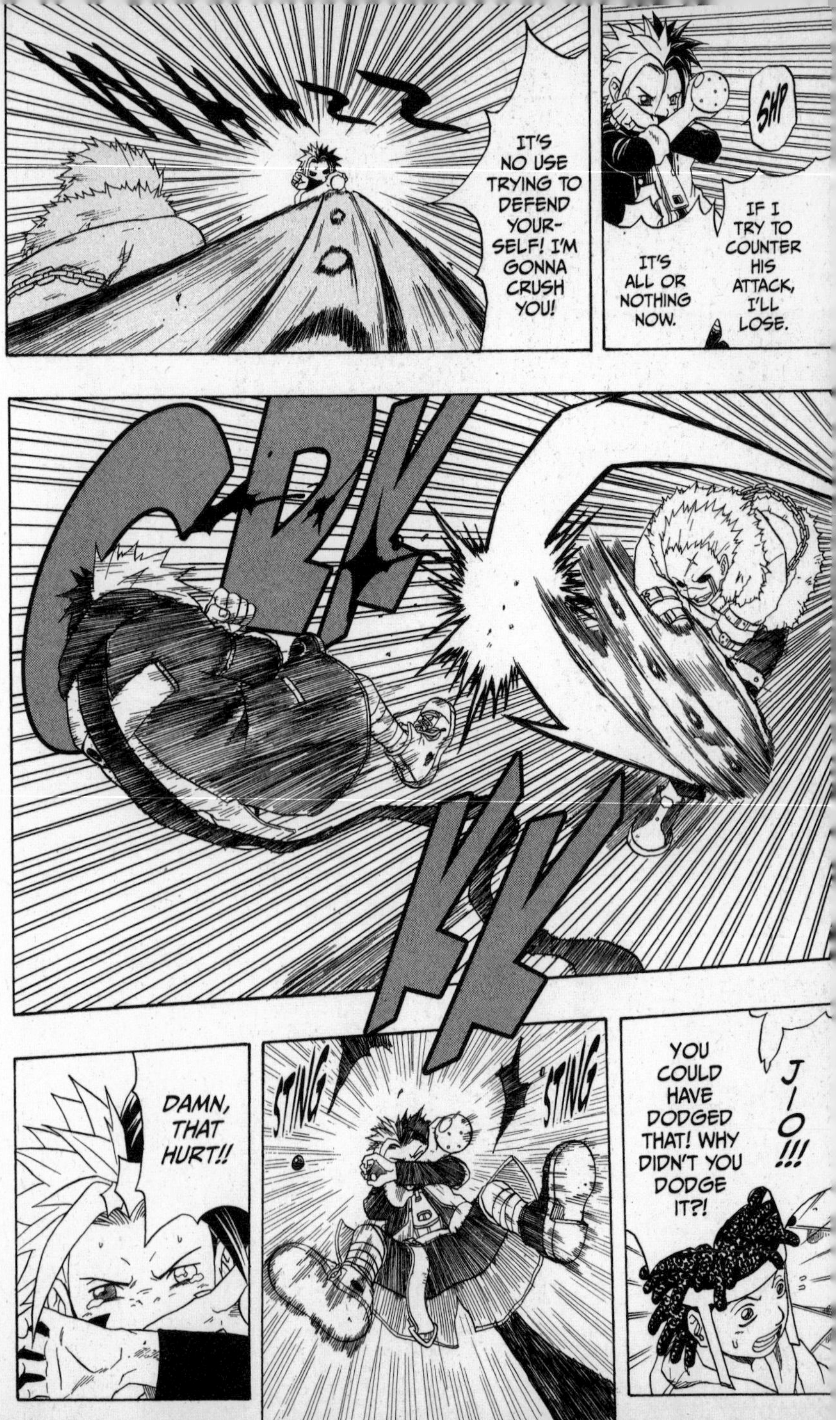
SHP
IF I TRY TO COUNTER HIS ATTACK, I'LL LOSE.
IT'S ALL OR NOTHING NOW.
IT'S NO USE TRYING TO DEFEND YOUR-SELF! I'M GONNA CRUSH YOU!
J-I-O!!!
YOU COULD HAVE DODGED THAT! WHY DIDN'T YOU DODGE IT?!
STING
STING
DAMN, THAT HURT!!

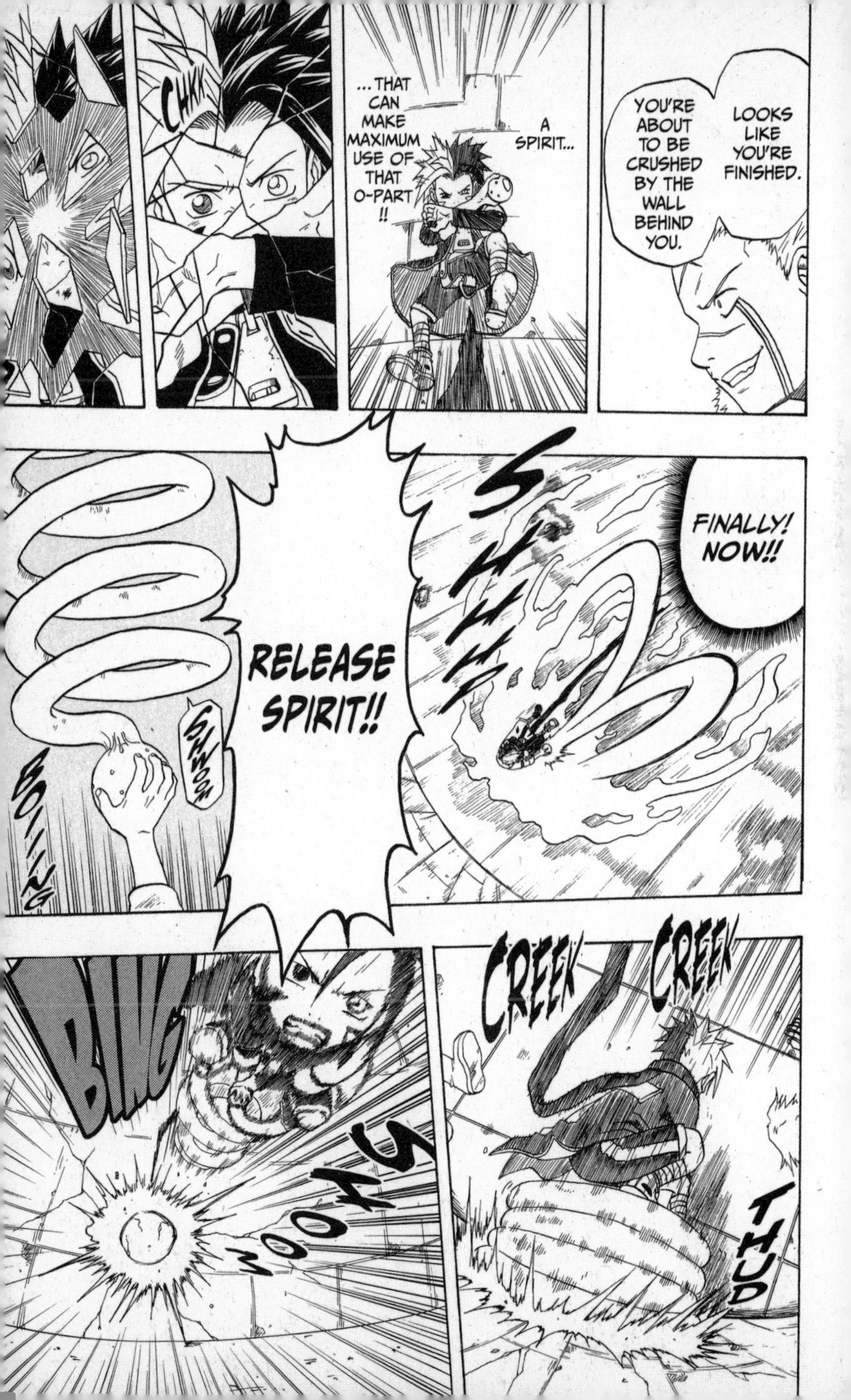
LOOKS LIKE YOU'RE FINISHED.
YOU'RE ABOUT TO BE CRUSHED BY THE WALL BEHIND YOU.
A SPIRIT...
...THAT CAN MAKE MAXIMUM USE OF THAT O-PART!!
CHKK
FINALLY! NOW!!
RELEASE SPIRIT!!
SHWOOM
BOIIING
CREEK
CREEK
THUD
BING
SHOOOM

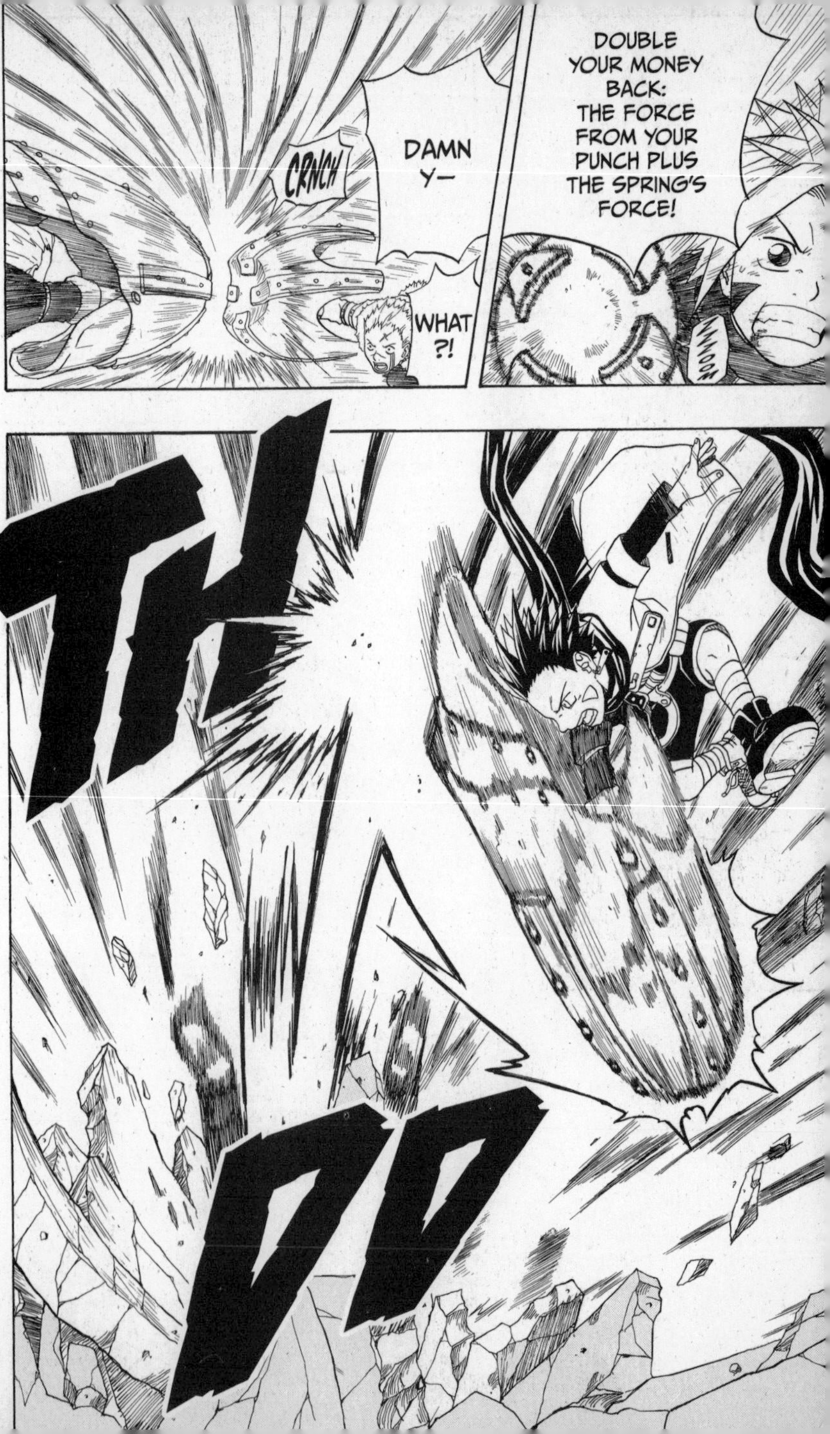
DOUBLE YOUR MONEY BACK: THE FORCE FROM YOUR PUNCH PLUS THE SPRING'S FORCE!
WHOOM
CRNCH
DAMN Y—
WHAT ?!

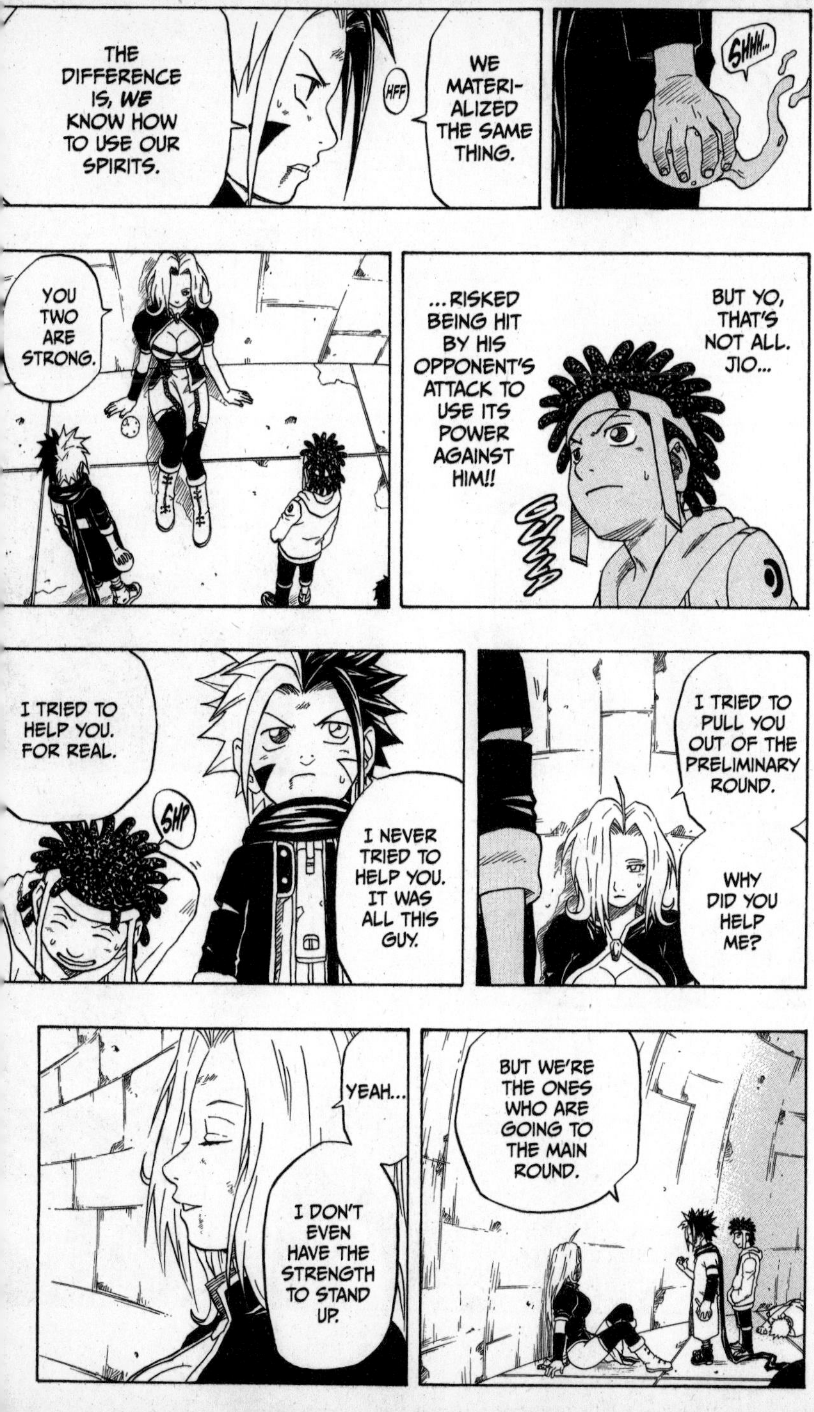
SHHH...
WE MATERI-ALIZED THE SAME THING.
HFF
THE DIFFERENCE IS, WE KNOW HOW TO USE OUR SPIRITS.
BUT YO, THAT'S NOT ALL. JIO...
...RISKED BEING HIT BY HIS OPPONENT'S ATTACK TO USE ITS POWER AGAINST HIM!!
YOU TWO ARE STRONG.
I TRIED TO PULL YOU OUT OF THE PRELIMINARY ROUND.
WHY DID YOU HELP ME?
I NEVER TRIED TO HELP YOU. IT WAS ALL THIS GUY.
I TRIED TO HELP YOU. FOR REAL.
SHP
BUT WE'RE THE ONES WHO ARE GOING TO THE MAIN ROUND.
YEAH...
I DON'T EVEN HAVE THE STRENGTH TO STAND UP.

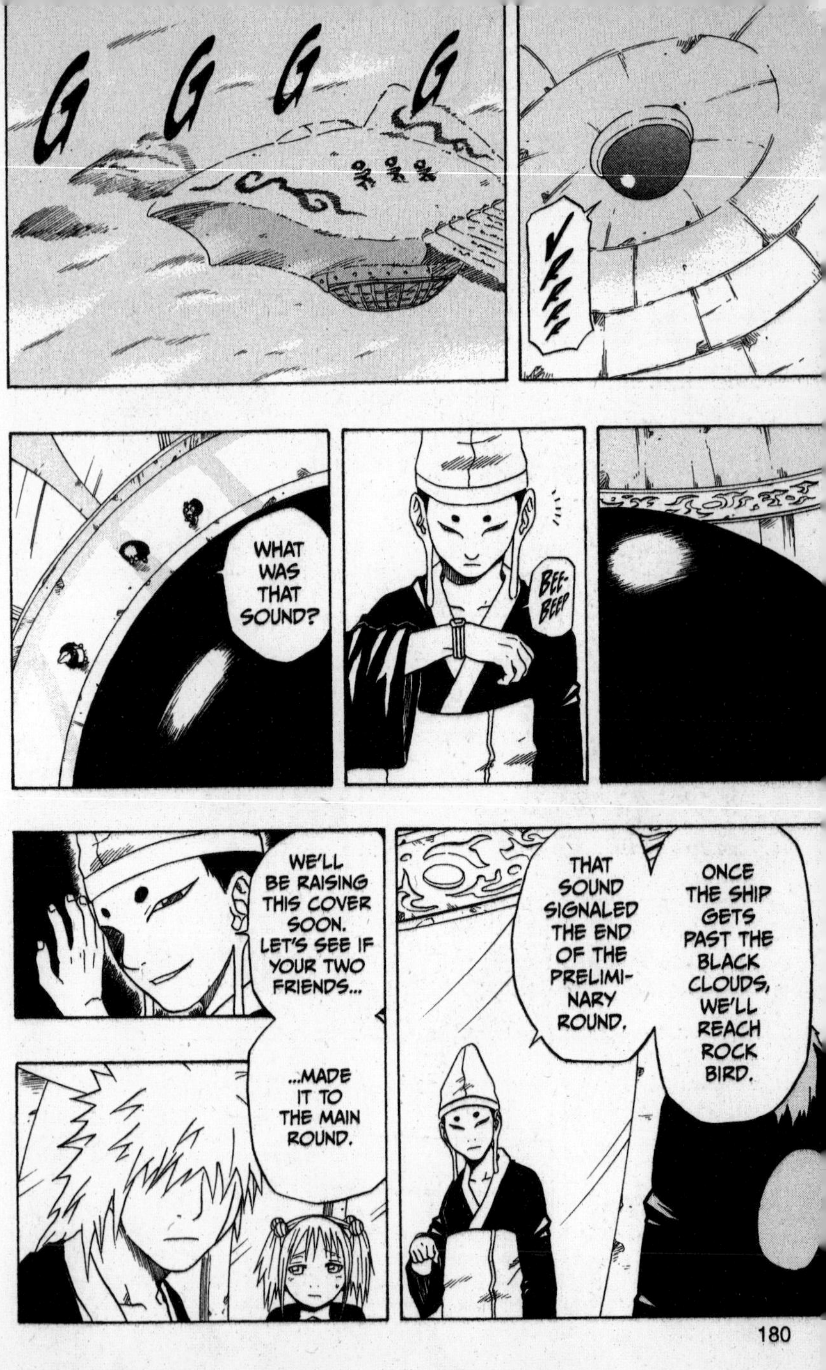
VRRRR
GGGG
BEE-BEEP
WHAT WAS THAT SOUND?
ONCE THE SHIP GETS PAST THE BLACK CLOUDS, WE'LL REACH ROCK BIRD.
THAT SOUND SIGNALED THE END OF THE PRELIMINARY ROUND.
WE'LL BE RAISING THIS COVER SOON. LET'S SEE IF YOUR TWO FRIENDS...
...MADE IT TO THE MAIN ROUND.

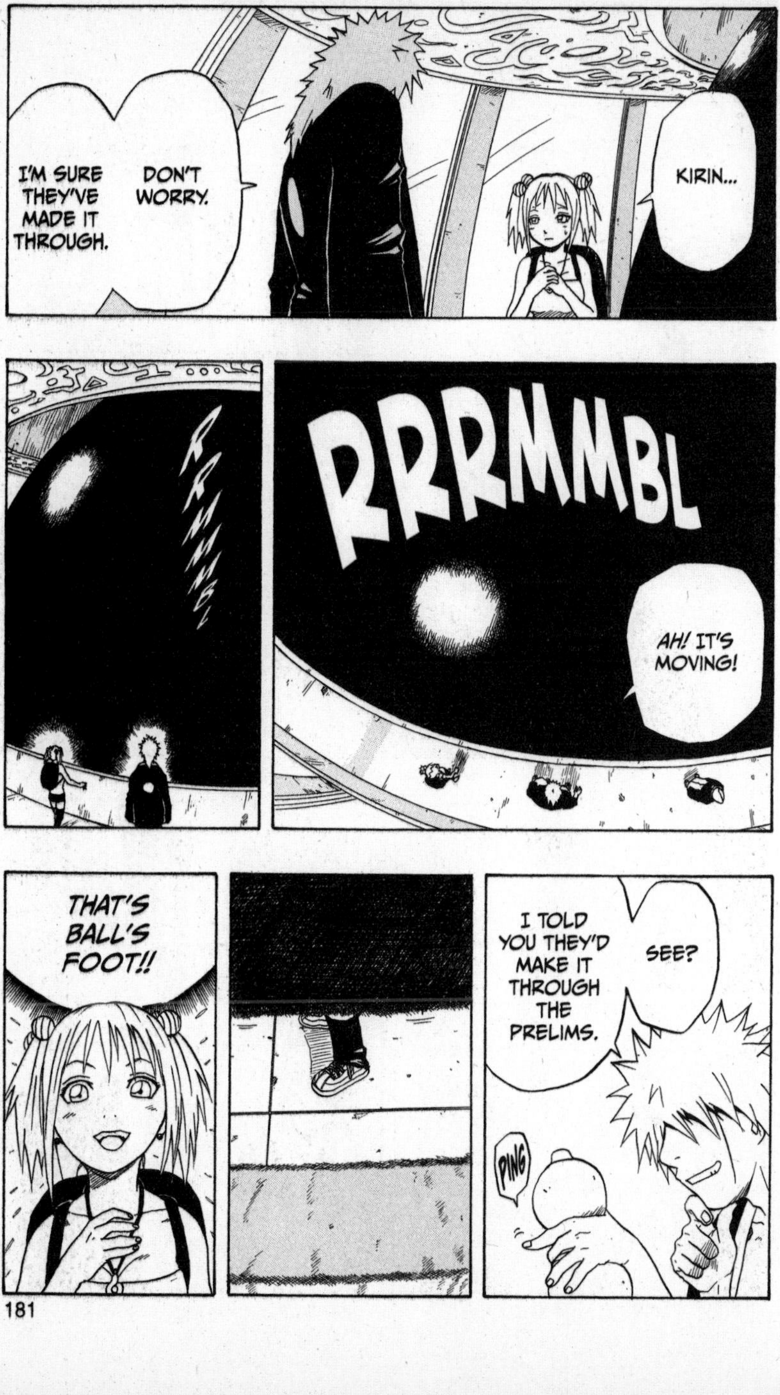
KIRIN...
DON'T WORRY.
I'M SURE THEY'VE MADE IT THROUGH.
RRRMMBL
AH! IT'S MOVING!
RRMMMBL
SEE?
I TOLD YOU THEY'D MAKE IT THROUGH THE PRELIMS.
PING
THAT'S BALL'S FOOT!!

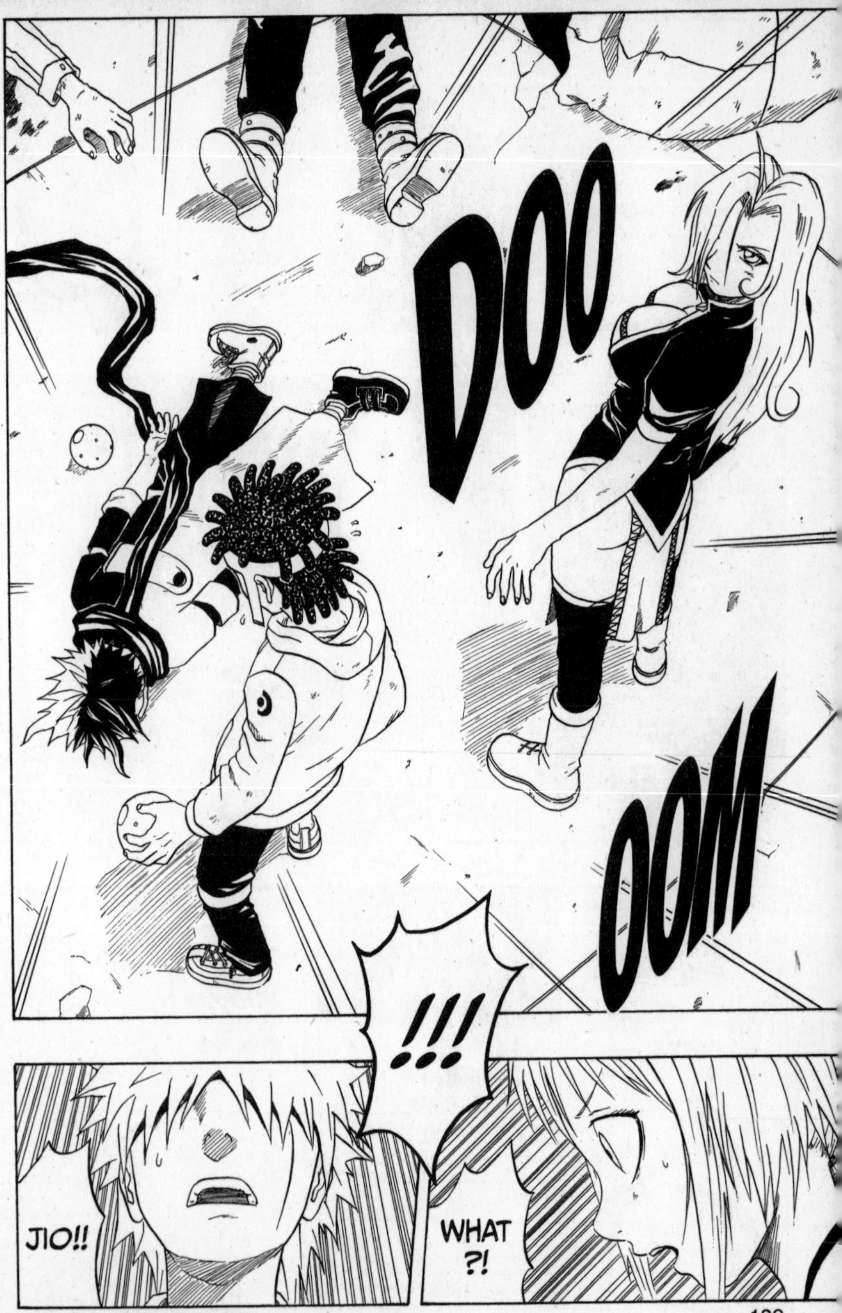
DOOOOM
!!!
WHAT ?!
JIO!!

TO BE CONTINUED...

O-PARTS HUNTER

CHARACTER FILE①

JIO FREED

AGE:	13
HEIGHT:	4'8"
WEIGHT:	77 LBS.
BLOOD TYPE:	O
GOAL:	WORLD DOMINATION.
LIKES:	MONEY, SCARVES, WOLVES.
DISLIKES:	CATS, KIRIN'S PICKLES, ZENOM SYNDICATE.
PERSONALITY:	BASICALLY SELFISH.
	HARDLY DOES ANYTHING FOR OTHER
	PEOPLE.
	CHILDISH.
	TALKS TOUGH.
	AT LEAST HE HAS THE MANNERS
	TO PROPERLY GREET PEOPLE.

O-PARTS HUNTER

CHARACTER FILE ②

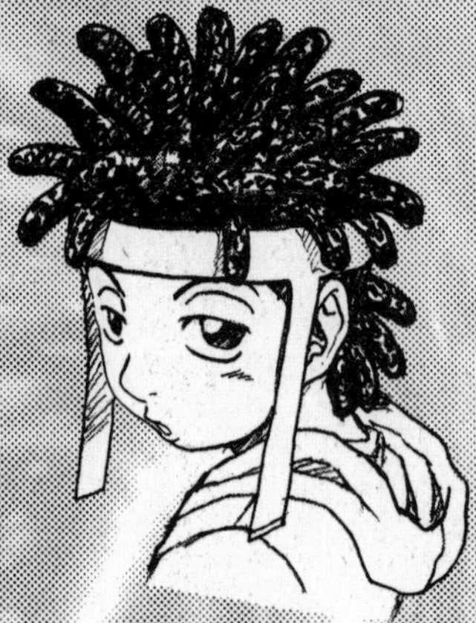

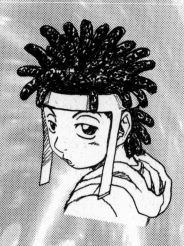

BALL

AGE:	13
HEIGHT:	4'11"
WEIGHT:	84 LBS.
BLOOD TYPE:	O
GOAL:	NOW THAT HE'S FULFILLED HIS LIFELONG DREAM OF BECOMING AN O.P.T., HE WANTS TO SAVE OTHER TOWNS LIKE ENTOTSU CITY. OH, AND HE'S PLOTTING TO MAKE RUBY HIS GIRLFRIEND.
LIKES:	YO-YO, BASKETBALL.
DISLIKES:	JAJA-MARU BEING SMUG, ANYTHING SQUARE, KIRIN'S PICKLES.
PERSONALITY:	A COWARDLY TYPE WHO WANTS ALL THE ATTENTION. YO, BUT WHEN PUSH COMES TO SHOVE, HE'S WILLING TO FACE THE MUSIC!! CHERISHES FRIENDS AND FAMILY TIES.

O-PARTS HUNTER

CHARACTER FILE③

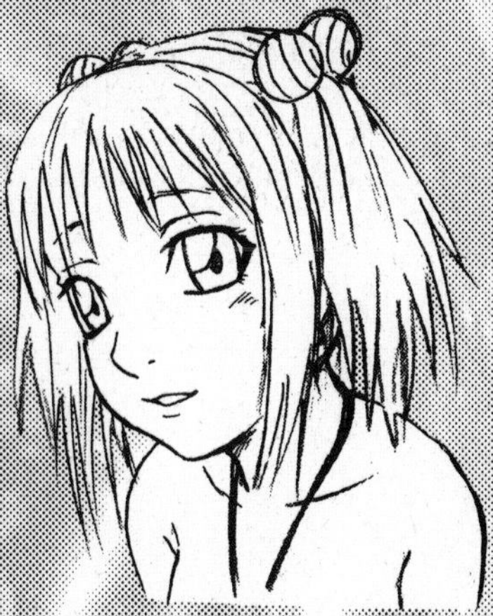

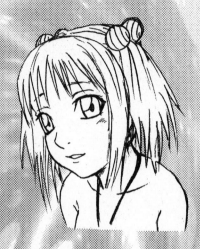

RUBY CRESCENT

AGE:	15
HEIGHT:	5'1"
WEIGHT:	88 LBS.
BLOOD TYPE:	O
GOAL:	TO BECOME A TREASURE HUNTER LIKE HER FATHER AND FIND THE LEGENDARY O-PART.
LIKES:	O-PARTS, CLOTHES.
DISLIKES:	PERVERTS, PEOPLE WHO DON'T LISTEN.
PERSONALITY:	VERY OUTGOING. A REAL TOUGH TALKER. BUT WHEN SHE'S WRONG, SHE'LL APOLOGIZE. SHE'S ACTUALLY PRETTY CUTE... EVEN IF SHE IS OFTEN THE "MANLIEST" ONE IN THE BUNCH.

O-PARTS HUNTER

CHARACTER FILE④

CROSS

AGE:	14
HEIGHT:	5'3"
WEIGHT:	104 LBS.
BLOOD TYPE:	A
GOAL:	TO KILL SATAN.
LIKES:	HIS SISTER, CHURCH, LILIES.
DISLIKES:	ADULTS, SATAN, HIS PARENTS.
PERSONALITY:	EVEN THOUGH HE SEEMS QUIET, HE'S ACTUALLY VERY STUBBORN. HE'S ESPECIALLY COLD TOWARD OTHER ADULTS. BUT UNDERNEATH IT ALL HE'S A KINDHEARTED BOY WHO WILL SACRIFICE HIMSELF FOR OTHERS.

SEISHI AND THE SPORTS DRINK

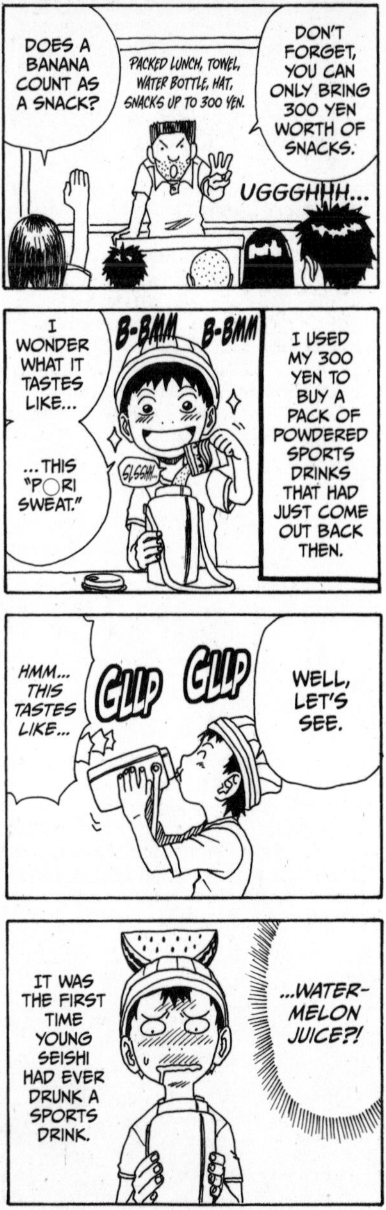
DON'T FORGET, YOU CAN ONLY BRING 300 YEN WORTH OF SNACKS.
PACKED LUNCH, TOWEL, WATER BOTTLE, HAT, SNACKS UP TO 300 YEN.
DOES A BANANA COUNT AS A SNACK?
UGGGHHH...
I USED MY 300 YEN TO BUY A PACK OF POWDERED SPORTS DRINKS THAT HAD JUST COME OUT BACK THEN.
B-BMM
B-BMM
I WONDER WHAT IT TASTES LIKE... ...THIS "P○RI SWEAT."
SLSSHH...
WELL, LET'S SEE.
GLLP
GLLP
HMM... THIS TASTES LIKE...
...WATER-MELON JUICE?!
IT WAS THE FIRST TIME YOUNG SEISHI HAD EVER DRUNK A SPORTS DRINK.

SEISHI AND JUDO

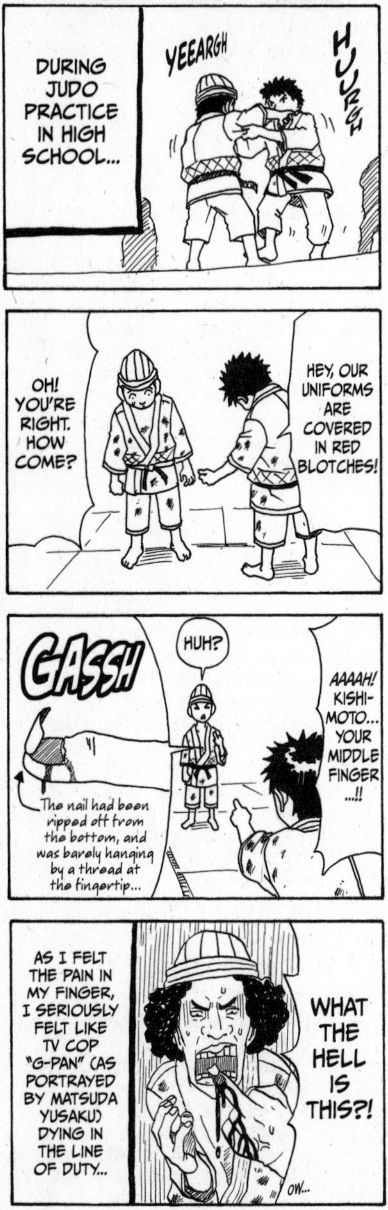
HJJURGH
YEEARGH
DURING JUDO PRACTICE IN HIGH SCHOOL...
HEY, OUR UNIFORMS ARE COVERED IN RED BLOTCHES!
OH! YOU'RE RIGHT. HOW COME?
AAAAH! KISHI-MOTO... YOUR MIDDLE FINGER ...!!
HUH?
GASSH
The nail had been ripped off from the bottom, and was barely hanging by a thread at the fingertip...
WHAT THE HELL IS THIS?!
OW...
AS I FELT THE PAIN IN MY FINGER, I SERIOUSLY FELT LIKE TV COP "G-PAN" (AS PORTRAYED BY MATSUDA YUSAKU) DYING IN THE LINE OF DUTY...

O–Parts CATALOGUE⑧

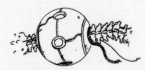

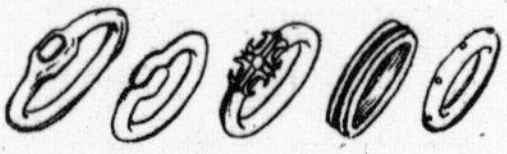

O-PART: JUSTICE
O-PART RANK: C
EFFECT: EARTH, ELECTRICALLY CHARGED WATER, WIND, ?, ?
THE FIRST O-PART PLACED UPON CROSS'S INDEX FINGER WAS FINALLY USED IN THIS VOLUME! ONLY CROSS CAN GATHER SO MUCH ELECTRICALLY CHARGED WATER FROM THE ATMOSPHERE.

O-PART: MUGEN
O-PART RANK: C
EFFECT: ENHANCE AND COMPRESS
THE O-PART BURIED INSIDE LIEUTENANT GENERAL MISHIMA OF THE STEA GOVERNMENT, WHO HAS A SEMI-CYBORG BODY. HIS POSITRON SHOT ATTACK IS MADE POSSIBLE BY CREATING POSITRONS INSIDE HIS BODY, THEN ENHANCING AND COMPRESSING THEM WITH THIS O-PART.

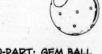

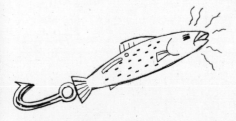

O-PART: SARDINE SWORD (WITH SESAME)
O-PART RANK: ?
EFFECT: SMELLS FISHY
AN O-PART WITH A REFINED, STREAMLINED FISH DESIGN. FUTOMOMO-TARO IS THE ONLY O.P.T. WHO CAN USE THIS SWORD. I LIKE THAT IT'S HARD TO TELL IF THIS O-PART IS ACTUALLY STRONG.♡

O-PART: GEM BALL
O-PART RANK: B
EFFECT: MATERIALIZATION OF ONE'S SPIRIT.
CREATED FROM GIL ORE. IT HAS A VERY POWERFUL EFFECT, BUT SINCE IT ATTACKS THE ONE WHO HOLDS IT, IT RANKS LOW AS A WEAPON. STILL, IT'S RANKED B.

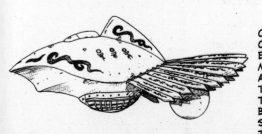

O-PART: BIG ORPHAN
O-PART RANK: B
EFFECT: SUPERCONDUCTIVE MAGNET
A MASSIVE FLOATING FISH THAT IS USED AS A VEHICLE TO GET TO AND FROM ROCK BIRD. THREE O.P.T.S MOVE IT, SO IT'S VERY, VERY TROUBLESOME.

Hurrrgk!
Blub blub
GAHH!
Shp!

SEISHI KISHIMOTO

The drunken businessman appeared!!

The drunken businessman used the attack spell of Barf!!

Kishimoto quickly dodged the attack!!

Kishimoto escaped!!

Dash!!

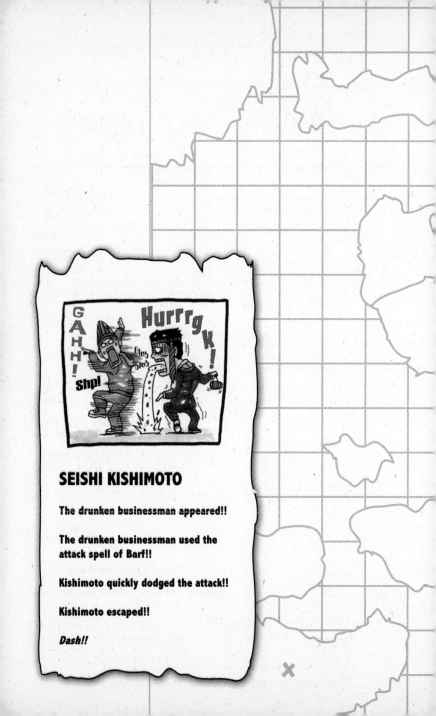

O-Parts HUNTER 8

VIZ Media Edition
STORY AND ART BY SEISHI KISHIMOTO

English Adaptation/Tetsuichiro Miyaki
Touch-up Art & Lettering/Gia Cam Luc
Cover Design/Amy Martin
Interior Design/Andrea Rice
Editor/Carol Fox

Editor in Chief, Books/Alvin Lu
Editor in Chief, Magazines/Marc Weidenbaum
VP of Publishing Licensing/Rika Inouye
VP of Sales/Gonzalo Ferreyra
Sr. VP of Marketing/Liza Coppola
Publisher/Hyoe Narita

Printed in the U.S.A.

Published by VIZ Media, LLC
P.O. Box 77010
San Francisco, CA 94107

10 9 8 7 6 5 4 3 2 1
First printing, February 2008

viz media
www.viz.com   store.viz.com

LOVE MANGA?
LET US KNOW WHAT YOU THINK!

HELP US ~~MAKE THE MANGA~~
YOU LOV~~E BETTER!~~

FULLMETAL ALCHEMIST © Hiromu Arakawa/SQUARE ENIX. INU YASHA © 1997 Rumiko TAKAHASHI/Shogakukan Inc.
NAOKI URASAWA'S MONSTER © 1995 Naoki URASAWA Studio Nuts/Shogakukan Inc. ZATCH BELL! © 2001 Makoto RAIKU/Shogakukan Inc.